Walt Disney World Guide

Open Road—More *and* Better Choices!

Open Road Travel Guides

Open Road Publishing has guide books to exciting, fun destinations on four continents. As veteran travelers, our goal is to bring you the best travel guides available anywhere!

No small task, but here's what we offer:

•All Open Road travel guides are written by authors with a distinct, opinionated point of view – not some sterile committee or team of writers. Our authors are experts in the areas covered and are polished writers.

•Our guides are geared to people who want to make their own travel choices. We'll show you how to discover the real destination – not just see some place from a tour bus window.

•We're strong on the basics, but we also provide terrific choices for those looking to get off the beaten path and experience the country or city – not just see it or pass through it.

•We give you the best, but we also tell you about the worst and what to avoid. Nobody should waste their time and money on their hard-earned vacation because of bad or inadequate travel advice.

•Our guides assume nothing. We tell you everything you need to know to have the trip of a lifetime – presented in a fun, literate, no-nonsense style.

•And, above all, we welcome your input, ideas, and suggestions to help us put out the best travel guides possible.

About the Author

Jay Fenster's previous Open Road guides were *Disney World & Orlando Theme Parks* and *Disney World with Kids.* Jay completely revamped his previous works so thoroughly that we made this a completely new book. You'll find many great new things to do in this guide, including unique money-saving ideas, ride ratings, average wait times at rides and attractions, new places to shop, other area theme parks, and thorough reviews of places to stay and eat in Walt Disney World and greater Orlando area. Of course, everything has been updated for this new edition!

Walt Disney World Guide

Open Road—More *and* Better Choices!

Jay Fenster

Open Road Publishing

Open Road Publishing

We offer travel guides to American and foreign locales. Our books tell it like it is, often with an opinionated edge, and our experienced authors always give you all the information you need to have the trip of a lifetime. Write for your free catalog of all our titles.

Open Road Publishing
P.O. Box 284, Cold Spring Harbor, NY 11724
E-mail: Jopenroad@aol.com

2nd Edition

Contents

1. Introduction   11

2. Overview   12
How to Use This Book   12
   Tips for Saving Money, Saving Time, & Having Fun   12
   Rankings & Ratings   12
   Hotels   12
   Theme Park Rides, Shows, Tours, and Exhibits   13
   Restaurants   13
   Abbreviations   13
   Feedback   14
What's New   14

3. The Best of Orlando & Disney World   15

4. The Magic Kingdom   20
Main Street, U.S.A.   21
Adventureland   23
Frontierland   26
LIberty Square   29
Fantasyland   31
Mickey's Toontown Fair   36
Tomorrowland   38
Entertainment   42
Where to Eat   44
Practical Information   49

5. EPCOT   52
Future World   52
Imagination!   57
The Land   58
Wonders of Life   60
The Living Seas   62
World Showcase   65

Entertainment   74
Where to Eat   75
Practical Information   81

6. Disney-MGM Studios   84
Hollywood Boulevard   85
Echo Lake/Streets of America   86
Mickey Avenue/Animation Courtyard   90
Sunset Boulevard   93
Entertainment   96
Where to Eat   97
Practical Information   100

7. Disney's Animal Kingdom   102
The Oasis   103
Discovery Island   103
Dinoland USA   105
Camp Minnie-Mickey   107
Africa   108
Asia   110
Entertainment   111
Where to Eat   112
Practical Information   115

8. Universal Studios Florida   117
Production Central   119
New York   120
San Francisco/Amity   122
World Expo   124
Woody Woodpecker's Kidzone   125
Hollywood   128
Where to Eat   129
Practical Information   132

9. Islands of Adventure   134
Port of Entry   135
Marvel Superhero Island   136
Toon Lagoon   138
Jurassic Park   139
The Lost Continent   141
Seuss Landing   143

Where to Eat   145
Practical Information   147

10. SeaWorld Orlando   150
Rides   151
Shows   152
Animal & Other Attractions   154
Animal Connections Programs   156
Educational Tours & Programs   156
Where to Eat   157
Practical Information   159

11. Where to Stay   161
Where Should I Stay?   161
Finding Discounts   163
Walt Disney World Resorts   163
Benefits of staying at WDW   163
Deluxe & Disney Vacation Club Resorts   166
Disney's Moderate Resorts   183
Disney's Value Resorts   186
Downtown Disney Hotels   187
Universal Orlando Hotels   191
Top Ten Lake Buena Vista Hotels   195
Top Ten Kissimmee Hotels   200
Top Ten International Drive Hotels   205
Off the Beaten Path   209
Chain Hotels   214

12. Where to Eat   216
Best of Theme Park Eats   216
Disney Character Dining   217
Disney Resort Dining   218
Downtown Disney Dining   220
Universal Orlando Dining   221
Kissimmee-Lake Buena Vista-Orlando   222
　　Gourmet   222
　　Surf & Turf   224
　　Teppanyaki   227
　　Asian Flavors   228
　　Innovative, International, & Islander   229
　　Italian   230
　　Southwestern Styles   232

Good Sports   233
Smoke 'Em If You Got 'Em   234
Casual Flavors & Comfort Foods   234
Pizza   236

13. Nightlife   238
Dinner Shows   238
Nighttime Attractions & Entertainment Complexes   245
Nightclubs & Bars   248

14. Shopping   254
Shopping & Entertainment Complexes   254
Malls, Marketplaces, & Outlet Centers   258

15. Fun In & On the Water   262
Water Parks   262
Orlando's Best Pools   268
Rent a Boat   268
Water Sports   269
Go Fish   269
Take a Cruise   271
Scuba, Snorkel, & Dive   272

16. Great Golf & More   273
Inside Disney World   273
Ouside Disney World   275
Spectator Sports   280

17. Amusements & Diversions   283
Busch Gardens Tampa   283
Daytona USA   285
Disney Quest   285
Haunted Grimm House of Old Town   286
Richard Petty Driving Experience   286
Seminole Hard Rock Casino   287
Skull Kingdom   287
Vans Skate Park   288
Miniature Golf   288
Movies   290
Midways, Carnivals, Go-Karts, & Stuff   291

18. Back to Nature 292

Bok Sanctuary   292
Central Florida Zoo   293
Cypress Gardens   293
Discovery Cove   294
Dinosaur World   295
Gator World   295
Green Meadows Petting Farm   296
Harry P. Leu Gardens   297
Horse World Riding Stables   297
Ivey Groves Fresh Citrus   297
Nature Conservancy's Disney Wilderness Preserve   298
Reptile World Serpentarium   298
Silver Springs   298
Wekiwa Springs State Park   299
A World of Orchids   300

19. Airborne Adventures 301

17. Music, Arts, & Culture 305

18. Science, Discovery, & Learning 315

PART 2: Planning Your Trip 321

When to Visit   321
Special Events   324
Preparation   333
Disney vs. Universal   333
Visitor Info & Discount Resources   334
Online Ticketing   337
Walt Disney World Ticketing   338
Universal Orlando/Sea World Ticketing   340
Package Deals   344
Getting to Orlando   346
Getting Around Orlando   350

Index 358

Maps

Central Florida   19

Magic Kingdom   165

Driving Around Orlando   351

Sidebars

Cinderella Castle   33

Hidden Mickeys   37

Overlooked Parade Vantages   43

Disney's FastPass   50

Wonders of Life – Exhibits   61

Kidcot Fun Stops   66

Kid's Discovery Clubs   105

VIP Tours of Universal   118

Protect Your Electronics from the Wild Waters!   138

Dine with Shamu   157

Sea World Traffic Tuesdays   160

Disney World Resort Reservations FAQ   164

Shades of Green   182

Another Option: Vacation Homes   210

Restaurant Price Key   217

Parental Parole   240

Inexpensive Gift Ideas   257

Flea Markets   259

Last Chance Souvenirs   261

Golf Gear   277

Orlando International Fringe Festival   307

Orlando Weather Chart   322

Your Planning Timeline   335

Web& Phone Visitor Info & Discount Resources   336

Packing Tips   346

Walt Disney World Guide

1. INTRODUCTION

This guide isn't for everybody. If you want to experience the same old things the same old way, get another book. If you want a one-sided, corporate-sanctioned, sanitized point of view, look elsewhere. Things you need in order to appreciate this book: a sense of humor, an open mind, an appreciation of value, and most of all, the desire for adventure and excitement. After all, that's what an Orlando vacation is for, right? If you wanted laid-back you should have gone to the beach.

A vacation is precious, and there's no reason to spend more than you have to, or waste time doing things that aren't what you want. I've been an Orlando junkie since my first visit at age 10, and I want to use my enthusiasm and experience to help you get the most out of your vacation.

You can expect a little bit of a different point of view from this guidebook than most others. I'm very opinionated. I'm a fan first and foremost – I wouldn't be writing this in the first place if there wasn't some love for the place – but I'm objective, brutally honest, and often irreverent.

I present a fresh, young, hip perspective on one of the country's favorite destinations. All the old favorites are covered – but there's only so much time you can spend there before a restless heart starts to wander. And when you decide you need a dose of *je ne sais quoi*, we'll show you where to find it.

Whether your perfect Disney vacation involves roller coaster adrenaline binges, fine dining, world-class golf, Florida's wild nature, or outlet shopping for your favorite brands, this guide will let you chase down your bliss. Only the area's top hotels made it into this book, so you can rest easy knowing that any accommodation you select from this book will be a handy base of operations for your trip.

Chapter 2

OVERVIEW

How to Use This Book

Before we start on our journey, I should explain a few things about the way that the information in this book is presented.

Tips for Saving Money, Saving Time, and Having Fun

Through the years, I've accumulated a lot of strategies, tactics, and tips for saving time, saving money, and having unexpected fun. These tips have been smoothly integrated into the text of the book, but you can spot them at a glance either with italics or in sidebars.

Rankings & Ratings

Information for theme park attractions, hotels, restaurants, and other features in this book are presented with basic information included in a consistent format. Most of the data presented is self-explanatory, but not all of it. So here's a primer on how I've presented the data:

Hotels

The hotels are divided into geographic areas and printed in order of their rank within that geographic area. Note that every hotel included in the book – regardless of rank – is still a hotel that I recommend for my readers. Four ratings are the heart of the hotel reviews: **Room Quality** represents the luxury, features, décor, and cleanliness of the guestrooms. The **Amenities** rating reflects the quantity and quality of activities and facilities available to guests. **Food** shows the quality of restaurants at the hotel. **Value** is an overall reflection of what you get for your money.

Theme Park Rides, Shows, Tours, and Exhibits

Fear Factor indicates how frightening a ride is. This scale runs from 1 to 5, from least to most frightening. Attractions deemed a 1 are safe for everyone. Fear Factor 2 attractions will only scare the youngest children. Fear Factor 3 rides and shows can be somewhat intense, and can rattle kids who spook easily. Fear Factor 4 means more intensity and a much higher age threshold for kids who'll tolerate it. Thrill junkies will want to bust out the yellow highlighters for Fear Factor 5 rides. The squeamish will want to give them a wide berth. Any special comments or notes about height and age requirements, FastPass or Universal Express ride scheduling, or other important details are also included in the capsules.

Restaurants

Orlando restaurants are not rated or ranked in their listings, but rest assured I will let you know if I don't consider a restaurant's food up to snuff. They are split into sections by dining type and cuisine. The reality of dining on an Orlando vacation is, at the end of a long day of theme park touring, most visitors are a lot less likely to seek out a particular restaurant than they are to just find something close and convenient to the hotel. Fortunately, the concentrations of hotels are interspersed with many quality restaurants, both national chains and independent local eateries. A restaurant's price range is represented by the number of dollar signs shown. $ indicates entrées under $10. $$ indicates entrées between $10 and $20. $$$ indicates entrées between $20 and $35. At $$$$ restaurants, you can expect to pay more than $35 per entrée. Next, accepted credit cards are listed:

AM American Express
DI Discover
MC Mastercard
VI Visa

Abbreviations

AK = Animal Kingdom
DD = Downtown Disney
I-Drive = International Drive
IOA = Islands of Adventure
MGM = Disney-MGM Studios
MK = Magic Kingdom
SWO = Sea World Orlando
UO = Universal Orlando

USF = Universal Studios Florida
WDW = Walt Disney World

Feedback

I value your feedback on this book, in order to keep evolving my guide to continue to meet my readers' needs and preferences. Feel free to email me with your comments, thoughts, and your own Disney experiences. Send your feedback to: orlandoguide@swina.com.

What's New?

This edition has undergone extensive revision following on-site visits and research in spring and summer 2005. All existing information has been verified, and additions to this edition include:

•Extensive information on Disney's new ticketing system, Magic Your Way
•12 new theme park attractions in Disney and Universal
•27 more Orlando area attractions, activities and diversions
•14 more hotels, including Disney's new Pop Century and Saratoga Springs resorts
•30 more restaurants
•12 more bars and nightclubs
•3 more dinner shows
•15 more annual special events
•6 more golf courses
•Enhancements to information on driving in Disney and Orlando
•Locations of designated smoking areas in all theme parks
•Expanded section on fishing camps, guides, and excursions
•Expanded section on water sports

Chapter 3

THE BEST OF ORLANDO & DISNEY WORLD

Here, at a glance, are my favorite Orlando and Disney World features:

Best Special Event, Disney: International Food & Wine Festival
Best Special Event, Universal: Halloween Horror Nights
Best Special Event, Non-Theme Park: Fringe Festival
Best Hotel, Overall: Gaylord Palms
Best Hotel, Disney: Animal Kingdom Lodge Resort
Best Hotel, Universal: Portofino Bay Hotel
Best Hotel, Lake Buena Vista: Hyatt Regency Grand Cypress
Best Hotel, Kissimmee: Gaylord Palms
Best Hotel, International Drive: Renaissance Orlando Resort
Best Hotel, Boutique: Celebration Hotel
Best Hotel, Convention Travelers: Peabody Orlando
Best Hotel, Couples: Royal Pacific Resort
Best Hotel, Families: Nickelodeon Family Suites by Holiday Inn
Best Hotel, Golfers: Hyatt Regency Grand Cypress
Best Hotel Pool, Aesthetics: Hyatt Regency Grand Cypress
Best Hotel Pool, Fun: Nickelodeon Family Suites by Holiday Inn

Best Hotel Restaurant, Disney: Victoria & Albert's, Grand Floridian

Best Hotel Restaurant, Universal: Tchoup Chop, Royal Pacific Resort

Best Hotel Restaurant, Lake Buena Vista: The Venetian Room, Caribe Royale

Best Hotel Restaurant, Kissimmee: Villa di Flora, Gaylord Palms

Best Hotel Restaurant, International Drive: Dux, Peabody Orlando

Best Theme Park: Universal Studios Florida

Best Theme Park Ride: The Adventures of the Amazing Spider-Man (IOA)

Best Theme Park Film: Terminator 2: 3-D Battle Across Time (USF)

Best Theme Park Show: Legend of the Lion King (AK)

Best Theme Park Restaurant: San Angel Inn (Epcot)

Best Theme Park Shop: The Emporium (MK)

Best Dark Ride: Pirates of the Caribbean (MK)

Best Interactive Attraction: Men in Black: Alien Attack (USF)

Best Nighttime Event: Fantasmic! (MGM)

Best Roller Coaster: Kraken (SWO)

Best Water Ride: Popeye & Bluto's Bilge Rat Barges (IOA)

Best Thrill Ride: Revenge of the Mummy (USF)

Best Water Park: Wet 'N' Wild

Best Airboat Operator: Glades Adventures

Best Art Gallery: Orlando Museum of Art

Best Golf: Championsgate

Best Hot Air Balloon Operator: Bob's Balloons

Best Live Music Venue: House of Blues

Best Live Performance: Cirque du Soleil: La Nouba

Best Miniature Golf: Hawaiian Rumble

Best Movie Theater: Universal Loews Cineplex

Best Rainy Day Option: Disney Quest

Best Zoo: Gatorland

Best Way to Kill an Extra Day: Kennedy Space Center

Best Way to Kill an Extra Hour: Ripley's Believe It... Or Not! Museum

Best Bar-B-Q: JT's Prime Time

Best Breakfast: Le Peep

Best Brunch: Atlantis, Renaissance Orlando Resort

Best Chinese Restaurant: Ming Court

Best Gourmet Restaurant: Victoria & Albert's

Best Healthy Eats: Seasons 52

Best Italian Restaurant: Christini's

Best Japanese Restaurant: Ran-Getsu

Best Latin Restaurant: Samba Room

Best Mexican Restaurant: San Angel Inn

Best Pizza: Fama's

Best Seafood Restaurant: Bonefish

Best Sports Bar: Orlando Ale House

Best Steakhouse: Vito's Chop House

Best Sushi: Amura

Best Theme Restaurant: Murray Bros. Caddyshack

Best Unusual Restaurant: Café Tu Tu Tango

Best Bar: Blue Martini

Best Dinner Show: Pirates Dinner Adventure

Best Nightclub: Cairo

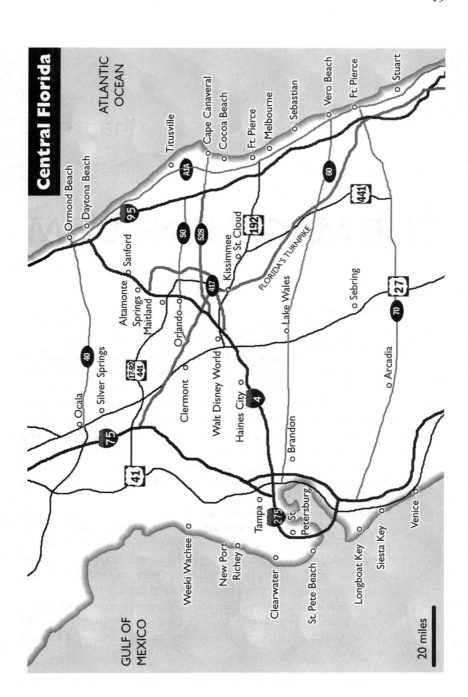

Chapter 4

THE MAGIC KINGDOM

Let's face it. This is why you're here. Everything else is gravy, but when people think Orlando or Disney World, chances are, the first image that pops into their head is that of Cinderella Castle – which ironically enough isn't even a ride or attraction. The iconic castle sits right on an island smack in the middle of seven themed areas covering 107 acres. Though this is the smallest of the Disney theme parks, it is without question the most difficult to tour efficiently. There are over 40 rides, shows, and attractions dotting the park, and a lot of them are relatively low-capacity enterprises. So whereas pretty much every other park in town can be toured in a single day during seasons of light to moderate attendance, there is no such luck here. The Magic Kingdom can get claustrophobically crowded even in the quieter months, thanks to consistent popularity among Florida residents. **Allow two full days to see everything**.

Similar (but not identical) to Disneyland, the Magic Kingdom focuses on family-friendly rides that feature some of Disney's best-loved characters. If your focus is on high-tech thrill rides, you'd be better off going to a Universal park. But if your kids want to get a hug from Mickey, an autograph from Donald, or a hug from Friar Tuck (don't worry, it's the chaste kind), the Magic Kingdom is the place best suited for the task.

The Magic Kingdom put Orlando on the map instantly on October 25, 1971, when it opened with this dedication from Roy O. Disney, the brother of the late and eponymous mousemaster, who died five years prior to completion:

Walt Disney World is a tribute to the philosophy and life of Walter Elias

Disney and to the talents, the dedication, and the loyalty of the entire Disney organization that made Walt Disney's dream come true. May Walt Disney World bring joy and inspiration and new knowledge to all who come to this happy place... a Magic Kingdom where the young-at-heart of all ages can laugh and play and learn together.

Truthfully, I have soured a bit on Disney World in general and the Magic Kingdom in particular in the past decade or so, compared to other parks both elsewhere in Disney and across town at Universal. The steady, thick crowds here make touring more frustrating than at many of the other parks, and compared to the technological marvels at Universal and even at Epcot. If you've been here a couple times before, you might get more out of your vacation by focusing your attention elsewhere. That being said, millions of people adore the Magic Kingdom and make pilgrimages there every year, every month, sometimes every week.

Main Street, U.S.A.

Based on Walt Disney's hometown of Marceline, Missouri, Main Street, U.S.A. is the gateway to the Magic Kingdom. Full of turn-of-the-century charm, merchandise, and snackery, it's a fun entrée to the Magic Kingdom that will excite you for the wonders to come further inside.

There's not a lot of worthwhile attractions here – a couple of momentary diversions and a couple of transportation devices disguised as rides. Skip these until you have the main-event attractions out of the way. Main Street does have some good eats, however, like the Crystal Palace, Tony's Town Square Restaurant, and the aromatic Main Street Bake Shop.

Shopping is the real raison d'être for Main Street USA, as seemingly endless shops wind from one end of Main Street to the other on both sides of the road. Again, don't waste time here in the mornings unless you're waiting for the rest of the park to open. If you do make a purchase here first thing in the morning, send your goodies to Package Pickup so you don't have to carry them around all day. Crowds are lightest in the shops here before 2:30pm and after 5pm.

Walt Disney World Railroad

Rating: C+

19-minute grand circle steam locomotive tour of the Magic Kingdom's perimeter.

Fear Factor: 1

Lightest crowds after 11am at Main Street station.

Come on ride the train ... and ride it. These four vintage steam locomotives, the Lilly Belle, Roy O. Disney, Walter E. Disney, and the Roger Broggie, were all built in Philadelphia between 1916 and 1928, and once hauled freight cars across Yucatan jungles.

There's not a whole lot of scenery on this train ride – no Grand Canyon Diorama or Primeval World like in Disneyland, and not much more than roundabout views of Splash Mountain, Fantasyland, Tomorrowland, and Mickey's Toontown, home of a second station. A third station sits beyond Splash Mountain in Frontierland. The tour is about a mile and a half long and is a relaxing way to get around the park, but in terms of an attraction – it's entirely skippable.

Main Street Vehicles

Rating: B-
Short one-way ride up or down Main Street.
Fear Factor: 1
Light crowds all day.

Enjoy a breezy ride up Main Street in a horse-drawn trolley, a refitted and modernized horseless carriage, jitney, an open-sided double-decker omnibus, or a bright red fire engine. A skippable diversion, but sometimes memorable for the close-up spectacle of a horse, ahem, doing his business in mid-ride.

Shopping

The **Emporium**, on the west side of Main Street, is the Magic Kingdom's largest gift shop, with 16,742 square feet of retail space featuring a huge selection of merchandise of all kinds, including stuffed animals, toys, t-shirts, sweatshirts, towels, handbags, hats, and Mousketeer ears, many adorned with Mickey, Minnie, or the WDW logo. Also, the store sells gifts, books, film, records, and sundry items. The linked stores on the east side of Main Street sell a wide variety of merchandise, less focused on souvenirs and character merchandise and more on specialty gifts. The **Chapeau** offers monogrammed hats and mouse ears. The **Confectionery** sells tempting candies, chocolates, candies, and snacks.

Crystal Arts features hand-blown glass. **Disney Clothiers** offers an array of apparel for men, women, and kids. **Engine Co. 71** sells *101 Dalmatians* merchandise. The **Main Street Athletic Club** offers athletic wear. **Main Street Cinema** sells collectible pins, music, and toys. **Main Street Gallery** offers art, posters, prints, and lithographs. **Uptown Jewelers** sells collectible gifts and jewelry. Last, but certainly not least, the **Harmony Barber Shop** offers shaves and haircuts along with – what else – a barbershop quarter, the Dapper Dans.

Services

The **Guest Relations** counter inside the MK is located here, at City Hall. There's also an information board at the end of Main Street closest to the castle. Main Street also hosts the **Stroller Shop, lockers,** and **lost and found** just inside the park entrance. **Package Pickup** can be found at Town Square. The Crystal Palace hosts the **Baby Center** and **First Aid.**

Adventureland

Going clockwise around the waterways at the center of the park, the first bridge you see leads to Adventureland, a tropical wonderland featuring some dynamite attractions and lush, tropical, inviting vegetation. The architecture recalls Indiana Jones and Romancing the Stone, and in one section, recreates Agrabah, Aladdin's desert home.

Some of the Magic Kingdom's best attractions can be found here, namely the Jungle Cruise and Pirates of the Caribbean. Adventureland is best experienced early in the morning or late in the afternoon. The Swiss Family Treehouse and more notably the Jungle Cruise have extremely slow-moving lines, but FastPass helps at the Jungle Cruise. A couple of fast food restaurants dot the landscape here, but nothing too compelling mealwise. (There is a great snack to be found here, but more on that later.) Shopping in Adventureland can be a lot of fun, with interesting imports from the seven seas available at the Persian-themed Agrabah Bazaar and the swashbucklin' Pirates of the Caribbean Plaza.

Pirates of the Caribbean

Rating: A+
8 minute "dark ride" in boats.
Fear Factor: 3
Lightest crowds early morning or late afternoon.

Classic Disney – this is exactly the kind of thing they do best. Pirates here plunder and burn a seaside village, tip back booze, and then auction off wenches (who then turn the tables) – and all of this mayhem is made completely innocuous by virtue of the infectious "Yo Ho (A Pirate's Life for Me)" tune that wafts through the ride.

The Audio-Animatronic pirates, townspeople, and animals who populate this ride are remarkable for their individuality, personality, and immaculate detail. Especially uncanny are the movements and noises (attitudes?) of the chickens, dogs, and pigs found throughout the attraction. The ride can be a little intimidating for the youngest of children, but even the spooky skull and crossbone scenes are completely nonthreatening. There's one slight drop (nothing like Splash Mountain) - a pitch-black plunge down a chute to the accompaniment of a roaring waterfall. But it's over before you know it.

Lines here move quick. Despite the popularity of this attraction, their is rarely a wait over half an hour, and then only during peak seasons. Be sure to put this on the top of your list.

Jungle Cruise
Rating: A
10 minute narrated boat trip.
Fear Factor: 2
Lightest crowds the hour after opening/before closing. Use FastPass.

You don't have to go on safari, the safari comes to you. Audio-Animatronic animals abound on this boat cruise, one of the few rides at WDW narrated and driven by a human. Everything else is fake though – the Jungle includes a family of bathing elephants, hippos, lions, and cannibals, also of interest is a section of the cruise that plunges cruisers into a dark Cambodian temple, home to a ferocious white tiger! Actually I lied. The tropical vegetation here is real and not robotic, and is kept warm in the winter by 100 heaters hidden in the rocks.

The boat pilots' spiel is corny but irresistibly funny. The pun-heavy prattle covers topics like previous guests who didn't make it, the headhunters, and the rest of the sights. The scenes are pretty realistic at times, and while a few kids are squeamish at first, but most soon sit back and enjoy the ride. Some of it is gruesome and odd, but it is all fun. Disney's FastPass is available here and recommended.

Swiss Family Treehouse
Rating: B-
Self-guided walking tour.
Fear Factor: 1
Lightest crowds before 11:30am and after 5:30pm.

This huge re-creation of the Robinsons' lost paradise has everything a marooned family could want in fine treetop living. Patchwork quilts, mahogany furniture, candles stuck in abalone shells, and a clever system of running water in each room.

Reaction to the Treehouse is mixed. Some people are turned off by all the stairs. For those who dare though, the view from the top is quite impressive. On the whole though, this isn't one of the more entertaining attractions here.

Tropical Serenade (Enchanted Tiki Birds)
Rating: C+
15 minute musical show.
Fear Factor: 2
Lightest crowds mid-afternoon.

Now under the "management" of Iago (Gilbert Gottfried, reprising his role from Aladdin) and Zazu (Rowan Atkinson, reprising his Lion King role), this venerable show has received a new lease on life, having grown somewhat tired since 1964. The birds now belt out songs like "In the Still of the Night," "Hot Hot Hot," "Do the Conga," and "Get on Your Feet." Hollywood-savvy guests will enjoy the irony of the pre-show, with two bickering birds who work as talent agents – named William and Morris. Be sure to note Ovitz the bird tossed out behind the building. Just kidding.

The Magic Carpets of Aladdin
Rating: C
2-minute Dumbo-type ride.
Fear Factor: 1
Lightest crowds the hour after opening/before closing.

A whole new world? I wouldn't go that far. If you've done Dumbo, you've done this. Passengers board 4-person "magic carpets" and circle around the Genie's lamp. Guests can use controls in the "carpets" to control the altitude of their flight, as well as pitching forwards and back. Music from the film is also featured in the attraction. While your kids may get a kick out of the spitting camels and the control factor, this is really a glorified carnival ride, and you can get away with skipping it if the line is prohibitive.

Shrunken Ned's Junior Jungle Boats
Rating: D
Remote control boats.
Fear Factor: 1
Visit midday when everything else is mobbed.

For $1, your kids can spend two minutes piloting a remote control boat around tiki gods and other obstacles. Your time is better spent elsewhere.

Shopping
The **Agrabah Bazaar** features merchandise and gifts with a Middle Eastern and African theme, safari apparel, and Aladdin merchandise. The

Pirate's Bazaar features "gemstones" by the bag, cutlasses, cannons, and other booty. That's pirate booty. Not the J-Lo variety. Yarr. **Island Supply Company** sells surfwear, grass skirts, leis, and sunglasses.

Frontierland

Craggy red rocks dominate the landscape here, with a landscape representing the Old West. The whole place looks like something out of a spaghetti western, with weathered buildings of stone and clapboard and cacti and sagebrush dotting the ground.

But more importantly than the scenery are the rides! Two of the Magic Kingdom's A-list attractions are located here – the Splash Mountain water thrill ride, and the Big Thunder Mountain Railroad roller coaster. These two attractions draw some serious crowds all day long, but FastPass makes them a little more manageable. The County Bear Jamboree is a perennial favorite as well. The venerable Diamond Horseshoe Revue here closed for good in October 2004.

There's some fun shopping to be done here – leather goods, Western wear, cowboy hats, toy guns, and Indian and Southwestern crafts are all available. There's a few quick service food options as well – the Pecos Bill Café is a particularly good burger bet thanks to their irresistible fixings bar.

Big Thunder Mountain Railroad

Rating: A+
Relatively tame but incredibly scenic and surprisingly long rollercoaster.
Fear Factor: 3
Use FastPass to avoid crowds, or visit in the first or last hours the park is open.

One of only two roller coasters in the Magic Kingdom, Big Thunder Mountain is an incredible experience for anyone. Don't be intimidated – the ride tops out around the 25mph mark, and the scenery is incredible. Adrenaline junkies will be nonplussed by the thrills, but anyone can appreciate the painstaking attention to detail and the wild scenes you careen through, around, over, and under this 197-foot mountain (Florida's third highest, although I don't think they count manmade) – including such potentially frightening sights as a bat cave (sit down, Alfred, it's not THAT Batcave, this isn't Six Flags), a rockslide, and a flood. It's all in fun though, and there's plenty of humor and innocuous sights – especially in the flooded-out town of Tumbleweed, in which a man sits, wearing his pajamas and a puzzled look as a Professor Cumulus Isobar's rainmaking machine sputters and pops, the flood beneath him. Geysers, partially unearthed dinosaur skeletons, and authentic mining equipment comprise some of the other eye candy on this 3 1/2 minute journey.

Be sure to check out the Railroad after dark, riding it at night is a completely different experience. Best times to hit this without lines are the first and last hours of park operation, unless you have a FastPass. Make sure you don't miss it though, it's one of the top five attractions here. Note that children must be 40" tall to ride, and must be accompanied by an adult under the age of 7. Child swap is available, to allow both parents of a child who does not meet riding restrictions to experience the attraction.

Splash Mountain

Rating: A

Fun 10-minute water flume ride through one of Disney's forgotten movie classics.

Fear Factor: 4

Use FastPass or visit during parades if you can't make it in the first/last hours.

Pop quiz. Sing the chorus of "Zip-a-Dee-Doo-Dah." Easy, right? Now tell me what movie it's from. AHA! Gotcha, didn't I? It seems surprising that one of the best and most popular attractions in Disney World would be based on a movie that people only remember for its controversial racial undertones – *Song of the South*. Another surprise is that, given this ride's theme song, it contains the single scariest thrill in all of the Magic Kingdom.

The ride retells the adventures of Br'er Rabbit as he indulges his wanderlust and gets into all kinds of trouble (mostly involving the scheming Br'er Fox and the hapless Br'er Bear) before making a triumphant, prodigal-wabbit return to the Briar Patch. The climax of the ride involves a wild and wet drop down a 52-foot, 45-degree chute. Reaching speeds of 40mph on the slope, the guest-filled logs hit the water with a splash and then seem to disappear under the surface of the water. No worries though – nobody drowns, and only Audio-Animatronic animals were harmed in the making of this adventure.

Compared to the Disneyland version, this is a slightly improved iteration of the experience. The pace through the mountain is slower and there's more focus on the actual scenery than the ride, so the story is told much more effectively.

A few important things to note: You WILL get wet. Deal with it. If you don't want to get wet, you NEED a rain poncho. They're available for $2 at 7-Elevens throughout town or more if you have to buy them inside the park. But a garbage bag works just as well.

As this is one of the most popular rides in Disney World, it gets crowded INSTANTLY, as many people make this their first stop of the day. To beat the crack-of-9 rush, there is a shortcut: rather than going through Liberty Square to Frontierland, go through Adventureland and turn right at the bathrooms across from the Swiss Family Treehouse. Run, Forrest, Run!

Country Bear Jamboree
> Rating: B+
> Entertaining musical show starring Audio-Animatronic bears.
> Fear Factor: 1
> Visit during the morning or after 5pm, or when people stake out parade seats.

Everybody seems to love the Country Bear Jamboree, where the eponymous woodland creatures perform like never before in a musical revue filled with fun. Led by Henry, the master of ceremonies, they kick up a storm. One bear has a knack for impersonating Elvis Presley, while three other bruins, Bubbles, Beluah, and Bunny, harmonize "Wish They All Could Be California Bears." Other performers include the heartthrob Teddi Barra, who sings in the rain a la Gene Kelly (complete with raincoat and galoshes), a country-western band known as the Bear Rugs: Zeb, Zeke, Ted, Fred, and Tennessee, Liver Lips McGrowl, Wendell, Gomer the pianist, Trixie the Tampa Temptation (a torch-song crooner), Melvin the Moosehead, and Big Al, who is nothing short of a cult hero at WDW.

Tom Sawyer Island
> Rating: B-
> Outdoor exhibit and play area.
> Fear Factor: 1
> Visit mid-day. Note that this attraction closes at dusk.

This attraction is incredibly popular with children, who can run and play and explore this fascinating and fun island in the middle of the Rivers of America, proving that you don't need robotic dinosaurs to have a good time. Diversions here include air guns, caves, bridges, mines, and cannons. Adults can get off their feet with a refreshing lemonade at Aunt Polly's Landing, combining with the shade to make this an attractive afternoon respite.

Frontierland Shootin' Arcade
> Rating: C
> Infrared target practice. Costs $.50 for 25 shots.

Fear Factor: 2
Visit anytime.

At this attraction, you can be the Lone Ranger, Clint Eastwood, or your favorite Western hero as you pick up a Hawkins 54-caliber buffalo rifle (modernized: they shoot infrared beams now) and can blow away any or all of almost a hundred targets, each one producing a different, often amusing reaction. Digital sound effects add to the "realism" of this arcade. Entertainment value is minimal here, but there's usually a minimal time investment as well, so knock yourself out. Just don't shoot your eye out.

Walt Disney World Railroad
The second of three stops on the Railroad is located between Splash and Big Thunder Mountains.

Shopping
The **Briar Patch** sells Splash Mountain gifts. At **Prairie Outpost and Supply**, Western themed toys like guns and horses; clothing such as boots, buckles, and moccasins; and provisions like venison chili and beef jerky. Kiosks and booths around Frontierland sell personalized wood carvings, hats, and other Western apparel.

Liberty Square

Celebrate America's Colonial heritage at Liberty Square, where patriotic melodies are piped through and Disney cast wander around in 18th-century dress. There's only really one attraction here that ties into that theme – the moving (but not always appreciated) Hall of Presidents show. If you're seeking a dose of red white and blue goodness though, check out the Liberty Tree, a 130-year old live oak that was found at WDW's southern fringe and transported to its present location twenty years ago. Thirteen lanterns hang on the tree, one for each of the original colonies.

The best attraction here is the Haunted Mansion, which often has formidable lines if you don't have a FastPass. There's only a few shops here, but there's one particularly good bet, where it's Christmas Eve 365 days a year. Liberty Square has some of the Magic Kingdom's best dining, both of the counter-service and sit-down varieties, including character dining at the Liberty Tree Tavern.

The Haunted Mansion
Rating: A+
7-minute classic Disney "dark ride" through a haunted house.

Fear Factor: 2
Visit before noon – FastPass is only necessary in the busiest seasons.

What's scarier than the decline of Eddie Murphy's taste in movie scripts? Not this classic attraction, which features incredible special effects that bring to life – and I use the term loosely – 999 ghosts, ghouls, and goblins. It's not scary at all though – kids might be a little a-feared in anticipation, but the sights on the ride itself are very tame, much more spooky than scary. Tame, yes. Simple? Not on your AFTERLIFE. There are a ton of details here that you won't notice your first time through – or your second, or your third, or even your fourth. Guests experience a 1 1/2 minute pre-show in a stretching room whose ceiling seems to rise – or is the floor sinking? The "doom buggies" just inside carry guests through elaborate Victorian sets that tell the story of a jealous groom and his suicidal bride, using clever displays and fascinating special effects most effectively. Best of all is the last effect – but telling would ruin the surprise. Just be sure your family doesn't pick up an extra member along the way. Lines are usually quick-moving here, so save your FastPass for another attraction.

The Hall of Presidents
Rating: B
23 minute tour of great moments in American history.
Fear Factor: 1
Visit anytime – you will rarely have to wait beyond the next showtime.

This attraction traces its red, white, and blue roots to one of the original Audio-Animatronic shows, *Great Moments with Mr. Lincoln*, from the 1964-65 World's Fair in Flushing, NY. It consists of a 70mm film about the historical importance of the Constitution, narrated by Maya Angelou. Then, an Audio-Animatronic Abe Lincoln and George W. Bush deliver speeches preceded by a roll call of all of America's leaders, from George 1 to Dubya 43, who delivers a 90-second spiel that reportedly has no malapropisms. The detail is impressive, as the chief executive officers fidget, nod, and whisper. Each president is dressed in authentic period costume, from his hairstyle to the fabric of his pants. Even their personal effects were painstakingly researched and recreated, like Washington's chair, FDR's leg brace, and the engraving on Dubya's watch.

If you are a history buff or just someone who feels especially proud of his red, white, and blue heritage, you will particularly appreciate this show. However, if you only have limited time and have seen the American Adventure at Epcot, you can skip this, especially if your kids are too young to appreciate history. Don't worry if there's a substantial line here: it turns over 700 people every 25 minutes.

Liberty Square Riverboat
> Rating: B-
> 16-minute circle tour of the Rivers of America.
> Fear Factor: 1
> Visit anytime.

The Richard F. Irvine steamboat chugs along the statuesque Rivers of America, providing lovely views of the Haunted Mansion, Big Thunder Mountain Railroad, Splash Mountain, Tom Sawyer Island, and more. This is a good bet to beat the heat and while away a few relaxing minutes on a sticky, crowded afternoon.

Shopping
> The **Yankee Trader** shop features kitchen goodies, like cookbooks and gadgets from the mundane to the sublime – everything from spatulas to soufflé dishes. There's also every Smucker's variety known to man. Best of all is **Ye Olde Christmas Shoppe**, where you can pick up all kinds of WDW and Disney character ornaments. **Heritage House** offers historical and American-themed gifts. Artists in Liberty Square also offer silhouette drawings.

Fantasyland

This is where dreams come true and fairy tales are personified. Fantasyland is truly the heart and soul of WDW. This is where Disney's best-loved characters, like Peter Pan, Alice in Wonderland, Cinderella, Dumbo, Snow White, and many more come to life. This is the favorite land of many children, as there are a few standout attractions here.

The buildings in which the adventures here are housed resemble an Alpine village. The adventures themselves are some of the most popular in Disney World, and thus crowds here can be downright suffocating at times. FastPass is available at the Winnie the Pooh and Peter Pan attractions and at the new Philharmagic film. **Ariel's Grotto**, located along the lagoon that formerly housed 20,000 Leagues under the Sea, is the foremost character greeting location in the Magic Kingdom.

Shops here feature a wealth of specialty character merchandise. Food options include character dining at Cinderella's Royal Table (inside her Castle) and several forgettable counter-service options.

Mickey's Philharmagic
> Rating: B+
> 12-minute 3D animated musical spectacular.

Fear Factor: 1
Visit in the afternoon or via FastPass.

Added in October 2003, Philharmagic features 3D animation of Disney's most beloved characters projected onto a 150 foot screen (one of the largest ever 3D projections), along with special effects and sensory tricks to enhance the experience. Probably the most surreal thing about this attraction is seeing characters from classic Disney animation rendered (for the first time ever!) in computer-animated 3D. I couldn't help but think how much Disney will miss Pixar.

There is a loose storyline, of course, involving Donald Duck frantically chasing a Fantasia MacGuffin, but it's just an excuse for classic Disney music and eye-popping 3D gags and effects. The movie's cast also includes Mickey (briefly, although the show bears his name), Jasmine and Aladdin, Ariel, Simba, and more. It's the most family-friendly of all the 3D movies in Disney, and offers a pleasant mix of nostalgia and effects. FastPass is available here.

Cinderellabration

Rating: N/A
18-minute live stage show.
Fear Factor: 1
Visit according to show schedules.

Imported from Tokyo Disneyland in May 2005 as part of Disney's "Happiest Celebration on Earth" birthday party, Cinderellabration is performed several times daily at the Castle Forecourt Stage. The show visits "Happily Ever After," as Prince Charming has married Cinderella, we pick up right before her coronation, with guest appearances from other Disney princesses, like Snow White, Princess Aurora (aka Sleeping Beauty), Belle, and Jasmine with elaborate costumes, special effects, and an original musical score incorporating classic Disney songs with new compositions. This show could not be reviewed before press time.

It's a Small World

Rating: B+
11-minute boat ride celebrating diversity.
Fear Factor: 1 (5 for the song!)
Visit after 12 noon.

Political correctness years ahead of its time, this saccharine-sweet attraction sets the frolicking of nearly 300 Audio-Animatronic dolls representing the cultures from all corners of the world. You'll find can-can

Cinderella Castle

The Castle is the iconic symbol of all Walt Disney World, but it comes as a surprise to many visitors that they cannot freely tour Cinderella Castle and that there is no ride or show in it. Still, it is arguably the most spectacular building in the whole World, and one of the most-photographed in the real world (as in the Earth!). The castle, whose gold, grey, and blue spires reach 189 feet over Main Street (100 feet higher than Sleeping Beauty Castle in Disneyland), is influenced by French palaces around the end of the 1100s, along with Mad King Ludwig of Bavaria's mansion and of course the castle from the 1950 Disney film.

Cinderella Castle is also the nerve center of the Magic Kingdom, both above ground and below it. Above Cinderella's Royal Table on the second floor are broadcast rooms, security centers (guardhouses, if you will), and a never-occupied apartment meant for the Disneys. Below ground Disney employees change out of their "real people" outfits (yes! they are real people, not Audio-Animatronics) and into a Mickey suit or khakis and a pith helmet. They then travel through underground corridors to their designated "land" and inconspicuously melt into the scenery.

What makes the castle Cinderella's besides the name? The restaurant in the castle features character dining with the princess herself, plus a series of five mosaic murals that depicting her familiar tale. The panels, measuring 150 square feet apiece, were designed by artist Dorothea Redmond and constructed by master craftsman Hanns-Joachim Scharff. They contain over one million tiny bits of Italian glass in 500 colors, plus bits of real silver and 14-karat gold.

dancers, Tower of London guards, leprechauns, Dutch kids with wooden clogs on their feet, Thai dancers, snake charmers, kite flyers, hula-dancing Polynesians, Don Quixote lookalikes, nursery rhyme characters, and countless others as your boat floats through various colorful themed rooms.

The dolls' costumes are particularly faithful, and the overall effect is glowing and alive with warmth. Just be aware though that the titular song will stick in your head like an ear infection. It can't be helped, so caveat emptor. The track, one of the most-recognized Disney tunes, was composed by Richard and Robert Sherman, the brother team who brought us Mary Poppins and other Oscar-winning music. The boat ride is particularly relaxing, and the oft-times mammoth lines move quickly, so there's rarely much of a wait. This ride was renovated and refreshed in 2004 and 2005, with a new mural by Mary Blair, a new color palette, hair and makeup touch-ups for the dolls, and upgraded lighting and soundtrack.

Peter Pan's Flight
Rating: B+
3-minute "dark ride."
Fear Factor: 2
Use FastPass or visit in the first or last hours of park operation.

Board a replica of Captain Hook's pirate ship and sail off into the London night on this ride, which transports you to Neverland and retells the Peter Pan legend in a spectacular fashion. You'll sail over the Thames, Big Ben, and Parliament, witness the sword fight between Pan and Captain Hook, and reach the satisfying finale: Hook nervously straddling the crocodile's jaws. WDW's most underrated attraction is toured much more easily with a FastPass, as Fantasyland "dark rides" tend to be crowded pretty much all day.

The Many Adventures of Winnie the Pooh
Rating: B
2-minute "dark ride."
Fear Factor: 1
Use FastPass or visit in the first or last hours of park operation.

The space formerly occupied by Mr. Toad's Wild Ride is this trip through the Hundred Acre Wood, which uses the old Mr. Toad ride mechanism, track, and concept to tell the story of Winnie the Pooh and the Blustery Day. Featuring Eeyore, Piglet, Kanga, Roo, and all the other characters, it's sure to please those with a fetish for Pooh – that's Pooh, with an H, you sickos. This ride is a particularly necessary FastPasser.

Snow White's Scary Adventures
Rating: B-
2 1/2 minute "dark ride."
Fear Factor: 2
Visit before 11am or after 4pm.

Probably the darkest of the Fantasyland rides, Snow White's Scary Adventures puts guests in mine cars that roll through dark tableaus that tell the often-gothic story of the sleeping princess, the seven dwarves, the wicked witch, the poisoned apple, and all of that good stuff. Definitely some spookiness to this one, so be sure your children have the fortitude for this sort of thing.

Dumbo, the Flying Elephant

Rating: C+
1 1/2 minute carnival-type ride.
Fear Factor: 1
Right after park opening or right before closing.

I'm not sure why this is such a classic, but for some reason it's part of the archetypal Walt Disney World experience. The youngest kids in particular love flying around in the elephants (although one particularly famous photo shows Muhammad Ali looking absolutely gleeful in one), using the buttons to raise and lower them as they circle around. It's only a 90 second flight, and since it's a low-capacity ride, lines seem endless. But for some reason this is unskippable for families with young kids. So do it first thing in the morning if you're dead set on it.

Cinderella's Golden Carrousel

Rating: C+
2 minute merry-go-round.
Fear Factor: 1
Visit after dark.

Much like the Swiss Family Treehouse, that places the emphasis not on action but on aesthetic beauty and attention to detail. Probably the most picturesque merry-go-round you will ever see, the Carrousel is a rarity in WDW - an authentic item, built in Philadelphia in 1917. Originally dubbed "Liberty", it had 72 horses and several stationary chariots on a 60-foot platform when it was discovered at Olympic Park in Maplewood, New Jersey. Disney replaced the chariots with more horses, and the mechanics were completely modernized. Each of the 90 white horses is slightly different, with details that lend personality and individuality to each. Look inward as the Carrousel circles and take in the eighteen hand-painted, six-square-foot scenes adorning the ride. The horses glide effortlessly to accompaniment from a band organ playing classic Disney tunes. This ride is especially breathtaking at night.

Mad Tea Party

Rating: C
1 1/2 minute carnival-type ride.
Fear Factor: 3
Visit before noon or after 5pm.

Even though it's loosely based on the Mad Hatter's unbirthday from Alice in Wonderland, you'll get déjà vu on this ride more likely than motion sickness. Of course you've seen this before. It's called the "Tilt-a-Whirl." Except that this one doesn't really tilt, it simply whirls riders around in spinning teacups. Oh well. It's still a fun little trifle if the line's not too bad, especially considering the wheel in the middle of the cups can be used to accelerate the spinning. Hey kids, wanna see Mommy's breakfast again?

Shopping

Fantasyland is a good place to shop for character merchandise, especially that of the various Disney princesses, whose regalia can be purchased for your daughters at **Tinkerbell's Treasures**. **Sir Mickey's** offers character merchandise, apparel, and toys. **Pooh's Thotful Shop** features a dynamite selection of goodies featuring the beloved characters from the Hundred Acre Wood. **FantasyFaire**, outside Philharmagic, sells Donald Duck swag.

Mickey's Toontown Fair

In 1988, a three-acre section of the Grand Prix Raceway was transformed into the Magic Kingdom's first new "land" since its opening in 1971 – Mickey's Birthdayland, commemorating the Mouse's 60th birthday. It later became Mickey's Starland and then Mickey's Toontown Fair, and is the best place in the park for your kids to get up close and personal with Mickey, Minnie, and the other big names of the Disney empire and take a tour of some of the "stars' homes." It's a fun diversion for everyone, especially the younger set, and definitely a bit of relaxation. Plus, this is the place to meet Mickey himself (at the **Judge's Tent**), Disney princesses (at the **Princess Room**), and heros, heroines, and villains (at the **Hall of Fame Tent**). There's no must-see attraction here, so you can skip this if you're pressed for time if you don't have younger children. There's one small shop here and a farmer's market serving refreshing produce.

The Barnstormer at Goofy's Wiseacre Farm

Rating: B
1 minute family roller coaster.
Fear Factor: 2
Visit before 11am or during parades.

The Barnstormer is a short, tame, and kid-friendly roller coaster that puts you in the hapless dog-type-thing's crop duster full of anthr— err – love, as you wind across a track that certainly earns the name Goofy.

Mickey's Country House & Judge's Tent
Minnie's Country House
Rating: B
Walk-through exhibits showing the "homes" of the celluloid mice.
Fear Factor: 1
Visit in the morning.

Call it "Behind the Mouseic." Call it whatever you like. If you ever wondered, "What is Mickey REALLY like at home? What kind of decorating taste does Minnie have? Well, your answers are all right here. Mickey's four-room cottage and Minnie's colorful pad offer plenty of opportunities for rambunctious fun, climbing, eye candy, and memorabilia spotting. Note that Mickey's Country House leads you into the queue for the Judge's Tent, which is where you can actually meet THE man, err, mouse of honor. So, check it out and get two Mickeyriffic experiences for the price of one.

Hidden Mickeys

One of the more intriguing running themes in a Disney World vacation is the eponymous nature of Mickey Mouse's distinctive silhouette. Sure, you'll see it in some obvious places, and some not-so-obvious ones, but there's a lot more than you might expect. In fact, some Disney veterans make the search for these "hidden Mickeys" an obsessive-compulsive quest during their trip. A fun activity for the whole family is to print a list beforehand of all the hidden Mickeys throughout the world, and see how many each person can collect. After all, what would a vacation be without a little good natured competition? To learn more about hidden Mickeys, read Stephen M. Barrett's *Hidden Mickeys: A Field Guide to Walt Disney World's Best Secrets*, or visit hiddenmickeys.org.

Donald's Boat
Rating: C+
Interactive playground.
Fear Factor: 1
Visit anytime.

This is a wet playground built around Donald's leaking boat. younger children especially love to splash and play here and you may need to drag them away eventually. This is especially enjoyable in the midday heat.

Walt Disney World Railroad

The WDW Railroad has its third stop on the outer fringe of the Toontown Fair.

Shopping

The only shop in Mickey's Toontown Fair is **County Bounty**, selling children's clothing, toys, and gifts.

Tomorrowland

Formerly a dull and monochromatic mass of concrete, Tomorrowland has been revamped and the focus changed from a "serious" look at the "real" future to the future envisioned by Jules Verne and other sci-fi writers of the 20s and 30s. It's now a sleek and somewhat sexy, neon-lined art-deco intergalactic spaceport. Dated attractions like Mission to Mars were replaced or renovated. The sum total effect of the renovations is that Tomorrowland actually feels like a futuristic city, rather than simply an abstract gray mess.

Space Mountain is one of the marquee attractions in all of Disney World, but beyond that, there's only one real must-see attraction, the interactive and fun Buzz Lightyear's Space Ranger Spin. Both offer FastPass. A few minor attractions and unremarkable shops also dot the landscape, as well as a couple of very good counter-service eateries.

Space Mountain

Rating: A+
3-minute indoor roller coaster.
Fear Factor: 4
Use FastPass or ride after 6pm.

Even though it only hits a top speed of 28 miles an hour, this unforgettable 3,188 foot long roller coaster is an absolutely sublime experience. It's positively other-worldly, with great sound and visual effects inside a dark, planetarium-like space, and the sounds of the trains clattering across the tracks and jubilant shrieks of riders are all you hear, it really feels like being out in deep space. While the thrill in conventional roller coasters lies in the actual twists, turns, drops, and loops, Space Mountain tries to terrify by sending you off through passageways of flashing lights, strobes, and strange sounds, and eventually into a cavernous place where the only thing you can see is the dark shape of a head in front of you. Unlike most coasters, these six-passenger cars have riders sitting single file, which reinforces the isolation of space travel.

Touring Space Mountain can be challenging due to its popularity. FastPass reduces the wait time considerably, but in the absence of that, your options are: ride first thing in the morning. Ride after dinnertime. Ride during a parade.

Note that due to the turbulent ride, there are some restrictions. Children must be 42" tall to ride, and the usual array of restrictions for pregnant women, back problems, heart issues, etc. apply here. Child swap service is available here to enable both parents of a too-small or too-scared child to experience the ride. Open during Extra Magic Hour.

Buzz Lightyear's Space Ranger Spin
Rating: B+
6 minute interactive "dark ride."
Fear Factor: 1
Use FastPass, visit before 11am, or after 6pm.

Based on the Toy Story movies, his fun, addictive ride follows the adventures of Buzz Lightyear's elite Space Rangers (that's you) in their fight to save the world from the evil intergalactic Emperor Zurg, who's plotting to take over the world by stealing batteries. You ride in cars that rotate 360 degrees and come equipped with lasers with which you can blast the enemy into submission. Your car keeps score of your progress, and as I found out… shooting aliens isn't as easy as it looks.

I will say this about Buzz Lightyear. As awesome as the concept is, and as much fun as the ride is, the ergonomics are EXTREMELY frustrating, as the laser guns are not very cooperative, they're often stiff and difficult to manipulate. I thought a lot more highly of this ride before I went on Men in Black: Alien Attack and saw how much more effectively executed that iteration is. Still, this is one of the wildest good times to be had in the Magic Kingdom and is strongly recommended.

Stitch's Great Escape
Rating: B-
15 minute long Audio-Animatronic show.
Fear Factor: 3
Visit during late afternoon or with FastPass.

This attraction, a prequel to the hit *Lilo & Stitch*, replaced the blood-curdlingly scary ExtraTERRORestrial Alien Encounter in 2004, hitting just the right tone to make this attraction a winner, unlike the last guy who lived here, who scared the living crap out of everyone who hadn't hit puberty yet and some who have. The scene of the attraction is the Galactic Federation Prisoner Teleport Center, a sort of intergalactic Guantanamo Bay. Skippy from Alien Encounter is still here, and is still being tortured like an enemy combatant. The mischievous Experiment 626, aka Stitch, is beamed into the facility, and proceeds to wreak havoc, eat chili dogs, and dodge two 1,600 pound "plasma cannons" before beaming himself down to Hawaii. Hey, I want to do that.

The show is fun, not to mention the goofy, adorable sort of thing that Disney hasn't been able to pull off in quite a while, although some guests find the ride to be dull, plotless, and anti-climactic, and some kids don't handle the moment of total darkness so well You can use FastPass here.

The Timekeeper
Rating: B
20 minute CircleVision 360 film and then some.
Fear Factor: 2
Visit during the crowded, hot midday hours.

For some reason this attraction is only open seasonally – this is a shame, as it's truly underrated, and a heartwarming good time with laughs and breathtaking sights, as 9-Eye, a flying, time-traveling robot with cameras spanning 360 degrees, and the Timekeeper, an Audio-Animatronic robot who looks uncannily like the man who provides his voice, Robin Williams. The film goes all the way back to prehistoric times, with a stop at Jules Verne's place on the way back to the future ... oh wait, that's another theme park.

Walt Disney's Carousel of Progress
Rating: B
Classic Walt-era 18 minute show.
Fear Factor: 1
Visit during the afternoon.

This happy show depicts the advancement of technology throughout the past hundred years, tracing an average family as they evolve from ice cubes and fans to air conditioning, from radio to television to the Internet, and so on and so forth. This attraction dates all the way back to the 1964-65 World's Fair, where it was called "Progressland." Open seasonally, this ride is a great bet for mid-afternoon heat-beating.

Tomorrowland Indy Speedway

Rating: C+
5 minute mock Indy car ride.
Fear Factor: 2
Visit before 11am or after 4pm.

I am not a huge fan of this attraction – it's loud, smells of exhaust, and the idea of putting around driving along a track at a whiplash-inducing 7mph really lost a lot of its appeal for me when I got my driver's license. But younger kids love it. The paradox here is that drivers must be 52" tall – so most of the ride's target audience has to sit shotgun. Oh well. One solution is to let your child sit on your lap and steer while you work the pedals, thus giving the illusion of driving to your kids. Consider this one skippable, unless your shorties tell you otherwise.

Tomorrowland Transit Authority

Rating: C
10 minute tour of Tomorrowland.
Fear Factor: 1
Visit anytime.

The TTA Metroliner Blue Line track can be seen winding all throughout Tomorrowland, but if you wish to ride, you have to go to the boarding area, near the AstroOrbiter. The quiet, environmentally friendly ride offers a narrated overview of Tomorrowland, with views of each attraction. Enjoyable, but not compelling in any way.

Astro Orbiter

Rating: D
1 1/2 minute carnival-style ride.
Fear Factor: 2
Ride before 11am or after 6pm.

These shuttles, modeled after Buck Rogers', make up a midway ride primarily for those kids between Dumbo and Space Mountain. Small aircraft circle a model rocket connected by large metal arms, and the height of your vehicle's flight can be altered. The shuttles rotate eleven times a minute for a top speed of 26 MPH, rising up to 80 feet. It's too tame for most people over twelve and is more time-consuming than most other attractions, being a slow-loading ride like Dumbo. Skip this one entirely if you can.

Shopping

The two major shops in Tomorrowland are **Mickey's Star Traders,** offering a very good selection of stuffed animals, clothes, collectibles, film, and sunscreen; and **Merchant of Venus,** offering kitschy futuristic gifts, toys, games, fashions, jewelry, and the like. The **Tomorrowland Power and Light Co.** features modern arcade fun.

Entertainment in the Magic Kingdom

There is always some sort of live entertainment going on around the Magic Kingdom. It ranges from character interaction to musical performance to stage show, but there's always something to keep you amused. Check your park map and entertainment guide for specific details of entertainment during your visit.

Meeting the Characters

For many children (and some adults), meeting Mickey himself, or any of dozens of other Disney characters, can be the highlight of the trip. But you have to know where to look for them. There are two major ways to meet the characters. One is at specialty dining experiences, and another is through meet-and-greets at specified times throughout the day. Get to the park before it opens and participate in a meet-and-greet with Mickey, Donald, Goofy at Main Street, USA's WDW Railroad Station.

Character dining is available at the following restaurants:
•**Cinderella's Royal Table:** Breakfast buffet featuring Cinderella and her Fairy Godmother as well as other princesses, like Belle, Aurora, and Snow White. $21.99 adults/$11.99 for kids under 12.
•**Crystal Palace:** Breakfast, lunch, and dinner buffets featuring Winnie the Pooh, Tigger, Eeyore, and Piglet. B: $17.99 adults/$9.99 kids. L: $19.99 adults/$10.99 kids. D: $22.99 adult/$10.99 kids.
•**Liberty Tree Tavern:** Dinner buffet featuring Mickey, Pluto, Donald, Daisy, Minnie, and more. $22.99 adults/$10.99 kids.

Character greeting areas include, but are not limited to:
•**Main Street, USA:** Town Square Exhibition Hall
•**Fantasyland:** Ariel's Grotto, Fantasyland Character Festival
•**Mickey's Toontown Fair:** Judge's Tent, Hall of Fame, Princess Room

Here's a hint on character meet-and-greets. Thick pens work better for autographs than thinner ones because of the thick gloves the people in the

mouse suits have to wear. Oops, did I just let the cat out of the bag? Sorry…
Don't ask me about Santa either.

Share a Dream Come True Parade

In October 2001, Disney World commemorated the centennial of
Walt Disney's birth with this new daily parade featuring Mickey Mouse and
a cast of 110, with Disney characters in tableaus that capture scenes from the
early days of Mickey all the way to the newest Disney films. Vignettes are
projected onto snow globes with Disney characters inside, with the first and
last floats containing especially amazing snow globes. The parade stops
intermittently to allow the characters and the audience to interact. It's fun,
but you can't help thinking that the folks in those snowglobes feel like ants
under a magnifying glass in the hot Florida sun. Definitely worth a viewing,
even if parade times are optimal times to tour popular attractions. The
parade starts at 3pm daily.

Overlooked Parade Vantages

Though Main Street, USA is often crowded with throngs of
parade-viewers, there are plenty of choice locations to stake out
some real estate for when the parade passes by. Some of these
include:

•At Sleepy Hollow, in Liberty Square close to the Hub, you can arrive
ten to twenty minutes early, buy some refreshments, and take a table
by the rail.
•Any spot on the pathway between Sleepy Hollow and the Castle on
the Liberty Square side of the moat.
•The covered walkway between Liberty Tree Tavern and the Diamond Horseshoe Saloon.
•The raised platform in front of the Frontierland facade.
•The central hub, between the Adventureland and Liberty Square
bridges.
•Waterfront at the Rivers of America.

SpectroMagic

This whimsical nighttime parade features over a million lights,
blinking, glimmering, and shining in bright white and fantastic color.
Characters in fiber optic suits interact with elaborate floats, to the
accompaniment of classic Disney music. Note that this parade only
functions when the park is open late.

Wishes

Replacing the 27-year-old Fantasy in the Sky fireworks show in 2003, *Wishes* is all about dreams coming true. Narrated by Jiminy Cricket, the 12-minute show sets perfectly choreographed explosions of sound and light and color with music and dialogue from classic Disney films, including Peter Pan, Aladdin, the Little Mermaid, Cinderella, Snow White, and Pinocchio. The quality of the fireworks themselves is much improved, and several of the pyrotechnic effects are making their WDW debut – pay particular attention to the "wishing star" and "Blue Fairy" fireworks. Just about the only thing kept around from Fantasy in the Sky is the opening – Tinkerbell zooming high above the Magic Kingdom, earthbound from the castle's spires. *Wishes* is performed most nights, but not when the park closes at its earliest hours.

Storytime with Belle

The beautiful heroine from *Beauty and the Beast* shares her magical story to enchanted children at Fairytale Garden in Fantasyland throughout the day, bringing them up to participate with costumes and props. Autograph and meet-and-greet opportunities also abound here.

Sword in the Stone

Every day, Merlin seeks the one who can remove the sword from the stone next to Cinderella's Golden Carrousel. Usually it's some lucky child who shall be amazed at his own strength as he is declared the "Leader of the Realm."

Flag Retreat

Every day at dusk or close to it, the Magic Kingdom Color Guard conducts a patriotic Flag Retreat ceremony at Town Square on Main Street. Military visitors are honored daily as the "Veteran of the Day," inquire at City Hall if interested.

Where to Eat in the Magic Kingdom

Food at the Magic Kingdom has gotten considerably better in recent years, as the variety available in the theme parks really makes it easy to find a tasty lunch. Sure, the burgers and hot dogs and pizza are all still here, and it's all passable, but you don't have to stuff your face with lowest-common denominator theme park food while you're here. Note: alcoholic beverages are not served in the Magic Kingdom. Reservations for sit-down restaurants are available 30 days in advance, 60 days for WDW Resort guests. Call 407/WDW-DINE for reservations.

In Main Street, U.S.A.

Crystal Palace

This gorgeous, airy landmark of a restaurant at the north end of Main Street features all-you-can-eat food and Pooh (That's Pooh, with an H - that joke never gets old), as the crew from the Hundred Acre Wood hang out here during all three meals. At breakfast ($17.99 adults/$9.99 kids), the menu includes an array of morning standards. Lunch ($19.99 adults/$10.99 kids) features sandwiches, salads, pasta, and entrees. Dinner ($22.99 adult/ $10.99 kids.) adds peel-and-eat shrimp, chef-carved ham and prime rib, arroz con pollo, BBQ chicken, and more. The kids' buffet at both meals includes chicken nuggets, macaroni and cheese, and pizza.

The Plaza Restaurant

Located at the north end of Main Street, this Art Nouveau restaurant that offers huge ice cream sundaes and frozen treats like floats and shakes. The choices at both lunch and dinner ($8.99-10.49) include 6 oz. burgers with your choice of toppings, turkey club or tuna sandwiches, and more adventurous offerings like chicken and strawberry salad with gorgonzola and white zinfandel vinaigrette; and portobello, hummus, and roasted red pepper wraps. The kids' menu ($4.99-5.49) includes hot dogs, hamburgers, and grilled cheese.

Tony's Town Square Cafe

You ever wonder why Lady and the Tramp didn't get marinara all over their faces? Spaghetti and meat-a-ball can't be a neat thing to eat if you have a face full of fur and no opposable thumbs. Tony's has leapt from the silver screen to the Magic Kingdom. The restaurant is elegantly Victorian, with polished brass, many windows, beautiful woodwork, and a terazzo-floored patio overlooking Main Street. The food is quality Italian fare. The lunch menu ($8.49-13.99) includes meatball subs, paninis, six-cheese pizza, and pasta primavera. At dinner ($18.49-24.99) the menu adds such daring choices as grilled veal T-bone on wild mushroom bread pudding, braised pork shank with red wine sauce and spinach gnocchi, and chicken Florentine topped with spinach, prosciutto, and cheese. The kids' menu ($4.99) includes spaghetti, ravioli, and pizza. Desserts here are great, and the glassed-in portion of the restaurant is perfect for parade viewing. Hint hint! Time a dinner here right and you'll have a perfect vantage point for the proceedings.

Casey's Corner

Hot dogs, corn dog nuggets, chili, fries, and drinks are offered up here ($3.29-3.89). This is another good spot for multitasking parade viewing with food.

Main Street Bakery

This cozy and oh-so-tempting little shop offers turnovers, danish, muffins, cake, and lots of Toll House cookies, along with espresso and cappucino. The freshly-baked cinnamon rolls are a real treat ($1.49-5.99).

Plaza Ice Cream Parlor

The ice cream parlor at the north end of Main Street serves up simple stuff – cones and sundaes, but mmmmmmm, are they good ($2.49-3.99).

In Adventureland

El Pirata y El Perico

Adventureland's only restaurant serves up tacos, taco salad, and beef empanadas with all the fixings ($3.49-5.79).

Aloha Isle

One of my favorite snacks in the Magic Kingdom is the Dole Whip, offered here – it's a soft serve combining vanilla and pineapple ice cream. Juice and pineapple spears are also available ($1.49-$2.99).

Sunshine Tree Terrace

This snack bar serves frozen yogurt, floats, and slushies ($2.59-3.29).

Egg Roll Wagon

Grab pork and shrimp egg rolls at this stand outside Aladdin's Magic Carpets ($2.50), open seasonally.

In Frontierland

Aunt Polly's Dockside Inn

Located on Tom Sawyer Island, this pleasant patio eatery delectable sundaes served on apple pie, brownies, or strawberry shortcake ($2.59-$3.99).

Pecos Bill Café

This is the park's best bet for burgers, served in 1/4 and 1/2 pound varieties, along with 1/3 lb. hot dogs, seasoned chicken wraps, and chicken salad. The fixings bar here is intense and includes sautéed mushrooms and onions ($4.69-7.49).

Frontierland Fries

McDonald's fries are served up here ($2.19).

Westward Ho
Frozen lemonade, chips, and drinks are available here ($2.39-3.29)

In Liberty Square
Liberty Tree Tavern
One of the best-liked sit-down restaurants in the Magic Kingdom, the Liberty Tree offers a character dinner featuring Mickey, Minnie, Pluto, Donald, Daisy, and Meeko. The prix fixe meal ($24.99 adults, $10.99 kids under 11) includes salad, roast turkey breast, carved beef, and smoked pork loin chops, mashed potatoes, vegetables, herb bread stuffing, mac & cheese, and warm apple crisp. Other desserts are available à la carte.

The restaurant doesn't have characters at lunch, but does have an appealing menu of sandwiches, burgers, and excellent regional American dishes like Colony Salad, with rotisserie chicken, Washington apples, sweet pecans, and applewood smoked cheddar over field greens; New England pot roast braised in a cabernet mushroom sauce; a grilled turkey panini, and a traditonal turkey dinner ($10.79-13.99). The children's menu at lunch includes mac & cheese, hot dog, hamburger, and chicken strips ($4.99).

Columbia Harbour House
This restaurant is one of the best bets for fast food at the Magic Kingdom. Highlights of the menu are the great ham and cheese sandwiches with broccoli slaw, tuna on toasted multi-grain, and hummus sandwiches (that's three separate meals, not one horrifying Frankensandwich) on artisan bread with broccoli slaw and tomatoes. Chicken strips and fish are also on the menu, but not recommended ($4.99-6.79).

Sleepy Hollow
This sesasonal stand offers funnel cake, caramel corn, ice cream cookies, and beverages ($2.79-4.29).

In Fantasyland
Cinderella's Royal Table
Located on the second floor of the Castle, a meal at this restaurant is often a vacation highlight for little girls enchanted by the princess. Diners actually have the chance to meet her (along with Snow White, Belle, Aurora, or others) at the character breakfast held here daily ($21.99 adults, $11.99 for children under 11). The meal is all you can eat fruit, eggs, bacon, sausage, cheese Danish, French toast, potato casserole, yogurt, coffee, and juice. Lunch and dinner don't have princesses.

They do have good stuff for carnivores. Lunch is prix fixe and offers "specialties of the castle" to start with, followed by your choice of grilled salmon with lemon buerre blanc, herb crusted pork tenderloin, and ham, turkey, and munster foccacia sandwiches and blueberry cobbler ($23.99 adults, $12.99 for kids 3-9).

Dinner is à la carte. Seafood cioppino with scallops, mussels, soft-shell crab, and fish; filet of beef; spice crusted Ahi tuna; and prime rib ($21-26). The kids' menu at lunch and dinner includes chicken strips, grilled cheese, and cheese dog rolls ($4.99).

Pinocchio Village Haus
This cavernous restaurant near It's a Small World features 1/3 and 1/2 lb. burger platters, turkey sandwiches, and hot dogs, as well as milkshakes ($4.69-7.29).

Enchanted Grove
Slushies and swirls are served here ($1.89-3.29).

Mrs. Potts' Cupboard
We all scream for shakes, floats, and sundaes, some on brownies or strawberry shortcake ($2.79-3.49).

Scuttle's Landing
Frozen Cokes, stuffed pretzels, and chocolate chunk cookees are sold here ($1.59-3.29).

In Mickey's Toontown Fair
Toontown Farmer's Market
Apples, bananas, grapes, and fruit cups make this a great stop for refreshing, healthy, cheap snacks ($.99-3.29).

In Tomorrowland
Cosmic Ray's Starlight Café
This is an oversized and excellent food court offering something for everyone – ribs and rotisserie chicken, chicken strips, grilled chicken sandwiches, turkey bacon wraps, and burgers ($5.69-13.89).

Tomorrowland Terrace Noodle Station
Located on the outskirts of Tomorrowland, this new restaurant features shrimp, chicken, and vegetarian noodle bowls as well as pad thai and other Asian dishes ($6.49-7.99).

The Lunching Pad at Rockettower Plaza
Beneath the TTA and Astro Orbiter, this counter offers filling smoked turkey legs, BBQ pork shank, chips, and frozen drinks ($2.39-5.19).

Auntie Gravity's Galactic Goodies
Auntie Gravity's is a guilty pleasure for soft serve, floats, sundaes, and smoothies ($2.79-3.29).

Practical Information

Getting In
For information on Walt Disney World's new Magic Your Way ticketing options, refer to Part 2, pages 338-340.

Getting There
The Magic Kingdom is easily accessible via I-4 exit 64B (US 192 West). It's the first exit and is unmissable, unless you're Rain Man. (Although, he did claim to be a good driver, so...) It's also easily accessible from inside WDW. Take the monorail or motor launch from the Grand Floridian, Polynesian, or Contemporary. Boat service is also available from Fort Wilderness and the Wilderness Lodge. Bus service connects all other Disney resorts to the Magic Kingdom.

Guests driving to the MK park at the Ticket and Transportation Center, and reach the park from there via ferry or monorail. The monorail runs on two tracks – an express connecting the TTC to the MK, and a local loop including the Polynesian, Contemporary, and Grand Floridian. The TTC offers bus service to all other Disney World areas.

Hours
The Magic Kingdom opens at 9am daily, with gates (and Main Street, U.S.A.) 30 to 60 minutes earlier, except on Morning Extra Magic Hours, when park access is limited to WDW resort guests from 8 til 9. Closing time varies by season, from 7pm to 11pm. Disney resort guests can take advantage of Evening Extra Magic Hours, which keep the parks open three hours past public closing. Bring your room key to specified locations in the park within two hours of public close to get a wristband granting you access. The specific days each park offers as morning or evening Extra Magic Hours varies by season, so check on www.disneyworld.com close to your departure to check the dates for your stay.

Do yourself a favor and show up on time – in fact, show up before the gates open. The least crowded time of the day in the Disney theme parks is the first hour (except on Extra Magic Hour mornings). Monday, Thursday, and Saturday tend to be the least crowded days of the week here.

Parking

The Transportation and Ticket Center parking lot is enormous – so be sure to write down where you park. Daily parking fees are $8 for non-Disney resort guests.

Money

Walt Disney World accepts American Express, MasterCard, Visa, Discover, Diners Club, JCB, and the Disney Credit Card, as well as travelers' checks and cash, even at counter-service eateries. There are Bank One ATMs located at the main entrance, by Frontierland Shootin' Arcade, and by the Tomorrowland Arcade. Guests staying at Disney resorts can also make theme park charges to their room.

Disney's FastPass

This system allows you to bypass the line at selected major attractions in the theme parks. Visit the FastPass distribution kiosks at participating attractions. Check the one-hour return time displayed for the ride. If returning then works for your agenda, insert your admission ticket. You will be issued a voucher with the assigned time printed on it. Return to the ride during this hour and bypass the standby line – this can usually save you quite a bit of time, but it does not guarantee that you will get right on the ride. In fact, often times FastPass lines merge with standby lines at a point closer to the boarding area, so the benefit isn't always as great as you might think. But there's no question that FastPass is the only way to go when it comes to riding FastPass attractions.

Why? Simple reason. **Everyone with a FastPass will be in line in front of you.** However, if the wait is 15 minutes or less, just hop in line. Here is one very important caveat. You can not get a second FastPass until the start time on your first one. That means if your FastPass time is eight hours away, you're screwed til then. The exception is for shows utilizing FastPass. You can get a second one an hour after getting a FastPass for a show. At press time, FastPass was available at: Big Thunder Mountain Railroad, Buzz Lightyear's Space Ranger Spin, the Haunted Mansion, Jungle Cruise, Many Adventures of Winnie the Pooh, Mickey's Philharmagic, Peter Pan's Flight, Space Mountain, and Splash Mountain, and Stitch's Great Escape. **Note that everyone in your party must have his or her own FastPass.**

Package Pickup

Each theme park offers package pickup service, where rather than lugging your purchases around all day, you can send them to a centralized package pickup center near the entrance to the park. Disney resort guests can have their packages sent directly to their hotels. Note that package pickup locations are most crowded between 5 and 6pm and/or one hour before the theme parks close. The Magic Kingdom's is located next to City Hall on Main Street.

Security

Bag/backpack/package searches are now performed at Disney World. Allow a few extra minutes to get through them.

Smoking

By law, all Florida restaurants and bars are now non-smoking. Smoking is only allowed in selected areas of the park. Smoking areas are located:

•**Main Street, U.S.A.:** Next to Tony's Town Square Restaurant.

•**Adventureland:** By the bathrooms just over the bridge from Main Street U.S.A., and next to Pirates of the Caribbean.

•**Frontierland:** At the north end of thre park, past Big Thunder Mountain Railroad.

•**Liberty Square:** Just over the northern bridge from the central hub.

•**Fantasyland:** Behind the castle, across from Philharmagic.

•**Mickey's Toontown Fair:** Near the train station.

•**Tomorrowland:** Adjacent to the Grand Prix Raceway entrance and to the Carousel of Progress.

Check the park map for exact locations.

Chapter 5

EPCOT

On October 1, 1982, Disney opened a $1.4 billion park then known as EPCOT Center – a vestigal acronym meaning Experimental Prototype Community of Tomorrow. Walt Disney had envisioned it as a geometrically compelling planned community and church of industry, but it wound up being more of a sort of permanent world's fair, comprised of two sections, **Future World** and **World Showcase**. (Incidentally, the planned community showed up 20 years later at Celebration.)

Future World's pavilions aim to educate and entertain in various subjects from all corners of modern civilization, including agriculture, communications, energy, and medicine. World Showcase features pavilions representing eleven nations with authentic food, music, art, fashion, and merchandise.

It's definitely got a different vibe than the Magic Kingdom. More serious, but still with plenty of whimsy – fascinating, spacious (spread over 300 acres), uncluttered, modern, and sleek, the park is much more of an "adult" experience. Not to say that it's not great for kids, it is. It just has a different presentation.

Future World

Modern architecture, lots of glass, grays, purples, blues, and warm pastels dominate the landscape here, as strikingly designed buildings conceal incredible adventures within. Never before has edutainment been so entertaining. During my last visit, I had several touches of cynicism that Exxon sponsoring the Universe of Energy and General Motors hosting Test Track seems a bit propagandic, but if you can look past that, there's plenty of fascinating stuff here. Don't confuse this area with Tomorrowland at the MK – while Tomorrow is a whimsical, sci-fi vision of the future through the eyes of writers and dreamers of the past, this area represents more of a look at the past, present, and future of various aspects of modern civilization, presented in a light-hearted and often very compelling fashion. Much like Tomorrowland, recent renovations have added splashes of color to the previously metal-tone buildings. It's a very pleasant place to spend a morning.

Crowds tend to move on to World Showcase after 230pm or so, doubling back around at this point can yield surprisingly quick wait times. Test Track and Mission: SPACE are crowded all day, but crowds tend to be manageable elsewhere. There's several decent dining options here – the Living Seas and Garden Grill offer excellent sit-down meals (with character interaction at the latter), while the Sunshine Season Food Fair food court is a personal favorite Epcot eatery. The only shopping of note in Future World is the Mouse House character shop, which is absolutely massive – rivaled only by World of Disney in Downtown Disney Marketplace for selection.

Mission: SPACE
>Rating: A
>Big-ticket, state-of-the-art 7-minute thrill ride.
>Fear Factor: 4
>Use FastPass or the single rider line to minimize your wait time.

Epcot's newest attraction opened in 2003, and received raves as the best attraction in Epcot, and possibly the best thrill ride in all of WDW. I think that's maybe a bit too much praise. While the ride creates an intense sensation, I found it a bit anti-climactic and simplistic overall, it feels like a good ride that could have been a great one. However, I seem to be in the minority

This is a simulated astronaut experience, created in conjunction with former NASA advisors, astronauts, and scientists, and starring Gary Sinise. It sets guests in 2035, when space travel is more a routine part of life. The queue area enters the "Sim Lab," which features fascinating real and imagined training gear and plaques commemorating various space "firsts." Guests are dispatched in ten "shuttles" of four at a time after learn the specific roles that they will be asked to fulfill – either as Commander, Pilot, Navigator, or Engineer. Basically, each of these roles involve pressing a button when you receive an audio cue.

When the actual ride begins, a 2G shuttle blastoff and simulated weightlessness are experienced, along with computer-generated photo-realistic graphics, followed by "hypersleep" hibernation for the long trip to Mars (involves total darkness), and after being awakened from your space nap, everything goes wrong – as has a tendency to always happen on simulation thrill rides, you ever notice that? But quick thinking and fast reactions from your crew will help you land safely on the Red Planet's surface.

After the ride, you exit into an interactive **Advanced Training Lab** containing the Space Base play area for young children, the Mission: SPACE Race, a video game mission allowing guests to compete against users on disney.com, email video postcards, and 60-person rocket races. Allow yourself 45 minutes to see everything here, not counting line time.

As this is the newest attraction here, it is also the most popular. FastPass, FastPass, FastPass. Otherwise be prepared for a long wait – in spite of its 2,000-an-hour capacity. Note that you must be 44 inches tall to ride, and the usual heart/back problem/pregnancy/motion sick crowd is exempt as well. Different people report various reactions to the ride – while the spinning and intensity are too much for some (especially small children and the elderly), many guests with motion sickness issues report being able to ride without a problem. Just remember to keep looking straight ahead (and not to the side) during the ride, if you can't see the ride spinning, it's easier for your body to ignore it. While the ride is nothing that would be classified as rough, it does put your body through unusual positions and sensations probably not outlined in the Geneva Conventions – but just be aware that it may discombobulate the crap out of you.

Spaceship Earth
Rating: A
16-minute ride detailing the history of communication.
Fear Factor: 1
Visit before 11am or after 5pm.

As the Magic Kingdom is iconified by Cinderella Castle, so is Epcot by the building housing this attraction. It looks like a gigantic golf ball – a geodesic dome 180 feet high and 164 feet in diameter, with Mickey's distinctive hand waving a wand at the whole thing. The monorail winding almost silently around the base of the structure completes the dazzling sight that first greets visitors who walk through the turnstiles.

One of Epcot's original attractions and still one of its best, I was really amazed at how well this attraction has held up with time. It was revamped slightly several years ago to reflect the incredible advances in communication and information technology that have broken through since 1982, and Jeremy Irons replaced Walter Cronkite as the narrator.

The heart of the ride remains the same, however, a sensory immersion that sends "time machines" to the Cro-Magnon era 40,000 years ago, where blacklit displays reveal the earliest cave drawings. The ride progresses through time, from Egyptian hieroglyphics to the first written alphabet, from the 9th-century BC, and to the Roman Empire and the advent of drama. Marching forward we witness the birth of the printing press and the birth of newspapers, radio, television, and finally the Internet. The ride culminates with an absolutely unforgettable planetarium-like starscape at the apex of the dome. As the time machines descend to earth, they witness a fanciful vision of the way we might interact with one another in the future. The whole ride is very moving and awe-inspiring at times.

Beyond the impressive quality of the attraction, it draws large crowds by virtue of its location. However, this is one of the fastest-loading rides in all of WDW, so lines melt away pretty quickly. Do NOT make this your first stop once you get into the park. Mission: SPACE and Test Track should be your top priorities – don't do this first just because you get here first.

The Spaceship Earth ride lets out into the **Global Neighborhood** exhibit, featuring family-friendly applications of community technology and simple video games that illustrate the information superhighway.

Test Track
> Rating: B+
> 5 1/2 minute sorta-thrill ride simulating automotive testing.
> Fear Factor: 4
> Visit first thing in the morning, after Mission: Space, or with FastPass.

This much-hyped attraction replaced the venerable World of Motion with a simulation of the rigorous testing that prototype automobiles go through. While an intriguing theory, the ride itself is for the most part disappointing and gimmicky, and has the oily car-dealer stench of promotional General Motors slick.

Following a pre-show you board a six-passenger car and climb thee stories at a 15 degree pitch for the Hill Climb Test. The Suspension Test sends your car over various rough road surfaces. Next, the brake test demonstrates the effect of anti-lock brakes, sending you into a tailspin without and to a complete stop with. The Environmental Chamber test exposes the car to searing heat, frigid cold, and then an acidic mist. Hope you brought your anthrax mask. The Ride Handling test sends you up and down a "switchback" hill and into the path of an oncoming truck and then through a crash barrier in the Barrier Test. Fun for the whole family. Up to here, the ride is pretty tame, and is mostly forgettable. At this point during my first ride, I was ready to declare it the dud of the year. Fortunately, it is redeemed by the High Speed Test, where you race around the exterior of the building in open air at 65 mph, navigating 50 degree banked curves along the way. It's exhilarating but before you know it, you've reached the end of the mile-long ride, where interactive exhibits and a GM showroom await. Avoid the Dream Catchers exhibit – it looks like a VR exhibit but is just a cartoon plugging GM cars.

This ride is insanely popular and often has 90-minute waits during times of the year when you can walk onto any other ride on the premises. Honestly, I don't feel like the ride is good enough to justify the wait. But you're going to ignore me and ride it anyway, because it's the Next Big Thing at Disney. So here's how to do it with the minimum of a wait. You can either get there first thing in the morning, reserve a FastPass time, or opt to split your party up and each of you ride alone. There is a separate entrance for single riders, who fill in available spaces on the cars. Your wait in the single rider line varies but is almost always shorter than the main line. FastPass is available here, and you pretty much need it if you want to hit this ride without waiting two hours. Guests must be 40" tall to ride.

Ellen's Energy Adventure (Universe of Energy)
Rating: B+
45 minute multimedia theater presentation and ride.
Fear Factor: 3
Visit before 10:30am or after 4:30pm.

This ExxonMobil sponsored look at the history of energy takes a whimsical and entertaining approach to a subject that's really only exciting if you own Halliburton stock, resulting in a presentation that actually succeeds both from the educational and entertainment perspectives. This is best known as Epcot's "dinosaur ride," not to be confused with the actual Dinosaur ride at the Animal Kingdom. But we'll get to that.

In the show opening, comedienne Ellen DeGeneres is watching Jeopardy and flubbing all the questions in the Energy category. Her neighbor, Bill Nye (the Science Guy) comes over to borrow supplies for an experiment, and is appalled by her lack of knowledge. To inspire her, he shows her an eight-minute presentation in which vivid images of falling water, fire, burning coal, and piles of logs show today's energy sources. Ellen doesn't care.

The presentation then moves to a seemingly normal theater with room for 600 in bench seats. Ellen falls asleep in front of the TV and dreams that she is on Jeopardy, facing off against Albert Einstein and her college roommate (played by Jamie Lee Curtis). At the end of the first round, Ellen's roommate is running away with the game, Einstein's at zero, and Ellen's in the red. Thankfully, Bill arrives and whisks Ellen off for a crash course in the history of fossil fuels.

This is the part of the attraction that most wows visitors. The theatre splits into smaller cars that slowly enter a world where the air is rich with sulfur and the sky flashes with lightning. The profile of a brontosaur is visible in the distance. Fog fills the warm, dank air and lava bubbles next to the cars. The lava is so realistic that few guests are convinced when informed that its main ingredient is hair gel. Audio-Animatronic dinosaurs battle on a rocky ledge, a mighty allosaurus against the armored stegosaurus. There are 250 prehistoric-looking trees, all manmade, and various other creatures of the era, from millipedes to pteranodons. An elasmosaurus sticks his head out of a lagoon. The dinosaurs here are frighteningly realistic, some of Disney's best Audio-Animatronic figures. And sure enough, Ellen manages to get trapped by one of them, and it's Science Guy to the rescue. Ellen returns from the past in time to win Double Jeopardy.

There's a joke somewhere in the juxtaposition of rainbow colored flourishes to the outside of the attraction, and the addition of Ellen DeGeneres to the presentation. I was very pleasantly surprised the first time I saw it after the renovation that added her – while it seems a bit silly to see an Audio-Animatronic Ellen cowering in fear from a dinosaur, she is really much funnier here than I ever remember her being on her sitcom.

Imagination!

This pavilion contains several attractions paying tribute to that greatest of gifts, the root of all creativity, Imagination. Someone must have had their thinking cap on backwards when imagining the waterfalls and fountains here, some defying logic and seemingly gravity. A fountain shoots blobs of water at regular intervals, most kids can't help but smack the blobs. My personal favorite is the Leap Frog Fountain, which winds across a landscaped courtyard, shooting streams of water from one planter to the next to the next, even over paths (and often guests' heads as well!).

Honey, I Shrunk the Audience
Rating: A+
20 minute 3D movie.
Fear Factor: 4
Visit with FastPass or after the rest of Future World closes.

Rick Moranis stars with Monty Python's Eric Idle in this hysterical, completely unexpected spinoff of the movies *Honey, I Shrunk the Kids* and *Honey, I Blew Up the Baby*. Without giving away any of the delightful surprises this movie holds, let me just say that it will leave your knees shaking with excitement. In-theater technology, computer-enhanced 3D effects, and "sneaky tricks" combine to make this an exhilarating, hilarious movie experience.

The plot, or more accurately, the pretense of the film is a ceremony honoring Professor Wayne Szalinski (Moranis) as "Inventor of the Year." Demonstrating his incredible shrinking machine, he accidentally shrinks the audience to the size of a bread box. The unsuspecting vacationers are then beseiged by tennis shoes, huge dogs, scurrying mice, and no longer-small bratty children. This unforgettable interactive theatre production makes previous 3D feel archaic, and accordingly, is very popular. It is most crowded during the afternoon hours, but FastPass is available.

Journey into Imagination with Figment
Rating: B
8 minute ride celebrating the power of imagination.
Fear Factor: 2
Visit before 11am or in the last hour Future World is open.

WELCOME BACK! Disney fans everywhere breathed a sigh of relief when Disney replaced the putrid "Journey Into Your Imagination" ride with this iteration, which is a happy medium between the original attraction's exuberance and the scientific approach taken in the new one. It's a satisfying attraction again thanks to the return of Figment, the mischievous purple dragon who crashes the party as Idle reprises his role as Dr. Nigel Channing, hosting an open house at the Imagination Institute. The sight, sound, and smell labs all show fun but genteel demonstrations of sensory stimulation, and then Figment has to show up and "Be That Guy." Next thing you know, the Taste and Touch sections of the tour are out the window, and instead, Figment is bringing you home to check out HIS pad. Much more fun than it was before they re-inserted Figment and a reworded version of the "One Little Spark" song – before, it almost hurt to ride it, knowing how far it had fallen from its original glory. But Disney has done right by the li'l purple guy.

The ride exits into the **What If? Labs**, a "creative playground of the future" that allows kids from one to one hundred to flex their imaginary muscles at interactive displays that will amaze, amuse, and entertain. Located at the exit from Journey Into Your Imagination, it can also be accessed from outside the pavilion.

The Land

This 6-acre pavilion includes a real greenhouse with actual cultivation going on inside it. Even better than the growth of food here is its consumption, as the Garden Grill offers character dining and the Sunshine Seasons

Food Fair offers great options for all palates. Because of the restaurants, the attractions here are often crowded at mealtimes. The new Soarin' hang sliding simulation ride also is a magnet for the mobs.

Soarin'
Rating: N/A
10 minute experience including 5 minute flight and pre-show.
Fear Factor: 1
Visit before 11am, or with FastPass.

In May 2005, Epcot opened its edition of the Soarin' Over California attraction found in Anaheim at Disney's California Adventure. The attraction combines motion-base simulation (to represent hang-gliding) 40 feet above an oversized screen that fills the 80-foot dome projection screen spreading in front, to the sides, and underneath you. Sensory effects like wind and the scents of orange groves, pine forests, and ocean spray to create a sensory kaleidoscope to convey the beauty of the Golden State, all filmed from a helicopter with IMAX cameras and presented at a rate of 48 frames per second, twice that of normal motion pictures, resulting in crisper images with extraordinary definition.

While this does simulate motion, it is much easier to handle than that of Mission: SPACE, Star Tours, or any of the other thrill rides. This ride had not opened in time to be reviewed for this edition. As Epcot's newest (and to some, its best) attraction, crowds can be expected to be formidable the whole day. Visit early in the morning or via FastPass. Avoid this pavilion during peak mealtimes, as the Sunshine Seasons Food Fair draws crowds of its own, who then mosey into line for Soarin'. Single rider lines are also available, and there is a 40" minimum height requirement.

Living with the Land
Rating: B+
14 minute boat ride through various agricultural settings.
Fear Factor: 1
Visit after 3pm, or with FastPass.

The only ride in Epcot narrated by a real live human being, Living with the Land is a boat ride that introduces guests to Audio-Animatronic biomes recreating the African veldt, the American prairie as it used to be, and a turn-of-the-century farm.

After that introduction, boats then pass through a variety of real agricultural environments, including three greenhouses – tropical, temperate, and a production house that generates much of the produce eaten at Epcot; the Aquacell fish farm, and the Creative House, where hydroponics, suspension, and other innovative agricultural technologies are demonstrated. If you'd like to know more about the topics discussed here, sign up for the 60 minute Behind the Seeds Tour at the Green Thumb Emporium. Cost is $8 per adult, $6 per child.

This is a pleasant and informative ride, but not an A-lister. Nonetheless, it draws steady crowds throughout the day, especially with Soarin' open across the pavilion. FastPass is available here, but crowds are only truly unmanageable at mealtimes.

Circle of Life

Rating: B

18 minute film combining 70m nature footage and Lion King characters.

Fear Factor: 1

Visit anytime besides lunch.

The stars of Disney's animated megahit *The Lion King* return in this new adventure, delivering a compelling, entertaining, and emotional parable about environmental conservation in the face of overdevelopment and industrialization.

Now king of the Pridelands, Simba (Matthew Broderick) walks in just as a cry of "Timber!" echoes, followed by the splash of a fallen tree. It seems that carefree slackers Timon and Pumbaa (Nathan Lane nad Ernie Sabella) have begun clearing the savannah to construct "Hakuna Matata Lakeside Village" — a timeshare community! (I'm surprised they didn't use it as a Disney Vacation Club plug.) Simba responds with a story told by his father of a creature that forgets that everything is connected in the great Circle of Life. "That creature," he explains, "is man." The 70mm footage that follows was taken from the "Symbiosis" film that previously occupied this theater. This film is especially notable for its presentation. The subject matter is serious, but the tone is optimistic and it encourages individuals to make a difference. This film can still be seen virtually anytime without much of a wait, except possibly at lunchtime.

Wonders of Life

The pavilion flanked by a 92-foot DNA strand houses attractions and exhibits related to health and the human body. Although the hype for this pavilion was huge upon its opening in 1989, it has since grown tired and dated, and as of January 2005, it remains closed most of the year, only open "seasonally" during periods of the highest attendance.

Wonders of Life – Exhibits

In addition to the attractions listed below, Wonders of Life also includes several interesting exhibits and minor diversions. They include the Fitness Fairgrounds, comprised of:

•**Frontiers of Medicine:** Serious exhibits featuring cutting-edge technology.

• **Sensory Funhouse:** Lots of hands-on exhibits dealing with one of the five senses and the tricks they can play on your mind.

•**Goofy about Health:** Seven-screen presentation depicting Goofy as he replaces bad habits with good ones, using original and long-lost animation.

Cranium Command

    Rating: A-
    20 minute multimedia presentation about brain chemistry.
    Fear Factor: 2
    Visit anytime when open.

This was one of my favorite attractions at Epcot – humorous, touching, and educational, Cranium Command stars an Audio-Animatronic rookie brain pilot named Buzzy, who, in order to earn his stripes, must guide a twelve-year-old boy through his daily routine. Gasp! A drill sergeant type named General Knowledge barks out the assignment to Buzzy in the witty pre-show. Buzzy balks at the idea, but changes his mind when threatened of being put inside the head of a chicken. Note that if you miss the preshow, you'll have a harder time understanding the rest of the presentation. If you arrive as the preshow is ending, it'd probably be a better idea to wait for the next show.

In the main theater, Buzzy sits in a captain's chair that allows him to oversee various organs – such as the left brain (Charles Grodin), the right brain (Jon Lovitz). the stomach (George Wendt), the heart (played by Kevin Nealon and Dana Carvey in their Saturday Night Live personas. Hans and Franz), and a hyperactive adrenal gland (Bob Golthwait, of course). This unlikely team wakes up inside the head of a 12-year-old, goes to school without eating breakfast, fights off bullies, impresses a beautiful female classmate, and does all the other things that twelve-year-old boys do. It is easy to get into the story and relate to Buzzy's charge, but if you've forgotten what it was like to be twelve, you may be less enchanted.

Body Wars
> Rating: C
> 5 minute motion simulator ride.
> Fear Factor: 5
> Visit anytime when open.

Here, at Epcot's first thrill ride, you are placed in one of four 40-passenger flight simulators and "miniaturized" in order to be injected into a patient, where you pick up the intrepid Dr. Lair (Elizabeth Shue) who has been examining a splinter imbedded just under the skin. A normal day in the office for anyone, right? But something is bound to go awry, as is the Disney thrill-ride tradition, and the ship's pilot (Tim Matheson) almost reaches Dr. Lair when whoosh, angry white blood cells and electrical failure threaten the whole mission, but all's well that ends well. This ride has been up and running since 1989, and truthfully it's starting to look quite dated. The storyline is tired and the effects pale next to modern CGI masterpieces.

Physically, this is a very rough ride, much worse than Star Tours, so be sure to buckle your seat belt when they instruct you to do so, even though the cars only travel a few feet in any direction, the ride does cause some motion sickness. In fact, they sometimes have to shut down one of the cars to remove, ahem, a souvenir left by the last unfortunate rider. If you start feeling queasy, close your eyes. Much of the thrill is visual, so if you take out one sense, it'll feel better. Guests must be 40" tall to ride.

The Making of Me
> Rating: C+
> 14 minute live-action film.
> Fear Factor: 2.
> Visit anytime when open.

Glenn Gordon Caron directed this funny film starring Martin Short as a man who ponders his conception, and not being one to leave us hanging, travels back in time to watch his parents date, fall in love, marry, and eventually decide to have him. There is actual footage of a developing fetus and yes, the birth. The sexual information necessary to a production like this is handled tastefully. Just be aware that if you're not ready to have "The Talk" with your kids, this one might raise a few questions.

The Living Seas

If you're looking for me, you'd better check under the sea. This recently refreshed $100 million pavilion features a restaurant, the world's largest salt water aquarium, and several exhibits focused on marine ecology and biology. This attraction gained a lot more charm when Disney introduced characters from the animated Pixar hit *Finding Nemo* to the pavilion, giving a family-friendly perspective to what was at one time Epcot's most arcane exhibit. We used to call this skippable, not so much anymore. If you prefer your marine biology on a plate, the renowned Coral Reef restaurant might be worth a looksee.

Seabase Alpha
Rating: B-
3-minute ride and interactive exhibits on marine biology,
Fear Factor: 1
Visit anytime.

Seabase Alpha is introduced with a 7-minute film that lauds the pioneers of undersea research and describe the oceans as a resource. These sometimes go over the heads of younger kids. Guests then board "hydrolators," elevators that simulate a plunge of many fathoms while in truth, descending about 2 inches, depositing you at Sea Base Alpha. a model undersea research facility consisting of life support system exhibits, video presentations, mammal viewing habitats, an observation deck for researchers, manatees, and an aquaculture exhibit. The aquariums here include a coral reef with over 2,000 fish representing more than 70 species. Exhibits on the two floors include Nemo-themed habitats and an interactive play area starring Bruce the shark. Much improved with the infusion from the cute Pixar feature.

Turtle Talk with Crush
Rating: B+
Interactive exhibit where the surfer turtle from *Finding Nemo* interacts with guests.
Fear Factor: 1
Visit early to mid-afternoon..

A new exhibit in 2005 is **Turtle Talk with Crush**, starring the 152-year old sea turtle from *Finding Nemo* who sounded so much like Jeff Spicoli. Crush interacts with guests, calling them by name and laughing and joking with them via voice-activated animation and digital projeection in live, unscripted conversations in this first-of-its-kind interactive attraction. The theater only holds about 40 people, so this overlooked attraction digests crowds slowly, but is well worth the wait.

Innoventions
Innoventions is a must-see for those who insist on staying on the crest

of the technological wave at all times, as it showcases new technologies in an entertaining and educational way as you wander along "The Road to Tomorrow." Although exhibits are constantly changing, here's an idea of what you can expect to find.

Innoventions East (green signs)

1. ThinkPlace: Send email postcards, experience voice recognition software, and virtually explore the Hermitage Museum in St. Petersburg, Russia.

2. Ultimate Home Theater Experience: 20-minute presentation on HDTV, DTS, Dolby Digital, DVD, plasma, lights, sound, drool.

3. The Great American Farm: Learn about biotechnology and food production here, including information about cutting-edge "smart farms."

4. Video Games of Tomorrow: Disney Interactive titles for all game platforms (including ESPN X-Games and Kingdom Hearts) are demonstrated here.

5. Tom Morrow's 2.0 Playground: Video games, the Aibo robotic dog, interactive play areas, state-of-the-art sound and light, including a Disneyfied Dance Dance Revolution.

6. Where's the Fire?: Enjoyable interactive game that teaches the basics of fire safety for the whole family, and a maze just for kids under 5.

Innoventions West (blue signs)

7. Welcome Center: Cast members are on hand to demonstrate the Segway HT.

8. Forests for our Future: Sustainable forest exhibits and trivia games.

9. Innoventions Internet Zone: Video e-mails and disney.com content.

10. Fantastic Plastics Works: Here you can virtually design a robot to compete in a race, then actually assemble the robot and take him home! It's you're your own Johnny Five, only without the Steve Guttenberg factor.

11. House of Innoventions: 15 minute walking tour of a "smart home" and new product showcase.

12. Opportunity City. This exhibit, based on the Hot Shot Business simulation game, teaches kids about entrepeneurship by running a virtual business.

13. Test the Limits Lab: Six kiosks demonstrate some of the abuse that goes along with product testing.

The fountains outside Innoventions feature a water ballet every 15 minutes, and is the site for live entertainment throughout the day. Consult with your park guide for a current entertainment schedule.

Shopping

MouseGear is Epcot's largest shop, features a massive selection of character merchandise of all kinds, including a phenomenal array of collectible items focused on specific attractions – perfect for the amusement park and Disney geeks among us. Also at Innoventions is **Art of Disney**, selling animation cels, posters, prints, and other collectibles, and the **Pin Station**, Epcot's headquarters for pin trading.

The **Green Thumb Emporium** at the Land sells placemats, refrigerator magnets, books, topiaries, hydroponic plants, and mementos. Located at Spaceship Earth are two shops – **Gateway Gifts**, featuring a small selection of souvenirs and sundries, and the smaller **Gift Stop**, which also hosts package pickup. There's also a gift shop at the **Living Seas**.

World Showcase

The other half of Epcot is a celebration of the cultures and people of the world community. The architecture, culture, history, music, and people of eleven nations are spotlighted here in pavilions staffed by natives of the countries represented.

Note that many of the pavilions do not have any attractions per se, just shops and exhibits. Don't dismiss these though in your rush to the next E-ticket attraction, as these are some of the most fascinating parts of WDW, and there's aesthetically pleasing stuff and authentic detail everywhere you look. Of course, that's not going to be enough to keep a lot of kids' attention. Maelstrom is the only attraction that draws serious lines, and appropriately, is the only FastPass attraction here.

Touring World Showcase is pretty straightforward on account of its layout – eleven nations are situated on the shores of World Showcase Lagoon, so either go clockwise or counterclockwise and do your thing. Boats travel from World Showcase Plaza (between Canada and Mexico) to the Germany and Italy pavilions, offering a shortcut and a nice ride.

World Showcase opens at 11am daily and is least crowded early in the day, getting progressively more packed throughout the day, culminating with Illuminations, the night-closing fireworks display and multimedia show that takes place on the water. Authentic entertainment is featured daily at all eleven pavilions, and immersive shopping and dining experiences abound at each of the eleven nations. The best food is in Mexico, Norway, Morocco, France, and Canada. The best shopping is in Mexico, China, Germany, Japan, France, and the United Kingdom.

Showcase Plaza

The entryway to World Showcase, the Plaza has two shops worth a look – **Disney Traders** offers character souvenirs, collectible gifts, and clothing emblazoned with flags of the eleven Showcase nations; and **Port of Entry**, offering sundries, convenience items, and gifts.

Kidcot Fun Stops

Each nation in World Showcase has a Kidcot Fun Stop area where your kids can interact with natives of each land and make some kind of fun craft or souvenir to take home. Check the park map for specific locations. These usually operate during afternoon hours only.

MEXICO

This pavilion is housed inside a pyramid whose Meso-American likenesses date back to the third century A.D. As you walk inside, it immediately becomes dusk. The air is filled with the excitement of a Mexican mercado (marketplace) and the romance of the San Angel Inn. The inside is beautiful on a grand scale and amazing in its intricate detail. Inside the pyramid are an open-air market and a street café, as well as rotating art exhibits. At press time, the gallery was featuring **Animales Fantasticos,** a folk art exhibit of wood-carved animals, humans, and creatures of myth.

Shops here include **Artesianas Mexicanas,** featuring ceramics and onyx ashtrays, plaques, chess sets, and bookends; **El Ranchito del Norte**, offering Northern Mexican items and hand-crafted rings; **La Familia Fashions,** offering apparel and accessories for women and children; and **Plaza de los Amigos,** offering clothing, baskets, papier-maché, pre-Colombian artifacts, paper flowers, wooden housewares, and piñatas. The **Mariachi Cobre** 12-piece combo performs inside and outside the pavilion.

El Rio del Tiempo

Rating: A-
7-minute boat ride.
Fear Factor: 1
Visit before 7pm.

This pleasant boat ride is suggestive of It's a Small World in the Magic Kingdom, only less cloying and more scenic. The first sights you see are the placid San Angel Inn and a glowing volcano, departing on a journey through the past and present of Mexico. Boats sail past artifacts and scenes representing the Mayan, Aztec, and Toltec peoples, meshed with video screens that give the attraction a less whimsical, more ethereal feel. There are dolls of children at play, your Small World moment. Don't hum it. Don't even think it. This ride, like the rest of the pavilion in which it resides, is a blissful escape from the rat race outside. You're humming it, aren't you?

NORWAY

Added to the park in 1986, World Showcase's newest pavilion is one of its best, featuring a fun (albeit too short) adventure boat ride, one of the World's most exciting restaurants, and a vivid blend of architectural styles. The Restaurant Akershus is named for the Norwegian castle of the same name, built in Oslo's harbor in the 1300s and still standing today, a wood-stave church mimicking the Gol church built around the year 1250. Incidentally, when Viking kings adopted Christianity and spread it throughout Scandinavia, the presence of churches of this type was confined to Norway. Very few still exist. On the Lagoon sits the Norseman, a 50-foot ship duplicating a thousand-year-old Viking ship. This was given to the pavilion by a Norwegian maritime group.

This pavilion only has one shop, but it's a good one – the **Puffin's Roost** offers offering clothing, jewelry, pewter candlesticks and tableware, glassware, blankets, wood carvings, decorative gifts, candy, and toys like the famous and popular-once-more trolls and Playmobil sets. The **Spelmans Gledje** quintet performs Norwegian folk music. The Akershus restaurant offers a Princess Storybook Breakfast daily.

Maelstrom

Rating: B
4 minute boat ride followed by 5 minute film.
Fear Factor: 3
Visit after 6pm or use FastPass.

Maelstrom puts you on a 16-passenger boat with a dragon's head carved onto it for a journey through the mythology and the reality of Norse culture. After passing a 10th century Viking village, you meet up with a three-headed troll who obviously got up on the wrong side of the bed. The troll puts a spell on you and you speed towards a waterfall that looks like you will be dumped into the courtyard below, but at the last moment, the boat reverses direction and accelerates down a chute into the wind-swept North Sea. You pass a drilling platform and get out of your boat in a recreation of a harbor village, and just once the ride has gotten interesting, it's over. Afterwards there's a 5-minute film on the sea's effect on Norwegian life, but it's nothing too special – a lot of repeat visitors just do the ride part and walk straight through the theater afterwards. Perhaps that's why Disney is planning on replacing this film in late 2005.

CHINA

As aesthetically pleasing as any of the other pavilions, China features a half-sized replica of Beijing's Temple of Heaven, a pond, and a courtyard suitable for resting up with a red bean ice cream or a Chinese beer while others in your party shop. The pavilion includes the **Land of Many Faces** exhibit, detailing the myriad of ethnic groups that comprise the 1 billion people of China, and the **Yong Feng Shangdian** department store, offering silken robes, prints, paper umbrellas and fans, purses, glassware, and as you climb up the price ladder, dolls, jewelry, figurines, rugs, porcelain masks, carved chests, and antique tables and chairs. For the younger set, toys include nunchuks, ninja swords, and toy snakes. Entertainment in China is provided by **Dragon Legend Acrobats** and classical music performed on authentic instruments by **Si Xian.**

Reflections of China
> Rating: B+
> 19 minute Circle Vision 360 film.
> Fear Factor: 1
> Visit anytime.

In May 2003, director David Katzman updated the 20-year old Wonders of China film with new footage including 360-degree views of Hong Kong and Macau as well as a much more modern glimpse of the nation than the old film, while still including landmarks such as the Forbidden City of Beijing, the vast plains of Inner Mongolia, the 2,400-year-old Great Wall, Tiananmen Square, Harbin, and Urumqi. Note that this is a standing presentation, and showtimes are every half hour.

GERMANY

Germany is quite the festive pavilion, with the constant Oktoberfest and the charming architecture, amalgamated from towns on the Rhine, in Bavaria, and the north of the nation, with some influence from Frankfurt and Rothenberg. The centerpiece on the plaza, St. Georgsplatz, is the Biergarten, an Olde World tavern where authentic German fare and authentic German entertainment are presented. The merry atmosphere is helped by communal seating and huge steins of beer. There are constant musical performances from the **Alpine Trio**, strolling accordionists, and the Oktoberfest band. Snow White makes appearances in the Germany pavilion.

Shopping here is a treat – **Sussigkeiten** features chocolates, candies, and cookies. **Weinkeller** features wine tastings (I recommend the red wine flight), bottles of German wine in a wide price range, as well as beer steins, wine glasses, goblets, decanters, and cheeses. **Glaz und Porzellan** sells Goebel giftware and ceramics (including Hummel figurines).

Die Weinachts Ecke celebrates Christmas 365 days a year, with nutcrackers and other traditional German gifts and ornaments. **Volkskunt** sells cuckoo clocks, ceramics, and random gift items. **Der Bucherwurm** offers English-language books on Germany as well as housewares and gifts adorned with the images of German cities, along with hand-painted Faberge eggs; **Der Teddybar** for toys including trains, dolls, and the eponymous stuffed animals; and **Kunstarbeit en Kristall**; with a selection of glassware.

ITALY

Italy, like its next-door neighbor in World Showcase, Germany, is a festive pavilion featuring fine dining, shopping, and street entertainment. A campanile atop the detailed replica of the Doge Palace towers over the pavilion, along with pedestals on which St. Mark the Evangelist and his lion companion stand, as in the square named for the apostle in Venice. In the Lagoon, there are peppermint-striped poles to which gondolas are tethered, and around the piazza, a fountain and cheery landscaping liven up the atmosphere.

Entertainment in this pavilion includes the ornately costumed **Character Masquerade** dancers, a juggler on weekdays, and the **Imaginum** living statue act. Shops here include **Delizie Italiana** for Perugina chocolates, Italian candies, and cookies; **Il Bel Cristallo** for Capodimonte ceramic flowers and figurines, Venetian glass paperweights, lead crystal bowls and candlesticks, alabaster figurines, and inlaid wood music boxes; and **La Cucina Italiana** for pastries, gourmet foods, cookware, and wines.

U.S.A.

When a dinner party is held, the host sits at the head of the table. In this World Showcase, it is only fitting that America serve as the centerpiece. With a facade comprised of 110,000 bricks, the pavilion's main building houses a fast food restaurant, one shop, and the titlular attraction. Entertainment here is provided by the **Voices of Liberty**, who do à capella performances of patriotic standards; the **American Vybe** vocal group, performing original American styles of music like jazz and gospel; and the **Spirit of America Fife and Drum Corps.**

This pavilion's only shop, **Heritage Manor Gifts**, offers hand-crafted goods and pre-1940s Americana items including glassware, food, toys, porcelain, and replicas of historic documents like the Constitution and the Declaration of Independence.

The American Adventure
Rating: A+

29 minute Audio-Animatronic show.

Fear Factor: 1

Visit before noon or after 3:30pm.

This moving presentation. hosted by Mark Twain and Benjamin Franklin, begins with the Pilgrims' arrival at Plymouth Rock. It then progresses to reveal the evolution of America's soul. In one scene, Franklin walks up a flight of stairs to visit Thomas Jefferson as he opines over the Declaration of Independence.

All over, the realism is incredible. Mark Twain smokes a cigar. Audio-Animatronic figures of Nez Perce Chief Joseph and Susan B. Anthony repeat the words of the originals. The voices of the robot Will Rogers and Franklin Delano Roosevelt are their own, the price of gas in the Depression scene is an accurate eighteen cents. The sets include a nearly life-size replica of Independence Hall in Philadelphia, Philly's Centennial Exposition, and a roadside gas station during the Depression, where one man strums a banjo, humming "Brother, Can You Spare Me a Dime?" Their antique radio plays a speech from FDR.

The music is a big part of this attraction's appeal. The Philadelphia Symphony Orchestra's performance of the finale, "Golden Dream," is absolutely breathtaking, presented along with video clips of the Eagle moon landing, John F. Kennedy's inaugural, and Dr. Martin Luther King's "I have a dream" speech. This moving, stately conclusion often brings people to tears.

This attraction is extremely popular and with the popularity of the nearby Liberty Inn as a lunch option, it's quite crowded between noon and 330pm, so plan to witness the production outside those hours. Even during peak hours, the huge capacity of the theater effectively manages crowds.

JAPAN

A five-story, blue-roofed pagoda, modeled after an eighth-century building in the Horyuji Temple in Nara, majestically overlooks the rest of Japan, easily distinguished from the other World Showcase countries by the torii gate at the edge of the Lagoon. The bright red torii was designed like the one at the Itsukushima Shrine in Hiroshima Bay. Perhaps the most beautiful and soothing part of the pavilion is the lovely garden, with streams and waterfalls, boulders, evergreens, and a small pond filled with koi, Japanese goldfish.

The **Bijutu-Kan Gallery** rotates exhibits of Japanese art and culture, the latest exhibit displaying the tin toys found in japan over the last century. Frantic drumming from **Matsuriza** can often be heard around the pavilion, and **Miyuki**'s candy artistry show is particularly intriguing. The **Mitsokushi** department store offers everything from dolls, bonsai, kimonos, and wind chimes to J-Pop goodies, everything from Yu-Gi-Oh and Pokémon to Iron Chef and Dragon Ball Z.

MOROCCO

This replicated Arabian village courtyard will throw some cinematic imagery into your mind, with architecture representing Casablanca, Fez, and Marrakesh. This pavilion includes some fascinating shops and a daring and delicious restaurant offering authentic but accessible Moroccan cuisine. The **Treasures of Morocco Tour** provides 45 minutes of narration on the culture, history, and people of Morocco.

If you look carefully at any of the tile pieces that make up the 9 ton facade, you would notice a flaw or imperfection with every single piece. This was done purposely by the Moroccan artists imported to construct the pavilion because the Islamic holy book, the Koran, says that only Allah may create perfection. This touch adds to the authenticity and apparent age of the pavilion, whose sights include recreations of the Koutoubia Minaret, the landscaped Medina, and the Bab Boujouloud gate. The **MoRockan** troupe performs contemporary Arabic music, and the **Gallery of Arts and History** hosts an ever-changing collection of Moroccan art, artifacts, and costume.

Shops of Morocco include **Berber Oasis**, selling baskets, leather, brass, jewelry, and curios; **Brass Bazaar**, with pottery alongside pitchers, planters, vases, trays, and serving sets of brass and copper; **Casablanca Carpets**, offering wall hangings, prayer rugs, throw pillows, and Berber and Rabat carpets; **Medina Arts**, for woodcrafts, jewelry, apparel, and gifts; and **Tangier Traders** for clothing and accessories. Jasmine and Aladdin can be found here throughout the day.

FRANCE

I know it's not a hip thing to do in 2004 to sweat France, but this is a lovely pavilion. Even if you're Boycott Bill O'Reilly, you don't have to feel guilty about enjoying a croissant or pastry here. Or even a gourmet meal at one of two great sit-down restaurants.

The pavilion features narrow streets, quaint sidewalk cafes, fountains, and shopping boutiques. The architecture is turn-of-the-century Paris and is towered over by a replica of the Eiffel Tower, which, ironically, is visible from everywhere in World Showcase except the France pavilion. There is a small enclave by the river connecting the International Gateway to the Epcot Resorts, this enclave housing a beautiful, small park inspired by A Sunday Afternoon on the Island of La Grande Jatte, Georges Seurat's famed painting. The park is relaxing and peaceful, but if exciting and breathtaking is more your cup of tea, try the gorgeous film playing at the Palais du Cinema theater towards the rear of the pavilion.

Authentic French entertainment is provided by – what else? **Le Mime Roland**. No explanation necessary, right? There's also audience participation during the daily performances of **Cyranose de Bergerac**. A few worthwhile shops here include **Gallerie des Halles** for impressionist art; **La Casserole** for cookwares; **La Signature** for Guerlain cosmetics, perfumes, and accessories; **Les Vins du France** for wine and sommelier accessories; and **Plume et Palette** for art, crystal, and fragrances. In addition to two award winning restaurants there's the sinfully good **Boulangerie Patisserie**.

Impressions de France
Rating: A
18 minute wide-angle film.
Fear Factor: 1
Visit after 7pm.

Like the two CircleVision 360 films found elsewhere in World Showcase, *Impressions de France* is a travelog type presentation with superb musical accompaniment. The differences however are major: while *O Canada* and *Reflections of China* show a fully panoramic view of their subjects, the huge screen on which *Impressions de France* is shown covers only 200 degrees. Because viewers need not stand to see a full circle, HALLELU-JAH – this theater has seats.

The film is absolutely stunning, featuring picturesque footage from Versailles, the Eiffel Tower, Mont St. Michel, Cannes, the Alps, and 43 other locations. A highlight, for sure, is the beautiful music, played by the London Philharmonic Orchestra and composed in the classic style by Frenchmen who lived in the late 1800s and early 1900s, including Jacques Offenbach, Charles-Camille Saint-Saens, Claude Debussy, and Erik Satie.

International Gateway
Located between France and the UK pavilion, Epcot's second entrance serves the Epcot Resorts and the Disney-MGM Studios. There are two shops here: **Showcase Gifts** for sundries, film, and convenience items and **World Traveler** for Epcot mementos and character merchandise.

UNITED KINGDOM
"Hey look kids, Big Ben, Parliament!" The United Kingdom pavilion recreates architectural styles ranging from 1500 to 1800, and includes lovely shops and an authentic pub on the shore of World Showcase Lagoon, a great place to relax with a pint and take in Illuminations at the end of the day. Some British characters flock to the UK pavilion – Peter Pan, Mary Poppins, Alice in Wonderland, and Pooh's posse can bw found here throughout the day.

British entertainment is courtesy of the **British Invasion,** performing the music of the Beatles; and the **World Showcase Players,** an improvisational street theater troupe. There's also a pianist at the Rose & Crown Pub. Shops here include **Crown & Crest** for fragrances; **Magic of Wales** for candy, music, and housewares; **Sportsman Shop** for sweaters, woolens, kilts, and tartans; **Queen's Table** for china; **Tea Caddy** for afternooning needs, candies, and chocolates; and **Toy Soldier** for books, stuffed animals, games and toys.

CANADA

Canada's landscape features the Victorian Gardens, an attractive little park based on the Butchart Gardens in British Columbia, a replicated Quebec hotel, towering elegantly over the pavilion, a stream, waterfall, and a small Rocky Mountain. The pavilion represents French Canada, the Canadian Rockies, the gardens of the city, and other areas, all of which are revealed in all their wacky Canuck glory in the CircleVision 360 movie here. Shopping here is limited to **Northwest Mercantile** for maple syrup and lumberjack shirts; and **La Boutique des Provinces** for Québecois merchandise, but the excellent Le Cellier Steakhouse makes up for any shortcomings in that department. **Off Kilter** performs new age, high-energy Celtic music here throughout the day.

O Canada!

Rating: B
17 minute Circle Vision 360 film.
Fear Factor: 1
Visit after 3pm.

In a theater tucked away in the side of a mountain, this CircleVision 360 film is dramatic and truly awesome at points. All of Canada's famed landmarks are featured, plus some not-so-famous locales where the wilderness is still king. Footage also includes the Royal Canadian Mounted Police (better known as Mounties), pristine woodlands, a rodeo, the Calgary Stampede, and Montreal with all its Old World charm. This film is very well done, but since it is right at the center of the park, seeing it without a crowd can be difficult unless you check it out in the late afternoon or early evening.

Entertainment in EPCOT

In addition to the events and shows listed below, each pavilion of World Showcase has its own authentic, native entertainment. See the individual pavilion capsules for full details.

Illuminations: Reflections of Earth

Introduced in 2000, the latest iteration of the Illuminations evening celebration and fireworks display captures the primal emotion of man sitting around a roaring fire, as the middle of World Showcase Lagoon is the setting for 15,000 LEDs wrapped across a floating globe, over 1,100 explosive shells, four fountain barges shooting 4,000 gallons of water skyward each minute, four color custom lasers, and an inferno barge shooting 40-foot flames from 37 nozzles. The show is incredible, moving, uplifting, and the perfect coda for any Epcot visit. **Your visit to Epcot is not complete if you do not experience IllumiNations.** Illuminations is performed at 9pm nightly or at closing time if later. Arrive 45 to 60 minutes early to stake out the prime real estate for the show. Best viewing spots include the Rose & Crown Pub and Cantina de San Angel, Italy's gondola landing, Germany's boat dock, and the island between the UK and France pavilions.

Jamminators

This group performs comedic percussion on trash can looking things.

Kristos

Performing at Innoventions Plaza throughout the day, this "visiting alien" dance trio combines ballet, contortion, and feats of strength.

Orisi Risi

At World Showcase Outpost is an interactive drum circle and African folklore.

Meeting the Characters

Long gone are the days when there was no sign of the Disney characters at the scholarly, straight-laced Epcot. Now, the **Characters on Holiday** bus transports various Disney characters around World Showcase Lagoon, stopping at various locations to interact with guests.

Character dining is available at the following restaurants:
•**Restaurant Akershus:** Breakfast buffet featuring Belle, Jasmine, Mary Poppins, Snow White, and Sleeping Beauty. $21.99 adults/$11.99 kids under 12.
•**Garden Grill:** Family-style lunch and dinner featuring Mickey, Chip, and Dale. L: $19.99 adults/$10.99 kids under 12. D: $21.99 adults.$10.99 kids under 12. The Garden Grill also hosts an Ice Cream Social meet & greet with Mickey at 3pm daily ($6.99).

Where to Eat in EPCOT

Epcot is home to many of Disney's finest restaurants, mostly those in World Showcase. Priority seating is available for any sitdown restaurant, call 407/WDW-DINE to make yours.

In Future World
Garden Grill Room (The Land)
This revolving restaurant that overlooks the Living with the Land boat ride, whose greenhouses provide much of the produce served here. Chip 'N Dale's Harvest Feast stars Mickey and Pluto and is offered at lunch and dinner. (L: $19.99 adults/$10.99 kids 3-11. D: $21.99 adults.$10.99 kids 3-11). The menu for both includes bread with three dips to start, your choice of beef strip loin, chipotle rotisserie chicken, seafood cioppino, grilled red snapper, and mushroom asiago ravioli, with chocolate fondue for dessert,. The kids' menu includes mac and cheese and chicken strips.

Coral Reef (The Living Seas)
Here, guests overlook the 5.7 million gallon aquariums of the Living Seas while dining on les fruits de mer. The view is impressive and the food is excellent (executive chef Keith Keogh won the Florida Seafood Chef of the Year award twice), but it is mostly overpriced. The lunch menu includes grilled mahi mahi, shrimp, or New York strip steak, an irresistible barbecue salmon sandwich, and seared lobster tail ($13-24), with a delectable array of starters including blue crab cakes and Hawaiian sausage salad. The dinner menu adds things like grilled wild king salmon and filet mignon ($16-31). The kids' menu includes grilled chicken, grilled mahi, pizza, and pasta ($4.99-8.99). The chefs introduce a new entrée for lunch and dinner every month. Though this is an excellent restaurant, there are other seafood joints in Orlando which are just as good if not better, plus cheaper and easier to get a table. Go elsewhere for your seafood fix.

Sunshine Seasons (The Land)
This highly recommended food court was reworked during this pavilion's 2005 renovation, offering soups (including a chicken chile garlic noodle bowl), salads (including seared tuna on mixed greens with sesame rice wine dressing), sandwiches (like veggie Cubans and a turkey and Muenster foccacia ($5.59-$9.99). The kids' menu includes chicken legs, mini subs, mac and cheese, and chicken stir fry ($3.99).

Electric Umbrella (Innoventions East)
Future World's best breakfasts are available here – omelets, bagel

sandwiches, French toast stocls, cereal, fruit, and more ($1.99-5.29). The lunch and dinner menu includes smoked turkey and Muenster sandwiches, bacon double cheeseburgers, roast beef and provolone, island chicken salad, and more ($4.29-7.99). Kids' meals include chicken nuggets and mac & cheese ($3.99).

Fountain View Espresso & Bakery (Innoventions West)
Breakfast pockets, croissants, bagels, and pastries are offered along with desserts like coconut flan, Boston cream pie, and cheesecake ($2.29-$4.49).

Cool Wash Pizza (Test Track)
Located outside the Test Track pavilion, this stand offers 7" cheese or pepperoni pizzas ($5.75-6.00).

In World Showcase
San Angel Inn (Mexico)
This is undeniably Epcot's most romantic restaurant, with the dining area overlooking the tranquil Rio del Tiempo, where boats sail past a volcano and away through a jungle. The atmosphere is that of a quaint but bustling Mexican village just after perpetual sunset.

Even better than the atmosphere is the stellar and authentic Mexican food. The lunch menu includes tacos al carbon, beef burritos and flautas, chicken nachos, carne asada, and roast pork with sweet and sour tamarind sauce ($10.75-18.50). The dinner menu focuses on grilled beef tenderloin, shrimp, or chicken breast. Mole poblano is authentic and tasty, Leave room for dessert—you won't be sorry ($17.95-23.95). The children's menu at both includes chicken strips, quesadilla, and cheeseburger ($4.99-5.99).

Cantina de San Angel (Mexico)
The tables at this counter-service restaurant on the waterfront at the Mexico pavilion offer the single best vantage for Illuminations. The menu includes stacked Cantina nachos, tacos al carbon, wet burritos, and frozen margaritas ($6.79-7.99). Arrive at least 45 minutes prior to Illuminations to stake out a table for it.

Restaurant Akershus (Norway)
Named after the castle overlooking the harbor in Oslo, this surprisingly intimate smorgasbord offers a family-style character breakfast featuring all-you-can-eat breads, bacon, eggs, sausage, French toast, potatoes, and fruit, along with visits from Jasmine, Belle, Snow White, and other princesses ($21.99 adults/$11.99 kids 3-11).

The lunch hot-and-cold buffet includes salads, cheeses, smoked salmon and eggs, and entrée selections like braised lamb and cabbage, salmon Nicioise salad, savory vegetable tart, and fettucine with vegetables in a Chardonnay cream sauce, and a dessert plate including lingonberry tart, rice cream, and chocolate mousse ($23.99 adults/$12.99 kids 3-11). The dinner menu adds smoked mackerel and salmon, seafood salads, poached cod, and venison stew ($27.99 adults/$12.99 kids 3-11).

Kringla Bakeri og Kafe (Norway)
This counter-service bakery offers sweet pretzels, strawberry-topped waffles, potato bread, double chocolate cake, rice cream, and open-faced sandwiches of salmon and eggs, ham and Jarlsberg, or smoked turkey breast ($1.49-5.59).

Nine Dragons (China)
Blending Szechuan, Cantonese, Kiangche, and Mandarin cuisines, the Nine Dragons offers dim sum at lunch along with sampler platters and traditional entrees like fried rice, General Tso's, pepper beef, and sesame chicken ($10.99-21.95). Dinner expands the menu with lamb chops, Beijing duck, and steamed fish in five flavor sauce ($12.99-38.75). For kids, there's a fried rice/spring roll combo and sweet and sour chicken ($4.75-8.75).

Lotus Blossom Café (China)
China's counter service eatery offers rice bowls, lo mein, salad, egg rolls, and ice cream ($4.50-6.59).

Refreshment Cool Post
Waffle cones, floats, slushes, and energy mix are available here ($2.99-3.69).

Biergarten (Germany)
Oktoberfest entertainment and belly-bombing food combine to make this a bigtime favorite for many festive Epcot guests. The half-hour show with yodelers, dancers, singers, and an oompah band, all clad in lederhosen, serves as an amusing backdrop for dining festivities. The lunch buffet consists of sausages, roast pork, rotisserie chicken, schnitzel, stuffed cabbage, cheeses and cold cuts, salads, breads, and desserts ($14.59 adults, $7.99 kids 3-11). At dinner fish and sauerbraten are added to the buffet ($20.99 adults, $8.99 kids 3-11). Beck's beer is on tap, and wine is available.

Sommerfest (Germany)

This courtyard stand offers chicken schnitzel, bratwurst, hot dogs, ham sandwiches, pretzels, and desserts ($2.89-5.99).

L'Originale Alfredo di Roma Ristorante (Italy)

World Showcase's most popular restaurant is a safe, if not always standout bet for finicky families. Accordionists stroll and waiters and waitresses will occasionally burst into Italian traditional, opera, and classical songs. The scenery is beautiful, decorated with murals that give the impression of real scenery instead of the two-dimensional flats on the walls.

The lunch menu includes tomato mozzarella and chicken Caesar salads, personal pizzas, pasta dishes (including the eponymous fettucine Alfredo), gnocchi, and chicken parmesan ($10.95-22.95). The dinner menu also includes bacon-wrapped filet mignon, veal chops, and more ($18.50-34.95). A little sticker shock, for sure – once again, better and far cheaper Italian can be enjoyed outside the parks. The kids' menu includes spaghetti, lasagna, and chicken nuggets ($4.99-6.99).

Pasticceria Italiana di Alfredo di Roma (Italy)

On World Showcase Promenade, this stand offers desserts from Alfredo's kitchen, including tiramisu, cannoli, and chocolate mousse ($1.50-3.95).

Liberty Inn (U.S.A.)

It's kind of disappointing that there's not more imaginative and off-the-beaten-path American fare here, but there is certainly a segment of the crowd who will appreciate a menu of burgers, hot dogs, chicken strips, and turkey sandwiches ($5.69-8.99). Vegetarian and chicken salads are also available.

Mitsokushi Restaurant (Japan)

These five rooms offer teppan table cooking, where the chefs chop, toss, juggle, sizzle, and stir-fry chunks of steak, chicken, vegetables, and seafood on the tables. Lunch runs $13.99-34.99, while dinner will set you back $15.99-34.99.

Tempura Kiku (Japan)

In this corner of the Mitsukoshi dining complex you can order up tempura, those tasty, battered-and-deep-fried chunks of beef, chicken, seafood, and vegetables ($8.95-13.75). Sushi and sashimi appetizers are also available, along with Kirin beer, sake, plum wine, and Japanese spirits. Dinner offers more seafood options ($15.95-24.75).

Matsunoma Lounge (Japan)
A good selection of sushi and sashimi is offered here ($3.75-21.75). This lounge offers an excellent view for Illuminations.

Yakitori House (Japan)
Skewered beef and chicken is the specialty here, along with udon noodles ($1.79-7.49).

Kaki Gori (Japan)
A stand along the waterfront offers ice slush concoctions called kaki-gori during hot weather and waffles with red bean paste during colder times ($2.25).

Restaurant Marrakesh (Morocco)
This excellent restaurant provides an exotic taste of Morocco available in few other locations in Orlando. The surroundings are foreign and as zestful as the food, and entertainment is provided by beautiful belly dancers and a live three-piece Moroccan combo or piped-in music.

The food is served up in tasty, heaping portions and the lunch menu includes roast lamb, lemon chicken, kebabs, and cous cous, a filling dish of steamed semolina topped with vegetables, chicken, beef, or lamb ($12.95-22.95). Dinner adds broiled salmon, Mediterranean seafood platter, and two excellent grand-tour prix fixe sampler dinners ($16.95-29.95). Since Moroccan cuisine is virtually unknown to most people, this restaurant rarely fills up in advance. The kids' menu includes hamburgers and kebabs ($4.95-5.95).

Tangierine Café (Morocco)
More familiar Mediterranean fare is offered up here, including shawarma sandwiches and platters with hummus and tabouleh, saffron rotisserie chicken, wraps, meatball sandwiches, pizza, and pastries ($6.95-11.95).

Les Chefs de France (France)
This is one of Epcot's most popular restaurants, and for good reason: The master chefs here are a renowned trio: Roger Verge, Paul Bocuse, and Gaston LeNotre. Bocuse and Verge each operate three star restaurants, on the Riviera and near Lyon, respevtively. LeNotre operates six Paris bakeries and is generally acknowledged as one of the world's top pastry chefs. The three collaborated on the menu and often make visits to Chefs de France to make changes to it. The atmosphere is Victorian-era continental, accented with wood paneling, brass light fixtures, etched glass, linen table cloths, and a diligent staff dressed in formal wear.

The lunch menu is a great bet for families, with salads, ham and cheese or tuna sandwiches, eggplant and zucchini lasagna, macaroni and Gruyère, steak, chicken, grilled shrimp, and salmon ($9.95-17.95). The dinner menu dispenses with the lighter fare and concentrates on braised, roasted, and grilled meats and seafood, including tuna skewers, lamb shank, and chicken cordon bleu ($15.95-27.95). Save room for the famous LeNotre pastries and a hot mug of cafe filtre, a strong, thick coffee similar to Italian espresso. The children's menu here includes chopped steak sandwich and chicken strips ($5.45-5.85).

Bistro de Paris (France)
Located upstairs from Chefs de France, the Bistro serves upscale, gourmet French cuisine from the same trio – Verge, Bocuse, and LeNotre. Open for dinner only, the Bistro's menu includes Bahamian lobster tail, seared scallops, lamb loin, and ribeye ($23-32). Note that there is no children's menu here.

Boulangerie Patisserie (France)
This magnificent and irresistible bake shop at the back of the France pavilion sells some of the best pastries known to man. Popular for breakfast, lunch, and dessert, the fare includes quiche, croissants stuffed with ham and cheese or chocolate, a delectable strawberry-topped cheesecake called schuss, and more goodies to wreck any diet. Absolutely not to be missed ($1.95-4.95).

Crèpes des Chefs de France (France)
This stand offers ice cream and thin pancakes known as crèpes, served with chocolate, strawberry, or orange ($4).

Rose & Crown Dining Room & Pub (UK)
This authentic British taproom offers traditional British cuisine like fish and chips, Guiness stew, bangers and mash, and cottage pie at lunch ($11.99-15.99). The dinner menu includes a few extra choices, like steak and prawns, pan-seared salmon, and roasted chicken ($14.99-26.99). The kids' menu includes pasta, pizza, and ribeye steak ($4.99-6.50).

Yorkshire Country Fish Shop (UK)
Harry Ramsden's fish and chips are sold at this counter on the promenade ($6.49).

Le Cellier (Canada)
This steakhouse offers intriguing Canadian cuisine, including seared trout or beef tenderloin salad, French dip sandwich, soft shell crab sandwich,

steakburgers, and vegetable lasagna ($6.99-21.99). At dinner, bigger, more flavorful steaks are trotted out along with Canadian king salmon, Prince Edward Island mussels, and grilled pork tenderloin ($15.99-34.99). The kids' menu includes steak, cheeseburger, grilled chicken, hot dog, and more ($4.99-8.99).

Trapper Bob's (Canada)
This stand serves up pretzel breadsticks along with traditional Canadian beer and wine ($4).

Refreshment Port
Located in Showcase Plaza, this stand offers Chicken McNuggets, McDonald's French fries, and McFlurries ($2.69-3.99).

Practical Information

Getting In
For information on Walt Disney World's new Magic Your Way ticketing options, refer to Part 2, pages 338-340.

Getting There
Epcot is easily reached from I-4 exit 67. Coming from Kissimmee, the WDW Maingate offers the easiest route here. International Drive guests can avoid I-4 entirely by taking I-Drive to SR 536 and turning right.

The park is connected to the TTC (and to the MK and Contemporary, Polynesian, and Grand Floridian resorts, with a transfer) via monorail; to Disney-MGM, the Yacht and Beach Club, Dolphin, Swan, and Boardwalk via boat launch (from the International Gateway entrance); and to all other WDW resorts via bus.

Hours
Epcot has staggered hours – Future World is open from 9am to 7pm in off-peak seasons, 9pm in peak seasons. World Showcase opens at 11am and closes at 9pm in off-peak seasons and 11pm in peak seasons. Note that several of Future World's most popular attractions are open the whole time – they are Honey, I Shrunk the Audience, Mission: SPACE, Spaceship Earth, and Test Track.

Parking
The 162-acre Epcot lot has 9,000 spaces and costs $8 per day, free for WDW resort guests and annual passholders.

Money

Walt Disney World accepts American Express, MasterCard, Visa, Discover, Diners Club, JCB, and the Disney Credit Card, as well as travelers' checks and cash, even at counter-service eateries. There are Bank One ATMs located at the Main Entrance, between Future World and World Showcase Plaza, and at the American Adventure. Guests staying at Disney resorts can also make theme park charges to their room.

Package Pickup

Each theme park offers package pickup service, where rather than lugging your purchases around all day, you can send them to a centralized package pickup center near the entrance to the park. Disney resort guests can have their packages sent directly to their hotels. Note that package pickup locations are most crowded between 5 and 6pm and/or one hour before the theme parks close. Epcot's package pickup is located at Gift Stop, by the main entrance.

Security

Bag/backpack/package searches are now performed at Disney World. Allow a few extra minutes to get through them.

Smoking

By law, all Florida restaurants and bars are now non-smoking. Smoking is only allowed in selected areas of the park. Smoking areas are located:

•**Outside the park:** On the west (left) side of the main entrance plaza.

•**In Future World:** Scattered across the middle trails between the inner loop (Spaceship Earth, Innoventions) and outer loops of the attractions (Living Seas, Land, Imagination, Test Track, Mission: Space, and Universe of Energy). There's also one next to Innoventions, east of the fountain.

•**In World Showcase:** Smoking areas are located in Mexico, China, Germany, Italy, U.S.A., Japan, and France, as well as near Showcase Plaza and the International Gateway.

Check the park map for exact locations.

Disney's FastPass

See Chapter 4 for details on how FastPass works. Epcot attractions utilizing FastPass were Honey, I Shrunk the Audience, Soarin', Living with the Land, Maelstrom, Mission: SPACE, and Test Track. Note that Test Track FastPasses disappear quickly – mid-afternoon may be too late to get one.

Services

The **Guest Relations** counter is located on the east side of Spaceship Earth. The **lost and found** is located at Guest Relations as well. **Lockers** are available at both the main entrance and International Gateway. The Odyssey Complex hosts **baby services, first aid**, and a **lost child resource center.**

Chapter 6

DISNEY-MGM STUDIOS

Forty years ago, Walt Disney wanted to open up the world of the studio backlot tour to more than just the privileged few, and so put in motion the idea that eventually became the Disney-MGM Studios Theme Park, which opened to great fanfare in May 1989. In the 15 years since, the popular park has doubled in size. The park, commemorating "the Hollywood that never was and will always be," includes stunt shows, thrill rides, behind-the-scenes tours, and lots more educational and entertaining experiences. In terms of the vibe offered here, it's halfway between the whimsy of the Magic Kingdom and the scholarly presentation of Epcot.

Compared to Universal Studios.......... Well. I know that this book is called "Disney World Guide," but the fact of the matter is, I prefer Universal. Better thrill rides, less waiting, more spectacular aesthetics, and a much smarter, more adult experience. That being said, Disney-MGM is a great park with lots of fun attractions, including my absolute favorite WDW attraction, the Twilight Zone Tower of Terror. It's definitely a stacked day of touring.

Disney-MGM is a working production studio as well – the facility's resumé includes animated features such as *The Little Mermaid, Pocohontas, Aladdin, Lilo and Stitch*, and *Brother Bear* (although Disney moved its entire animation operation to California); live action films such as *Oscar, Passenger 57, Quick Change,* and *Marvin's Room* (I didn't say they were good films); and TV shows like *Full House, Wheel of Fortune, WCW Nitro/Thunder, Talk Soup, Live with Regis & Kathie Lee,* and *ER.* Although admittedly, you can't help but think, when the backlot tour makes note of the houses from *Ernest*

Saves Christmas and *Empty Nest,* it becomes apparent that it's not MUCH of a working studio.

Hollywood Boulevard

Much like Main Street, USA, this entryway into the park is loaded with retail therapists (aka: stores) and places to satisfy sweet teeth on the way into or out of the park. Instead of quaint turn-of-the-century Missouri, we get fabulous 1930's L.A. Art deco, chrome, and neon buildings and creeping characters straight out of a film noir make you feel as if you've walked into Roger Rabbit. The characters, dubbed **Streetmosphere**, are detectives, starlets, directors, and other unsavory types.

The Great Movie Ride
Rating: A+
22-minute ride through great movies throughout history.
Fear Factor: 3
Visit after 5pm.

Behind the gigantic Sorcerer Mickey hat is a full-scale replica of Grauman's Chinese Theater, in which live guides, Audio-Animatronic figures of movie stars, elaborate sets, and meticulously recreated costumes, take guests through various genres – starting with musicals, like a scene from the Busby Berkeley musical *Footlight Parade* where sixty dancers kick and move atop a revolving cake. Gene Kelly then croons "Singin' in the Rain." Then to a scene from *Mary Poppins*, where Julie Andrews floats, singing "Chim Chim Cher-ee" while Dick Van Dyke dances on a rooftop. A gangland ambush nearly occurs, but they decide you're not worth their time. A shootout occurs and you are forced to detour into the Wild West, where the Duke sits on a horse, brandishing a rifle while he talks to the audience. A little later, a bank heist goes down and the robber's Audio-Animatronic accomplice fires at the crowd. The bank blows up, and the flames can be felt as you ride by. Overhead, hay begins to smolder.

Now, there are two different things that happen in the gangster/ western scene. In the bank heist or the shootout, your driver-emcee-actor stops the car and goes in to investigate. But then, a robber or gangster runs out, brandishing a tommygun or a rifle and commandeers the vehicle. She/ he leaves the driver and takes off with guests as hostages, entering the spaceship Nostromo (of *Alien* fame), where Ripley stands with weapon in hand, sweating and leaning against the wall of a corridor. reach Harrison Ford and John Rhys-Davies lifting up the ark from *Raiders of the Lost Ark.* When the cars reach an Egyptian scene with a huge gem on an idol, greed will get the better of the driver, who runs up to grab the gem, not hearing a belated warning about a curse. Evil is punished, good triumphs, same old story, thank you, drive through. Later, Tarzan swings on a vine over Cheetah and Jane.

Next stop, Casablanca. The plane's engine sputters, the propellors whirl, and Rick bids Ilsa farewell. Then, it's off to a happy place. You hear Munchkins sing "Ding dong, the witch is dead," and the subject of the song's sister pops out of a puff of smoke, threatening your driver. You leave the frightened Munchkins and follow the yellow brick road (well, what else would you do?), where you see Dorothy, Toto, the Tin Man, Scarecrow, and Cowardly Lion gaping at the Emerald City. The finale of the ride is an impressive montage of 90 Academy Award-winning films squeezed into three minutes. This tribute was created by Oscar-winner Chuck Workman. As you exit, the driver yells after you to remember them "when Oscar time comes around!" This ride is not to be missed, but crowds up pretty steadily all day. If the line extends outside the theater, you will have a twenty-five minute wait or more.

Shopping

Shops on Hollywood Blvd. include the **Darkroom** for cameras, film, and accessories; **Celebrity 5 & 10** for studio logo souvenirs, **Cover Story** for Photoshopped magazine cover photo ops; **Keystone Clothiers** for men's and women's fashions and accessories; **L.A. Prop Cinema Storage** for kids' fashion and souvenirs; **Mickey's of Hollywood** for character merchandise and plush toys; and **Sid Cahuenga's One-of-a-Kind** for cinematic collectibles.

Echo Lake/Streets of America

Echo Lake is a small body of water around which several major restaurants and attractions sit, including Star Tours and the Indiana Jones Epic Stunt Spectacular. The Streets of America use forced perspective and other tricks to recreate portions of the New York skyline and various landmarks. Attractions here include Jim Henson's Muppet*Vision 3D.

Jim Henson's Muppet*Vision 3D
Rating: A+
Hilarious 25-minute 3D movie.
Fear Factor: 2
Visit before 11am or after 3pm.

This wild insanity of an attraction goes WAY beyond 3D, as the film is supplemented by the presence of Audio-Animatronic figures, live characters, and dazzling, live special effects like bubbles raining down on the audience or a gentle spray of water when Fozzie Bear shoots water from a corsage, plus a theater that actually changes as the show goes on. These must be some of the "cheap 3D tricks" to which Kermit assures you that "we will at no time be stooping." The plot of the story is thin, but done in spectacular fashion. Most of it's just a pretense for abusing Miss Piggy.

After explaining the technology behind Muppet*Vision with help from Dr. Honeydew and the long-suffering Beaker, the Muppets attempt to mount a musical production, but run into the usual mishaps, prompting the show to screech to a halt when Bean Bunny runs away with Waldo, the computer-generated "spirit of 3D." The Muppets roam the theater looking for them. Bean pops up in the upper balcony and there is a happy, albeit destructive ending with more shooting than a John Woo film and an explosive finale at the hands of the Swedish Chef.

The pre-show is equally amusing, held in a warehouse filled with crates to be delivered to the Muppets. The Muppets cavort about three television screens overhead, preparing for the show. Disney prepared for the large crowds who frequent the theater by making it large enough to accommodate them. The only time when you may experience a wait of more than twenty minutes is immediately after the nearby Indiana Jones Epic Stunt Spectacular! discharges an audience.

Star Tours
> Rating: A
> 7-minute Star Wars themed simulator ride.
> Fear Factor: 4
> Use FastPass or visit before 10am.

A model Ewok village and an Imperial Walker sit in front of this, one of Disney's most breathtaking works, a sensational flight simulator adventure called Star Tours. The ride is based on the Star Wars trilogy (seemingly set around the time of Return of the Jedi) and was created by Disney and George Lucas. Dozens of Audio-Animatronics droids, including C3P0 and R2D2 occupy the queue area and get you in a Millennium Falcon state of mind before you even board. The displays on either side of the queue are fascinating and make long waits in line somewhat bearable. Threepio, Artoo, and the other robots converse while they, among other things, prepare the Starspeeders for takeoff.

Your pilot is a robotic rookie played by Pee-Wee Herman. Your trip gets off to a bumpy start almost immediately as you make a wrong turn and almost smash the ship before you even take off. But you eventually get your bearing and fly straight to the Moon of Endor. But unfortunately, you wind up taking a detour through an asteroid field and into a comet. As you smash through the wall of the comet, you are out in open space, just you, the pilot, and an Imperial TIE fighter! The fighter fires on you and you somehow wind up in the tractor beam of the Death Star. But a Rebel pilot steers you out of the tractor beam and leads you on an attack on the Death Star. After one more near miss, your Starspeeder docks and you get off saying with a huge grin on your face, "Let's do it again!" as you exchange high-fives. Although admittedly, this ride has started to look a bit dated, having debuted before Lucas so much as spruced up Episodes IV-VI, but Lucas has made statements hinting at an "overhaul" for the ride, indicating that perhaps an Episode III tie-in is possible. The Anakin Skywalker Volcano Adventure Grill perhaps? This is one of the more popular rides in the Disney-MGM Studios and is most crowded early in the day. If you are not at the gate by 10am, expect a sizable wait, so use FastPass.

Indiana Jones Epic Stunt Spectacular
> Rating: B+
> 22-minute live-action stunt show.
> Fear Factor: 2
> Arrive 30-45 minutes prior to showtime or use FastPass.

This show recalls the archaeologist's misadventures to demonstrate how fights, explosions, and other movie magic are safely performed. The show opens with a Harrison Ford lookalike gently replacing a golden idol with a bag of sand, then getting chased down an incline by a huge, 12-foot high stone ball.

The production crew explains how movie stunts are done and then proceeds to make a fiery demonstration thereof. The two other scenes are the Cairo marketplace where Indy is ambushed by sword-wielding acrobats, and then to a scene with an attempted escape with a Nazi plane, the runaway truck, and the explosive finale. There are machine gun battles and a climax of unbelievable magnitude. In case you were wondering, everything is real. You will realize that after the first explosion when heat hits your face. The stuntmen have been hurt on more than one occasion, but the production usually goes off without a hitch. The one and only flaw of this production is the slow pace of the narration between the action sequences. A retooled script could breathe new life into the show.

At the beginning of the show, ten extras are selected from the audience to perform in the show, but don't worry, there is absolutely no danger for nine of the extras. The tenth is used to demonstrate how to "take a punch." But don't worry, this one's a plant. You'll know which one he is because of the comments about his wardrobe. Look on your entertainment schedule or on the board outside the attraction for showtimes, plan on arriving 30 minutes beforehand and you will have little or no wait. If before the house is opened, the line extends to the dinosaur at the shore, you probably will not be seated in the next show. FastPass is available here.

Lights, Motors, Action! Extreme Stunt Show
Rating: N/A
30-minute stunt show featuring automobiles of all kinds.
Fear Factor: 2
Visit late or with FastPass.

Imported from Disneyland Paris to a 6.5 acre stage surrounded by a new 5,000 seat amphitheater (complete with giant LCD screen for optimum viewing from anywhere), LMAX features a cast of over 30 stunt drivers, technicians, actors, and stunt managers blend with over 30 featured vehicles to create a fast-paced show full of pyrotechnics, humor, surprises, and action. The premise of the show is the filming of a European spy thriller. Drivers perform high-speed spins, two-wheel driving, jumps, and high falls. FastPass is available at this attraction. It opened in May 2005, too late to be reviewed in this edition.

Honey, I Shrunk the Kids Movie Set Adventure
Rating: B
Walk-through playground built to ridiculous scale.
Fear Factor: 2
Visit before 11am or after 4pm.

This playground based on the motion picture *Honey, I Shrunk the Kids* allows yours to play among 20-foot tall blades of grass, rolls of film to play in, huge bugs, enormous Legos, and a garden hose that drips on unsuspecting passers-by. It's fun, but nonessential, and worth skipping if there are no children in your party.

Sounds Dangerous
Rating: B-
12-minute theater presentation demonstrating high-definition ste-reophonic sound.
Fear Factor: 3
Visit anyime.

This often-hilarious attraction stars Drew Carey as a hapless police officer who wears a hidden camera and attempts to bust a jewel smuggling ring. All of it is captured on a hidden camera for a show called Undercover Live – at least until Drew breaks the camera, and all that's left is the sound.

You're in a darkened auditorium, listening through headphones to a spatially programmed soundtrack. That's the rest of the show. It's still quite a bit to take in, if you're not a terribly visual person, anyway. After the show, you'll be shuttled into the Sound Works area, where you can participate in hands-on exhibits and edit your own soundtracks. You can also enter this section of the attraction from the street.

Shopping

Shops in this area include **Golden Age Souvenirs**; **Indiana Jones Adventure Outpost**, selling adventure gear, pith helmets, fedoras, whips, and snakes; **It's a Wonderful Shop**, carrying a year-round selection of Christmas merchandise; the **Stage 1 Company Store**, featuring Muppet merchandise; and **Tatooine Traders**, offering a wide selection of Star Wars merch.

Mickey Avenue/Animation Courtyard

Winding along the back edge of the theme park, Mickey Avenue plays home to several major attractions.

Who Wants to Be a Millionaire? - Play It!
Rating: A-
30-minute interactive version of the popular TV game show.
Fear Factor: 1
Visit with FastPass or after 5pm.

You don't have to be a Millionaire fan to enjoy this attraction – I loathe the TV show but found myself completely sucked into the game. Disney faithfully reproduced the look and feel of ABC's hit game show, right down to the lighting effects and the music. Sure, you won't really have Regis throwing out the questions, and you won't actually win a million dollars, but audience members play along for the chance to sit in the hot seat and answer questions for points that can earn you some cool prizes, especially if you actually make it near the million. The grand prize package at press time included a Disney cruise for 4. Other prizes included pins, hats, and t-shirts. You'll have three lifelines, 50/50, Poll the Audience, and Phone-a-Complete-Stranger. Instead of a friend, you'll be placing a call to someone random outside the theatre. During special events like Star Wars Weekends, the game features special questions geared towards the subject matter.

Voyage of the Little Mermaid
Rating: A-

17-minute mixed-media musical show.
Fear Factor: 2
Visit with FastPass or before 10am.

This dazzling show features songs from the movie, puppets, live actors, and Audio-Animatronic characters, including a 12-foot high Ursula singing "Poor Unfortunate Soul." Ariel and Sebastian sing other songs from the movie. It's a fascinating show, with great effects and a well-executed juxtaposition of different media. The only flaw I can really point out in the show is that the story feels rushed – the entire second act of the movie is pretty much condensed into a 30 second animated clip. The special effects are incredible here, creating the illusion of wind, rain, bubbles, and undersea detail. Black light scenes will also wow viewers. So will the realization that Ariel is only 16 years old. I feel sorta dirty now.

Walt Disney: One Man's Dream
Rating: B
25-minute film and extensive exhibits.
Fear Factor: 1
Visit during the midday.

This attraction commemorated the creativity and spirit of Walt Disney as part of the 100 Years of Magic festivities. The multimedia exhibit includes artifacts dating back to the early days of Disney including the man's desk, office chair, and cabinet, the Oscar he won in 1954 for *20,000 Leagues Under the Sea*, props from *Snow White* and *Pinocchio,* and models of attractions ranging from Peter Pan's Flight to Sleeping Beauty Castle and the Tree of Life, over 400 items in all. Perhaps most interesting of all is the demonstration of how a skeletal Audio-Animatronic robot moves. As you wander through the exhibit, you can trace the entire life and career of Disney and even the posthumous accomplishments of the company that bears his name, and then share a 25-minute film in which Disney narrates his own life story – up til the part where he died. Michael Eisner took over from there, and managed to sound vaguely evil without even trying.

Playhouse Disney: Live on Stage
Rating: B-
20-minute live stage show featuring Disney animation characters.
Fear Factor: 1
Visit anytime.

This show, featuring characters from Bear in the Big Blue House, Rolie Polie Olie, the Book of Pooh, JoJo's Circus, and Stanley, is extremely popular with younger children, who thrill to singing, dancing, and playing with their heroes. The focus of the show is on the importance of friendship, and there's a storyline about Tutter the mouse getting over his inhibitions about dancing in front of friends. It's pleasant and a must-see for fans of the Disney Channel's animation block. For best seating, arrive 15 minutes prior to showtime.

The Magic of Disney Animation
Rating: C+
15-minute tour and discussion of how animation is created.
Fear Factor: 1
Visit anytime.

With the mass layoff of Disney's Florida animation studio in 2004, this was revamped and reworked to an attraction featuring a live artist who interacts with the animated Mushu, the dragon from Mulan, for a 10 minute segment called "Drawn to Animation" that talks about character development, followed by a walk-through the ghost town that used to be the animators' workspace, and the Animation Academy, which allows guests to create their own Disney character artwork with the help of a Disney artist. The old video presentation with Walter Cronkite and Robin Williams is gone along with the animators, so this isn't nearly as compelling an attraction as it used to be.

Backlot Tour
Rating: D
35-minute walking and tram tour of backlot facility.
Fear Factor: 2
Visit anytime, or better yet, never.

What a stinker Disney-MGM has turned this attraction into. Whereas before the combination of the walking and tram tour contained lots of interesting information and fun sights, now most of the sights seem dated, and most of the tour seems to be spent waiting in line for the next part. The first part of the tour is the special effects water tank, where Michael Bey introduces the world of FX in the context of what he did to "make Pearl Harbor realistic." Incredibly, he said it with a straight face. Volunteers are drafted from the audience and stuck into the picture, where they invariably get wet and/or shot at.

Next, you wind through the prop storage room, which is just a queue area to get on the tram for the final portion of the tour. And the tram ride isn't all that impressive. While seeing the houses from *Ernest Saves Christmas* and *Empty Nest* might have been cool in 1989 – ok, ok, they were LAME even back then – but now it's just laughable and dated that in 2003 one of the world's biggest entertainment conglomerates is bragging that a Jim Varney movie and a bad Saturday night sitcom were filmed on its lot.

The tour takes guests past the wardrobe and scenic departments, basically warehouses containing stockpiles of properties, set pieces, and costume items. The Boneyard is the most interesting part of the tour, as this is the resting place for vehicles from such movies as *Who Framed Roger Rabbit, Return of the Jedi, Flight of the Navigator*, and many more. Next it's off to Catastrophe Canyon. The guide warns you at the beginning of the tour, "Those of you on the right side of the cars are going to get a little wet, those of you on the left are going to get soaked." This is the place he meant. You enter an oil drilling operation, only to be hit by rain, earthquakes, fires, explosions, and flash floods (sounds like California!) and then suddenly, it's over, just as quickly as it began. You've survived, and you can't help but notice that the effects weren't all that impressive.

Your last port of call is New York Street, where a technique called forced perspective turn two blocks of two-dimensional "buildings" into a cityscape. This attraction has been tinkered with and altered some, and it's a shame – because previously this was one of my favorite attractions, one I rated "not to be missed." But now I just feel like it's mostly a waste of time.

Shopping

Shopping in this area of the park is limited to a handful of shops, including the **AFI Showcase Shop** featuring specialty movie memorabilia and the **Animation Courtyard Shops**, offering cels and original artwork as well as souvenirs and costumes from classic Disney films.

Sunset Boulevard

The first major expansion to the Disney-MGM Studios, Sunset Boulevard plays host to the two wildest thrill rides in all of WDW – the Rock 'n' Roller Coaster starring Aerosmith, and the heart-stopping Twilight Zone Tower of Terror. There's also a lot of shopping and snacking opportunity along this path.

Twilight Zone Tower of Terror
Rating: A+
8-minute thrill ride culminating in a 13-story drop.
Fear Factor: 5
Visit second thing in the morning or with FastPass.

This ride is diabolical, now that Disney Imagineers have reprogrammed it so that the ride experience is never the same twice. The thrill ride puts you into an episode of the Twilight Zone, introduced by none other than Rod Serling. The storyline is detailed in an 88-second pre-show narrated by Serling and a sound-alike (Serling died in 1975 – his introduction was taken from a 1961 episode). In 1939, a Hollywood couple, a bellboy, a child actress, and her governess boarded the elevator in the Hollywood Tower Hotel and as the elevator rose, it was struck by a bolt of lightning. The elevator vanished and its occupants with it. As the protagonist in "tonight's Twilight Zone," you must venture up to the top of the hotel in service elevators to find out what exactly happened on that stormy night. Unfortunately, the ride does not follow through on the storyline as much as it could, glossing over the disappearance. There is one stop in a corridor in which spectral images of the missing passengers gesture to you and then disappear into the starry night, followed by the entire corridor. It's amazing. The next stop is the "fifth dimension." where holographic projections, lights, mirrors, and other effects simulate "The Twilight Zone."

Fortunately, the best is yet to come. After some more deadpan narration, you find yourself at the top of the Tower – and here's where it gets fun. There's a 13-story drop, right? Always has been. Then they added a secondary drop. Then the Imagineers added a random element so that the drop sequence is different every time – special effects, long drops, rises, short drops, catches – it's all here and it's never the same twice. If you get here early enough you can ride it repeatedly and see for yourself how different the ride experience is. Note that you must be 40 inches tall to ride this. FastPass is available here. Even though lines here tend to move relatively quickly (when all the elevator cars are running, at least), this is definitely an attraction that benefits from its use.

Fantasmic!
    Rating: A+
    25-minute nighttime spectacular.
    Fear Factor: 3
    Get here 60 minutes prior to show time!

Fantasmic! is without question the 800 pound gorilla of nighttime shows at Disney World. Performed at least once nightly (more in peak seasons), the show is a simple good-vs-evil conflict that puts Sorcerer Mickey against some of Disney's most nefarious villains from *Fantasia*, *Aladdin*, *Pocahontas*, and many more, brought to life with fireworks, music, water screens, and larger-than-life characters. Monstro the whale, a 40-foot Maleficent dragon, and the evil queen from Snow White all make appearances. While Disney's budget cuts in recent years have hit nighttime fireworks shows hard, Fantasmic! proves that you don't need to go all-out with the explosions to make a quality show. The character-laden boats swooping across the lagoon, the good vs. evil conflict in the show, and its nearly unmitigated thematic darkness (bad guys are winning for probably about all but 5 minutes of the show), make this one of Disney's most remarkable experiences.

This show is INCREDIBLE and is not to be missed. Be aware that it fills up quickly and you really do need to arrive an hour or more showtime. An option is to purchase a Fantasmic! dinner package, which allows reserved seating at the show and a meal at a sit-down restaurant in the Studios for $22.99-36.99 adult/$10.99 and up kids 3-11. Call 407/WDW-DINE. A snack bar in the Hollywood Hills Theater offers a limited menu of snacks, soft drinks, and beer.

Beauty & the Beast – Live on Stage
   Rating: A
   25 minute stage show.
   Fear Factor: 1
   Visit anytime.

This moving, mesmerizing live show relives the romance between Belle and the Beast, along with the rest of the characters from the movie – Lumiere, Chip, Mrs. Potts, and the rest. The music from the film is featured. Check the park map for performance schedules. Note that the Tower of Terror and Rock 'n' Roller Coaster are both inundated with crowds immediately after a performance lets out. To be guaranteed a seat here, try to arrive 20 minutes prior to showtime. Disney recently changed the show's schedule from five days a week to seven.

Rock 'n' Roller Coaster Starring Aerosmith
   Rating: B+
   2 minute indoor roller coaster.
   Fear Factor: 4
   Visit first thing in the morning or with FastPass.

Disney's first roller coaster to venture out of the realm of the tame, the Rock 'n' Roller Coaster is one of the best things that Disney has done in years. That being said, it's still not a HUGE thrill for coaster junkies, especially those who've already experienced Islands of Adventure's Hulk Coaster or the Kraken at Sea World.

The pre-show winds through G-Force Records' offices, with displays showing the history of recorded music, from wax canisters to minidiscs. You then arrive at Aerosmith's Los Angeles studio where they are finishing up recording. They're about to head out to a concert, and guess what, you're invited. Their manager balks. Aerosmith insists. How kind of them. Next thing you know, you're boarding a long roller coaster train in the shape of a super-stretch limousine. You move around the boarding area, which resembles an underground garage, and wait at a red light. You can hear the engine running until the light turns green. Tires squeal and you're off, flying from 0 to 60 in 2.8 seconds and 5 G's with "Sweet Emotion" or one of four other Aerosmith tunes blaring from 120 onboard speakers.

The 3,400 foot coaster features two rollover loops and a corkscrew as well as black light décor recalling California landmarks such as the Hollywood Hills, masterfully carrying the theme throughout the entire attraction. The only downside to the attraction is its length – it's just under two minutes from beginning to end, and unlike the Hulk Coaster, which isn't all that much longer, this ride *feels* short, but it's smooth, fast, and pretty darn wild.

Entertainment at Disney-MGM Studios

There's less of a focus on random live entertainment here, partly because there's so much live entertainment built into the actual attractions. But there's a couple of options. Be sure to catch the *Beauty and the Beast* and *Fantasmic!* shows, as well as *Playhouse Disney* if you have pre-school kids.

Hollywood Boulevard is a good place to catch musical performances from the likes of the Screen Extras Band, the Tubafours Quartet, and the Toontown Trio, while Streetmosphere characters entertain daily. Celebrities also descend often upon the Studios.

Disney Stars and Motorcars Parade
Introduced in October 2001, this parade consists of a motorcade of customized cars themed after things like Andy's bed from Toy Story and the Genie's lamp in Aladdin. Favorite characters from the small and large screens ride around and interact, including Luke Skywalker, Miss Piggy, Mary Poppins, the Power Rangers in their morphing car, and finally Mickey and Minnie in a 1929 Cadillac. It's a fun parade that definitely has less of a magical vibe than Share a Dream Come True, but is entertaining in its own way. Strongly recommended. The parade winds down Hollywood Blvd and in front of Echo Lake, eventually disappearing behind Star Tours.

Meeting the Characters
There is less character interaction at Disney-MGM than at the other parks, but the characters are still here – their most notable appearance is in the daily Disney Stars & Motorcars Parade, but there is no meet-and-greet there. Daily character greeting opportunities are available with characters from Pixar movies, Star Wars, Disney villains, and the usual gang of

characters, usually at Animation Courtyard. Check your entertainment guide for character specifics and times.

Where to Eat at Disney-MGM Studios

Fantasmic! priority seating packages are available at all full-service restaurants and can be booked 90 days in advance by calling 407/WDW-DINE.

On Hollywood Boulevard
The Hollywood Brown Derby

The spirit of the original 1930 Vine Street establishment has been transplanted to Florida at this, the Studios' signature restaurant, and one of Disney's closest reproductions. There's the Wall of Fame, covered with caricatures faithfully remade from the originals. Louella Parsons and Hedda Hopper even hang out here, or at least actresses representing them. The atmosphere is such that you are tempted to just scan the restaurant from stars.

The lunch menu includes the classic Cobb salad, topped with chicken or or sesame-seared tuna, a Thai noodle bowl, New York strip steak, and salmon bruschetta ($12.99-23.99). The dinner menu is daring and tasty, with such items as pan-fired grouper, rotisserie chicken, center cut filet, and more delectable options ($16.99-27.99). Be sure to leave room for the grapefruit cake, a Brown Derby original. Available here is a children's menu consisting of mac and cheese, burgers, hot dogs, and grouper strips ($1.99-5.99).

Starring Rolls Bakery

Located next to the Hollywood Brown Derby, this spot offers great breakfasts and pastry options. Starting at 8:30 AM, there are Danishes, rolls, croissants, fruit tarts, and bear claws. After breakfast, there are sinfully delicious cookies, cakes, and pies ($.99-6.99) as well as veggie pitas, tenderloin sandwiches, and Cobb salads..

On Echo Lake/Streets of America
50s Prime Time Cafe

This popular restaurant is the Studios' best bet for family-friendly dining. Nostalgia in served in heaping platefuls along with good, homey dishes. The atmosphere is enhanced by Fiesta Ware plates, and TV trays straight from a 50's sitcom kitchen. Televisions show clips from classics like Leave It to Beaver. The waitresses insist on being called "Mom," they check for dirty fingernails before dinner, and then announce to the fellow diners when one of the "kids" clears a plate. The menu is identical at both lunch and dinner and includes June Cleaver specialties like meatloaf, pot roast, BBQ char-grilled chicken, fried chicken, vegetarian stuffed peppers, and more ($12.49-19.99). The kids' menu here includes chicken nuggets, PB&J, and hot dogs ($4.99).

Hollywood & Vine

This restaurant features good, unpretentious American dishes served up in an all-you-can-eat setting decorated with 8-foot murals depicting Hollywood landmarks like the original Hyperion Avenue Disney Studios, Columbia Ranch, the Warner Brothers Studio, and the Cathay Circle Studio. Open for dinner only, the menu changes daily but includes sirloin steak, catch of the day, vegetable lo mein, grilled sausage, and pasta and veggies Alfredo ($22.99 adults, $10.99 kids 3-11). The kids' menu includes meatballs, citrus chicken legs, and mac & cheese.

Mama Melrose's Ristorante Italiano

This restaurant, located on New York Street, offers wood-fired flatbreads and standard Italian dishes like eggplant parm, sausage and peppers, fra diavolo, and penne puttanesca ($11.79-14.99) Dinner adds charred sirloin steak, veal osso buco, and more ($11.79-21.99). The kids' menu includes burgers, chicken nuggets, pasta, and pizza ($4.99).

Sci-Fi Dine-In Theater

This restaurant is on a soundstage designed to resemble a drive-in where it is perpetually night. Diners enter through the ticket lobby, sit in classic automobiles and watch a 45-minute montage of clips and trailers from movies like *Attack of the 50-Foot Woman, Invasion of the Saucer People*, and other classic "B" science fiction and horror films. Carhop waitresses complete the scene. The Sci-Fi serves smoked turkey, Reuben, or flatiron steak sandwiches, burgers, ribs, and shrimp penne pasta ($10.99-16.99), and pan-fried catfish, chicken Caesar salad and seared salmon at dinner ($11.99-16.99).

ABC Commissary

This huge 550-seat restaurant offers cheeseburgers, fish and chips, Cuban sandwiches, tabouleh wraps, and more ($5.49-6.89). Breakfast is offered seasonally ($3.39-$5.99).

Backlot Express

This "scene shop" located near Star Tours serves up double cheeseburgers and andwiches stuffed with grilled veggies or grilled turkey and cheese, sesame chicken salad, hot dogs, and chicken strips ($5.69-6.99).

Toy Story Pizza Planet Arcade

This backlot pizzeria and arcade, themed after the 1996 Pixar hit, offers cheese, pepperoni, and veggie pizzas and salads ($5.29-8.19).

Studio Catering Co.

This counter-service eatery offers Mediterranean dishes like lamb kebob, marinated chicken with yogurt, steak gyro style, and Greek salad ($5.99-6.99). The children's menu includes chicken or smoked ham wraps ($3.99).

Dinosaur Gertie's Ice Cream of Extinction

The huge brontosaurus that looms over Lakeside Circle chews on greens and conceals a stand offering soft serve cones and ice cream sandwiches ($2.39-3.69).

Min and Bill's Dockside Diner

This snack bar on Lake Echo represents "California Crazy" architecture in the form of a tramp steamer, the *S.S. Down the Hatch*. Min and Bill serve up stuffed pretzels and vanilla and chocolate shakes ($2.69-3.29).

Peevy's Polar Pipeline

Located near Echo Lake and Hollywood Boulevard, this is the spot for slushies ($2.39).

Dip Site

Open seasonally, this stand near Indiana Jones offers cheesesteaks, chips, and drinks ($2.39-6.79).

On Sunset Boulevard

Catalina Eddie's

This stand on Sunset Blvd. offers cheese, pepperoni, and BBQ chicken pizzas ($5.49-8.19).

Rosie's All-American Café

Burgers, hot dogs, and chicken strips are sold here ($5.79-6.79). The kids' menu includes chicken nuggets and mac & cheese ($3.99).

Toluca Legs Turkey Co.

Turkey legs and foot longs with chili and cheese ($3.89-5.19).

Anaheim Produce

Fruit cups and whole fruit, pretzels, pickles, and drinks are sold here ($.99-2.99).

Fairfax Fries
McDonald's fries and drinks are sold here ($2.39).

Hollywood Hills Theater (Fantasmic!)
The snack bar at the Fantasmic! venue offers spicy chicken ranch wraps, pretzels, and kids' box lunches ($2.50-5), as well as beer and hard lemonade for mom and dad..

Hollywood Scoops
Hand-dipped ice cream cones are sold here ($2.59).

KRNR Station
Located in the plaza outside the Rock'N'Roller Coaster, this stand serves frozen lemonade, smoothies, and blended frozen desserts served in a waffle cone ($3.59-3.79).

Practical Information

Getting In
For information on Walt Disney World's new Magic Your Way ticketing options, refer to Part 2, pages 338-340.

Getting There
Disney-MGM is easily reached from the WDW maingate, on US 192 east of I-4 exit 64B. Via Kissimmee, the Osceola Parkway offers an alternative to US 192. The park is connected to Epcot and the Yacht and Beach Club, Dolphin, Swan, and Boardwalk via boat launch; and to all other WDW resorts via bus.

Hours
The Disney-MGM Studios theme park opens at 9am daily. It closes at 7pm during off-peak seasons, later when crowds are heavier.

Parking
Disney-MGM Studios parking is $8 for guests not staying at WDW resorts.

Money
Walt Disney World accepts American Express, MasterCard, Visa, Discover, Diners Club, JCB, and the Disney Credit Card, as well as travelers' checks and cash, even at counter-service eateries. There are Bank One ATMs

located at the Main Entrance and at Toy Story Pizza Planet. WDW resort guests can also charge to their rooms.

Package Pickup

Each theme park offers package pickup service, where rather than lugging your purchases around all day, you can send them to a centralized package pickup center near the entrance to the park. Disney resort guests can have their packages sent directly to their hotels. Note that package pickup locations are most crowded between 5 and 6pm and/or one hour before the theme parks close. The Studios' package pickup is located next to Oscar's, by the main entrance.

Security

Bag/backpack/package searches are now performed at Disney World. Allow a few extra minutes to get through them.

Smoking

By law, all Florida restaurants and bars are now non-smoking. Smoking is only allowed in selected areas of the park. Smoking areas are located:

•**Hollywood Boulevard:** Next to the Darkroom shop and just south of the Great Movie Ride.

•**Echo Lake/Streets of America:** Next to Dinosaur Gertie's, the Dockside Diner, and Toy Story Pizza Planet.

•**Mickey Avenue/Animation Courtyard:** Near the entrance to the Backlot Tour, and next to the studio arch.

•**Sunset Boulevard:** Next to Keystone Clothiers and outside the Hollywood Hills Ampitheater, Tower of Terror, and between Hollywood Scoops and Catalina Eddie's.

Check the park map for exact locations.

Disney's FastPass

See Chapter 4 for details on how FastPass works. At press time Disney-MGM attractions utilizing FastPass were Indiana Jones Epic Stunt Spectacular, Rock 'n' Roller Coaster, Star Tours, Twilight Zone Tower of Terror, Voyage of the Little Mermaid, and Lights, Motors, Action! Stunt Show.

Services

The **Guest Services** counter is located to the left of the main entrance. **First aid** and **baby services** are located in the same place. **Lockers** can be rented on the opposite side of the entrance plaza.

Chapter 7

DISNEY'S ANIMAL KINGDOM

Disney's fourth Florida theme park, the Animal Kingdom, opened amid great hoopla in April 1998. The theme park combines classic Disney atmosphere with the excitement and wonder of a zoological park. The park is themed to tell the story of all animals, real, imaginary, and extinct, with attractions, dramatic landscapes, and close encounters with exotic creatures.

However, Disney's high hopes for the park have been dashed, as attendance shrunk over the past few years, as have park hours. Frankly, you only need a couple of hours to get through everything here – making the park something of a disappointment for those who were expecting a full-day affair like Disney's other parks.

The 500-acre park is home to over 1,000 live animals representing 200 different species, representing one of the largest zoo migrations in history. Many of the animals can be viewed running free in the 100-acre grassland and forest designed to replicate the African savannah.

The Animal Kingdom consists of six themed areas. The Oasis is the entry point, offering essential services and a smooth, tropical transition from the outside world to the adventure inside. Discovery Island sits on the island in the middle of the Discovery River and serves as the hub between the lands. It's also home to the Tree of Life, the park icon. Dinoland U.S.A. celebrates America's fascination with dinosaurs, showcasing interactive adventures and thrill rides in a kitschy roadside attraction sort of way. Camp Minnie-Mickey features live shows featuring characters from the Lion King and Pocahontas along with Disney characters waiting to meet your kids. Africa plays host to a walk-through safari attraction, a jeep adventure, and a train to Conservation Station, an interactive, educational pavilion devoted to teaching about saving the earth and its inhabitants. Asia features the Kali River Rapids flume ride and another walk-through.

Touring this park requires an entirely different mindset than the other theme parks. This one is less about relentless go-here-see-this-do-this-turbo-death-race-kamikaze touring and more about stopping and smelling the flowers. There are only a few major attractions here where you'll encounter any kind of a wait, and if you're in such a hurry to put those particular notches in your belt, you'll miss what makes this park special – the lush vegetation and the amazing menagerie of animals who roam the park.

The Oasis

This placid, tropical garden serves as a buffer/transition from the urban world to this one, with lush vegetation, flowers, waterfalls, streams, rocky grottos, and colorful wildlife such as wallabies, tree kangaroos, anteaters, giant sloth, Chinese deer, exotic birds, and more. There aren't any attractions per se here, but walking around the maze of trails is as good a way as any to spend a half-hour. Don't even think about skipping this land in your rush to do everything else.

Shopping
Garden Gate Gifts, located at the entrance to the park, offers character and park merchandise as well as basic services, stroller/wheelchair rental, film developing, and more.

Discovery Island

Borrowing its name from the defunct nature conservatory in the middle of Bay Lake, The central hub of the Animal Kingdom, this land has restaurants and shops at every turn, along with tempting trails where you can see lemurs, kangaroos and capybaras. This is also the home of the Tree of Life, the iconic 14-story landmark that best conveys the theme of the park. This artificial tree is the icon of the Animal Kingdom, with representation of over 325 animals carved into the massive branches and roots. Each morning, 15 minutes before opening, Mickey, Minnie, Pluto, and Goofy stop by for a meet-and-greet.

It's Tough to Be a Bug
Rating: A+
15-minute 3-D film.
Fear Factor: 3
Visit early in the day or with FastPass.

This is a fascinating computer-animated 3D movie that spins off from *A Bug's Life*, as Flik (Dave Foley) emcees a talent show designed to show the interaction between bugs and the rest of the world. The megalomaniacal Hopper (Kevin Spacey) irately usurps the proceedings when Flik declares the audience "honorary bugs," but of course, eventually he gets his karmic retribution. It's one of the park's premier attractions - a great film with really good visuals, Audio-Animatronic figures, and in-theater effects, a step up from the similar technology used at *Honey, I Shrunk the Audience*.

Drama buffs will appreciate posters from the Tree of Life Repertory Theatre's past productions, shows like "A Cockroach Line," "My Fair Ladybug," and even "The Dung and I." While waiting to enter the theatre, guests are entertained by musical numbers from the aforementioned shows, sung by buzzing, humming insects.

Discovery Island Trails
Rating: B+
Walking trails.
Fear Factor: 1
Visit anytime – animals are most active early in the day.

Surrounding the Tree of Life is one of the park's nicest diversions– a series of waterfront trails with habitats for Galapagos tortoises, lemurs, kangaroos, and golden top tamarins. Alas, the original Discovery Island – a zoological park in the middle of Bay Lake, near the Magic Kingdom and Fort Wilderness – closed as a tourist attraction when the Animal Kingdom rendered it redundant, with most of the resident animals making their new home here.

Shopping
The Animal Kingdom's best souvenir and character shopping can be found here. The **Beastly Bazaar** offers safari hats and personalized items as well as chocolates and home décor. **Disney Outfitters** offers Pooh gifts, apparel, watches, housewares, and animal-themed gifts. **Island Mercantile** offers a huge selection of character merch. **Creature Comforts** offers plush toys, gifts, and kids' wear.

Dinoland U.S.A.

With the quirky design of roadside Americana – Dinoland offers an array of entertaining looks at the ancient creatures that have fascinated us for millennia – the dinosaurs. Blinking, shimmering carnival rides and midway games further capture the kitschy motif of the land. Some of the most popular rides in the park are here – the Dinosaur thrill ride and the two kid-friendly rides, Primeval Whirl and TriceraTop Spin, found in the dinosaur-themed carnival midway area, Chester and Hester's Dinorama.

Plenty of lower-key sights can be found here as well. Paleontologists in residence work in the Fossil Prep Lab, where Dino Sue was prepared to meet her public – the largest, most complete T-Rex skeleton ever found, she measures 40 feet long and 13 feet tall with an estimated live weight of 6-8 tons. Be sure to walk around the Cretaceous Trails to see some of the plants that existed alongside the dinosaurs way back in the day.

Dinosaur
Rating: A
7-minute thrill ride to the prehistoric era.
Fear Factor: 5
Visit first thing in the morning or with FastPass.

Until Expedition: Everest opens, this is the only thrill ride in the park, but it's a doozy. Guests board time machines and hurtle back in time to the late Cretaceous period – just minutes before the cataclysmic asteroid hits the earth and puts the dinosaurs in the history book. God bless renegade science – as a rebel sends you back in time to retrieve a herbivore and bring him back to the present. Unfortunately, you're threatened by both the Carnotaurus, a fierce meat eater, and by the asteroid itself. You race around an apocalyptic scene tracking a homing beacon placed on the dino and barely escape with your lives. Some of the effects are similar to those found in the Indiana Jones ride at Disneyland.

While this is a wild ride, it's not nearly as bumpy a ride as simulator rides like Body Wars, it's still more than enough of a jolt for those with less of a taste for the action. As you exit the ride, don't miss the video monitors overhead — they show the amusing coda to the story of the attraction. Children must be 40" tall to ride.

Kid's Discovery Clubs

Spread across the park are six Discovery Clubs, interactive learning stations where kids aged 4-8 can assemble a pile of dinosaur bones, play "wildlife detective," or see the world from a bug's point of view. Check the park map and times guide for hours and locations.

Tarzan Rocks!
Rating: B
30-minute live stage show.
Fear Factor: 1
Visit anytime.

This high-energy show features the music and characters of Disney's recent animated feature *Tarzan*, including Jane, Terk and a cast of "jungle gymnasts" in a four-act show featuring five songs from the soundtrack, including "You'll Be in My Heart." The show includes rock-concert spectacle as 27 performers sing, dance, and execute stunts like rappelling over the audience and dancing an airborne ballet. This lively and amusing show will shut down sometime in early 2006, when the Theater in the Wild is scheduled to be fully enclosed.

The Boneyard
Rating: B-
Interactive playground.
Fear Factor: 1
Visit anytime.

This creative, interactive playground lets kids wander through a dig site, slide down oversized bones, play xylophones on other bones, and participate in fossil digs.

Primeval Whirl
Rating: B-
2-minute family roller coaster.
Fear Factor: 1
Visit early morning or with FastPass.

This is a bright, colorful, whimsical family-friendly roller coaster – no loops, steep drops, or other excitement – just the twin themes of time travel and dinosaurs. There are a few interesting elements, as the cars U-turn and spin around at various points in the ride. It looks like something straight out of a Dr. Seuss book. It's extremely popular and thus rather crowded in spite of being a continuous-loading ride, so using a FastPass is highly recommended here.

TriceraTop Spin
Rating: C+
2-minute Dumbo-type ride.

Fear Factor: 1
Ride early morning or at the very end of the day.

Another Dumbo-type ride. In this one, 4-person vehicles circle around a structure that reveals itself to be a toy top containing a dinosaur. This ride suffers from the same slow-line syndrome as the others of this ilk, so be aware that including this in your touring agenda requires a significant investment of time.

Shopping

Themed after a tacky 50s gift shop, **Chester and Hester's Dinosaur Treasures** sells toys of all kinds, plus books, models, t-shirts, hats, magnets, bean bag dolls, and other goodies. The **Dino Institute Shop** at the exit of the Dinosaur thrill ride contains attraction swag and dinosaur gifts.

Camp Minnie-Mickey

This woodsy, frontier-evocative, but not quite Western land is geared more towards children, with shows based on *The Lion King* and *Pocahontas* as well as extensive opportunities to meet Disney characters along the Character Trails, where individual characters get their own designated chillout zones and themed queue areas.

Festival of the Lion King

Rating: A+
25-minute live show celebrating the story and music of the Lion King.
Fear Factor: 1
Visit anytime.

This is the best stage show at any WDW theme park. Truly inspiring, uplifting, and joyful, this evocative stage show includes tons of audience participation and a talented cast of trapeze artists, singers, dancers, and actors, showing flashes of Bob Fosse and Cirque du Soleil while drawing heavily from the Broadway production of *The Lion King* to produce a moving, beautiful, colorful show that is festive enough to earn the title of "festival." Check the park guide for performance times. You should try to arrive at least a half hour before showtime to ensure your chances of getting the best seats.

Pocahontas and her Forest Friends

Rating: B-
20-minute live stage show.

Fear Factor: 1
Visit anytime.

Pocahontas and Grandmother Willow search for the protector of the forests in this cute but boring children's show featuring a host of live animals. Don't expect many characters from the movie to make an appearance, nor much music, only "Colors of the Wind" is present. This one's strictly for fans.

Africa

Inspired by the Kenyan town of Lamu, the African village of Harambe features a walk-through safari, a jeep safari, and exceptional shopping, as well as the opportunity to learn about conservation. The Dawa Bar here is a pleasant place to kick back with a tasty adult beverage in mid-safari.

Harambe also hosts a train station from which guests can visit Rafiki's Planet Watch. The 7-minute Wildlife Express takes guests to this remote area of the park, which features lots of exhibits, a petting farm, and a walking trail featuring golden-top tamarins, but no "attractions" in the traditional sense. Rafiki's Planet Watch is skippable if you are pressed for time.

Kilmanjaro Safaris
Rating: A+
26-minute jeep safari.
Fear Factor: 2
Visit as early in the day as possible.

The Kilmanjaro Safaris attraction is the signature experience of the Animal Kingdom. Guuests board open-air jeeps and ride across the African savannah, passing elephants, giraffes, apes, lions, and more. Who knows, you might even get to chase down a poacher or two. This is the best ride in the park, hands down. Charismatic cast members, breathtaking vistas, and endearing animals all combine to make this ride a truly memorable experience. This ride is best experienced early in the day, as many of the animals are most active then, and some in fact sleep during the hotter parts of the day. Mid-early afternoon can sometimes also work well. Because of the variables of the drivers and the activity level of the animals, this ride can be different every time you experience it.

Pangani Forest Exploration Trail
Rating: A-
Self-guided walking safari tour.

Fear Factor: 2
Visit in the morning.

One of the Animal Kingdom's many walking trails, this one allows you to view animals native to Africa, including mountain lions, gorillas, hippos, birds, and more. Be sure to take your time walking through this exhibit, as sometimes the animals are not readily visible at first glance. Patience is rewarded, though, as guests can see animals in their natural habitats doing all kinds of animal things. Particularly interesting are a wall containing a blind mole rat colony, as well as stations for underwater viewing of hippopotami. Keep in mind that animals are generally most active early in the day, and many of them sleep away most of the afternoon. So plan accordingly.

Conservation Station
Rating: B-
Exhibits on animal research and conservation.
Fear Factor: 1
Visit anytime.

This is the main part of the Planet Watch area, featuring webcams showing the animals in their habitats and interactive exhibits about veterinary science, training, and feeding. There's also the Sounds of the Rain Forest show, where Grandmother Willow narrates and small groups of guests hear sound effects that transport them to the Amazon.

Affection Section
Rating: C+
Petting farm.
Fear Factor: 1
Visit anytime.

The Animal Kingdom's only petting zoo features sheep and San Clemente goats among other creatures. Sheep are beautiful creatures!

Shopping
The Africa section of the park contains some great shopportunities, most notably the African gifts and souvenirs available at **Mombasa Marketplace** and **Ziwani Traders**, who also offer safari gear, apparel, books, and toys. **Duka La Filimu** offers last-minute film and camera supplies for Safari-bound guests. The only shop at Rafiki's is **Out of the Wild**, offering unique and earth-friendly gifts including Forest Pure lotions and shampoos, candles, and a small selection of toys, snacks, and apparel.

Asia

The Animal Kingdom's most recent addition, this land recalls the hustle and bustle of India and the southeast of Asia, complete with ruins and authentic architecture. Attractions include a white water rafting ride, another walk-through safari, and a bird show. A new thrill ride is coming in 2006.

Expedition: Everest
Opens in 2006

The Animal Kingdom's next $100 million thrill ride, Expedition: Everest, will take guests on a roller coaster through bamboo forests, waterfalls, and glacier fields to the base of a 200-foot high recreation of Mount Everest, where the track ends at the hands of the Yeti – the abominable snowman. This family thrill ride will climb to 120 feet, drop as far as 80, and reach speeds of 50 mph. It will also feature backward drops, but no inversions, so it may be more palatable than the Rock 'N' Roller Coaster. This will be a FastPass attraction, and guests must be 44" or taller to ride.

Maharajah Jungle Trek
Rating: B+
Self-guided walking safari tour.
Fear Factor: 2
Visit in the morning.

The second walk-through safari, this one sends you through the Royal Forest of Anandapur, a fictional Asian nation with some serious wildlife. The animals cavorting here include Malaysian simians, Vietnamese white cheeked gibbons, Komodo dragons, endangered Malayan tapirs, Rodrigues fruit bats and Malayan flying foxes, six tigers, a field of elk and antelope, as well as a bird sanctuary. Between the animals and the intricate ruins along the trail, this is one of the most breathtaking spots in the Animal Kingdom.

Kali River Rapids
Rating: B
10-minute whitewater raft ride.
Fear Factor: 3
Visit during the heat of afternoon, with at FastPass.

This is a raft ride similar to those found in many other theme parks, putting eight guests in a circular raft bound for swirling white water. The ride starts promisingly, with the rafts being elevated up an incline shrouded by mist... once the 12-passenger rafts reach the top of the attraction and start floating downstream, it goes a bit... shall we say... downhill. While most Disney rides have a nicely developed story behind them, this one is but skin and bones, one scene showing deforestation by logging companies, followed by a scene of an overturned logging truck set ablaze... and that's pretty much it. The ride is all too short, all too plain, and nowhere near wet enough. Popeye and Bluto's Bilge Rat Barges at Islands of Adventure is a far better incarnation of this kind of ride, as is Grizzly River Rapids at Disney's California Adventure.

Flights of Wonder
Rating: B-
30-minute bird show.
Fear Factor: 2
Visit anytime.

This amusing, light-hearted show features a colorful variety of birds and showcases their natural behaviors, along with lively narration and storyline. "Flights of Wonder" takes place at Caravan Stage, a theatre carved out of the stone ruins. Birds performing include barn owls, West African crowned cranes, parrots, and birds of prey.

Shopping
The only shop in the Asia section, **Mandala Gifts** offers authentic African and African-themed gifts including wind chimes, carved wood items, print shirts and dresses, candles, and more.

Entertainment in the Animal Kingdom

The featured performers at this park are the animals, so that's why there's less in the way of HUMAN live entertainment here.

Mickey's Jammin' Jungle Parade
Safari vehicles, abstract puppets, dancing, music, and Disney characters combine to throw an "interactive island street party." The parade features over 60 performers as well as rickshaw taxis, character-based safari vehicles, animal puppets, 16 Disney characters, "party animal" stilt-walkers, and "party patrol." The parade is held at 4pm daily.

Live Street Entertainment
Unbelievable – that's the word you'll use to describe **DeVine**, a

performance artist, who walks around the Animal Kingdom in a sheath of vegetation, a walking, living, plant creature – absolutely fascinating and a great photo op. There's also often authentic music and dance performances from native African and Asian cultures (including two percussion groups, the Beatniks and Mor Thiam), as well as small animal handler demonstrations and lots more. Some favorites include **Wes Palm**, the talking palm tree who wanders the Oasis, and **Pipa**, the talking recycling can, at Conservation Station.

Meeting the Characters

The Animal Kingdom offers an area specifically designed for character interaction. The **Greeting Trails** at Camp Minnie-Mickey offer four characters at a time – including Mickey, Minnie, Pluto, Goofy, Pooh, and Tigger in a dedicated chillout area. Other characters can be encountered at **Character Landing** on Discovery Island, across from the Flame Tree Barbecue. There is also a character breakfast buffet, **Donald's Breakfastosaurus**, daily at Restaurantosaurus. It features Donald, Mickey, Goofy, and Pluto ($17.99 adults, $9.99 kids 3-11).

Where to Eat in the Animal Kingdom

In the Oasis
Rainforest Café

This wildly popular theme restaurant, which was named AOL Cityguide's most family-friendly Orlando eatery, has two locations in Disney World, one at the Marketplace and one just outside the gates to the Animal Kingdom. The restaurant combines a conservation theme and wild rainforest décor with unusual twists on classic food items, but for as daring as this restaurant wants to be, a lot of the menu items just don't have as much flavor as their names. I can't really advocate eating here for the atmosphere either, because as far as robotic animals are concerned, Rainforest Café definitely gets taken to school by Audio-Animatronic.

The food's kinda eh, but inoffensive: French toast, eggs Benedict, steak and eggs, waffles, fruit platters, and breakfast burritos in the morning ($8.99-12.99); and a huge menu the rest of the day consisting of all-natural veggie and 1/2 lb beef burgers, buffalo fried chicken salads, turkey or BBQ wraps, grilled veggie, crab cake, or Cajun chicken sandwiches, exotic and traditional pizzas, and assorted steak, chicken, seafood, and pasta dishes ($9.99-39.99).

A kids' menu is available to those 12 and under, it includes pizza, mac & cheese, mini-hot dogs or burgers, popcorn shrimp, and chicken tenders, and even a couple of special desserts ($5.99-6.99).

To trump the crowds and guarantee your own priority seating, join the Rainforest Café Safari Club. For $10 you get a $10 certificate, 10% off up to four entrees, merchandise, and express seating. Note that the benefits don't take hold until your next visit, so sign up at the Downtown Disney or hometown location to use it at the AK restaurant.

On Discovery Island
Flame Tree Barbecue
This irresistible counter offers fresh-from-the-smoker beef brisket, chicken breast, and pork shoulder along with St. Louis ribs and BBQ chicken salad in a toasted garlic shell. Just try to resist their aromatic siren song ($6.79-8.49).

Pizzafari
This huge restaurant features intricately themed rooms and a simple but effective menu of chicken Caesar salads, pizzas, and a hot sandwich stuffed with ham, turkey, Swiss, and provolone, topped with pesto marinated tomatoes and Caesar salad ($3.99-6.99).

Safari Barbecue
Pick up a turkey leg here ($4.49).

Safari Coffee
Shade grown espresso and cappuccino and assorted pastries ($1.49-3.99).

Safari Pretzel
Pretzels and drinks are sold here ($2.89).

In Dinoland USA
Restaurantausaurus
Home of Donald's Breakfastasaurus, a character buffet featuring Mickey, Pluto, and Goofy. The all-you-can-eat feast includes donuts, breakfast pizza, quiche, omelets, bacon, sausage, oatmeal, grits, French toast, and lots more ($17.99 adults, $9.99 kids 3-11). The rest of the day, this eatery offers veggie burgers and 1/2 lb. cheeseburgers and hot dogs, Chicken McNuggets, and Mandarin chicken salad ($5.49-6.79). McNugget Happy Meals are available for kids ($3.99).

Dino Bite Snacks
Hand-scooped ice cream, shakes, floats, and sundaes are offered along with chips, popcorns, yogurt, cookies, and beer ($1.49-3.49),

Dino Diner
Soft-serve ice cream floats and waffle cones are available ($3.49-3.59).

Petrifries
McDonald's fries and chocolate chip cookies are sold here ($2.39).

In Camp Minnie-Mickey
Chip & Dale's Cookie Cabin
Fresh baked sugar, oatmeal, and chocolate chip cookies and ice cream sammiches are offered here ($1.49-3.49).

In Africa
Tusker House
This large restaurant is the one of the only quick service breakfast options in the park, with scrambled egg platters, muffins, cereal, and biscuits and gravy ($1.99-5.29). Lunch and dinner see an intriguing array of grilled salmon, rotisserie chicken, and sandwiches like fried chicken or marinated veggie ($6.99-7.99). A children's menu includes mac and cheese and a chicken drumstick ($3.99).

Dawa Bar
Adjacent to Tusker House, this open-air bar offers beer, wine, and mixed drinks.

Harambe Fruit Market
Fresh fruit, pretzels, and juices are sold here ($.99-2.89).

Kusafiri Coffee Shop & Bakery
Assorted pastries, muffins, cookies, cakes, and yogurt-topped fruit cups are served here along with shade grown espresso and cappuccino ($1.49-4.29),

Tamu Tamu Refreshments
Fruit smoothies, soda floats, and sundaes are available here ($3.49-3.79).

In Asia
Anandapur Ice Cream
Grab a float or soft-serve cone here ($2.59-3.49).

Chakrandi Chicken Shop
This stand offers stir fry chicken, Thai beef salad, lo mein noodle salad, and pot stickers ($3.99-5.99) and child chicken noodle soup ($3.99).

Sunaulo Toran Fries
McDonald's fries are sold here, as well as 1/2 lb. hot dogs ($2.39-5.69).

Practical Information

Getting In

For information on Walt Disney World's new Magic Your Way ticketing options, refer to Part 2, pages 338-340.

Getting There

The Animal Kingdom is easily accessible from I-4 exit 65. Via Kissimmee, the Osceola Parkway offers an alternative to US 192. The park is connected to all WDW resorts and the TTC by bus.

Hours

The Animal Kingdom opens at 9am daily and closes at 5pm. daily. Hours are sometimes extended slightly during peak seasons. More so than any other park, it is important to get here as early as possible, because the animals in the habitats are almost always more active early in the day.

Parking

Parking in the Animal Kingdom's 6,000-car lot costs $8 for guests not staying at WDW resorts.

Money

Walt Disney World accepts American Express, MasterCard, Visa, Discover, Diners Club, JCB, and the Disney Credit Card, as well as travelers' checks and cash, even at counter-service eateries. There is a Bank One ATM located at the main entrance. WDW resort guests can also charge to their rooms.

Package Pickup

Each theme park offers package pickup service, where rather than lugging your purchases around all day, you can send them to a centralized package pickup center near the entrance to the park. Disney resort guests can have their packages sent directly to their hotels. Note that package pickup locations are most crowded one hour before the theme parks close. The AK's package pickup is located at Garden Gate Gifts, at the main entrance.

Security

Bag/backpack/package searches are now performed at Disney World. Allow a few extra minutes to get through them.

Smoking

By law, all Florida restaurants and bars are now non-smoking. Smoking is only allowed in selected areas of the park. Smoking areas are located:

- •**Discovery Island:** Next to Safari Barbecue and Flame Tree Barbecue.
- •**Camp Minnie-Mickey:** Next to the restrooms.
- •**Africa:** Next to the Dawa Bar, at Rafiki's Planet Watch, and north of the main trail to Asia.
- •**Asia:** Next to Sulano Toran Fries and next to the eastern bridge over the Discovery River.

Check the park map for exact locations.

Disney's FastPass

See Chapter 4 for details on how FastPass works. At press time Animal Kingdom attractions utilizing Fastpass were Dinosaur, It's Tough to Be a Bug, Kali River Rapids, Kilimanjaro Safaris, and Primeval Whirl. Expedition: Everest will use FastPass when it opens in 2006.

Services

The **Guest Relations** counter is located to the left of the main entrance. **First aid** and **baby services** are located in Safari Village. **Lockers** can be rented on the opposite side of the entrance plaza.

Chapter 8

UNIVERSAL STUDIOS FLORIDA

In 1994, Universal Studios opened up a $630-million Orlando location to bookend the popular Hollywood attraction. In a town dominated by Disney, it seemed like a scrappy foothold, an end-of-the-week diversion when you're bored with Disney. My, what a difference a decade makes. The eye-popping Universal Studios Florida is the crown jewel of a resort juggernaut that provides a real alternative to Walt Disney World, as opposed to simply an add-on. The 2,300-acre **Universal Orlando** complex also includes the cutting-edge Islands of Adventure park, three sumptuous luxury hotels, and the CityWalk entertainment complex.

Many theme park aficionados, myself included, consider Universal Studios Florida to be the #1 theme park in Orlando. *Fodor's,* in fact, called it the best theme park in the world. It's a reasonable choice for the distinction: between breathtaking thrill rides, genre-bending multimedia, top-notch entertainment, shockingly realistic street scenes, and diverse food choices, you'd be hard pressed to find anything at this park that isn't done well. You won't get the Disney characters, of course, and the Universal staff, while professional and friendly, aren't as over-the-top nice and helpful as their counterparts down the road. But if you care about rides, if you care about shows, if you care about excitement more than whimsy, this is the place for you.

For more information about Universal, visit www.universalorlando.com, call 407/363-8000, or mail 1000 Universal Studios Plaza, Orlando, FL 32819.

Universal Express

Universal Express is a similar system to Disney's FastPass, with one significant difference: this is practically EVERYWHERE, not just on a handful of attractions. Pretty much every attraction that COULD theoretically utilize the system does. Another significant difference: Universal Express kiosks let you select your ride time window from one of several options.

Like Disney's FastPass, you can only have one Universal Express pass at a time. You can get a new one after using the first one, after the time window on the first has expired, or two hours after getting the pass. Universal resort guests get Express access to all participating attractions all day by showing their room key.

VIP Tours

There is an option that allows you and your party to experience Universal Studios and Islands of Adventure with guaranteed no-line, no-wait access to everything, any time of year. Of course, it'll cost you a pretty penny, but if you've got the means, it's definitely a way to accomplish more during your peak-season trip. VIP Tours are non-private five hour tours for up to 12 guests and include guided walking tours with front-of-the-line access to at least eight attractions. Exclusive VIP Tours are up to eight hours long and private, including only your group – up to 12 people. A tour of either theme park costs $100 per person, the exclusive tour costs $1400 per group. A six-hour VIP tour of both parks (with a one-hour break in between) costs $125 per person. Eight hours of Exclusive VIP access to both parks cost $1700 per group. The Ultimate Escape Tour offers unlimited park-to-park access and front-of-the-line privileges into the attractions of your choice at both Universal Studios and Islands of Adventure for two days. Price on this package is $2600 per group.

The tours do not include park admission, but do include valet parking, bottled water and coffee on check-in, one free soft drink coupon, exclusive access to select backstage areas, discounts on food and merchandise, and a complimentary Universal Music CD. For reservations, call 407/363-8295 or email viptours@universalorlando.com.

Production Central

The entry area to Universal backs onto several working soundstages (not open to the public) and hosts two brand-new attractions based on recent animated TV and movie hits. While you're here, be sure to check out Soundstage 54, where you can see vehicles from Universal movies like the *Mummy Returns, Jurassic Park III, The Fast and the Furious, Blue Crush,* and *The Bourne Identity.*

Shrek 4-D
Rating: A
15-minute 3D movie.
Fear Factor: 2
Visit early.

The stars of the hit movie – Mike Myers, Cameron Diaz, John Lithgow, and Eddie Murphy, reunite in this new attraction, featuring 15 minutes of all-new 3D animation that continues the story of Shrek and Fiona, set between the events of Shrek and Shrek 2.

Wickedly funny and brilliantly animated, with several subtle jabs at Disney, Shrek 4-D is a winner. Like the hit films on which it is based, expect off-color humor and hilarious pop culture references to Star Wars, the Blues Brothers, the Matrix, and the Sixth Sense. Presented in "OgreVision," the film combines with theater effects to create a total sensory experience for 1,200 guests an hour. Compared to the Disney 3D movies, Shrek is truly in a class apart. Expect some jostling and bumping in the seats, this is much more high-powered than WDW's 3D. Note that Shrek does **not** offer Universal Express access.

Jimmy Neutron's Nicktoon Blast
Rating: A
Motion-simulator seat ride combined with CGI film.
Fear Factor: 1
Use UE or visit early.

What a pleasant surprise this new attraction turned out to be! Replacing the Hanna Barbera attraction, this smart and funny attraction combines hydraulic-powered moving seats, neat-looking computer animation, and Nickelodeon favorites like Spongebob Squarepants, the Rugrats, the Fairly Odd Parents, and the Wild Thornberrys.

Jimmy, his devoted robot dog Goddard, and hapless buddy Carl attempt to save the earth from the nefarious alien Ooblar using the stolen Mark IV spaceship to terrorize the Nickelodeon studios backlot. With wry, outrageous, and sometimes meta humor ("Hello supporting characters!"), brilliantly synchronized seat effects, and a riotously entertaining twist at the end, the Nicktoon Blast is one of Universal's best rides. Since this is closest attraction to the park exit, it remains crowded most of the afternoon. Visit early or with Universal Express.

Nickelodeon Studios

Rating: C+
35-minute walking tour of Nickelodeon Studios facility
Fear Factor: 1
Visit in the afternoon.

This tour takes guests through Nickelodeon's hair, makeup, and dressing rooms, soundstages, wardrobe, and prop departments, and then to the Game Lab, where kids can check out prototypes for new Nickelodeon fun. This tour is unmemorable compared to the Disney-MGM Studio Tour, unless a show is in production when you visit. However, there's no chance of getting slimed at MGM. To find out whether a show will be in production at the time of your visit, call 407/224-6355 or visit the Studio Audience Center just inside the main park turnstiles. There are only about 150 to 200 tickets for any event, so they go quickly.

Shopping

Production Central shops include the **Universal Studios Store**, home of the park's largest selection of Universal mementos, apparel, and souvenirs, **On Location** for film and sundries, **Studio Sweets** for fudges, candies, cookies, and caramel apples, and **It's a Wrap** for last-chance gifts. **NICKSTUFF** offers Nickelodeon swag. **Shrek's Ye Olde Souvenir Shoppe** offers character merchandise for the lovable ogre.

New York

This recreation of some of New York City's more flavorful neighborhoods is so authentic, you'll almost feel Rudy Giuliani trying to clean up your act. This area contains some excellent restaurants as well as one of the park's most incredible attractions. While here be sure to catch a performance of Street Breakz, as dancers spin, pop, lock, and defy gravity in this true American original style. In 2004, the park's first roller coaster, the wild Revenge of the Mummy ride opened here.

Revenge of the Mummy
Rating: A+
4-minute roller coaster with special effects galore!
Fear Factor: 4
Visit early in the day or with UE.

An absolutely mind-blowing roller coaster that redefines the whole genre, combining dark ride elements, state of the art coaster technology, pyrotechnics, special effects, primo sound, and incredibly sophisticated robotic figures, including a 6'8", 650 lb. mummy. Authentic Egyptian artifacts were recreated with assistance from London's British Museum and leading experts in the study of the ancient civilization.

The ride features incredibly creepy sequences in between coaster sequences, and one wickedly funny twist that it would be a shame to spoil. The technology at work includes linear-induction tracks, backward drops, electromagnetic propulsion launch inspired by magnetic levitation trains, and soundproofing to maximize the volume of your screams. Audiophiles will have their minds blown by surround sound from 22 speakers on board the cars, and 200 more pumping out 18,000 watts around the track. Absolutely not to be missed if you can stomach the adrenaline.

Twister...Ride It Out
Rating: A
10 minute tornado experience.
Fear Factor: 4
Visit after early afternoon.

Honestly, I don't remember the last theme park attraction that legitimately frightened me before this one. I don't know if there's been one. That's how realistic and incredible this ride is. Based on the 1996 film starring Helen Hunt and Bill Paxton, this is one of the most technologically advanced theme park attractions anywhere. After a short and foreboding preshow and a queue through realistically themed sets, guests are herded into the main auditorium, where you will witness an honest-to-god tornado. A five-story twister, 12 feet wide, the largest indoor tornado ever created.

The amazingly realistic effects are created by a combination of 18 seven-foot fans, 110 decibels of sound effects pumped through a 42,000-watt sound system with 54 speakers, and hundreds of xenon strobe lights. Without giving away the surprises that make this attraction so terrifying, let me simply say that Universal truly has gone all out on this one.

The Blues Brothers
Rating: B

20 minute live performance.
Fear Factor: 1
Visit anytime.

Doppelgangers for Jake and Elwood Blues perform songs like "Think," "(Almost) Everything I need," "Soul Man," and many more several times daily on Delancey Street, on a mission from God to save their alma mater. They promote the show by driving across the New York area in the Bluesmobile.

Extreme Ghostbusters: The Great Fright Way

Rating: B-
Live performance
Fear Factor: 2
Visit anytime.

Extreme Ghostbusters, eh? That sounds like the animated New WKRP in Cincinnati. Anyway, in this live show, the gang's assignment is none other than Beetlejuice – constructing a nefarious plan to turn the 'busters into a boy band. Only in Orlando.

Shopping

Aftermath offers educational gifts about tornados as well as *Twister* merch. **Sahara Traders** offers Mummy-themed stuff.

San Francisco/Amity

The architecture and sights in this land seamlessly blend two coastal communities – San Francisco and Amity, the Maine town best known for its encounters with an scary and ornery shark. And about five ornery but less interesting sharks after the first one. Including one really crappy one in 3-D.

Jaws

Rating: B+
5-minute boat ride adventure.
Fear Factor: 4
Visit with UE or before 11am.

This ride is a fun and pretty scary adventure that pits a plucky tour boat against the ravenous great white. Boats leave from Amity Harbor, ostensibly for a guided tour, but no sooner do you make the first turn that you spot the wreckage of another boat. A dorsal fin pops up and chases you into a boathouse, where you can await backup safely. Yeah, right. Jaws busts through the side of the boathouse and it's on the run again. Your captain picks up a grenade launcher that conveniently happens to be located on the boat and fires it at Jaws. Explosions? Special effects? Fearsome robot sharks? Yes please! This ride is best seen before 11am. Universal Express is available.

Earthquake: The Big One

Rating: B
23-minute multi-part presentation.
Fear Factor: 4
Visit before noon.

Earthquake uses various technologies to simulate an 8.3 earthquake while guests ride on the BART train en route from Oakland to San Francisco. This is a frightening, intense culmination after more low-key demonstrations of how stunts and special effects are created. The best view during the ride can be had in the second car from the front (on your left). Try to sit in the middle of the car, as the view from the front is somewhat obstructed. Universal Express is available here.

Beetlejuice's Graveyard Revue

Rating: B-
18-minute musical stage show.
Fear Factor: 3
Visit in the afternoon.

This all-new show features singing, dancing, special effects, and pyrotechnics as Beetlejuice makes like Elwood and tries to get a rock band going with the Universal Monsters, including Frankenstein and the missus, the Wolfman, and Dracula. Universal Express is available here.

Fear Factor Live

Rating: N/A
Interactive version of the thrillseeking game show.
Fear Factor: 2 to watch, 5 to participate!
Visit in the afternoon.

Smell the NBC Universal synergy! Guests compete against one another in gravity-defying and gross-out stunts in front of a studio audience at this based on the popular NBC show. Up to 48 guests each day – six per show - will be "cast" in one of three stunts that include squid-flinging and dangling 30 feet in the air. Fear Factor Live opened in June 2005, too late to be reviewed for this edition.

Shopping

Quint's Surf Shack offers surf swag and apparel. The **Oakley** store sells shades and accessories. **Shaikens' Souvenirs** offers Universal souvenirs. The **San Francisco Candy Factory** offers bulk candies, candy apples, fudge, confections, cookies, and more. Also, the **Amity Games** midway offers plenty of chances to win cool prizes.

World Expo

Reminiscent of the 1964-65 New York World's Fair (and at times more like the old Convention Center on I-Drive), the Expo Center area contains two of the most jaw-dropping thrill rides in the park.

Men in Black: Alien Attack

Rating: A+

Wild interactive 5-minute dark ride.

Fear Factor: 3

First thing in the morning or after 2pm, or use UE or single rider line.

This ride is – bar none – the most fun I have ever had in a theme park. Six-passenger cars equipped with guns are dispatched in a *Men in Black* training mission that is quickly interrupted by aliens of the non-training variety. Of course, riders are quickly deputized by Will Smith and Rip Torn (reprising their MIB roles) and sent to combat the menace. Like Buzz Lightyear's Space Ranger Spin at the MK, the object here is to rack up as high a score as possible by shooting the aliens who have crash-landed in New York City.

Compared to Buzz Lightyear though, it's like the difference between a 4th grader's diorama science project and a demonstration at DARPA. Tremendously detailed, hilarious, and exciting, this ride is populated with hundreds of wild-looking bugs who react amusingly when neutralized with a shot to the eyes (shoot until the green turns to red.). The ride culminates with an unfortunate encounter with a warehouse-sized creature, the largest animatronic ever built – 30 feet high, with 8 foot teeth and 12 foot claws. Who's got the Raid? The coolest thing about this ride is that there are dozens of different endings, depending on how you and the other people in your car score. This ride can become something of an obsession. When I visited last, my brother and I rode seven times in a row, the last six of which were spent with me vainly trying to end my emasculation by topping my kid brother's score.

The Single Rider Line at MIB is a great way to bypass the lines almost entirely, if you're not against the idea of splitting your party up. When my brother and I visited, we were able to walk right on using the Single Rider Line six consecutive times in less than an hour. Most of the time we ended up in different rows of the same car, or in the second car dispatched at the same time anyway, so the splitting turned out to be a moot point.

Back to the Future… the Ride!

Rating: A

4 1/2 minute IMAX/simulator thrill ride.

Fear Factor: 4

Visit before noon or use UE.

This ride can be summed up in one word: WOW! The *Back to the Future* trilogy was one of the most popular series of its time, and the best-of-breed thrill ride almost serves as yet another sequel, except that it stars park guests as the intrepid time travelers. You will wander the halls of the Institute of Future Technology to reach a pre-show area where Doc Brown (Christopher Lloyd) informs you that he has completed a batch of faster, more efficient, eight-passenger Deloreans-turned-time machines.

He also glumly tells you that Biff Tannen (Thomas Wilson) has broken into the Institute and is plotting something not quite kosher. Guests hop into time machines and set off into a hemispherical, seven-story Omnimax theater with incredible flight-simulation effects. The liquid-nitrogen fog, the perfectly-timed hydraulic jolts, the 70mm film, and the multi-channel stereo surround sound all enhance the astonishing realism of the production. On your journey, you chase Biff back past Leonardo da Vinci, the Wright Brothers, and over waterfalls, cliffs, and canyons, eventually into the mouth of a Tyrannosaurus Rex, over the lip of a volcano, and… well, let's just say that this is a quite intense ride from beginning to end. Kids over eight will usually love this ride, however, with younger ones, the fright potential is very high. Although this ride feels a bit dated compared to the Mummy and MIB, it's still a classic and draws the crowds befitting such a crowd favorite.

Shopping

MIB Gear offers action figures, toys, and souvenirs from the Men in Black, including neuralizers and Ray-Ban sunglasses. **Back to the Future: The Store** sells gifts and memorabilia from that franchise.

Woody Woodpecker's Kidzone

This is the foremost area for family-friendly attractions here at Universal. Whereas a lot of the emphasis elsewhere is on thrills, the rides and shows here are suitable and enjoyable for the whole family.

E.T. Adventure
Rating: A-
5 minute dark ride on flying bikes.
Fear Factor: 2
Visit after 12 noon.

Arguably Steven Spielberg's crowning achievement, *E. T.* serves as the basis for this spectacular ride adventure, in which guests board a pack of flying bikes and set off through a redwood forest, escaping the clutches of the Man and soaring through space to E.T.'s home planet. Once there, you meet E.T's playmates and planetmates, which include some exotic flora and fauna. At the end of the ride, E.T. thanks you personally for your help. Original music for this ride was composed by John Williams, another nice touch.

Curious George Goes to Town
Rating: B+
Awesome, wet, interactive play zone.
Fear Factor: 1
Visit during the afternoon heat.
Combine 12,000 balls, 15,000 gallons of water, and a monkey, and what do you get? No, not Michael Jackson's pool party, but good answer... Curious George, the most mischievous monkey of them all, roosts in this huge, multi-level playground where foam ball pits are taken to the next level with cannons and clever dumping mechanisms, and combined with water pumps, cannons, and dump buckets. A great way to cool off in the afternoon heat or to drain off some of that excess ADD. Personally I love this attraction even though I'm way outside the target demographic. Maybe it's because I love monkeys.

Animal Planet Live!
Rating: B
20-minute trained animal show.
Fear Factor: 1
Visit in the afternoon.

This attraction, new in 2003, combines video clips, live animal performances, and audience participation to reveal how animal interaction improves quality of life in this show, based on many of Animal Planet's hits like "Emergency Vets," "The Jeff Corwin Experience," and "Wild on the Set." Many of the domestic animals in the show are shelter rescues, adding a heartwarming layer of good karma to the show. Universal Express is available here.

Woody Woodpecker's Nuthouse Coaster
Rating: B-
1 1/2 minute family roller coaster.
Fear Factor: 1
Visit during the afternoon.

This is a wacky, junior-sized kids' roller coaster straight out of the world of Woody Woodpecker. Climb into coaster cars shaped like crates of nuts – mixed, salted, and certifiable. The 800 foot, 90-second ride only reaches 22mph, and so is suitable for just about everyone, but is extremely big with the littlest.

Fievel's Playground
Rating: B-
Interactive playground.
Fear Factor: 1
Visit during the afternoon.

This is a "mouse-eye view" playground, similar to the Honey, I Shrunk the Kids Movie Set Adventure at MGM. Only this one seems much more detailed and diverse in the types of stimuli offered, including water-based fun, rope climbs, bridges, and slides. Note that there is usually a wait for the waterslide, but none otherwise.

A Day in the Park with Barney
Rating: C
25-minute show starring the purple dino and his friends.
Fear Factor: 1
Visit anytime, but only if your kids insist.

My rating here is terminally biased due to the fact that Barney makes my skin crawl. But younger children, understandably, love this show, where Barney combines fun and education while interacting with Baby Bop, BJ, and the rest of the gang, including a new character, Mr. Peekaboo. At the end of the show Barney walks along the audience and greets and hugs kids. This is a highlight for children who drink the Barney Kool-Aid, but if you're more the Rainbow Randolph type, skip this one.

Shopping
The **Barney Store** lets you show Barney that you love him too, in the most old-fashioned way – by giving him your money. **E.T.'s Toy Closet** offers E.T. photos and gear. The **Universal Cartoon Store** has memorabilia from the cartoon characters featured throughout the park.

Meeting the Characters

Universal does have several notable characters that your kids may want to meet. **Nickelodeon** characters like Jimmy Neutron and SpongeBob SquarePants hang out on Plaza of the Stars Blvd. near the entrance of the park. Woody Woodpecker and lots of other Hanna-Barbera cartoon characters hang out in **KidZone**. Shrek characters can be found at Ye Olde Souvenir Shoppe. Additionally, Barney does a meet-and-greet at the conclusion of every performance of A Day in the Park.

Hollywood

This art-deco wonderland looks like Hollywood Boulevard at MGM, and much like that section of that park, this one feels more like a "transition" land than a destination on its own right. Although it does possess one of the most bad-ass theme park attractions anywhere.

Terminator 2: 3-D Battle Across Time

Rating: A+

20-minute 3D movie.

Fear Factor: 5

Use UE or go after 3pm.

One of the top attractions in all of Orlando, this *Terminator 2* sequel reunites the Governator (aka Arnold Schwartzenegger) with Edward Furlong, Linda Hamilton, and Robert Patrick in this eye-popping 3D movie, shot on 65mm film by James Cameron. The film combines amazing action shots, elaborate sets, computer imaging, and three fifty-foot screens to wow the audience, along with live actors, effects, and menacing in-theater robotic Terminators make the show literally leap off the screen. This is one of the world's largest 3D theatres and the first to use the triple screen. This is an absolutely unbelievable film. There just aren't enough words. Just see it. Again and again. Wow. It's that good.

Universal Horror Makeup Show

Rating: B

25-minute behind-the-scenes look at makeup effects.

Fear Factor: 4

Visit anytime.

This well-conceived, well-done show focuses in on the make-up effects that make films like *Van Helsing, Beetlejuice, The Fly*, and *The Exorcist* so successful. The humor is tongue-in-cheek, and there's more than enough gore to satisfy anyone's craving for it. The best thing about this worthwhile show is the fact that it is pretty much a sleeper, thus receiving few of the gigantic herds that plague many of the other attractions.

Lucy: A Tribute
Rating: C+
Exhibit of memorabilia from the first lady of comedy.
Fear Factor: 1
Visit anytime.

Universal pays homage to Lucille Ball with this exhibit, featuring classic show clips, costumes, scripts, rare home movies, and more.

Shopping
Cyber Image sells Terminator merchandise and No Fear apparel. **Brown Derby Hat Shop** offers headgear of all kinds. **Silver Screen** sells classic souvenirs featuring Lucille Ball, Betty Boop, and Alfred Hitchcock.

Where to Eat at Universal Studios

AAA members and Universal Annual Passholders receive a 10% discount at restaurants here and at Islands of Adventure. Don't forget that you can always duck out at lunchtime and enjoy a meal at one of the many restaurants at CityWalk.

In New York
Finnegan's Bar & Grill
Finnegan's Pub is one of the most convincing spots in Universal, portraying accurately a friendly, Irish pub straight off the streets of Manhattan, complete with authentic live and recorded Irish music. There's a full bar, of course, and friendly service. The menu consists of 10 oz. sirloin steak, bangers and mash, Dublin and shepherd's pies, fish and chips, corned beef, smoked turkey, or grilled chicken sandwiches, burgers, and more ($9.25-21.95). The kids' menu includes eight choices including chicken fingers, fish and chips, PB&J, burger, or steak and cheese ($4.99-7.99).

Louie's Italian Restaurant
Pick up pizza by the slice or pie, meatball subs, and fettucine Alfredo or spaghetti & meatballs at this aromatic counter ($3.49-15.99).

In San Francisco/Amity
Lombard's Seafood Grille

Fisherman's Wharf hosts the "only restaurant in Florida with views of the Pacific and the Atlantic" – the casual, classy Lombard's Landing. Enjoy meals like Ipswich clams, San Francisco cioppino, shrimp Alfredo, a ginger chicken stir fry, seafood salad sandwich, and pasta with three sauces ($9.95-19.95). The kids' menu includes burgers, linguine, fried fish, and chicken nuggets ($6.75-6.95).

San Francisco Pastry Co.
Everything looks so good here, it's hard to know where to start. Here's a hint: mousse, kiwi tarts, cheesecake ($1.99-7.29). Oversized ham and swiss or turkey croissant sandwiches are also served.

Richter's Burger Co.
At Lombard's Landing, this joint serves up singles, doubles, grilled chicken, and veggie burgers ($6.69-8.79).

Capt. Quint's Seafood & Chowder House
From the makers of Steve Irwin Croc Nuggets, this shop serves up fried shrimp, scallops, and chicken, as well as clam chowder, cole slaw, fries, and peach cobbler ($4.99-9.99).

Chez Alcatraz
This eatery and full bar on the San Francisco waterfront offers peel and eat shrimp cocktail, chili in a bread bowl, turkey wraps, seafood chowder, California rolls, and nachos ($4.99-6.99).

Boardwalk Funnel Cake Co.
Carvel ice cream and funnel cakes with delicious toppings are sold here ($3.29-4.99).

Brody's Ice Cream Shop
Milkshakes, floats, banana splits, and more frozen goodness ($2.59-4.79).

Midway Grill
Nathan's hot dogs are served up plain or with chili and cheese, Chicago style, Reuben style, or with slaw. Cheesesteak sandwiches and corn dog nuggets are also sold here ($4.99-6.79).

In World Expo
International Food and Film Festival
Five counters here offer various cuisines to guests. The American stand offers cheeseburgers and southern fried chicken. The Asian counter serves

orange chicken, pepper beef, and wonton soup. The Italian counter offers pizza, chicken parm, and penne with meatballs. The Salad stand offers fresh fruit platter, chef's salad, and Mediterranean tuna salad. The Dessert stand offers strawberry cheesecake, apple pie, chocolate butterscotch pudding, and more ($3.49-8.29).

In KidZone
Animal Crackers
This stand serves up chicken fingers, hot dogs, tuna conewiches, and turkey drumsticks ($4.89-7.49).

In Production Central
Monsters Cafe
This restaurant offers pizza rotisserie chicken, and chef and chicken Caesar salads ($5.99-7.49).

Bone Chillers
Full bar service is available here.

In Hollywood
Café La Bamba
This festive waterfront eatery offers rotisserie chicken, baby back ribs, cheeseburgers, BBQ pork sandwiches or chicken wraps, and a daily happy hour ($7.49-10.99).

Mel's Drive-In
This nostalgic 50's-style diner offers burgers, chicken sandwiches, chili, hot dogs, and more ($5.99-7.69).

Schwab's Pharmacy
The emphasis here is on the old-school ice cream fountains, but you can also grab ham, chicken salad, or ham sandwiches here ($2.69-5.99).

Beverly Hills Boulangerie
Located at the corner of Plaza of the Stars and Rodeo Drive, this is a great place to pick up sweets like éclairs, cookies, and pies, as well as turkey or ham and cheese croissant sandwiches ($1.99-7.99).

Practical Information

Getting In

For information on Universal Orlando ticketing options, refer to Part 2, pages 340-344.

Getting There

Universal Orlando is easily accessible via I-4 Exit 75A (SR 435/ Universal) if you're coming from the Disney/Kissimmee/LBV area. From downtown Orlando and Daytona, use Exit 74B. From International Drive, go one block east to Universal Blvd. and take that north all the way to the parks.

Hours

Universal Studios Florida opens at 9am daily. Closing hours vary by season from 6pm to 11pm.

Parking

Universal Orlando has a huge parking garage structure, enclosed from the elements, surveyed by 200 cameras, and easing your journey with escalators and moving sidewalks. Parking is $8 per day.

Money

Universal accepts Visa, Mastercard, American Express, Discover, and Diners Club, as well as personal, cashier's, and traveler's checks. There are ATMs at the main entrance and near Jaws in Amity.

Package Pickup

Any merchandise you pick up in the park can be sent to the Universal Studios Store at the entrance, awaiting your retrieval.

Security

Bag/backpack/package searches are now performed at Universal. Allow a few extra minutes to get through them. Universal forbids coolers, outside food and beverage, weapons, alcohol, illegal drugs, duffel bags, folding chairs, and large umbrellas.

Smoking

By law, all Florida restaurants and bars are now non-smoking. Smoking is only allowed in selected areas of the park. Smoking areas are located:

•**Production Central:** At the corner of Nickelodeon Way & Plaza of the Stars, and just inside the park entrance, next to first aid, and on Amblin Ave. across from Twister.

•**New York:** On Park Ave., at the corner of South St. and 7th Ave.,

•**San Francisco/Amity:** Next to Earthquake and next to Fear Factor Live.

•**World Expo:** Next to the International Food and Film Festival.

•**Woody Woodpecker's KidZone:** Next to Animal Planet Live.

•**Hollywood:** Next to Lucy: A Tribute.

Check the park map for exact locations.

Chapter 9

ISLANDS OF ADVENTURE

In May 1999, Islands of Adventure became Universal's second Orlando theme park, and according to some, the best theme park in the area. Great themes, technologically brilliant and unique attractions, memorable characters, decent food, and some of the best thrill rides around make this park absolutely mindblowing.

With Steven Spielberg serving as creative consultant, this park features groundbreaking technology plus adventures based on characters like the Cat in the Hat, Popeye, Spider-Man, The Incredible Hulk, Jurassic Park dinosaurs, and more.

There are six themed Islands here. Port of Entry prepares adventurers for the goodies beyond. Marvel Superhero Island is the home of amazing attractions based on Marvel comic adventures. Toon Lagoon offers several water rides themed after cartoons and newspaper comic strips. Jurassic Park contains adventures based on the Spielberg film. The Lost Continent takes adventurers to a mystical time and place with medieval and mythical themed adventures and thrills. Seuss Landing is the only place in the world where your kids can meet the characters of Theodore Geisel's fabled books.

Islands of Adventure is most comparable to the Magic Kingdom in terms of its presentation – it's a strictly-for-fun park, no pretense of education, just pure, unadulterated enjoyment. One key difference between the two parks, similar to the contrast between Universal Studios and Disney-MGM … the Disney parks tend to be much more geared to a younger demographic, while older children and adults will get more enjoyment out of the Universal experiences. Spiderman alone is practically worth the price of admission, and 2 out of the 3 wildest roller coasters in Orlando are located here.

Touring tips: since the park is laid out around a circular lagoon, a la World Showcase, you either go clockwise or counter-clockwise. The first lands in each direction appeal to a different group – Marvel Superhero Island is aimed at older kids and adults, while Seuss Landing is the most kid-friendly land around. Both contain rides whose lines add up pretty early on in the day, so you pretty much have to choose between one or the other to experience first, without crowds, and deal with 'em at the other.

For more information about Islands of Adventure, visit universalorlando.com, call 407/363-8000, or mail 1000 Universal Studios Plaza, Orlando, FL 32819.

Universal Express

Universal Express is a similar system to Disney's FastPass, with one significant difference: this is practically EVERYWHERE, not just on a handful of attractions. Pretty much every attraction that COULD theoretically utilize the system does. Another significant difference: Universal Express kiosks let you select your ride time window from one of several options.

Like Disney's FastPass, you can only have one Universal Express pass at a time. You can get a new one after using the first one, after the time window on the first has expired, or two hours after getting the pass. Universal resort guests get Express access to all participating attractions all day by showing their room key.

Port of Entry

Recreating a statuesque and weathered seaside village, Port of Entry is quite appealing – you almost want to stop and explore everything here when you first arrive. Stay focused though. Though the shopping here is great and the architecture is gorgeous, you've got places to go, things to do, minds to blow! Essential services such as ATMs, lockers, stroller/wheelchair rental, and package pickup are available here, as well as some tasty dining and an information booth by the water at portside. Island Skipper Tour boats ferry passengers on a scenic route between here and Jurassic Park.

Shopping

The immense **Islands of Adventure Trading Company** offers merchandise from every Island including apparel for men, women, and children, accessories, jewelry, gifts, toys, stationery, and themed collectibles. The

Ocean Trader Market offers imports from around the globe. **De Foto's Expedition Photography** offers film, batteries, and equipment.

Port of Entry Christmas Shoppe offers awesome ornaments all year round. **Island Market & Export** offers candy, fudge, and character goodies. **Port Provisions** is a last chance shop outside the entrance to the park, offers a limited selection of t-shirts, caps, and other last minute souvenirs.

Marvel Superhero Island

Based on the adventures of classic comic book protagonists like Spider-Man, the Fantastic Four, X-Men, and the Incredible Hulk, the attractions here are among the most technologically advanced in the world and rival any thrill ride in the world for sheer adrenaline. The architecture is a sort of art-deco comic-book motif, with some buildings painted with chrome-illusion paint that changes colors depending on angle. Many of the characters represented here, also represent here – hanging out, signing autographs, and giving hugs.

The Amazing Adventures of Spiderman
    Rating: A+
    The most advanced and incredible theme park ride ever built.
    Fear Factor: 3
    Ride this right after Hulk or with UE.

This absolutely incredible ride combines rapidly moving, highly mobile ride vehicles with 3D action and pyrotechnics, vivid scene sets, and more. You wander along queue lines through the Daily Bugle and then chase off with Spider-Man as he tries to recover the Statue of Liberty, which has been stolen by Dr. Octopus and his anti-gravity ray. The ride rotates a full 360 degrees, surrounding guests with 3D animation projected onto 25 huge screens and dozens of smaller ones. After the climactic battle between Spidey and Doc Ock, the ride culminates with a must-be-seen-to-be-believed 400-foot drop, and a satisfying "take this job and shove it" coda from Spidey's alter-ego.

It's a wild ride, but it's not the least bit rough or uncomfortable, so even the most chicken-hearted should have no more than a quickened pulse at the end of this one. I can not express what a mind-blowing attraction this is. It combines so many different attraction technologies so seamlessly, with a compelling and exciting storyline – this ride pushes the envelope in so many different ways, it is unlike anything you will experience in Disney or anywhere else on earth, unless you yourself get bitten by a radioactive spider. **Do not miss this!** Unless you're under 40" tall. In which case, sorry. You're not getting on. Using the Single Rider Line can greatly reduce your wait time here.

Incredible Hulk Coaster

Rating: A
The second-best roller coaster in Orlando.
Fear Factor: 5
Ride this first thing in the morning or with UE.

Don't be expecting anything jolly about this green giant, towering 150 feet over the park. This is an awesome, sleek, modern 2-minute roller coaster that will satiate any adrenaline junkie. Here's the key specs: 0-40 in 2 seconds, straight into a zero-G heartline roll. 105-foot death drop. Two underground tunnels. Top speed of 60mph. Seven inversions. Bring extra underpants. Free lockers nearby give you a place to stow your stuff while you ride. You must be 54" tall to ride. Unsure about this one? Preview the ride via Quicktime or Windows Media on the IoA website.

Storm Force Accelatron

Rating: B-
2-minute carnival ride.
Fear Factor: 2
Ride before 11am.

The Storm Force is essentially an X-Men themed port of the Mad Tea Cups ride, with sound effects and lightning accenting Storm's battle against the evil Magneto. It's one of the few truly kid-centric rides in Islands of Adventure. Universal Express is available here.

Doctor Doom's Fearfall

Rating: C
Freefall drop ride.
Fear Factor: 4
Ride before 9:30am or with UE.

These two 200-foot towers of steel are Dr. Doom's newest creation – a device designed to suck every last drop of fear out of riders, channeling it into a massive weapon. Sounds more like Dr. Evil than Dr. Doom to me. Anyway, it certainly does suck - it's not all that frightening, considering it has the word FEAR in its name. The 16-seat rings are shot skyward and sent towards the ground at breakneck speed, then bounce up and down a bit after the initial drop. The view from the top is cool, and the sensation of a fall is fun, but this ride isn't anywhere near worth the long waits it often attracts. You must be 52" tall to ride.

Shopping

Shopping here has, as you might expect, a comic book theme. The **Comic Book Shop** has, well, comic books. Worst. Description. Ever. The **Marvel Alternaverse** store offers superhero and supervillain costumes along with clothing, accessories, mugs, keychains, jewelry, collectibles, and artwork.

There is an **Oakley** shop here, as well as the **Spider-Man Shop** for web-fingered swag. **Kingpin's Arcade** boasts exclusive Marvel Super Hero Island and Doctor Doom Freefall merchandise and current arcade games.

Toon Lagoon

Characters from classic Saturday morning cartoons and newspaper comics populate this Island. Exaggerated cartoon buildings dominate the landscape along with panels from featured strip. How do you feel about getting wet? If you respond to water like a cat, you may want to invest in a rain poncho before you hit this Island – because soaking, dripping, sopping wet is the rule here, not the exception.

Popeye and Bluto's Bilge Rat Barges

Rating: A-
4 1/2 minute whitewater raft ride.
Fear Factor: 3
Ride before 10:30am or in the heat of afternoon with UE.

Popeye and his nemesis, the rotund Bluto, battle for the love of Olive Oyl and Swee' Pea in this whitewater rafting adventure. Longer, faster, and wetter than the similar Kali River Rapids at the Animal Kingdom, this offers big drops, water cannons, and a fully functional boat wash. In fact, this is probably the wettest ride like this I've been on anywhere. It's all in fun though. It's especially fun for the diabolical folks standing up on the Olive, shooting water cannons at smug-looking riders excited at having been missed by the gushing water. You must be 42" tall to ride.

Protect Your Electronics from the Wild Waters!

You may be waterproof, but your camera, cell phone, two-way, or PDA may not be. Take it from someone who's lost more waterlogged cell phones than he'd care to admit. Don't forget.

Dudley Do-Right's Ripsaw Falls
Rating: B+
5-minute log flume ride.
Fear Factor: 3
Ride before 11am or after 4pm.

Dudley Do-Right must save Nell from the dastardly Snidely Whip-lash in this log flume ride named for the city in 1960s cartoon Rocky and Bullwinkle. The 12-man rafts follow the hapless Do-Right's attempt to save the day, culminating in a 60-foot drop where the level of incline steepens from 45 to 50 degrees halfway down, under the surface of the water into total darkness and up a roller coaster hill. A damn fun ride. You must be 44" tall to ride. Universal Express is available here.

Me Ship the Olive
Rating: C+
Interactive play area.
Fear Factor: 1
Visit in the afternoon.

Popeye's three-story boat is a family-friendly interactive area to explore, with dozens of things to get into, like cargo nets, a crane where you can drop a BOX OF WATER on Barge riders, and much more. A fun way to while away a few minutes, but not worth a trip on its own.

Shopping
The **Betty Boop** store sells goods emblazoned with the iconic character. **Gasoline Alley** offers resortwear, towels, and sandals. **Toon Extra** offers personalized gifts, collectibles, and apparel.

Jurassic Park

Jurassic Park brings guests face to face with "living, breathing" dinosaurs who blink their eyes, flinch at your touch, and even spit. Here you will find some of the most technologically advanced animatronics figures anywhere. Be sure to check the entertainment schedule for a chance to meet the park's 2 1/2 month old (at press time) "trike" babies, Sadie and Savannah.

Jurassic Park River Adventure
Rating: A
Boat tour-cum-thrill ride through Jurassic Park.

Fear Factor: 4
Visit before 11:30am or with UE.

Climb aboard for a peaceful 7-minute boat ride through the herbivore pens at Jurassic Park. Peaceful? Yeah right. Thanks to some unruly animals, your boat is diverted through the storehouses and loading docks of the island, as your radio crackles with panicked staff. Boats sail through velociraptors and spitters who stalk the grounds, and then finally right at a huge tyrannosaurus rex. Only one way out, and that way is an 85-foot plunge down the fastest, longest, steepest water descent ever built. The T-Rex doesn't sound so bad now, does it?

This is one of the marquee attractions here, and for good reason – the dinosaurs look incredible, much more menacing and intimidating than those you see at Epcot or even the Animal Kingdom. The ride is well executed but seems over a bit too quickly, although that's a minor complaint. You must be 42" tall to ride.

Triceratops Encounter
Rating: B-
Animatronic dinosaur display.
Fear Factor: 1
Visit in the afternoon.

At this pleasant and intriguing attraction, guests can pet a "living" dinosaur. This feed and control station contains a life-sized animatronic triceratops. Guests can learn about the history of the creature from trainers who explain everything from his emotional state to feeding habits. The creature's responses to touch include blinking his eyes and flinching his muscles.

Jurassic Park Discovery Center
Rating: B-
Edutaining exhibits on dinosaurs.
Fear Factor: 1
Visit in the afternoon.

This massive building hosts laboratories where biochemists create the technologies that bring these dinosaurs to life, plus interactive opportunities to manipulate dinosaurs' DNA and create their own dinosaur, plus a T-Rex skeleton and a Raptor hatchery.

Camp Jurassic
Rating: C+

Interactive play area.
Fear Factor: 1
Visit in the afternoon.

This interactive playground gives kids the opportunity to check out rainforests, lava pits, amber mines, decks, caves, and quarries.

Pteranadon Flyers
Rating: D
Uneventful glide over the Jurassic Park area.
Fear Factor: 2
Visit in the afternoon, if at all.

Guests soar strapped into pteranadons who glide along an aerial track over the Jurassic Park compound. The line for this ride practically moves backwards, it's so slow, and the ride is intended mainly for small children. Skip it. Guests must be 36"-56" to ride without a child.

Shopping
Jurassic Outfitters offers River Adventure merch and attraction photos. The **Dino Store** offers dinosaur-themed toys and gifts.

The Lost Continent

Mythology, mysticism, and magic come to life at this exotic corner of the park, with Middle Eastern, Greek, and Arthurian themed attractions and architecture along with more high-tech fun. So get ready to get medieval. There are games of skill here as well as the attractions and shops listed below.

Dueling Dragons
Rating: A+
Two intertwined and awesome roller coasters.
Fear Factor: 5
Ride before 11am with UE.

The 105-second Fire and Ice coasters represent twin dragons who scorch and freeze the forests, you learn as you walk through the dark, eerie, and LENGTHY queue area, as it winds through a castle and into the dungeon before reaching the boarding area. This is a "dueling" roller coaster whose two coasters fly fast and furious at each other, missing by a mere 12 inches at points. The rides are computerized and timed according to passenger weight to ensure the timing of the fly-bys. Three near misses, a zero-gravity toll, corkscrews, and five inversions (at up to 50 mph) later, you're breathless and racing to get back in line for the other train. Reaching a top speed of 60 mph and 125 foot heights, this roller coaster is almost the adrenaline rush of the Hulk but not quite. Ride this one twice if you can, the Fire and Ice rides are completely different.

Poseidon's Fury: Escape from the Lost City
Rating: A-
15-minute special effects extravaganza.
Fear Factor: 3
Visit after 2pm.

Intense special effects, innovative and dynamic sets, and frantic narration from tour guide Taylor make this attraction a winner. A professor has gone missing, and your guide foolishly leads you into the bowels of a temple to look for him. Of course, you have to go further into the depths before finally making your escape. Along the way you pass through an an amazing 42-foot vortex of water to witness an epic battle between Poseidon and his arch-enemy, Lord Darkennon. Guests are trapped in the middle of a fierce fight that combines 350,000 gallons of water with 200 flame effects including 25 foot fireballs. This presentation may be too intense for younger kids.

The Flying Unicorn
Rating: B-
Kids' roller coaster.
Fear Factor: 2
Ride before 11am.

Next to Dueling Dragons is a family-friendly roller coaster whose unicorn-shaped cars reach a top speed of 22mph and a top height of 40 feet, perfect for rollercoaster cherry popping. Universal Express is available here.

The Eighth Voyage of Sindbad
Rating: C+
20-minute live stunt show.
Fear Factor: 2
Visit after noon.

This stunt show follows mythical sailing hero Sindbad as he struck out once again on his search for enormous riches. Along the way he encounters an evil sorceress who has taken a beautiful princess hostage, but the storyline is secondary to the stunts, battle scenes, and 50 pyrotechnic effects including a 10-foot circle of flames. Universal Express is available here.

Shopping

Visit the **Dragon's Keep** for merchandise themed on Fire and Ice dragons, as well as books, magical tricks, games, toys, crystal balls, and pewter mugs are sold here. The **Coin Mint** offers hand-crafted metal coins. **Historic Families** will provide you with information about your family name or coat of arms. **Star Souls** is the place for psychic readings and Henna body art. **Chimera Glass** blows their own goods. **Treasures of Poseidon** offer aquatic-themed gifts at the exit to the attraction.

Seuss Landing

Children go bug-eyed at this land, with the opportunity to rub elbows with the Cat in the Hat and other Dr. Seuss characters for the first time. The whimsical architecture of Theodore Geisel's books is recreated here. In keeping with the no-straight-lines theme, the palm trees found here were bent nearly in half by Hurricane Andrew.

One caveat: the bright colors of Seuss Landing do a really good job of reflecting sunlight, so on bright days this area can be Sunburn Central. Prepare accordingly.

Meeting the Characters

Character sightings here can be a particular treat for a certain segment of the audience, as the Marvel superheroes appear daily all across their Island. Spiderman can be found at the Marvel Alternaverse store. The characters upon whom Toon Lagoon and Seuss Landing are based also make appearances the whole day long in their respective locales.

One Fish Two Fish Red Fish Blue Fish

Rating: B+
2-minute Dumbo ride, with a bonus.
Fear Factor: 1
Ride before 11am.

This is a Dumbo-like ride, where guests board Seussian fish and fly, rising or descending up to 15 feet from the ground. Water is squirted out of several strategically placed fish. You can avoid getting wet, but it'll take a little work. A rhyme broadcast during the ride gives instructions you can follow to stay dry. Universal Express is available here.

The Cat in the Hat
Rating: B
5-minute dark ride.
Fear Factor: 2
Ride before noon.

Couch potatoes of the world unite! Here guests board a sofa and take a chaotic journey through Seuss's most famous book, with 130 ride effects and 30 animatronic characters along the 18 show scenes, including the Cat in the Hat, Thing 1 and Thing 2, and the hapless goldfish entrusted with the job of keeping the house in order. It really is something else to see one of your favorite childhood books brought to three-dimensional life. No word yet on when to expect a ride based on the Cat in the Hat Comes Back, aka the *Caddyshack II* of children's literature. Universal Express is available here.

Caro-Seuss-El
Rating: B
4-minute merry-go-round ride.
Fear Factor: 1
Ride before 11:30am.

This heart-warming merry-go-round features 54 different mounts representing seven Seuss characters like cowfish from "McElligot's Pool," Elephant-birds from "Horton Hatches an Egg," AquaMop Tops and Twin Camels from "One Fish Two Fish Red Fish Blue Fish," Dog-a-lopes and Mulligatawnies from "If I Ran the Zoo," and Birthday Katroo from "Happy Birthday to You." Universal Express is available here.

If I Ran the Zoo
Rating: C+
Interactive play area.
Fear Factor: 1
Visit anytime.

Eponomously based on the story of Gerald McGrew's quest to create a zoo of strange and unusual animals, this interactive playland features 19 interactive elements in the Hedges, Water, and New Zoo areas.

Shopping
Cats, Hats, and Things offers apparel, gifts, and toys based on the famous feline. **All the Books You Can Read** offers the full selection of Seuss books, DVDs, videos, and software. **Snookers & Snookers** is like an opium

den for the sweet tooth. The **Mulberry Street Store** sells Cat in the Hat and Grinch goodies.

Where to Eat at Islands of Adventure

In Port of Entry
Confisco Grille & Backwater Bar
This full service restaurant near the park's entrance offers chicken stingers, Buffalo wings, wood oven pizza, chicken Caesar, sizzling steak, or Chinese chicken salad, mahi fajitas, pad thai, and burgers, as well as a full bar and daily happy hour from 3-5pm ($7.99-18.99). Breakfast is also served here.

Croissant Moon Bakery
Fresh baked pastries including the eponymous crescent rolls and desserts are sold here along with specialty sandwiches ($1.99-6.79).

Arctic Express
Funnel cakes, waffle cones, and soft serve sundaes ($2.99-4.99). Yum!

Cinnabon
Cinnamon rolls and other Cinnabon classics are served here ($2.89-3.79).

In Marvel Superhero Island
Café 4
Pizza by the slice or pie, chicken Caesar salad, spaghetti and meatballs, and fettuccine are offered here ($3.49-8.69).

Captain America Diner
Burgers, chicken sandwiches, apple pie, and other red-white-and-blue favorites are served here ($5.99-7.69).

Chill Ice Cream
Sundaes, floats, and cake cones are available ($2.49-4.49).

Cotton Candy
Pick up the eponymous sugary snack or churros ($2.19-2.69).

Fruit
Whole fruit and fruit cups are available here ($.99-2.99).

In Toon Lagoon
Comic Strip Café
This is a food court with funny page wallpaper and stands offering Chinese, with sweet and sour chicken, broccoli beef, shrimp and scallop lo mein, fried rice, and wonton soup; Fish & Chicken, offering popcorn shrimp hoagies, chicken tenders, and cheesesteaks; Mexican, offering fajitas, soft tacos, club wraps, and nachos; and Pizza & Pasta, offering 9" pies, spaghetti and meatballs, fettuccine Alfredo, and Italian deli or meatball sandwiches ($6.99-8.79). Desserts are also available, as is a kids' menu featuring pizza or PB&J ($5.49-6.29).

Blondie's: Home of the Dagwood
Huge sandwiches are served up here, as you might expect, including the Dagwood, a monstrous concoction of ham, salami, bologna, turkey, Swiss, and American. Half-pound chili dogs are offered, as are meatloaf and American, smoked turkey and Swiss, and tomato mozz sandwiches ($5.99-7.29). Bologna and cheese sandwiches are available for the kids ($5.49).

Wimpy's
Burgers, of course, and chicken fingers, wraps, and hot dogs too ($5.79-7.99)

Cathy's Ice Cream
Ack out on your diet with the house specialty hot fudge sundae ($3.59-4.99).

In Jurassic Park
Thunder Falls Terrace
This seasonal restaurant, which is sometimes reserved for corporate events and private parties, offers rotisserie chicken, ribs, wings, and salads ($6.99-10.99).

The Burger Digs
Big burgers, chicken sandwiches, and milkshakes are on tap here ($6.69-7.49).

Pizza Predatoria
Personal pizzas, meatball and sausage sandwiches, and Caesar salads are available ($5.29-6.99).

The Watering Hole
This stand offers beer, wine, a full bar, and frozen drinks as well as a happy hour from 2-4pm daily.

In the Lost Continent
Mythos Restaurant
Voted the best theme park restaurant in the US for both 2003 and 2004 by *Theme Park Insider,* this full-service restaurant offers continental and Mediterranean dishes like gnocchi with shrimp, risotto, grilled chicken with pasta, boneless BBQ ribs, cedar planked salmon, and many more ($9.95-21.95). The kids' menu includes pizza, BBQ chicken, and linguine ($5.95).

Enchanted Oak Tavern & Alchemy Bar
This restaurant, located inside a huge oak tree, features smoked chicken, turkey legs, BBQ ribs, bacon cheeseburgers, and smoked chicken salad, plus a full bar with a happy hour from 3-5pm daily ($7.69-10.99).

Fire-Eater's Grill
Gyros, chicken stingers, and chili cheese dogs are offered here ($6.29-7.99).

Frozen Desert
Enjoy soft-serve strawberry and pineapple sundaes and Eskimo pies ($2.49-4.49).

In Seuss Landing
Circus McGurkus Café Stupendous
At this large restaurant kids thrill to pizza, fried chicken, lasagna, and spaghetti ($5.99-7.49).

Green Eggs & Ham
You can procure the eponymous sandwich here as well as cheeseburgers and chicken sandwiches ($5.59-8.49).

Hop on Pop Ice Cream Shop
Brownie, waffle cone, and stick sundaes are sold here ($3.59-5.29).

Moose Juice Goose Juice
No meese and geese in the drinks here – just fresh or frozen tangerine or green apple drinks plus churros and light snacks ($1.99-3.79).

Practical Information

Getting In
For information on Universal Orlando ticketing options, refer to Part 2, pages 340-344.

Getting There

Universal Orlando is easily accessible via I-4 Exit 75A (SR 435/ Universal) if you're coming from the Disney/Kissimmee/LBV area. From downtown Orlando and Daytona, use Exit 74B. From International Drive, go one block east to Universal Blvd. and take that north all the way to the parks.

Hours

Islands of Adventure opens at 9am daily. Closing hours vary by season from 5pm to 11pm. Plan on getting here a half hour before the gates open. Doing so will enable you to beat all of the crowds and knock off most of the major-wait attractions in the park before everyone else even gets through the turnstiles.

Parking

Universal Orlando has a huge parking garage structure, enclosed from the elements, surveyed by 200 cameras, and easing your journey with escalators and moving sidewalks. Parking is $8 per day.

Money

Universal accepts Visa, Mastercard, American Express, Discover, and Diners Club, as well as personal, cashier's, and traveler's checks. There is an on-site Wachovia Bank to the right of the turnstiles, as well as ATMs at the main entrance and at the Enchanted Oak Tavern in the Lost Continent area..

Package Pickup

Any merchandise you pick up in the park can be sent to the park entrance while you frolic.

Security

Bag/backpack/package searches are now performed at Universal. Allow a few extra minutes to get through them. Universal forbids coolers, outside food and beverage, weapons, alcohol, illegal drugs, duffel bags, folding chairs, and large umbrellas.

Smoking

By law, all Florida restaurants and bars are now non-smoking. Smoking is only allowed in selected areas of the park. Smoking areas are located:

•**Port of Entry:** To the right of the main gate and at the edge of the lagoon.

•**Marvel Super Hero Island:** Next to the Cotton Candy Shop and the Comic Book Shop.

•**Toon Lagoon:** Next to Me Ship, the Olive and on the passage to Jurassic Park.

•**Jurassic Park:** On the passage to Toon Lagoon, outside the Discovery Center, and by the lagoon.

•**The Lost Continent:** Near the entrance to the Flying Unicorn, outside Mythos, and near Poseidon's Fury.

•**Seuss Landing:** Next to the Mulberry Street Store and the Snookers & Snookers Sweet Candy Cookers.

Check the park map for exact locations.

Chapter 10

SEAWORLD ORLANDO

Central Florida's other "World" is devoted to marine life, and is the most popular marine attraction in the world, with over 4 million visitors each year. **SeaWorld**, with more than 200 acres, has a completely different feel to it than WDW. The pathways are wider, the pace of things more leisurely, more Floridian. Oh, did I mention that there are no Audio-Animatronics here? Every animal is real.

When seen towards the end of your vacation, SeaWorld serves almost as a decompression chamber, to allow you to recover from the vacation. Most of the attractions are shows held in stadiums big enough to accommodate several thousand people at once, so lines are rare.

Touring SeaWorld is less complicated than other theme parks, due in large part to the fact that the majority of attractions are shows playing at specific times or continuous exhibits, which means that you'll spend a minimum of time in line here. That being said, note that the few rides at the park – Wild Arctic, Kraken, and Journey to Atlantis – are crowded most of the day, so ride 'em early. Most of the attractions here are completely family friendly, there are only a few rides that will even raise the question, and they're clearly noted below

During summertime and holiday seasons when the park is open late, the night is closed with a **musical fireworks** display.

For more information about SeaWorld, visit www.seaworld.com, call 800/423-8368 or 407/351-3600. You can also write 7007 SeaWorld Drive, Orlando, FL 32821.

Rides at Seaworld

Journey to Atlantis
> Rating: A+
> Thrilling 6-minute water coaster.
> Fear Factor: 3
> Ride this after Kraken. Avoid it if it's cold and windy!

This "water coaster" puts guests right in the crossfire of an epic clash for the lost city of Atlantis, as the Sirens will do anything to keep tourists from invading their home, which has risen out of the harbor of a Greek fishing village. The 6-acre, 10-story Atlantis is glorious from the outside – with classic Mediterranean architecture and Greek temples poking out of rocky cliffs. The ride itself teams guests with Hermes, who attempts to lead the travelers to safety, and includes some genuine thrills, impressive special effects including lasers, holograms, and LCD lights, two near-freefalls, and some roller coaster elements at the tail end of the ride – with more splashy wet goodness than you can shake a stick at – which is great if you're a hot, sweaty, cranky traveler, and not such a good thing if you're a travel writer with a week's worth of notes inside a now-soaked backpack. Not that I would know anything about that sort of thing.

This is one of the best water rides in the Orlando area, and is one of SeaWorld's top attractions, living up to all the hype surrounding it. I recommend this attraction as not to be missed. Children must be 42" tall to ride.

Kraken
> Rating: A+
> Orlando's coolest roller coaster.
> Fear Factor: 5
> Ride this first thing in the morning.

When this ride opened last year, it became Orlando's fastest, tallest, and longest roller coaster, weighing in at 65 mph, 151 feet, and 4,177 feet, respectively. It's a floorless coaster with open-sided seats riding on a pedestal suspended over the track. Themed after the massive sea serpent kept by Poseidon, this ride includes a 144-foot suicide drop, seven inversions including vertical loops, dive loops, camelback/zero-G rolls, cobra rollers, and flat spins, high G-forces, weightlessness, three underground plunges, and portions where riders look down and see nothing but water. This is the best roller coaster in town, and as one of the only marquee rides here, lines can get long, so see this early or late in the day. Guests must be 54" tall to ride.

Wild Arctic
>Rating: B
>Simulator ride and Arctic exhibit.
>Fear Factor: 3
>Ride after the Kraken and JTA.

This multi-faceted adventure attraction serves to unravel the mystery of the Arctic, combining a thrilling flight over the frozen north with encounters with animals who reside there. Wild Arctic combines high-definition film with high-powered flight simulation, simulating the jet helicopters Borealis and Snow Dog taking off and race against an incoming storm. Breathtaking vistas are blended with suspense while dangerous Arctic hazards are experienced before guests are delivered safely to the research center.

There, guests enter Base Station Wild Arctic, built (according to legend) around a 150-year old British exploration ship. Guests view polar bears, walruses, beluga whales, and seals from bot habove and below water level as they forage for food, dive, swim, and interact with Base Station workers in a 900,000 gallon ecosystem. It's a fascinating look at a habitat which remains an enigma to us. Guests must be 42" tall to ride. You can access the exhibit part of Wild Arctic without riding the simulator.

Shows at Seaworld

Shamu Adventure
>Rating: A+
>30-minute show starring the eponymous killer whale.
>Fear Factor: 1
>See anytime, according to schedule.

SeaWorld's living, breathing answer to Mickey Mouse, Shamu, has his own amazing show, narrated by animal expert Jack Hanna. The show explores the similarities between killer whales in the ocean and at SeaWorld and uses the huge ShamuVision high-definition video screen to transport guests to Alaska, Norway, the Crozet Islands, and more. The demonstrations are truly fascinating, and the show is heart-warming. Note that you will likely get wet in the first 14 rows of the stadium.

Clyde and Seamore Take Pirate Island
> Rating: A-
> 25-minute Sea lion and otter show.
> Fear Factor: 1
> See anytime, according to schedule.

This fun and funny new incarnation of the park's sea lion and otter show features trainer Eric Lang and his first mate, Clyde the sea otter. Clyde and his cohorts team up for swashbuckling action on an awesome set. This show is quite enjoyable and well worth your time, with fun, cheesy humor and cast members acerbic enough to turn the wit cannons on the audience when they fail to respond.

Shamu Rocks America
> Rating: A-
> 20-minute nighttime show.
> Fear Factor: 1
> According to schedule.

This nighttime show combines the killer whale and trainers with rock and roll and theatrical special effects.

Odyssea
> Rating: B+
> 30-minute non-traditional circus show.
> Fear Factor: 1
> See anytime, according to schedule.

Drawing inspiration from Cirque du Soleil, the Odyssea troupe combines acrobatics, comedy, costumes, music, and special effects to transport guests to an underwater fantasy world. Acts include "penguins" bouncing, tumbling, and flipping on trampolines, aerial performers, and contortionists.

Pets Ahoy
> Rating: B-
> 20-minute domestic animal show.
> Fear Factor: 1
> See anytime, according to schedule.

This entertaining show is performed by an array of domestic animals, many of whom were rescued from area shelters. The case includes 18 cats,

12 dogs, birds, rats, pigs, and even a horse performing vaudeville. The show was totally revamped in June 2001.

Blue Horizons
Rating: N/A
Fear Factor: 1
See anytime, according to schedule.

Breakthrough Broadway-reminescent show featuring live mammal interaction within a storyline emerging from a young girl's imagination, her dreams of the place where the sea meets the sky. The dazzling display includes exotic birds, dolphin, and false killer whales along with a few humans – arialists and divers who plunge into the water. During the "Mystify" show here, 60 foot mist screen projections are used alongside flame and fireworks. This opened in summer 2005, too late to be reviewed in this edition.

Animals & Other Attractions

Clydesdale Hamlet
The eight-horse hitch often seen pulling the wagon across the park resides here, in this walk-through facility. Daily posing and petting sessions offer unforgettable photo-ops.

Key West at SeaWorld
This 5-acre section of SeaWorld is devoted to the southernmost city in the United States, featuring a trio of naturalistic new animal habitats hosting several of the Keys' most popular species, including Atlantic bottle-nose dolphins, stingrays, and endangered sea turtles. There's also a nightly *Sunrise Celebration* here with entertainers, live bands, and more.

Manatee Rescue
This new exhibit immerses guessts in the beautiful underwater world of the endangered Florida manatee with creatures acrually rescued by SeaWorld.

Pacific Point Preserve
Here you can come nose-to-soggy-nose with a variety of animals including turtles, dolphins, stingrays, and seals. You can feed them, touch them, pet them, and learn about the species represented here.

Shark Encounter

Guests ride a moving sidewalk through an aquarium featuring the deadliest creatures to ever roam the oceans. That's right, through the aquarium. There's 500 tons of sea water above and around you along with creatures like the surgeon-fish, sharks, lionfish, puffer-fish, scorpion-fish, and more.

Dolphin Nursery

Home to new moms and their calves.

Penguin Encounter

A moving sidewalk carries you past over 200 penguins, plus puffins and other Antarctic sea birds. The indoor, glassed-in "penguin pen" is so Antarcticly chilly that it actually snows. "It's ninety-five in the shade out here, and those penguins get a ski slope," summer visitors often lament.

Caribbean Tidepool

Hands-on experiences with sea urchins and other creatures.

Tropical Reef

The Reef is a 160,000-gallon pool illuminated by neon coral bigger than a house. The exhibit's inhabitants include raccoon butterfly-fish, morey eels, lobsters, surgeon-fish, clownfish, Florida alligators, fanged baby sharks, and more. This exhibit is to conventional aquariums what Space Mountain is to conventional roller coasters. It's something special, one of the reasons people pay to get in.

Turtle Point

Key West's animal attraction features sea turtles, of whom over 30 were rehabilitated by Sea World.

Shamu's Happy Harbor

Rating: B

This 3-acre play area includes four stories of cargo netting, steel drums that guests can smash away on, a water maze, radio-controlled cars, an air bounce, slides, crow's nests, ball crawls, and vinyl mountains. There are restrooms and an abundance of shaded seating. Boogie Bump Bay, a smaller area, is intended specifically for kids 42" or less and features scaled-down versions of most of the equipment.

Anheuser-Busch Beer School

Rating: B-

"Beer school" is where SeaWorld's corporate daddy leads guests through the beermaking process, right up to that most important step where you get to sip free samples of Anheuser Busch brews. Much like college however, you don't need to go to class in order to drink.

Animal Connections Programs

Beluga Interaction Program

Participants meet the whale's trainer and learn how to communicate with them. Following this training, guests don wetsuits and dive into a Wild Arctic tank where you will touch and feed the beluga whales, and help trainers communicate with them via hand signals. This costs $130 and is available to guests over 13. Park admision is extra.

Sharks Deep Dive

Guests put on wetsuits and either snorkel or scuba dive in a shark cage, encountering over 50 sharks. This program includes a t-shirt and a shark booklet and poster, but does not include park admission. Cost is $150 for scuba, $125 for snorkel.

Marine Mammal Keeper Experience

This nine-hour program allows guests to experience the thrill of working alongside SeaWorld's staff of trainers, learning firsthand about the experiences of the animal care specialists. The program includes lunch, a t-shirt, a career book, a souvenir photograph, and a seven-day pass to SeaWorld for $399 per person.

Educational Tours & Programs

Adventure Express Tour

Take this six-hour tour and enjoy express access to rides, reserved seating at shows, special animal feeding opportunities, and a knowledgeable tour guide to escort you across the park. Cost is $89 per adult, $79 per child, in addition to park admission.

Polar Expedition Tour

This 60-minute tour goes behind the scenes at Wild Arctic and the Penguin Research Facility. Prices are $16 adult, $12 child.

Predators
Explore the world of sharks and killer whales in this 60-minute tour. Prices are $16 adult, $12 child.

Saving a Species Tour
Visit rescue and rehab facilities where endangered manatees and sea turtles are given medical treatment. Guests can also hand-feed birds in Sea World's exlusive open aviary. Prices are $16 adult, $12 child.

SeaWorld Adventure Camp
SeaWorld's education department offers over 200 programs, including day camps, resident camps, sleepovers and family adventures. Call 407/ 363-2380 for details.

Where to Eat in Seaworld

In addition to the restaurants listed here, there's also the Makahiki Luau Dinner Show, Tel. 407/351-3600, covered in the Nightlife chapter. Note that admission to the park is not required to check out the Luau.

Sharks Underwater Grill
Open for lunch and dinner, Sharks offers a Coral Reef like aquarium surrounding along with Floribbean fare, including fresh seafood, prime beef, and chicken entrees. Signature dishes include Caribbean seafood pasta, oak grilled filet mignon topped with jerk spices, and pork medallions with black bean sauce ($17.45-24.99).

The Spice Mill
The newest restaurant at the Waterfront, Spice Mill offers flavorful items like jerk grilled chicken, a habanero chicken tender sandwich, Cajun jambalaya, Philly cheesesteak, and muffaletta sandwiches ($6.79-8.99)

Dine with Shamu

OK, so this is an interesting twist on character dining. This adventure offers guests the opportunity to eat alongside killer whales, mingle with Shamu trainers, and observe training sessions in an intimate area at Shamu Stadium. The buffet dinner accommodates 200 guests per seating and includes salads, pasta, chicken, beef, and seafood entrees, as well as a separate children's buffet. The cost is $32 for adults, $18 for kids 3-9, 10% less for passmembers. Park admission is required.

Smoky Creek Grill

Here, you can fill up on barbecue platters with cole slaw, a roll, and ribs or chicken, picnic-style. Guests dine on umbrella-covered outdoor tables by Atlantis Lagoon ($8.39-9.99).

Waterfront Sandwich Grill

This lagoon-view restaurant offers hamburgers and sandwich platters, including the California Light, a turkey breast with sprouts and cheese. A children's platter with a turkey sandwich, fruit salad, and a cookie is available. Guests can sit at closely-spaced indoor tables or more spacious outdoor, dockside areas ($6.39-7.39).

Seafire Inn

This new eatery in the Waterfront offers a character breakfast featuring Shamu, Dolly Dolphin, Pete and Penny Penguin. The buffet includes eggs, pancakes, biscuits and gravy, and fruit ($14.95 adult, $9.99 kid). At lunch and dinner, half-pound burgers, tropical chicken stir fry, coconut fried shrimp, and chicken cordon bleu sandwiches make the bill ($6.99-10.99).

Voyagers Wood Fired Pizza

The Waterfront offers hand-tossed pizzas, grilled salmon, orange-wood smoked chicken, and foccacia club sandwiches ($7.99-14.95).

Smugglers Feast Snacks

Snack away on smoked turkey legs, pizza pockets, apple cider, and caramel apples on the waterfront ($2.99-5.99).

Sand Bar

Located at the base of the 400 foot Tower, this restaurant offers sushi, shrimp cocktails, seared sesame ahi tuna, and fruit and cheese platters ($4-10).

Mango Joe's Café

Sizzling beef and chicken fajitas, fajita samdwiches, Cajun shrimp po boy, and veggie wraps and club sandwiches ($5.49-9.99).

Capt. Pete's Island Eats

This surprising little kiosk offers up conch fritters, turkey drumsticks, smoothies, key line funnel cakes, and more, representing Key West cuisine to its fullest ($4.99-6.99).

Mama's Kitchen

Cheesesteaks, turkey sandwiches, citrus BBQ pork, and Cajun shrimp Caesar salad are available here ($4.49-7.49).

Smoky Creek Grill

Smoky chicken, beef brisket, spare ribs, and baby backs are served up at this tempting counter ($7.99-11.99).

Hospitality Deli

This pleasant lunchtime locale offers hand carved turkey and roast beef sandwiches plus bratwurst sandwiches, stacked deli clubs, chicken Caesar salads, and desserts ($5.79-7.29).

Mama Stella's

The fare in this restaurant includes muffaletta, cheesesteak, and jerk chicken sandwiches, as well as chili and chicken tenders. This restaurant is extremely popular in spite of its somewhat questionable quality ($6.29-7.99).

Cypress Bakery

Various pastries, muffins, and bagel sandwiches are served up at this shop by the main entrance ($1.99-3.99).

Polar Parlor

A variety of frozen treats and ice cream novelties are offered at this eatery by the main entrance ($3.29-4.99).

Practical Information

Getting There

Sea World is located at 7007 Sea Harbor Drive, just off southern International Drive, south of the Bee Line Expressway. To get here from Disney World or Kissimmee, take I-4 east to exit 71 (Central Florida Parkway/Sea World). From Universal take I-4 west to exit 72 (SR 528/Bee Line Expressway), take the International Drive exit, turn left, and take I-Drive south, turning right on Sea Harbor Drive.

Getting In

For information on Sea World's ticketing options, refer to Part 2, pages 340-344.

Hours

SeaWorld opens at 9am daily. Closing hours vary by season from 6pm to 10pm.

Parking

SeaWorld parking offers 6700 spaces at $8 per day.

Money

SeaWorld accepts Visa, Mastercard, American Express, and Discover. There are ATMs at the main entrance, Key West, by Shark Encounter, and by Wild Arctic.

Package Pickup

Any merchandise you pick up in the park can be sent to Shamu's Emporium at the park entrance.

Security

Bag/backpack/package searches are now performed at Universal. Allow a few extra minutes to get through them. Sea World forbids coolers, outside food and beverage, weapons, alcohol, illegal drugs, duffel bags, folding chairs, and large umbrellas.

Smoking

By law, all Florida restaurants and bars are now non-smoking. Smoking is only allowed in selected areas of the park. Smoking areas are located:

•On either side of the entrance plaza, next to the Tropical Reef, next to Coconut Bay Traders, at the corner closest to Journey to Atlantis, by Dolphin Cove, by Dolphin Stadium, across from Friends in the Wild, next to Seaport Theater, outside Voyagers, next to the Seafire Inn, and next to underwater viewing for Shamu.

Check the park map for exact locations.

Sea World Traffic Tuesdays

Something special for older guests, this weekly program geared to a 50+ crowd, includes hour-long symposiums on health, horticulture, and animal training, and the AARP discount is raised to $8.

Chapter 11

WHERE TO STAY

After the question of timing, this is the most important factor in how your trip will be remembered. A nice hotel with a clean room and a well-kept pool becomes a haven of a home base from which to weave your dreams. Too loud, too run-down, too far away, and you'll start and end each day on the wrong foot.

There are hundreds of hotels, motels, resorts, condos, vacation homes, and other lodging establishments in and around Orlando. Some of them are really nice. Some of them look like something out of a Norman Bates B-movie ripoff. But rest assured, we've already done the heavy lifting, you won't find any of the latter in this book.

That frees you up to pick your hotel based on your specific desires and preferences for the trip. There's something for everybody – and this chapter will show you the best of the best, as well as showing specific ways to get discounts at each hotel.

Where Should I Stay?

For practical purposes, we divide the hotels into seven geographic concentrations. Your entertainment agenda should drive your lodging decision. Those areas are:

Walt Disney World. The 43 square miles of "Vacation Kingdom" include over 30 hotels, ranging from budget to luxurious. Three hotels are connected to the Magic Kingdom via monorail. Five more are connected to Epcot and MGM via boat. There are significant benefits to staying on-site at Disney, discussed later. There are also the Official Hotels in Downtown

Disney, which provide proximity but not the level of service of those hotels owned and operated by Disney itself.

Kissimmee. The gateway to the World, the Kissimmee-St. Cloud area is an old-school, but recently freshened tourist drag packed with souvenir shops, cheap motels, and chain restaurants. In recent years improvements to the main tourist strip (US 192) and new development along it have made this a much more desirable destination than in years past.

Lake Buena Vista. At the back side of WDW, adjacent to Downtown Disney, this area includes some of the area's finest luxury properties, as well as lots of all-suite hotels in one of the area's last underdeveloped areas. Direct access to I-4 is a plus.

Universal. The Universal Orlando resort includes three full-service, luxury hotels – the Royal Pacific, Portofino Bay, and Hard Rock Hotels. They provide a similar level of luxury and amenity as the Disney Deluxe Resorts, and a marvelous attention to detail and atmosphere. Plus, Universal provides easy access to I-4, providing a quick trip west to WDW.

International Drive. A marvelous, visually striking tourist drag of the greatest magnitude (imagine the Vegas Strip, only for kids), I-Drive is home to some of Orlando's coolest attractions, most memorable restaurants, and best-bet hotels. The north end is closest to Universal, but is older, more congested with traffic, and a generally less appealing place to stay than the southern end, which benefits from tree-lined medians, better urban planning, and generally a less hokey flavor of cheese. The south end of International Drive also provides quick commute to Sea World and Disney World.

In each area, we list the Top Ten choices in our order of preference. Some of the things that drive our decision making are:

•**Spacious rooms.** When piled on top of one another, even the Cleavers can snap into axe-murderers. Room to breathe takes a lot of the stress off family vacations.

•**In-room amenities and perks.** Things like high-speed Internet access, video games, coffeemakers, and refrigerators allow you to enjoy the comforts of home.

•**Special pools.** Waterslides, whirlpools, themed play areas, and other goodies can transform a mundane midday break into a memorable vacation highlight. In recent years more hotels have been snazzing up their pools in order to differentiate themselves from the pack.

•**Dining options.** Breakfast buffets and food courts make for affordable family-friendly dining, while many of the best restaurants in Orlando can be found in its hotels.

•**Exceptional value.** You won't find any of the super-low budget places listed in this guide book, but you will find plenty of options that give you bang for the buck.

Finding Discounts

You don't need to pay rack rate for hotel rooms in most places around Orlando. (WDW lodging discounts take a little more wiggling, but it can be done.) The **Orlando Magicard** yields deep discounts at area hotels and especially at vacation homes. Websites like **Hotels.com, Priceline,** and **Hotwire** offer good prices too – Priceline and Hotwire feature name-your-own price deals.

AAA also offers discounts of up to 20 or 30% at many nationwide chains and independent hotels, and **AARP** members often reap similar discounts. The **Official Visitor Center** is a good place to find same-day deals – as well as coupon books and publications with ads from local hotels working against the clock to fill empty rooms. Special discounts are often also offered to military, government, and senior citizens. Inquire about corporate or promotional rates. **TripAdvisor.com** aggregates hotel deals from across the Internet. Many hotel chains guarantee that their best available online rate is offered on their website. This can save plenty of time and searching, but be aware that coupons and special group discounts can sometimes beat the so-called "best available" rate.

Walt Disney World Resorts

You've got to hand it to Disney, they sure know how to create a mood. This is evidenced in the diverse hotels on the property, as they bring to life locales as exotic as the South Seas and New Mexico, and as varied as New England and Palm Beach. From rustic park lodges to imaginative and modern high-rises, there's a Disney resort for every taste. And with the addition of value-priced Quonset quasi-motels, the All-Star and Pop Century Resorts, it's now possible to reap the benefits of staying on-site at a reasonable cost.

All resorts have a check-out time of 11am, with 1pm checkout usually available upon request. Most Disney resorts have a check-in time of 3pm, although Fort Wilderness has a 1pm check-in, and the All-Star and Disney Vacation Club resorts have a 4pm check-in.

Benefits of staying at WDW

If you're looking at your first trip to Disney World, you may be asking yourself, "What's the big deal about staying in Disney World?" First of all, Disney is renowned for its service, cleanliness, and friendliness – and there's just something in the air at Disney resorts. Call it pixie dust, call it magic, call it whatever. It's just a different world when you're staying inside WDW. And besides the fancy-tickling theming of the hotels, significant tangible benefits to staying on-site include:

•Closest possible proximity to WDW theme parks.

•Guaranteed admission to the parks, even when they are full.

•Resort ID can be used as admission media and carry charging privileges (meals, shops, recreation).

•Extra Magic Hour early admission to theme parks.

•Free parking at all theme parks.

•Room delivery of purchases.

•Priority dining reservations – same-day or up to 120 days in advance.

•Priority tee times – 60 days in advance.

•Unlimited use of all boat, bus, and monorail transportation inside WDW.

•Pets can be boarded overnight at WDW kennels.

•Wake-up calls from Mickey and the gang.

•Bedtime stories in-room all night long.

•Several entertaining and informational closed-circuit park and resort information channels.

•Complimentary customizable voice mail.

Of these, the biggest bonus is the Extra Magic Hour, which gives early rising Disney guests exclusive access to the park for an hour before it opens

Disney World Resort Reservations FAQ

Q. How can I reserve a room at a Disney resort?
A. You have several options, described below.
•Online: www.disneyworld.com, or sites like AAA, Expedia, and Travelocity.
•By phone: 407/W-DISNEY. Hours are 7am to 10pm weekdays, 7am to 8pm weekends. *Do not call the hotels directly for reservations.*
•By mail: Walt Disney World, Box 10100, Lake Buena Vista, FL 32830
•In person: Ocala Information Center, I-75. Call 352/854-0770.

Q. How far in advance can I reserve?
A. Generally, reservations can be made through the end of the following calendar year. Note that for the most popular accommodation choices during the Christmas season, you need to book as close out to that one-year mark as possible.

Q. What kind of deposit do I need?
A. You need to leave a deposit in the amount of one night's accommodations, plus 11-12% tax, either at the time of your reservation for arrivals within 30 days, or within two weeks of making your reservation for bookings more than 30 days out.

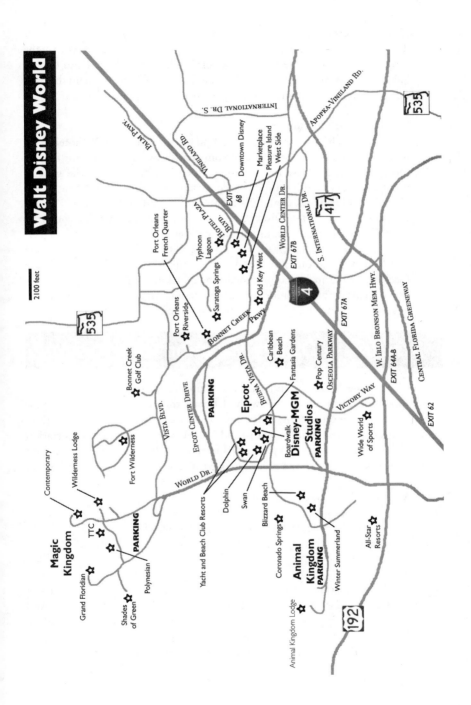

Walt Disney World

2100 feet

to the general public. They rotate the parks so only one is open early on each day of the week. Note that if you're not staying at a Disney resort, you might want to steer clear of the theme park hosting the Extra Magic Hour on any given morning, as even if you get through the turnstiles the moment the park opens, there's still hundreds of people already with a jump on you.

WDW Resort Discounts

It's much more challenging to find discounts for WDW hotels than it is for most off-site hotels due to consistently strong demand for rooms. Disney generally doesn't make room discounts available to the general public, but they do offer specific discounts to certain groups: **AAA** members (10-20%), **Florida residents** (30-45%), **annual passholders** (30-45%), and the **military** (30-40%), Disney also sends out postcards with personalized promo codes to people on its various mailing lists.

WDW divides their resorts by the level of service provided – Deluxe and Disney Vacation Club Resorts are at the top of the heap. Moderate Resorts provide quality accommodations at reasonable prices. Value Resorts provide bare-bones amenities and garish design but gets you all the benefits of staying on-site at a fraction of the cost of your other options.

Deluxe & Disney Vacation Club Resorts

Disney's Deluxe and Vacation Club Resorts provide spacious, well-appointed accommodations with elaborate themed pools, plenty of full-service restaurants, room service, luggage service, valet parking, babysitting, concierge, fitness centers, tennis, and bus, boat, or monorail transportation (depending on hotel and park). Deluxe resorts also have concierge service available. Expect to pay a premium of $150-200 for a concierge level room.

ANIMAL KINGDOM LODGE
$199-620
2901 Osceola Parkway, LBV, 407/938-3000
Room Quality: B   Amenities: A-
Food: A+   Value: C

The great thing about Disney resorts is the way that they just take you elsewhere. A different time, a different place … therein lies the magic. And out of all Disney's wondrous hotel fantasies, none transports you quite like the Animal Kingdom Lodge, from the moment you step into the cavernous, dark-hued, and surprisingly intimate thatched-roof open-air lobby. Perhaps that's why Fodor's named the AKL one of the Top 20 Hotels in the World for 2005.

So what's so special here? Imagine, if you will. You're laying on the bed after a long day of theme park fun. You hear a noise outside your window - a weird bleating noise. So you open the sliding glass door and step out into the mild night air, and stare out at the savannah beneath and beyond your balcony. And what do you see, but a half dozen wildebeests gracefully chasing one another back and forth across the grasslands, honking exuberantly. This is the kind of experience that you can't find at any other hotel in town, and it's a truly special thing to behold. Over 100 grazing animals and over 130 birds populate the three savannahs surrounding the hotel, which total 74 acres. Each contains different animals and foliage, and all of them feature artificial moonlight for nighttime viewing. AKL Concierge floor guests have exclusive access to the Wanmaya Safari, a 3 1/2 hour experience including a guided tour of the savannah. Three nights a week, up to eight guests board a specially designed pop-top vehicle and tour the wildlife reserve. The tour costs $150 per person, and includes a customary South African "sundowner" with juice, dried beef, fruits, and nuts, followed by dinner at the resort's signature restaurant, Jiko.

The 1,293 rooms are among the smallest of the Deluxe resorts at 344 square feet, but the décor is particularly appealing, with the African theme carried throughout, with colorful jewel-toned bedspreads, mosquito netting (for effect only, not function!), and playful tiles in the bathrooms. It's attractive and understated, but if you've got a family of five, it might be a little cramped. Note that all rooms do not have savannah views. If you want to overlook one of the three savannahs, you need to specify that when you reserve your room. And of course, you'll pay a premium for the privilege. However, keep in mind, there are public viewing areas that provide excellent vantage points of the savannah – so even if you don't have a savannah view room, you can still enjoy the incredible vistas.

The AKL boasts two excellent restaurants that serve daring, authentic, and surprisingly family-friendly African cuisine – which makes more sense when you realize that WDW's Vice President of Food and Beverage, Dieter Hannig, once was a chef at a hotel in Kenya. The AAA Four Diamond Award-winning **Jiko – The Cooking Place** serves up flavorful "New African" cuisine with an emphasis on freshness, simplicity, and light flavors. **Boma** is a bountiful family-style buffet surrounding a show kitchen complete with wood-burning grill and rotisserie. Cultural enrichment here isn't just limited to your taste buds. Storytelling happens at the Arusha Rock Firepit behind the lobby at 7:30pm every night – fascinating stuff for grown-ups and kids alike. Light snacks and quick meals can be found at **Mara**, serving inside or by the pool, while drinks can be enjoyed at **Victoria Falls Lounge** in the lobby or **Uzima Springs** at poolside.

And speaking of poolside ... let's talk about the pool, shall we? **Uzima Springs** is the largest pool you'll find at any WDW Resort, covering 9,000 square feet. There's a zero-entry area where the pool slopes gently, enabling accessibility for mobility-challenged guests. There's two relaxing whirlpools and a wading pool around the fringes of the themed area.

The **Zahanati Massage and Fitness Center** features Cybex weights and cardio equipment plus aromatherapy, massage therapy, body treatments, and more. Be sure to check out the **Zawadi Marketplace** shop in the lobby. At 5,300 square feet, it boasts one of the best selections you'll find at any WDW resort. Beyond the obvious, you'll find authentic African crafts, artwork, and souvenirs.

Simba's Clubhouse is the AKL's child activity center, where $8 an hour buys parents freedom and quiet (we know you need it, it doesn't make you a bad person.) and gets your 4- to 12-year old kids dinner, snacks, Disney movies, toys, games, and supervision. Because dammit, it's YOUR vacation too!

WILDERNESS LODGE/VILLAS @ WILDERNESS LODGE
$199-490/$284-1,015
> 901 Timberline Dr., LBV, 407/824-3200
> Room Quality: B+   Amenities: B+
> Food: A-   Value: C+

The Wilderness Lodge is one of the most aesthetically pleasing places in all of Disney World. This loving recreation of Yellowstone's Old Faithful Lodge (circa 1904) feels so secluded and placid, you'd never realize that it was just a stone's throw from the Magic Kingdom. But it is – and even the fact that the Lodge is connected to the MK by boat reinforces that far-away-from-it-all feel.

The lobby is breathtakingly magnificent and homey at the same time, featuring a six-story atrium decorated with totem poles and strewn with porches and libraries for guests to discover. The focal point of the lobby is the 82-foot tall, three-sided fireplace, representing 2 billion years of geology with fossilized animal and plant life throughout the colorful strata (not to mention a hidden Mickey or two), re-created in the same proportions that occur in the Grand Canyon. Even the musical score that plays in the common areas evokes thoughts of the old West, drawing themes from *Dances with Wolves, Silverado, How the West Was Won*, and more classic westerns. There are two daily walking tours offered here. The 9am tour discusses the architecture, landscaping, and art of the Lodge. The 3pm tour goes behind the scenes at the hotel's restaurants, and allows you to sample Artist Point's signature salmon dish.

If the fireplace is the Wilderness Lodge's heart, Silver Creek is its soul. A spring fountain in the lobby feeds a stream that runs down to the pool, and the run-off from the pool trickles down to Bay Lake. (Environmentalists and people who like swimming in clean water, don't worry, there's actually three separate water systems.) Every hour on the hour, the geyser behind the hotel erupts 120 feet in the air. Cool!

The Wilderness Lodge's 728 rooms are the smallest of Disney's Deluxe resorts (340 square feet), decorated in browns, greens, and beiges, with red accents on windowpanes that recall the architecture of Frank Lloyd Wright. Patchwork quilts, artwork depicting the mystery of the old West, and light-wood armoires with etchings of mountain scenes enhance the homey feel of the rooms. Most rooms have balconies that overlook waterfalls, geysers, courtyards, lodgepole pine forests, or Bay Lake. Sleeping options include a king size bed, double-queens, or two bunk beds and a queen.

In 2000 Disney opened the 136-unit Villas at Wilderness Lodge, with accommodations including:

• Studios that sleep four adults, measuring 356 square feet, including microwave, fridge, coffeemaker, private porch ($284-449);

• One-bedroom villas that sleep four adults, measuring 727 square feet, with a king sized bed, whirlpool tub, refrigerator, stove, microwave, washer and dryer, and a private porch ($390-580); and

• Two-bedroom villas measuring 1,080 square feet, sleeping up to eight in one king, two queens, and a queen sleeper sofa, with all the amenities of a one-bedroom villa, with extra space ($570-1,040).

The Villas also have their own quiet pool.

Artist's Point is the Wilderness Lodge's premier restaurant, serving the house specialty, cedar plank roasted Cypress Island salmon, along with steak, seafood, chicken, and game selections cooked over a hardwood flame. The other full-service restaurant, **Whispering Canyon Café,** is a fun place for family style dining, with all-you-can-eat skillets served on a lazy-susan in the middle of your table. À la carte items are also available. Late night needs can be accommodated at **Roaring Fork Snacks** and breakfast items are available at **Coffee Express.** Need to sip something stronger? Check out the **Territory Lounge** – they feature their own micro-brew plus a lunch menu and evening appetizers. There's also the **Trout Pass Pool Bar** outside.

The **Silver Creek** themed pool is not as spectacular as some of the others, but it's one of WDW's prettiest – complete with a waterslide seemingly carved out of the rocks. There's two hot tubs and a stretch of white sand along Bay Lake. Enjoy the outdoors further on the half-mile jogging trail, the hires at **Teton Boat & Bike Rental,** or the guided fishing excursions. You can also catch a workout at the **Sturdy Branches Health Club** or enjoy the game tables in the **Iron Spike Room.**

The **Cub's Den** is a supervised dining and entertainment program for kids 4 to 12, open 5pm til midnight daily. Parents get a breather from all that quality time, and kids get video games, movies, arts and crafts, and animals to play with. The **Flag Family** program's cast members escort one family each morning to the roof of the Lodge, where together they raise the American and state flags, the Disney flag, and two Wilderness Lodge flags. You'll get a souvenir photo and a certificate to commemorate the occasion. The **Electrical Water Pageant** floats by here at 9:35 pm nightly.

YACHT & BEACH CLUB RESORTS/BEACH CLUB VILLAS
$294-680/$294-1,040
Yacht Club: 1700 Epcot Resorts Blvd., LBV, 407/934-7000
Beach Club: 1800 Epcot Resorts Blvd., LBV, 407/934-8000
Room Quality: A   Amenities: A
Food: A   Value: C-

Now you don't have to be a WASP to vacation like one! You can live the good life at these luxurious resorts, designed by Robert A.M. Stern to recall the New England beachfront resort towns of the late 19th century. Not only are these some of the nicest accommodations in Disney World, but they are perfectly situated – walking distance to Epcot and a quick boat ride to MGM. Even better – some of the best restaurants in WDW are here.

Inside and out, the hotels' styles complement one another nicely. The Beach Club's blue and white stick house architecture blends amiably with its sister hotel's gray clapboard. The Yacht Club's bright, airy, 380 square foot rooms have a nautical flair and muted rose and cobalt colors seem all the more brilliant against fresh white walls with blue trim, a contrast to the Beach Club's pastels and natural finish furniture. Rooms at both are very spacious – sleeping up to five adults – and feature double sinks, brass trimmed mirrors, ceiling fans, refrigerators, coffeemakers, and chess and checker sets.

In 2002 Disney opened the 205-unit Beach Club Villas, with accommodations including:
•Studios that sleep four adults, measuring 356 square feet, including microwave, wet bar, fridge, coffeemaker, and private porch ($305-475);
•One-bedroom villas that sleep four adults, measuring 727 square feet, with a king sized bed, whirlpool tub, a fully equipped kitchen, DVD player, washer and dryer, and a private porch ($410-605); and
•Two-bedroom villas measuring 1,080 square feet, sleeping up to eight in one king, two queens, and a queen sleeper sofa, with all the amenities of a one-bedroom villa, with extra space ($575-1,070).

The Villas also have their own pool.

The Beach Club side of the resort has volleyball and white sand, while the Yacht Club side features a marina where personal craft can be rented by the hour. The two sides of the complex are joined together thematically and literally by **Stormalong Bay**, the breathtaking 3-acre swimming complex, featuring a 750,000 gallon pool along the shores of Crescent Lake. This dazzling feature pool comes complete with waterslides, shipwreck, whirlpools, bubbling jets, "rising sands," and a quiet lagoon. Each resort also has a quiet pool. This complex is also home to the **Beaches and Cream Soda Shop**, an old-school ice cream parlor, and **Hurricane Hanna's Grill**, a poolside destination for fast food favorites.

The full-service restaurants here are particularly impressive. The **Yachtman Steakhouse** features aged, grain-fed beef carved by a house butcher and grilled over sweet, smoky oak. The **Yacht Club Galley** features à la carte and buffet breakfasts as well as sandwiches and light entrees for lunch. On the Beach Club side of the resort, the **Cape May Café** is a culinary highlight – clambakes! If you're not into clams, there's plenty of other seafood on the buffet – which is extremely popular for good reason. Landlubbers can chow down on beef, ribs, chicken, and veggies. There's also a daily character breakfast here. The new **Beach Club Marketplace** offers gourmet sandwiches, soup, salad, and desserts.

Each resort has two small, relaxing bars – there's the **Crew's Cup Lounge** sports bar and hidden-away **Ale & Compass** lounge at the Yacht Club and the **RipTide Lounge**, featuring frozen fruity drinks, and the **Martha's Vineyard** wine bar at the Beach Club.

The resorts have tons of fun waiting to be had – there's a marina with water mice, sailboats, pontoon boats, pedal boats, and rowboats. On the Yacht Club side, naturally. The Beach Club has, duh, a beach, along with volleyball, croquet, and two tennis courts. In the central area are the **Ship Shape Health Club** is a full facility complete with spa, steam room, and saunas; as well as the **Lafferty Place Arcade** gameroom. The **Sandcastle Club** is the kids' activity center here, for nightly quality time without the kids. Each hotel has a gift shop, and there's the Periwig Salon in the common area for all your grooming and beauty needs.

POLYNESIAN RESORT
$304-720
1600 Seven Seas Dr., LBV, 407/934-8000
Room Quality: A   Amenities: A
Food: A   Value: B

A venerable favorite, the Polynesian Resort has been wowing guests since its opening in 1971. With the lush tropical vegetation, waterfalls, and craggy rocks in the 250-square foot centerpiece of the Great Ceremonial House, you'll feel as if you've been transported to the South Seas the minute you walk in the door. And that's the whole idea – not to mention a good part of the charm.

This is one of the most convenient resorts to the Disney theme parks – it's on the monorail line, which means easiest possible access to Epcot and the Magic Kingdom. It's also one of the most luxurious – with great Pacific Rim cuisine, beautifully landscaped grounds that meander down to the Seven Seas Lagoon, and some of the best shopping you'll find in any Disney resort.

The hotel's rooms are among Disney's largest, measuring 409 square feet. Rooms are split between eleven two- and three-story "longhouses" named after Pacific islands. Magic Kingdom views can be enjoyed from the Hawaii, Tahiti, and Tuvalu buildings. Each room has two queen beds and a sleeper sofa, comfortably accommodating five. Each room also has a coffeemaker and refrigerator. Starting in May 2005, all guestrooms will be redecorated, updating the South Seas theme with flat-screen TVs, dark, hand-carved wood furniture and blues, greens, and brown bedspreads (with designer sheets), and wall coverings.

The culinary highlight of the hotel is 'Ohana Feast, where all-you-can-eat family-style goodness is cooked over an 18-foot fire pit grill, with meats sliced off 3-foot skewers in front of you. There's also a daily character breakfast here. The Spirit of Aloha dinner show recently replaced the Polynesian Revue (aka the Luau), and features authentic Polynesian music (plus "Hawaiian Roller Coaster Ride," from Lilo & Stitch) along with ribs, chicken, veggies, rice, and dessert.

The Kona Café is renowned for its "Tonga Toast," featuring bananas stuffed into sourdough, rolled in cinnamon and sugar – it absolutely lives up to the hype. You could do worse than to get up a bit early and stop here for a taste on your way to the Magic Kingdom one morning. Lighter fare can be had at Captain Cook's Snack Company, while libations can be enjoyed at the Tambu Lounge in the Great Ceremonial House, or the Barefoot Pool Bar outside.

Oh yes, I neglected to mention the pool. It rocks. Igneous rocks, if you want to be precise. New in 2001, the Nanea Volcano Pool is fed by streams starting at the Great Ceremonial House, trickling down to a pool with a towering 40 foot volcano (that even shoots lava!). Underwater jets, piped-in underwater music, extra heated areas, a kids' wet play area, and in-pool seating add to the uniqueness of this pool, which also features a zero depth entry. There's a quieter pool as well, plus Seven Seas Lagoon for the beach bunnies among you.

Other recreational activities and facilities include a 1.5 mile jogging trail, fishing excursions, waterskiing, parasailing, and Moana Mickey's Fun Hut 24-hour arcade. Kids can have safe, supervised fun, enjoying arts and crafts and Disney movies in the Neverland Club.

The Torch Lighting ceremony is based on a traditional Polynesian welcoming of the night and features authentic fire-knife dancing, chants, and drumming. The **Electrical Water Pageant** floats past the Polynesian each night at 9pm.

Seven shops in and around the Great Ceremonial House offer everything from resortwear (for both men and women), swimwear, and accessories to character and logo merchandise, snacks, sundries, newspapers, liquor, wine, and beer.

GRAND FLORIDIAN RESORT & SPA
$349-870
4401 Grand Floridian Way., LBV, 407/824-3000
Room Quality: A   Amenities: A+
Food: A+   Value: C

This gorgeous Victorian hotel is the opulent, showy crown jewel of the Disney hotel empire. Modeled after seaside resorts like the one Walt Disney's father ran in Daytona Beach around the turn of the 20th century, the Grand Floridian is steeped in luxury – from the pampering at the hotel's spa, to the area's only Five Diamond restaurant – from the moment you walk into the open, ornate, extravagant, 15,000-square foot Grand Lobby. While this is a more adult-oriented hotel than the other choices on the monorail, it features some of the most family-friendly activities, like the **Wonderland Tea Party** afternoon character tea party (130pm weekdays only), with cupcakes, lunch, storytelling, bouquet-making, and characters from Alice in Wonderland. The **Grand Adventures in Cooking** program lets kids get creative with chef's hats and aprons and read a story, then share their creations. Best of all is the **Pirate Adventure**, where children don bandanas and follow clues to search for treasure in the various resort marinas. Each program is $28.17 plus tax. The **Mouseketeer Club** gives kids supervised access to video games, movies, games, arts and crafts, and dinner for $10 an hour during the evening.

The lushly appointed 400 square foot rooms accommodate five, between two queen size beds and a sleeper sofa. Decorated features light oak armoires and furnishings, Victorian woodwork, ceiling fans, and marble-topped sinks. The walls are painted in delicate green and salmon. Most rooms have terraces, and each room also has a private pantry with sundries available for a fee.

The hotel's feature restaurant is the formal **Victoria & Albert's**, which has won numerous awards, including its fifth consecutive AAA Five Diamond award. In 2005 it was one of only 57 restaurants in North America to earn this distinction. This $95 prix fixe experience features seven courses of modern American cuisine, fine crystal, china, and silver, an extensive wine list, and an incredibly intimate setting. **Citrico's** features signature aperitifs and innovative Mediterranean-flavored dishes featuring ingredients from the sea, field, wood, and sky. **Narcoosee's** is the other top-notch restaurant here. Located on the fringe of the sugar-sand beach, the open-air kitchen churns out a seafood-centric menu with French and continental touches. **1900 Park Fare** offers a character breakfast starring Mary Poppins, plus a bountiful dinner buffet featuring Cinderella. The **Grand Floridian Café** offers casual dining for breakfast, lunch, and dinner, while the 24-hour **Gasparilla Grill** offers take-out self-service light meals and quick snacks.

The **Garden View Lounge**, in addition to being a pleasant watering hole, has a traditional afternoon tea with crumpets, scones, sandwiches, pastries, rich English desserts, fruits, and cheeses. Reservations are recommended.

Mizner's Lounge is a more bustling setting for a beverage, and the **Summerhouse** addresses dry mouths by the pool.

Unlike many of the other resorts here, the pièce de résistance of the Grand Floridian's recreation isn't a pool – it's the hotel's full-service health club and spa, which features massage therapy, skin care, hydrotherapy, body, hand, and foot treatments, and spa packages for individuals, couples, or families. There's also a new 5,000-square foot feature pool and a powder-sand beach on Seven Seas Lagoon, plus two clay tennis courts. The hotel's amenities are rounded out by six shops, a business center, and a barber/beauty shop. The Grand Floridian's guests can watch the **Electrical Water Pageant** each night at 9:15.

CONTEMPORARY RESORT
$244-695
4600 N. World Dr., LBV, 407/824-1000
Room Quality: B+   Amenities: A
Food: A   Value: B

Whoosh. The monorail trains gliding in and out of the aptly-named Grand Canyon Concourse at this sleek A-frame resort don't transport you to the future – they transport you to the Magic Kingdom, literally right next door. But the fact that the trains stop in the lobby certainly adds to the faux futuristic feel of the place. Much like those at MK's Tomorrowland, the recent renovations here have made this a much warmer atmosphere, more tongue-in-cheek futuristic, more subdued and soft than before, when people criticized the hotel for being stark and overly minimal. In 2005, the bright, bold future-past color scheme will be updated to black and white with muted color accents, and designer bedding and flat-screen TVs will be introduced.

Be sure to peep Mary Blair's 90-foot-high mural at the Grand Canyon Concourse. The floor-to-ceiling mosaic contains over 18,000 hand-painted tiles. The designs, inspired by Southwestern native American art, includes families, flowers, trees, and a five-legged goat.

The rooms, Disney's largest at 422 square feet, accommodate five and are split into two types: Tower rooms, which are located in the main building and bear the more striking views of the Magic Kingdom (complete with fireworks!); and Garden rooms, which are quieter and more relaxed. As for the views – some of the Garden rooms are right up close to the edge of beautiful Bay Lake, so unless you're given a parking lot view, you're golden. All the rooms have a day bed plus either a king or two queen beds. The bathrooms are large too, and nicely laid out. They each contain double sinks, a bathtub with a shower head, or a bathtub with a separate shower stall.

Dining at the Contemporary is a particular treat, most notably at the **California Grill**. Located on the 15th floor of the resort, the Grill has a dynamic menu that draws influences both from the eponymous Golden State, and the Pacific. **Chef Mickey's** features character buffets featuring Mickey himself at breakfast and dinner. Chef Mickey's is one of the best character breakfasts in WDW. The **Concourse Steakhouse** features breakfast staples; salads, burgers, and sandwiches at lunch; and steaks, ribs, and seafood at dinner. Coffee and accessories can be enjoyed at **Contemporary Grounds**, while snacks and quick meals can be enjoyed 24 hours a day at the **Food & Fun Center**. By the marina, the **Sand Bar & Grill** serves up snacks, sandwiches, and beverages. Thirsty? Make your way to the **Outer Rim** cocktail lounge, which boasts a stunning view of Bay Lake.

Good times aren't hard to come by here. The Contemporary boasts two swimming pools, a playground, hot tubs, a Bay Lake beach with volleyball courts, boat rentals, basketball hoops, waterskiing and parasailing through Sammy Duvall's Water Sports Centre, fishing excursions, a complete fitness center chock full of goodies, a massive 24-hour arcade that can be similarly described, and last but not least, six lighted clay tennis courts. The Contemporary's amenities also include six shops, including a Pin Trading Station. Catch the **Electrical Water Pageant** each night at 10:05 pm.

BOARDWALK RESORT & VILLAS
$294-690/$294-1,040
2101 Epcot Resort Blvd., LBV, 407/939-5100
Room Quality: A-   Amenities: A
Food: A+   Value: B-

Another one of the deluxe "Epcot resorts" surrounding Crescent Lake, the Boardwalk is a bustling place – a multi-use facility that includes a full-service hotel, Disney Vacation Club villa accommodations, and an eponymous waterfront strip of bars, restaurants, shops, and activities for the whole family. The look and feel evoke images of Asbury Park, New Jersey in its heyday. The atmosphere is comfortable, charming, and relaxed, with excellent public facilities and guestrooms.

The 378 rooms of the Inn proper feature two queen-sized or one king-sized bed plus a day bed, cherrywood furniture, ceiling fan, double vanities, and marble bathrooms. At 390 square feet, the rooms are spacious indeed. If that's not room enough for you, consider one of the 383 Boardwalk Villas:

•Studios that sleep four adults, measuring 359 square feet, including microwave, toaster, wet bar, refrigerator, and coffeemaker ($305-475);

•Studios that include a five-foot day bed allowing one additional child in the room;

•One-bedroom villas that sleep four adults, measuring 712 square feet, with a king sized bed, whirlpool tub, toaster, blender, pots and pans, DVD player, washer and dryer, and a private porch ($410-605);

•Two-bedroom villas measuring 1,071 square feet, sleeping up to eight in one king, two queens, and a queen sleeper sofa, with all the amenities of a one-bedroom villa, with extra space ($575-1,070); and

•Three-bedroom, three-bath Grand Villas measuring 2,142 square feet with private balconies, accommodating up to twelve adults ($1,395-2,020)

Villa guests who don't want to deal with the bustle and noise of the public areas of the boardwalk should request a Standard View, not a Water View room.

While there are no restaurants in the hotel itself, there are several great choices elsewhere in the Boardwalk complex. Tops are **Spoodle's**, featuring tapas cuisine, the open-kitchened **Flying Fish Cafe**, and the **Big River Grille and Brewing Works**, WDW's only brew pub. The **ESPN Club** offers a full range of unassuming American food and classic bar fare. For snacks, visit the **Boardwalk Bakery** or **Seashore Sweets**, or one of the many specialty food stands along the promenade.

The **Bellevue Room** is a lounge offering butler service in the main lobby of the Inn and on an outdoor balcony overlooking Crescent Lake. There is also a pool bar, **Leaping Horse Libations**.

The themed swimming area here is called **Luna Park**, themed after a turn of the century carnival, and features a Jacuzzi and a 200-foot water slide called Keister Coaster. There are two smaller pools as well, plus a playground called the Luna Park Crazy House. The **Muscles and Bustles Health Club** features Cybex weightlifting equipment, dumbbells, cardiovascular equipment, and massage services. Other activities available include tennis, volleyball, croquet, surrey bike rentals, and jogging.

There are daily activities for kids, like face painting, sand art, water balloon tosses, and fishing trips. Some of these require a fee, and the lineup changes frequently. There is one sundry shop at the resort, and three more shops on the Boardwalk.

OLD KEY WEST RESORT
$269-1,545
1510 N. Cove Rd., LBV, 407/827-7700
Room Quality: A+   Amenities: B+
Food: B   Value: B

The first WDW resort designed specifically for Disney Vacation Club travelers, this casual Floridian resort features some of the most spacious accommodations on the property, from studios to three-bedroom Grand Villas. Possibly due to the age of the property, the Old Key West offers lower rates than similar accommodations elsewhere in Disney. This resort is located near Downtown Disney and offers transportation there via pleasant pontoon boats.

The exteriors of the buildings are done in grays and pastel greens, with tin roofs, back porches, gazebos, gingerbread, and latticework abounding. Its architecture is somewhat reminiscent of the Yacht Club Resort. The one, two, and three-bedroom vacation homes are all decorated in a whimsical Key West motif, pinks and light greens dominating the color schemes here, the furniture bleached wood. amenities of the units include ceiling fans, full kitchens (including microwave oven, china, flatware, and cookware), TVs with VCR, hardwood floors, whirlpool tubs in the master suite, and full-sized washers and dryers. Windows are large and take advantage of the environment: each room has a view of either the forest, water, or golf course. Accomodation options include:

•Studios that sleep four adults, measuring 376 square feet, including a kitchenette with fridge, toaster, microwave, coffeemaker, and bar sink ($269-389);

•One-bedroom villas that sleep four adults, measuring 1,016 square feet, with a king sized bed, fully equipped kitchen, whirlpool tub, a laundry room, a large great room, very spacious bathrooms, and a private porch ($360-540);

•Two-bedroom villas measuring 1,322 square feet, sleeping up to eight in one king, two queens, and a queen sleeper sofa, with all the amenities of a one-bedroom villa, with extra space ($500-825); and

•Three-bedroom, three-bath, two-story Grand Villas measuring 2,265 square feet with private balconies, accommodating up to twelve adults ($1,100-1,545)

The hotel's one restaurant, **Olivia's Café**, features dining indoors and outdoors on a terrace and offers Key West specialties like conch fritters, homemade French fries, and Key Lime white chocolate mousse. The cuisine here is seasoned with spices straight from the restaurant's herb garden. There's a character breakfast three days a week. The poolside snack bar **Good's Food to Go** offers the usual lineup of fast food plus the house specialty, conch fritters. The **Turtle Shack** lounge offers pina coladas, daquiris, sandwiches, salads, and hot dogs. Overlooking the island-themed swimming area is the **Gurgling Suitcase**, an open-air bar serving a variety of mixed drinks, beer, and wine.

The resort's focal point is a unique facility called the **Clubhouse**, themed after a Key West retreat, with hardwood floors, historical photos, and Papa's Den: a comfortable reading room with bookshelves filled with the works of authors who once inhabited Key West. There's four pools here including an island-themed feature pool. Two tennis courts are available for use. **Slappy Joe's** is a health club complete with massage, free weights, exercise equipment, and sauna. Bicycles and boats can be rented as well. Other amenities include volleyball, shuffleboard, and two arcades. Daily children's activities are also offered and can vary, so ask upon check-in what's scheduled for your visit.

WDW SWAN

$339-454
1500 Epcot Resorts Blvd., LBV, 407/934-8000
Room Quality: A+   Amenities: B
Food: B+   Value: C+

The Westin-operated, convention-friendly Swan provides an appealing blend of convenience, resort amenities, fine dining, and luxurious accommodations, located right between Epcot's International Gateway entrance and the Disney-MGM Studios. A recently completed $75 million renovation here has added a touch more class to the décor and a lot more comfort to the rooms. Those familiar with the Westin chain of hotels know what sort of opulence and pampering to expect from them, but let me drop a little science for the rest of you.

If you're one of those finicky sleep types who needs to be pampered like the princess and the pea to get a good night's sleep, this hotel's beds will suit your taste like the third bowl of porridge. (Apologies for the mixed metaphor.) Westin's "Heavenly Beds" feature duvets, comforters, five pillows, and pillow-top mattresses and thread counts as high as 250. Original artwork, slate foyers, 27" televisions, great reading lighting, two-line speakerphones, and nightly turndown service set these rooms a cut above most of the others on site. Though rack rates here are severely overpriced here and at the Dolphin, discounts of up to 50% are readily available for AAA or AARP members, Government employees, teachers, nurses, or Disney annual passholders and via corporate rates, Entertainment books, and even on Priceline – searching for a 4-star hotel in Lake Buena Vista gives you a shot at a room at the Dolphin or Swan.

Note that rates do not include a $10 per day resort fee, which gives you access to the health club, daily newspaper delivery, use of the in-room coffeemaker, and up to 60 minutes of local, credit card, or toll free phone calls.

Like its adjacent sister property, the Dolphin, this hotel's mascots are perched 12 stories up, atop the building – 45 feet high, a pair of 14-ton swans. Decorated in coral, peach, and aqua, it's certainly eye-catching. Inside, the common areas have almost a Carnivàle feel.

Several special programs make kids feel right at home, like the Kid's Passport, which encourages youngsters to collect stamps from various locations across the hotel; a TV channel dedicated to bedtime stories, and **Camp Dolphin**, in the Swan's sister hotel, which includes a supervised environment for kids to enjoy dinner, video games, arts and crafts, and Disney movies.

Palio's is the premier dining experience here. This Italian bistro features wood-burning pizza ovens, ambitious entrees, phenomenal desserts, and strolling musicians. The **Garden Grove Café** offers a character breakfast buffet on Sundays as well as lunch and dinner and the self-proclaimed "most sinful pastries in town." **Gulliver's Grill** offers steak and seafood at dinner. **Kimono's** offers sushi, sake, and karaoke. The **Splash Grill** offers light snack fare at poolside. **Swan's Lobby Court** is the spot for an aperitif or dessert.

In addition to the eight tennis courts and 3-acre grotto pool shared with the Dolphin, the Swan's facilities include a quieter pool, boat rentals, volleyball, basketball, a small health club, and a gameroom. The Swan has two shops as well.

WDW DOLPHIN

$339-454
1500 Epcot Resorts Blvd., LBV, 407/934-4000

Room Quality: B	Amenities: B+
Food: A	Value: C

An odd jurisdictional juxtaposition, the convention-magnet Dolphin is located along the shores of Crescent Lake, within sight of Epcot and Disney-MGM (with boat transit to both), but is owned and operated by Starwood. It provides many of the deluxe amenities and perks of the Disney-owned-and-operated resorts, but has a distinctly different feel. It's got a pervasive tropical motif, but not quite enough to call it a themed hotel in the sense of the Polynesian, Beach Club, etc. Admittedly it's one of the more garish hotels in a town full of them, but a recent $75 million renovation project brought back original architect Michael Graves to upgrade and update the rooms and public facilities here and at the Swan.

The hotel is a landmark – the tallest resort on Disney property, with a soaring 27-story main building flanked by 55-foot dolphin statues. The grounds are lovely, with lush landscaping, grotto pools, and the shimmering Crescent Lake. The rooms are bright and cheerful, with spacious bathrooms and separate vanities, but note that they include two double beds, not two queens like elsewhere in Disney. The same remarks about available discounts and resort fees in the Swan section above also apply to the Dolphin.

Between the Swan and Dolphin, there's a whopping 17 lounges and restaurants. On this side of the complex are the elegant and eponymously basic **Shula's Steakhouse**, the convenient and tasty buffet-service **Fresh Mediterranean Market**, the 24-hour **Tubbi's Buffeteria**, the '50's diner knockoff **Dolphin Fountain**, and the poolside snack bar, **Cabana Bar & Grill**. In early 2004, renowned seafood chef **Todd English's bluezoo** opened, offering imaginative appetizers and breathtaking composed plates, as well as simply grilled, flavorfully sauced fresh fish. Prime venues for sipping include **Copa Banana's** and the **Lobby Lounge**.

Recreational opportunities abound at this hotel, including the striking grotto pool shared with the Swan, two quieter lap pools, eight tennis courts lit for night play, billiards, and a health club. The Dolphin also boasts four shops and **Camp Dolphin**, a supervised children's activity center where kids can enjoy video games, arts and crafts, and Disney movies while their parents can enjoy some blessed quiet.

SARATOGA SPRINGS RESORT & SPA
$269-1,545
1960 Broadway, LBV, 407/827-1100
Room Quality: A+   Amenities: B+
Food: C+   Value: B-

The first phase of Saratoga Springs opened in May 2004, and will total 828 units when completed in 2007, making it Disney's largest Vacation Club resort. With a "health, history, horses" theme and décor inspired by summer retreats like the eponymous upstate New York getaway, Saratoga Springs is comprised of 12 buildings on the site of the former Disney Institute and before that the Disney Village Resort.

A ten-minute walk from the excitement of Downtown Disney, Saratoga Springs offers sumptuous relaxation options at its full-service spa, options like massage therapies, hydro massage, body treatments, facials, hand and foot treatments, and special programs for kids and couples.

Lodging options are similar to the other Disney Vacation Club resorts:

•Studios that sleep four adults, measuring 355 square feet, including a refrigerator, microwave, and coffeemaker ($269-389);

•One-bedroom villas that sleep four adults, measuring 714 square feet, with a king sized bed, fully equipped kitchen, whirlpool tub, a washer and drier, and a private porch ($360-540);

•Two-bedroom villas measuring 1,075 square feet, sleeping up to eight in one king, two queens, and a queen sleeper sofa, with all the amenities of a one-bedroom villa, with extra space ($500-825); and

•Three-bedroom, three-bath, two-story Grand Villas measuring 2,113 square feet, accommodating up to twelve adults ($1,100-1,545)

The resort's one restaurant/shop is **Artist's Palette**, offering counter-service dining options like pizza, sandwiches, and family-size entrees as well as sundries, resortwear, character merchandise, and groceries. Libations can be found at the classy **Turf Club**, offering billiards and sports on the large-screen television; and at **On the Rocks**, at the complex's feature pool. Several quiet pools are also available.

That pool complex, High Rock Spring features a themed children's area, a waterslide, and impressive rock formations, as well as zero-depth entry and a whirlpool. There's also the **Win, Place, or Show** arcade, bike rentals, tennis courts, basketball, and shuffleboard. Ferry transportation to the Downtown Disney Marketplace and West Side is available, boats leave every hour on the half hour.

FORT WILDERNESS RESORT & CAMPGROUND
$234-339/$38-89
4510 N. Fort Wilderness Dr., LBV, 407/824-2900
Room Quality: B+*   Amenities: A+
Food: C   Value: A-

Fort Wilderness is the only campground accommodation available inside Walt Disney World, and as such has a very focused and particular appeal. In addition to campsite hookups, though, Fort Wilderness also consists of 407 spacious and well-equipped Wilderness Cabins that sleep six, offering families a real alternative to cramping into a standard hotel room. Boasting the best array of recreational activities in all of WDW, Fort Wilderness is a lovely natural enclave that's a short boat ride away from the gates of the Magic Kingdom. However, transportation to the other theme parks is a little more time-consuming, as they require a transfer from one of the three internal loop buses. Keep the increased commuting time in mind if you do decide to stay here.

The 788 campsites here are 25-foot high back-ins that combine a paved driveway and a sandy portion, and come with a picnic table, charcoal grill, electricity, and city water. Most of the sites have sewer hookups as well. Preferred campsites also include a cable TV hookup (and better location). Fifteen air-conditioned and controlled-access comfort stations provide showers, restrooms, laundry rooms, phones, and ice machines.

The attractive log-sided Wilderness Cabins measure about 12' by 42' and include a full bathroom, double bed, two bunk beds, and a Pullman, fully equipped kitchen, two TVs and a VCR, a dining table seating six, and a wood deck. Some of the furniture is themed to look like it's been carved from branches and logs.

There's not a lot of emphasis on dining here – you can cook your own using groceries from either the **Meadow** or **Settlement Trading Posts**. Crockett's Tavern offers pizza, quesadillas, and other simple snacks. **Trail's End** provides all-you-can-eat breakfast, lunch, and dinner. The **Hoop-Dee-Doo Revue** dinner show is also located here, and on certain nights the Fort Wilderness Pavilion hosts **Mickey's Backyard BBQ** character dinner buffet featuring a live country band and line dance instructors.

There's practically no end to the things you can do here. Swim in one of two pools. Play tennis. Go fishing on your own on the canals, or take a 2-hour excursion (there's even a weekend fishing program just for kids). Play volleyball, basketball, tetherball, shuffleboard, and horseshoes. Hike along Swamp Trail or sweat along the exercise trail. Rent bikes and boats and enjoy watersports like parasailing, waterskiing, and wakeboarding. Nightly wagon rides are offered, and depending on Magic Kingdom hours, sometimes Fireworks wagon Rides are available. Visit the petting farm and the Tri-Circle D Ranch. Ride a pony or a private carriage. There's also a nightly campfire program featuring movies, characters, and the **Electrical Water Pageant** floating past at 9:45pm. Oh yeah, and if you get bored with all of that, there's always the Magic something-or-other.

Shades of Green

Opened in 1971 as the Golf Resort and later rechristened the Disney Inn, Shades of Green is a resort leased by the Department of Defense for the use of vacationing active and retired military personnel as well as DoD civilians and U.S. public health officers. Shades of Green offers cheap rates ($72-114 for rooms, depending on rank/grade, $200-$225 for suites), Disney World's most spacious accommodations (480 square feet), and resort amenities, with most of the perks of being an onsite Disney guest (except for room charge privileges). For more information on Shades of Green, visit their website (shadesofgreen.org) or call 888/593-2242.

Disney's Moderate Resorts

Disney's Moderate Resorts offer essential amenities like full-service dining, pizza delivery, boat rentals, and pools with slides and whirlpools. Transportation to the theme parks is by bus, but those in the Downtown Disney area offer transportation to the Marketplace and West Side by boats.

PORT ORLEANS RESORT – FRENCH QUARTER
$139-215
2201 Orleans Dr., LBV, 407/934-5000

Room Quality: B	Amenities: B-
Food: C+	Value: B-

The charm and romance of New Orleans' more genteel side is brought to life in this moderate-priced resort in the Downtown Disney area, with wrought-iron railings, plantings, flower-lined boulevards, and murals creating a PG Mardi Gras kind of vibe. At the check-in area, designed to resemble a 1900-era mint, cast members check in guests from behind bank teller windows.

Renovated in 2004, the rooms, measure 314 square feet and accommodate up to four adults in either a double-double or king configuration. Each room now has a small refrigerator. This is an excellent mid-priced choice for couples – the grounds of the hotel are lovely, making this one of WDW's most romantic hotels. For extra romance, take an evening carriage ride through the two Port Orleans resorts. The 30-minute rides cost $30, and each carriage can accommodate four.

There's only one place to eat at the Port Orleans – the **Sassagoula Floatworks and Food Factory**, a 300-seat food court featuring burgers, pizza, salads, soups, and entrees. Room delivery of pizza is available. You can grab a beverage at **Scat Cat's Club** adjacent to the Floatworks, or at **Mardi Grogs** poolside.

The French Quarter's pool, **Doubloon Lagoon**, is a landmark. Check out Scales, the serpent whose tongue serves as a waterslide. Jazz-loving alligators haunt nearby. By virtue of the hotel's waterfront location, you can rent boats at Port Orleans Landing here. There's also a game room, croquet, bike rentals, cane pole fishing, and two-hour excursions, and one large shop.

PORT ORLEANS RESORT - RIVERSIDE
$134-215
1251 Dixie Dr., LBV, 407/934-6000

Room Quality: B	Amenities: B-
Food: B-	Value: B-

The former Dixie Landings Resort winds around the Sassagoula River, recalling the Mississippi bayou with structures and guestrooms designed in two distinct styles, the rugged Bayou and the dignified and stately Plantation. Both are aesthetic and attractive, and this resort provides easy boat, bus, or driving access to the wealth of activities, restaurants, and shops available at Downtown Disney.

The 314-square-foot rooms in the two sections differ most in terms of decor. Everything from the carpeting to the beds to the ceiling fans has its own specific flavor. Antebellum-style Plantation rooms are found in elegant estate homes with cream-colored siding and pale grey-shingled roofs. Brick chimneys, elaborate balconies and porches, and hanging flowers accentuate the genteel Southern feel. Bayou buildings are rugged and scruffy with tin roofs and weathered wood siding offering a sharp foil to the Plantation. Furnishings here include wood and tin armoires and tin lamps. The bedposts are textured and colored like logs. Bayou rooms can sleep an additional child under 9.

The hotel's full-service eatery, **Boatwright's Dining Hall**, features Cajun specialties and Southern dishes. The 480-seat food court, the **Captain's Cotton Mill**, offers Mexican food, burgers, sandwiches, pizza, pasta, baked goods, and ice cream. The **River Roost Lounge** is modeled after a cotton exchange and serves specialty drinks and appetizers. Next to the pool at Ol' Man Island is the **Muddy Rivers** bar. Carriage rides leave from Boatwright's from 6 to 930pm.

Ol' Man Island is the themed pool area here, but so much more – it also includes a spa, wading pool, playground, and a stocked fishing hole. Jogging trails, bike and boat rentals, and an arcade round out the recreational offerings. There is one shop here.

CARIBBEAN BEACH RESORT
$139-215
900 Cayman Way, LBV, 407/934-3400
Room Quality: B   Amenities: B-
Food: B-   Value: B-

Disney's first moderately-priced resort, the Caribbean Beach has become one of its best-loved. 2,112 rooms are split between six villages all situated around a 42-acre lake, Barefoot Bay. Each village is painted in a different set of pastels and named after a Caribbean island. This is a very large resort and your room may be some distance from the main guest areas. There is an internal bus route here.

The oak-furnished rooms here measure 340 square feet, larger than those at the other moderate resorts, and include spacious bathrooms. All of the rooms were renovated over the last couple of years, with the hotel's dining facilities refurbished and upgraded in 2002.

Old Port Royale is the focal point of the resort's activities and amenities, hosting the Asian- and island-influenced **Shutters** restaurant and the 500-seat **Old Port Royale** food court, which sells burgers, pizza, pasta, broiled meats, and pre-packaged sandwiches, salads, and drinks, plus the Straw Market Fruit Cart. Shutters offers a full bar, and the **Banana Cabana** offers drinks and snacks at poolside.

The Caribbean Beach boasts seven pools on its grounds, most prominently the feature pool at Old Port Royale, which includes a whirlpool, a wading pool, and fantastic décor that recalls a pirate stronghold. Each village has its own pool and a stretch of white sand along Barefoot Bay. There is also a gameroom, 1.2 mile jogging trail, and an array of boats and bikes for hire. There are also two gift shops.

CORONADO SPRINGS RESORT

$139-215
1000 W. Buena Vista Dr., LBV, 407/939-1000
Room Quality: B-   Amenities: B
Food: B-   Value: C+

Disney's newest moderate resort, the Coronado Springs, opened in 1997 with a 95,000 square foot convention center attached, making this the first Disney resort specifically built with conventioneers in mind. That being said, it still has all of the theming, amenities, and general bells and whistles of the other moderate resorts. However, this resort tends to get lower marks – both from Disney vacationers and business travelers who find it inconvenient and too spread out for its own good.

The resort is inspired by the travels of Francisco de Coronado, between the American southwest and northern Mexico. The rooms are split into three distinct clusters: Casitas, representing urban areas of the Southwest with festive plazas and fountains; Ranchos, recalling rural areas, with a Mission-style country ranch feel and rocky streams; and brightly colored, tropically themed Cabanas. The rooms are equally equipped, with two double beds or one king sized bed, and the rooms measure 314 square feet.

The **Maya Grill** features a menu from the same people responsible for Epcot's delicious San Angel Inn, with a wood-fired grill and a wine list including vintages from Chile, Argentina, and Mexico. The **Pepper Market** food court includes American cuisine, Tex-Mex, Asian stir-fry, and baked goods in a festive environment where guests and chefs interact. **Francisco's** is a 200-seat lounge offering hors d'oeuvres, snacks, and regional specialties, including a ceviche bar and more tequila than spring break. **Siesta's** is the Coronado Springs pool bar.

There are four pools here, three quiet ones scattered throughout the grounds, and the 272,000 gallon **Dig Site** pool, doubling as an archaeological dig site. The complex includes a 46-foot Mayan pyramid, the Explorer's Playground, a 123-foot water slide, a kiddie pool, and a 22-person jacuzzi, the largest outdoor spa on Disney property. There's also the 3,000-foot **La Vida** health club, a .9 mile walking/jogging trail, a nature trail, surrounding Lago Dorado, an arcade, rental boats, and beach volleyball. There is a 6,000 square foot gift shop and a convenience store here.

Disney's Value Resorts

Disney's Value resorts are large, motel-like complexes with themed pools, pizza delivery, and food courts. Transportation to other resort areas is by bus only, and these resorts tend to be a little more remote, thus requiring a little more time to get to most of the parks.

ALL-STAR SPORTS, MUSIC, MOVIES RESORTS
$79-137
Movies: 1991 W. Buena Vista Dr., LBV, 407/939-7000
Music: 1801 W. Buena Vista Dr., LBV, 407/939-6000
Sports: 1701 W. Buena Vista Dr., LBV, 407/939-5000
Room Quality: C+   Amenities: C
Food: C+   Value: B

These three resorts marked an intriguing concept for Disney. They spun them as paying homage to sports, movie, and music legends. Sounds like a fun theme for a resort. It's just too bad that the execution is so humdrum. For the first time, Disney has created an utterly ordinary hotel product. It will appeal to younger kids, and families on a tight budget, but unless that's you, move on. One common complaint about the All-Star resorts is that the bus service is not as efficient or quick as at other resorts.

The complexes are garishly painted in bright and neon colors and adorned with gigantic icons representing the names of the buildings, like 38-foot surfboards along the side of "Surf's Up," a size 270 cowboy boot on the side of the "Country Fair," and a 35-foot Buzz Lightyear on the "Toy Story" building. Other themes include baseball, basketball, football, and tennis at Sports, calypso, Broadway, rock, and jazz at Music, and 101 Dalmatians, Mighty Ducks, Herbie the Love Bug, and Fantasia at Movies. Other than the icons and the coat of paint on the walls, these three hotels are identical.

The brightly colored rooms are the smallest of the Disney empire, measuring 260 square feet, and are decorated like children's bedrooms. Note that the rooms nearest the pools or the resort activity centers are generally the loudest. Each resort has a food court with bakery, grill, pizza and pasta, market, and barbecue stands; as well as a poolside bar. Each hotel has two custom-shaped swimming pools, an arcade, and a gift shop.

POP CENTURY RESORT
$79-137
1701 W. Buena Vista Dr., LBV, 407/939-5000
Room Quality: B-   Amenities: C+
Food: C+   Value: B+

For a while this seemed like a tawdry albatross around Disney's neck – thanks to post-911 tourism slowdowns and the recession, Disney temporarily halted construction on this laughable 5,760-room value resort concept, with oversized icons representing each decade of the 20th century, so as you drove down the main access road, you saw the blight of large, empty buildings with 60s and 70s catch-phrases plastered all over them.

Disney eventually opened the first half of this 177-acre resort in December 2003. It seems that they have listened to some of the complaints that people had about the All-Star Movies, Music, and Sports Resorts, although this resort is often derided in comparison to the other Disney resorts and Comfort Inn-level hotels they seem to be assimilating. The 260 square foot rooms do have a 27-inch television, which is a step up from the All-Stars.

The Pop Century has a food court, **Everything Pop**, selling grilled foods, Asian fare, pizza, pasta, and baked goods; a bar called **Classic Concoctions**, and the **Petals Pool Bar**. The resort has three feature pools, the **Bowling Pin Pool, Hippy Dippy Pool**, and the **Computer Pool**. There is also a Goofy-themed playground.

Downtown Disney Hotels

The Downtown Disney Resort Area, also known as the Hotel Plaza, is a tree-lined boulevard surrounded by the seven Official Hotels of Walt Disney World, on-site but operated by others. These hotels share several key benefits with the Disney-owned-and-operated places, such as complimentary bus transportation, advance tee times, advance reservations at restaurants and dinner shows, and exclusive discounts and savings. Visit www.downtowndisneyhotels.com for details.

Compared to the Disney-owned hotels, you'll get more for your money here, plus an unbeatable location in the middle of Downtown Disney's excitement, just off I-4 and the myriad of shops and restaurants in

Lake Buena Vista. What you won't get are the elaborate themes, attention to detail, and Disney magic.

HILTON IN THE WDW RESORT

$134-279
1751 Hotel Plaza Blvd., LBV, 407/824-4000 or 800/774-1500
Room Quality: A+   Amenities: B+
Food: B+   Value: B
www.hilton.com

This 814-room hotel, winner of the AAA Four Diamond Award, underwent a $25 million renovation in 2004. It occupies 23 acres directly across the street from Downtown Disney Marketplace. Convenient, luxurious, and pleasant, this hotel includes nine restaurants and lounges and plenty of cool stuff to keep you occupied. The Hilton's rooms are loaded with amenities. In addition to the standard stuff, each hotel room offers a coffeemaker, two phone lines, high-speed Internet access (included in the optional $9 daily resort fee), video games, and a trouser press and iron. Some add CD and DVD players. You can even have a treadmill delivered to your room.

The Hilton offers 24-hour room service and eight restaurants, including **Benihana,** the famous Japanese steakhouse. **Finn's Grill** serves steak and seafood nightly along with specialty drinks in a Key West atmosphere, while **Covington Mill** combines New England ambiance and family fare, with a character breakfast on Sundays. The **Main Street Market** includes a deli with Boar's Head meats and Ben & Jerry's ice cream. There are also three specialty bars, two pools with whirlpool, fitness center (included in resort fee), arcade, volleyball, jogging trail, and billiards. Wireless Internet access is available in most public areas of the hotel. The Hilton is the only Downtown Disney "Official" hotel with access to the Extra Magic Hour feature. Discounts are available for AAA members and on the Hilton website.

WYNDHAM PALACE RESORT & SPA

$129-330
1900 Hotel Plaza Blvd., LBV, 407/827-2727 or 800/327-2990
Room Quality: A   Amenities: A+
Food: A   Value: B
www.wyndhampalace.com

The largest Downtown Disney hotel is also the most convenient hotel to Downtown Disney, just across the street from the Marketplace. The main tower is the highest point in all of WDW. The recently-renovated rooms are found in a 27-story tower and three smaller towers, while the 100 Palace

Suites are located on the recreation island in two five-story structures connected by a seven-story atrium building. The spacious rooms all have patios or balconies, pillowtop mattresses, and Herman Miller Aeron ergonomic chairs (I'm sitting in one now, let me editorialize: Ahhhhhh.). Some of the rooms have amazing views of Downtown Disney and Epcot.

Five restaurants include **Arthur's 27**, a gourmet rooftop restaurant offering artistic presentation and impeccable service along with Continental cuisine and a Gothic wine cellar; and the carnivorous **Outback Restaurant**. On Sundays, there's a character breakfast at the **Watercress Café**. The **Laughing Kookaburra** is a fun bar with 99 brands of beer. The **Top of the Palace Lounge** has an 800-bottle wine list and amazing views. The Palace's amenities include three swimming pools, volleyball, basketball, a 10,000 foot European-style spa, comprehensive fitness center, marina, three tennis courts, an arcade, steam rooms, and saunas. Discounts: AAA, AARP, Government military. Best rate guarantee on www.wyndham.com.

GROSVENOR RESORT
$79-159
1850 Hotel Plaza Blvd., LBV, 407/828-4444 or 800/624-4109
Room Quality: B   Amenities: B
Food: B-   Value: B+
www.grosvenorresort.com

The least expensive of the Hotel Plaza choices, the 19-story Grosvenor is especially family-friendly thanks to the pervasive Sherlock Holmes theming, in a broader British/colonial setting. The rooms, all of which have been recently redecorated, are nicely laid out with two double beds or a king-sized and a sleeper. The rooms have a slight Bahamas air to their decor, and amenities including a coffeemaker, high-speed Internet access, and refrigerators.

Restaurants include **Baskerville's**, a casual restaurant serving breakfast, lunch, and dinner amidst Sherlock swag. In the center of the restaurant is a glassed-in model of the parlor of 221B Baker Street. There's a character breakfast here three days a week. Friday nights feature live jazz and all-you-can-eat seafood. Every Saturday night, this restaurant hosts Murderwatch Mystery Theatre, a murder mystery dinner featuring prime rib and professional actors. Named for Holmes' nemesis, **Moriarty's Pub** features darts, billiards, and beverages.

For recreation, there's an aquatic center with a windmill-shaped pool, European thermal spa, volleyball, shuffleboard, and a bar, basketball courts, a small gameroom, handball courts, two tennis courts, a playground, volleyball, shuffleboard, racquetball, and horseshoes. Best rate guarantee on www.grosvenorresort.com.

DOUBLETREE GUEST SUITES RESORT

$125-368
2305 Hotel Plaza Blvd., LBV, 407/934-100 or 800/222-TREE
Room Quality: A   Amenities: B+
Food: C+   Value: C+
www.doubletreeguestsuites.com

This hotel, close to I-4 and SR 535, offers two-room, 600 square foot suites that sleep six on two double beds and a pullout sofa. Amenities include custom-designed furniture, two televisions, stocked refrigerators, coffeemakers, microwaves, and high-speed Internet access.

The Doubletree has particular appeal to kids, with warm chocolate chip cookies on check-in, a kids' theater, a gameroom, playground, and swimming pool with Jacuzzi and wader. The Doubletree also offers a pool bar, two tennis courts, an exercise center, and jogging trails.

Streamers offers in-room dining and features a breakfast buffet and regional American cuisine and wines, plus unique desserts. There's also a lounge and shop here. Discounts: AAA, AARP, Government, military.

HOTEL ROYAL PLAZA

$129-219
1905 Hotel Plaza Blvd., LBV, 407/828-2828 or 800/248-7890
Room Quality: B-   Amenities: B-
Food: C+   Value: B
www.hotelroyalplaza.com

With only 396 freshly renovated rooms in its tower and two extensions, this is the smallest hotel on the block, but it seems to buzz with energy, appealing to young adults, older children, and teenagers.

Pleasant rooms feature light wood furnishings, Roman tubs (some with whirlpools), and coffeemaker. The art-deco **Giraffe Diner** features a daily breakfast buffet and traditional American fare, there's also a deli and bar. Recreation options include a fitness center with saunas and a hot tub, shuffleboard, four tennis courts, a heated pool, a gameroom, and a salon. Discounts: AAA, AARP, Government, miliary, union, Florida resident.

BEST WESTERN LAKE BUENA VISTA RESORT

$119-399
2000 Hotel Plaza Blvd., LBV, 407/828-2424 or 800/348-3765
Room Quality: C+   Amenities: C
Food: C+   Value: C
www.orlandoresorthotel.com

Probably the plainest of the Downtown Disney hotels, the Best Western's rooms measure 325 square feet, and each room has two queen size beds, a balcony, in-room video games, and a coffeemaker. The hotel has two moderately priced restaurants, a lounge, a pool, playground, and gameroom.

HOLIDAY INN IN THE WALT DISNEY WORLD RESORT
$77-179
1805 Hotel Plaza Blvd., LBV, 407/828-8888 or 800/223-9930
Room Quality: N/A   Amenities: N/A
Food: N/A   Value: N/A
www.holidayinnwdw.com

The former Courtyard by Marriott (and before that, the Howard Johnson) property was severely damaged by 2004's hurricane season, and so Holiday Inn used that as an excuse to spend $6 million to refurbish all of the hotel's rooms and public spaces, essentially replacing everything but the concrete. It reopened in August 2005, too late to be reviewed in this edition.

The 323-room hotel features a 14-story atrium tower, two pools, a gameroom, exercise room, restaurant, deli, and lounge. Rooms offer high-speed Internet access, coffeemaker, in-room Nintendo, and all-day room service. Discounts: AAA, AARP, Entertainment card, Government, military. Lowest rate guarantee on www.holidayinnwdw.com.

Universal Orlando Hotels

The Universal Orlando complex is a full-service destination containing three eye-popping, AAA Four Diamond Award winning luxury hotels that easily compete with anything that the Mouse has to offer his sleepover guests. Much like the Universal parks, these hotels definitely seem geared towards an older crowd, but at the same time featuring plenty of activities and amenities for the whole family. Note that discounts for Universal resorts are available for Florida residents and for longer stays during off-peak seasons.

Benefits of Staying at Universal
Like the Disney resorts, Universal makes it worth your while to choose one of their resorts as your base of operations, and several of these value-added benefits are actually much more substantial than Disney's.
•Universal Express access everywhere, the whole day – simply show your room key. This is about the best perk anyone could possibly imagine to staying at a Universal resort, and Disney has absolutely nothing that compares. You'll save hours of time otherwise spent in line.

•Charge meals and purchases to your room.

•Priority seating at select restaurants.

•Send theme park and Citywalk purchases to your room.

•Early entry hours into theme parks (sometimes, promotionally).

•Complimentary boat or tram transportation to theme parks.

The company that runs the Universal resort hotels, Loews, provides some of the most luxurious accommodations and impeccable service of any national chain. Some of its exlusive services, available at all three Universal resorts, include:

•Loews Loves Kids program: special supervised activities and amenities for those traveling with children, things like special menus, game libraries, tours, welcome gifts, and childproof kits.

•Loews Loves Pets program: amenities and services for people traveling with pets, including dog-walking and pet-sitting, place mats, food and water bowls, toys, treats, and even pet room service!

•Did You Forget? closet with everything from computer accessories and cameras ti dog leashes and raincoats.

•Join the Loews First program before you leave, and reap benefits like a bottle of wine or milk and cookies at check-in, upgrades, late checkout, free fitness center access, and bonus airline miles.

•Valet, laundry and pressing services

•In-room video checkout

PORTOFINO BAY HOTEL
$264-434

5601 Universal Blvd., 407/828-2424 or 800/348-3765

Room Quality: A   Amenities: A-

Food: A+   Value: B-

www.universalorlando.com or www.loewshotels.com

The most aesthetically pleasing hotel in all of central Florida, the AAA Four Diamond rated Portofino Bay Hotel is patterned after the Italian seaside village of Portofino, with amazing attention to detail paid to the décor and architecture. Marble, topiaries, and huge chandeliers welcome you to the lobby, and the back of the hotel overlooks a shimmering bay with gondolas floating gently, moored to the docks. This was the only Orlando hotel named to Travel and Leisure's list of the top 100 hotels in America and Canada. It also made the T&L lists for Top 20 Family Friendly Resorts in America/Canada and Top 500 Hotels in the World (three years running). Condé Nast named the hotel to its Gold List of "World's Best Places to Stay" two years running.

The Portofino offers special services including Curbside Check In, which simplifies the arrival process and makes the obligatory stop at the front desk a thing of the past. Smart Rooms ensure state-of-the-art safety, security, and convenience, from the guest key, which doubles as your resort ID, to automatic temperature adjustment and monitoring of room vacancy to eliminate service-related disturbances. The 435-475 square foot rooms are luxurious, with rich Italian furnishings, custom made duvets and Egyptian cotton linens, a large television with in-room movies and Sony Playstation, two phone lines with data ports, high-speed Internet access, bathrobes, slippers, iron and ironing board, and coffee makers. Villa rooms feature full butler service, complimentary breakfast and evening cocktails, turndown service, in-room fax machine, and CD player. The rooms sleep five in either a king or two queens.

The Portofino Bay has eight restaurants and lounges, including recent addition **Bice Ristorante,** an internationally inspired upscale Italian restaurant with an 80-year tradition and unique dishes that feature local ingredients. Also worth a bite are **Mama Della's** family-style Tuscan restaurant, the family-friendly **Trattoria del Porto,** offering three meals, regional Italian specialties, and great antipasti and desserts. Casual bites can be enjoyed at **Sal's Market Deli, Gelateria Caffé Espresso,** and **Splendido Pizzeria.** Libations can be enjoyed with caviar at the sleek and upscale **Bar American** or with finger food at the casual dockside **Thirsty Fish.**

The signature amenity of the Portofino Bay is the **Mandara Spa,** a full-service spa offering massage, skin care, hair and nail care, steamroom, sauna, and fitness center. Other amenities at the Portofino include three beautiful swimming pools, an arcade, and a spa and fitness center complete with a full service salon, a children's activity center, 3 whirlpools, jogging, and 2 bocce ball courts, upscale shops and boutiques, and an art gallery. The **Campo Portofino** activity area is a supervised kids' haven to give Mom and Dad the opportunity for a night out.

ROYAL PACIFIC RESORT

$199-379 Way, 407/503-3000

Room Quality: A- Amenities: B
Food: A Value: C+
www.universalorlando.com or www.loewshotels.com

This 1,000-room Loews hotel, winner of the AAA Four Diamond Award, is a 1930s-era luxurious island paradise, sitting ashore a beautiful lagoon, complete with 90-foot seaplane. Walk inside and you'll discover lush vegetation and sublime décor, as well as one of the hottest tables in town, hosted by none other than Emeril Lagasse.

The rooms, Universal's smallest at 335 square feet, are accentuated with bamboo and furnished with hand-carved teak pieces, decorated with touches of light, casual island style, with refreshment pantries, separate vanities, coffeemakers, and high-speed Internet access.

Emeril's brand-new **Tchoup Chop** is a phenomenal Asian/Polynesian fusion restaurant, infused with the charismatic chef's distinctive personality and style. The restaurant is just as pleasing to the eyes as to the taste buds too, both in the décor and the presentation of the food. A shot across Disney's bow, the **Wantilan Luau** combines authentic Polynesian music and dancing with an exotic array of food plus unlimited soft drinks, beer, wine, and mai tais. The Wantilan Luau is held on Saturday nights year round and Fridays as well during the summer months.

The **Island Dining Room** offers a breakfast buffet and à la carte menus all day long. At poolside, the **Bula Bar & Grille** offers salads, sandwiches, wraps, and a delicious pressed Cuban. **Jake's American Bar** is an aviator-themed place to grab a drink. The elegant **Orchid Court Lounge** overlooks an indoor orchid garden.. For the sweet tooth, there's a branch of Boston's famous **Emack and Bolio** ice cream parlor.

Recreational activities available at the Royal Pacific include the Lagoon Pool, with an interactive water play area, sandcastle building, volleyball, shuffleboard, and ping pong. The **Green House Spa**, with massages, aromatherapy, facials, and more; and the 5,000 square foot **Gymnasium**, featuring steam, sauna, a complete cardio theater and circuit training equipment. There are also two shops here. Supervised childcare is available at the **Mariner's Club** after 5pm daily.

HARD ROCK HOTEL
$229-349
5800 Universal Blvd., 407/503-2000
Room Quality: A   Amenities: B
Food: B   Value: B
www.universalorlando.com or www.loewshotels.com

Music is the answer at this resort hotel, named a AAA Four Diamond hotel and one of Condé Nast Traveler magazine's 2005 Gold List of "World's Best Places to Stay." The Hard Rock captures all the spirit of the restaurant of the same name, surrounding you with over $1 million worth of memorabilia, and music piped through on audiophile systems. The theme is cemented by 42 intertwined bronze guitars at the entrance plaza's fountain, and even in the rooms themselves. The 365 square foot rooms and suites here (including Kid Suites) are all appointed rock-and-roll style. And we're talking "thematic décor" here, not "Keith Moon stayed here last night." Check out the guest services book, it's got relevant song lyrics printed on the pages for each amenity. A particular perk is the CD audio system in each room.

The Hard Rock's restaurants include the world-renowned **Palm Restaurant**, famous for its prime cuts of beef and Nova Scotia lobster; and the newly redesigned **Kitchen**, featuring a Chef's Table where visiting celebrities cook up their favorites and mount their cooking gear on the "Apron Wall." The **Beach Club** offers grilled food and drinks, nearby **Emack & Bolios** and **Starbucks** peddle their signature goodies.

Named Orlando's best hotel bar in 2002 and 2003, the **Velvet Bar** is stylish and swank, offering the once-monthly **Velvet Sessions** party, an invite-only cocktail party featuring beverage themes and entertainers like A Flock of Seagulls, Animotion, Quiet Riot, and musicians from Red Hot Chili Peppers, Deep Purple, and Twisted Sister. Visit www.velvetsessions.com for your invite.

The trademark amenity here is the themed sand-beach pool with piped-in music, a 260-foot waterslide, and private cabanas. The Hard Rock also has a fitness center, jogging paths, and a Hard Rock store. Parents can get peace and quiet by dropping the kids off at **Camp Lil Rock.**

Top Ten Lake Buena Vista Hotels

These are the ten best hotel choices in Lake Buena Vista:

HYATT REGENCY GRAND CYPRESS
$209-364
One Grand Cypress Blvd., LBV, 407/239-1234
Room Quality: B+   Amenities: A+
Food: A+   Value: B
www.hyattgrandcypress.com

The ultraluxe AAA Four Diamond Award winning Hyatt Regency Grand Cypress has 750 opulent and neatly appointed guestrooms, centered around a heart-stopping atrium complete with free-fly aviary. The 360-square foot rooms come equipped with video games, mini-bar, ceiling fan, and a balcony.

The 1,500-acre resort includes a half-acre grotto pool with two waterslides, three whirlpools, and 12 waterfalls, 45 holes of Jack Nicklaus golf, a golf academy, a racquet club with 12 tennis and 2 racquetball courts, a world-class equestrian center, and a spa featuring massage therapy, a beauty salon, manicures, and pedicures.

The Grand Cypress has several critically acclaimed restaurants, including seafood and steak with a water view at **Hemingway's** and innovative New World cuisine at **La Coquina**, which offers five-course Chef's Table dining four nights a week. The **White Horse Sports Bar** features a gourmet bar menu and sports on DirecTV. For a stellar dining experience, visit the **Black Swan** at the Villas of Grand Cypress, winner of the AAA Four Diamond award for ten consecutive years. Discounts: AAA, Government, senior over 62. Best rate guarantee on www.hyatt.com.

NICKELODEON FAMILY SUITES BY HOLIDAY INN

$117-575
14500 Continental Gateway, LBV, 407/387-5437 or 800/462-6425
Room Quality: A+   Amenities: B+
Food: B+   Value: A+
www.nickhotel.com

One of the best options in Orlando for families, the Nickelodeon Family Suites offers spacious accommodations, two over-the-top pools with more bells and whistles than you could possibly imagine, and unique Nick-themed fun. Suites include 1-bedroom kitchen suites and 2- and 3-bedroom KidSuites themed after Spongebob Squarepants, Jimmy Neutron, the Fairly Oddparents, Rugrats, and more. KidSuites feature multiple televisions, in-room game system, game table, refrigerator, microwave, coffeemaker, and a private bedroom for the grownups. The hotel also offers 1-bedroom kitchen suites with full kitchen including stovetop range and dishwasher; and 1-bedroom "Nick at Nite" suites with a heart-shaped whirlpool tub, dual-head showers, mood lighting, and 50" television with stereo.

Your kids are going to love the two themed pools – the **Lagoon**, a virtual waterpark with a four-story interactive water tower, 400-gallon dump tank, seven water slides and flumes, water jets, and zero-depth entry, climbing nets, miniature golf, and two giant whirlpools; and the **Oasis**, a water play area including an Olympic-sized lap pool, water flumes and slides, two whirlpools, and a sand play area. There's also a 3,000 square foot arcade and the exclusive **Studio Nick**, home to activities like interactive live entertainment to Nickelodeon-inspired games, and a **Kids Spa** offering hair braiding, airbrush tattoos, manicures, and pedicures.

The **NickToons Café** features a character breakfast daily, and as buffet or a la carte selections for dinner. Reservations are recommended, and the character breakfast is open to guests here only. Kids eat free at the **Buffet** restaurant, which is open for lunch and dinner. There's also a food court featuring A&W, Pizza Hut Express, and Barney's Coffee & Tea. Pool bars and snack bars round out the dining options.

ORLANDO WORLD CENTER MARRIOTT

$129-412
8701 World Center Dr., 407/239-4200 or 800/621-0638
Room Quality: B+   Amenities: A+

Food: A+   Value: B
www.marriottworldcenter.com

This AAA Four Diamond resort scores big with 18 holes of golf at **Hawk's Landing**, a luxurious full-service spa including a 4,000 square foot fitness center, massage therapy, body, hair, nail, and skin treatments, four tennis courts, four pools, six whirlpools, volleyball, basketball, six shops, children's activity programs, and a variety of restaurants ranging from casual to upscale, including **Ristoranté Tuscany**, with authentic regional Italian specialties and wines, the classy **Hawk's Landing Steakhouse** overlooking the golf course (two-time Wine Spectator Award winner), and **Mikado,** offering teppanyaki and sushi.

All of the Marriott's rooms include private balconies, Pacific Coast Feather down surround pillows and comforter, high-speed Internet access, mini-bar, and sitting areas complete with a sofabed. Discounts: AAA, Government, senior over 62. Best rate guarantee on www.marriott.com.

CARIBE ROYALE RESORT SUITES
$169-314
8101 World Center Dr., LBV, 407/238-8000 or 800/823-8300
Room Quality: A   Amenities: B+
Food: B+   Value: A-
www.cariberoyale.com

This resort and convention center, located on 45 lushly landscaped acres at the south end of International Drive, opened in 1996 and caters equally to families, business travelers, and leisure travelers; and as such provides an appealing blend of luxury and whimsy suitable for anyone.

One-bedroom suites sleep up to six in rooms with microwave, fridge, coffeemaker, wet bar, video cassette player, and high speed Internet access, and even optional Jacuzzi. Each room also has a full work area fur business travelers. Also available are two-bedroom villas with fully equipped kitchens and screened balconies. Dining options here include the sublime **Venetian Room,** winner of the AAA Four Diamond Award, the casual **Tropicale**, plus two casual eateries and a lounge.

Amenities here include concierge service, complimentary theme park transporation, a complimentary breakfast buffet, night-lit tennis courts, and three pools, including a huge, 250,000 gallon themed feature pool with a 75-foot waterslide. Golfers can take advantage of Caribe Royale's teetime privileges at several area courses.

BUENA VISTA SUITES
$89-159
8203 World Center Drive, LBV, 407/239-8588 or 800/537-7737
Room Quality: A-   Amenities: B
Food: C+   Value: B+
www.buenavistasuites.com

Located near the intersection of South International Drive and SR 536 just 1 1/2 miles from Disney, this is an attractive and very reasonably priced choice for families, as the two-room suites here sleep up to six and include coffeemaker, refrigerator, microwave, two TVs, and video games. Full American breakfast buffet and transportation to the Disney parks are included. Amenities include a pool, whirlpool, exercise room, and two tennis courts.

This is one of the quieter and more under-developed areas in the region, so the throngs of fast food and cheap shopping are a bit more remote from this establishment. Kind of a double-edged sword, but having a one-mile drive to get a burger instead of a half-mile drive really isn't that much of a price to pay for the increased peace and quiet.

EMBASSY SUITES LBV RESORT
$109-225
8100 Lake Avenue, LBV, 407/234-1144 or 800/257-8483
Room Quality: A-   Amenities: B
Food: B-   Value: B
www.embassysuitesorlando.com

Parents magazine recently listed Embassy Suites among the top hotels for families, and J.D. Power and Associates thanks to spacious two-room suites that offer welcome breathing room from the ones you love, along with refrigerators, microwaves, two cable TVs with VCR, and free transportation to the Disney theme parks. Like every Embassy Suites location, this hotel offers complimentary, cooked-to-order breakfast every morning and a reception every evening. Located just outside Downtown Disney, the hotel features two restaurants, a fitness center, tennis court, basketball court, and volleyball court. The Embassy Suites is a pet-friendly hotel.

RESIDENCE INN ORLANDO/LAKE BUENA VISTA
$105-169
11400 Marabella Palms Ct., LBV, 407/465-0075 or800/331-3131
Room Quality: A+   Amenities: B-
Food: C   Value: A
www.marriott.com

This installment of Marriott's spacious suite-only chain, about 10 minutes from Downtown Disney, features one- and two-bedroom suites with multiple televisions, video games, VCR, high-speed Internet access, and fully equipped kitchens, with a complimentary full American breakfast buffet every morning, complimentary shuttle transportation to Universal and Disney, an on-site restaurant, pool, and a full spa. Discounts: AAA, Government, military, seniors. Best rate guarantee at www.marriott.com.

HOLIDAY INN SUNSPREE RESORT LBV

$77-150
13351 Apopka-Vineland Road, LBV, 407/239-4500 or 800/366-6299
Room Quality: A-   Amenities: B-
Food: B   Value: A-
www.kidsuites.com

The SunSpree resort offers a mix of standard rooms with two queen beds and themed KidSuites with a king or queen size bed plus room for up to four kids, plus kitchenettes with microwave, refrigerator, and coffeemaker, video games, VCR, and stereo.

Special programs for kids abound - from special check-in just for kids and a movie theatre in the lobby showing free family flicks all day, to a Kids Eat Free program and Camp Holiday, a supervised activity program featuring arts and crafts, games, and movies. There's a buffet restaurant, deli, poolside bar, and lounge, along with a fitness room, landscaped pool area, and complimentary theme park shuttles. The Holiday Inn is pet-friendly. Discounts: AAA, AARP, Entertainment card, Government, military.

SHERATON SAFARI HOTEL

$95-135
12205 Apopka-Vineland Road, LBV, 407/239-0444 or 800/423-3297
Room Quality: B   Amenities: B-
Food: B   Value: A-
www.sheratonsafari.com

A cool African theme sets this hotel apart from cookie cutter motels, as does a primo location 1/8 mile from Disney World's Hotel Plaza entrance. Rooms feature Sheraton Sweet Sleeper beds, with plush top mattresses, fleece blankets, a duvet, and five soft pillows. You may never wake up. If you do, your room has high-speed Internet access, Playstation, and coffeemaker.

The hotel boasts a full-service restaurant, deli, and bar, a themed, heated outdoor pool with a 79-foot waterslide, a 24-hour fitness room, and complimentary transportation to the Disney parks. Kids 10 and under eat free here as well. Discounts: AAA, government, senior. Best rate guarantee at www.sheraton.com.

CLUB HOTEL BY DOUBLETREE

$84-180

12490 Apopka-Vineland Road, LBV, 407/239-0444 or 800/423-3297

Room Quality: B   Amenities: C+

Food: B   Value: B

www.doubletree.com

This colorful hotel with pineapples all over the wall looks like the kid brother of the Dolphin and Swan and features a convenient location near the Crossroads shopping center and Downtown Disney, along with light-hearted décor, high-speed Internet access, and best of all, a delectable Au Bon Pain for sandwiches and pastries. Discounts: AAA, AARP, Government. Best rate guarantee on www.doubletree.com.

Top Ten Kissimmee Hotels

GAYLORD PALMS

$199-319

6000 W. Osceola Pkwy., Kissimmee, 407/586-0000 or 800/423-3297

Room Quality: A+   Amenities: A

Food: A+   Value: B-

www.gaylordpalms.com

Unlike anything else in Orlando, this sister property of the Opryland in Nashville opened in 2002 with a mind-boggling four-acre atrium under glass, with themes recalling various locales of Florida, including St. Augustine, the Everglades (complete with live alligators!), and Key West, the latter of which actually has a 60-foot sailboat moored indoors. Absolutely incredible and absolutely immense, it'll take you ten minutes to walk from one end of the hotel to the other – but what a journey. The visuals here are more incredible that anything you'll find in a Disney or Universal hotel. As befitting the only AAA Four Diamond Award winning hotel in Kissimmee, the Gaylord Palms offers rooms that are spacious, opulent, and graciously equipped, more like suites - with in-room computer, refrigerator, coffeemaker, 2 phones per room including one cordless, CD stereo systems, lounge chairs and ottomans, and beautiful bathrooms with granite vanities, tubs, and glass shower enclosures. The resort fee adds high-speed Internet access, daily newspaper, use of the fitness center, Dasani water delivered to your room, complimentary park shuttle, a free bucket of range balls, and 20 minutes of local calls.

Dining here is a wonder, thanks to the expansive atrium, guests can enjoy climate-controlled al fresco dining experiences. The European market-inspired **Villa di Flora** restaurant offers a dazzling buffet at all three meals, with six chefs' stations, representing Italian, French, Spanish, and Greek cuisines. **Sunset Sam's Fish Camp** offers a nightly sunset celebration and delectable seafood specialties on the schooner in the shimmering waters of the Key West section of the hotel. In the rustic Everglades section, **Old Hickory Steakhouse** offers classic top-shelf Black Angus steaks, handcrafted after-dinner cheeses, and an extensive wine list, plus a **Ben & Jerry's** and several other eateries and bars.

The Gaylord Palms is stacked in terms of recreation as well. In addition to an expansive themed pool and a adults-only pool, the 20,000-square foot **Canyon Ranch Spa Club** offers Ayurvedic treatments, facials, body wraps, saunas, steamrooms, hot tub, a full salon, and a 4,000 square foot fitness center with cardio and strength equipment as well as a Pilates program. Just for kids age 3 to 14, **La Petite Academy** features themed activities and play stations in a supervised environment. There are a dozen shops of all kinds here, plus free-roaming artisans. Gaylord Palms guests also enjoy tee time privileges at the Falcon's Fire Golf Club.

CELEBRATION HOTEL

$179-439
700 Bloom Street, Celebration, 407/566-6000 or 888/499-3800
Room Quality: A-   Amenities: A+
Food: A-   Value: B
www.celebrationhotel.com

Located in Disney's master-planned community just east of I-4 and south of US 192, the AAA Four Diamond Award winning Celebration Hotel offers 115 spacious rooms and suites in 30 different configurations, decorated neatly with dark wood, rattan furniture, four-poster beds, and stone-tiled bathrooms with deluxe toiletries, plus video games and high-speed Internet access. Also a Four Diamond winner is the hotel's restaurant, the **Plantation Room**, which serves DeJuan Roy's blend of gorgeous New American cuisine (emphasizing seafood from the Gulf of Mexico and the Atlantic) in an intimate, upscale environment.

Recreation options include the **Celebration Golf Club**, where hotel guests have tee time privileges, the 60,000 square foot **Celebration Health Fitness Centre & Day Spa**, voted the best gym in town by the readers of Orlando Magazine. Right next door is **Salon 720**, a beauty and body spa. There's also a lakeside pool, plus nearby walking, bike, and nature trails, as well as downtown horse and carriage rides. Best rate guarantee at www.celebrationhotel.com.

WYNDHAM PALMS RESORT & COUNTRY CLUB
$100-351
7900 Palms Parkway, Kissimmee, 407/396-1311 or 877/747-4747
Room Quality: B+   Amenities: A+
Food: C+   Value: B-
www.wyndham.com

This lush new 600-acre resort consists of one- to three-bedroom villas complete with Jacuzzi, VCR, and fully equipped kitchens, accommodating 4, 8, and 12, respectively. Two- and three-bedroom units include a 52" television.

Resort amenities include the Mystic Dunes 18 hole championship golf course and clubhouse, tennis, basketball, bike rental, miniature golf, three heated pools, concierge service, family activities, a restaurant, pool bar, and Pizza Hut Express. Discounts: AAA, AARP, Government, military. Best rate guarantee on www.wyndham.com.

ORANGE LAKE RESORT & COUNTRY CLUB
$105-325
8505 W. Irlo Bronson, Kissimmee, 407/239-0000
Room Quality: A   Amenities: A+
Food: A   Value: B+
www.orangelake.com

The Orange Lake combines a full service resort with world-class recreational facilities. Studios, suites, and one- to three-bedroom villas provide tons of space and amenities like whirlpool bath, VCR, screened porch, coffeemakers, refrigerators, and in villas, full kitchens.

Orange Lake features three standard pools plus two themed swimming areas, Splash Lagoon, which features an interactive fountain, wade-in pool, and slides; and the 12-acre River Island (under construction at press time), which will feature a lazy river as well as pools, waterfalls, spas, and more. The resort also includes seven restaurants, 36 holes of golf (including 18 entirely renovated and redesigned in 2005), eight tennis courts, 27 holes of par-3 golf, 36 holes of miniature golf (host course of the Professional Putters' Association National Championship – snicker all you want, prize money topped $65k), volleyball, an 80-acre lake with a beach, fishing, and a a variety of watersports; racquetball, shuffleboard, playgrounds, arcades, a fitness center, croquet, badminton, and bike trails, plus activities and entertainment for kids and families alike, including movies, karaoke, live music, and lots more. Quite possibly the biggest array of recreational activities available at any resort or hotel in the area.

STAR ISLAND RESORT & CLUB
$102-248
5000 Avenue of the Stars, Kissimmee, 407/997-8000 or 800/423-8604
Room Quality: A+   Amenities: A
Food: C+   Value: A+
www.star-island.com

This Mediterranean-styled all-suite resort offers 1-, 2- and 3-bedroom villas with VCR, stereo system Jacuzzi, washer and dryer, and fully equipped kitchens and kitchenettes with dishwasher, microwave, coffeemaker, toaster. The resort's amenities include the full-service **Spa at Star Island** and **Celebrity Fitness Center** for pampering or pushing yourself, respectively. **Vic Braden's Tennis College** includes 8 courts, a stadium center court, practice lanes, and training from pros. Lake Cecile is available for fishing, waterskiing, and jetskiing. A wide array of activities are offered as well, like karaoke, face painting, ice cream socials, and arts & crafts. Note that maid service is available for a fee of $20-35.

AMERISUITES ORLANDO/LAKE BUENA VISTA SOUTH
$89-169
4991 Calypso Cay Way, Kissimmee, 407/997-1300 or 866/499-1300
Room Quality: B+   Amenities: B
Food: C+   Value: B+
www.amerisuites.com

Location, location, location. This all-suite hotel provides easy access to Disney via the Osceola Parkway, and to the smorgasbord of eating and entertainment options on US 192 and Lake Buena Vista via a relatively quiet stretch of SR 535, without the commotion and chaos of either tourist cluster. Accommodations include 26" television, microwave, fridge, coffeemaker, wet bar, continental breakfast, and transportation to the Disney parks. Resort amenitites include three pools (one with a waterslide), whirlpool, 18 holes of miniature golf, volleyball court, and fitness center. Discounts: AAA.

COMFORT SUITES MAINGATE EAST
$80-160
2775 Florida Plaza Blvd., Kissimmee, 407/397-7848 or 800/228-5150
Room Quality: B+   Amenities: C+
Food: C   Value: B
www.choicehotels.com

Opened in 2000, and awarded the chain's Inn of the Year award in 2002, this Comfort Suites location offers one- and two-bedroom suites with free high-speed Internet access, refrigerators, microwaves, and coffeemakers, as well as a fitness center, gift shop, game room, pool, hot tub, and tiki bar. This hotel offers complimentary continental breakfast and transportation to WDW, Universal, and Sea World. Discounts: AAA, Government, military, seniors (50+). Lowest rate guarantee on www.choicehotels.com.

LA QUINTA LAKESIDE
$49-109
7769 W. Irlo Bronson, Kissimmee, 407/396-2222 or 800/848-0801
Room Quality: B-   Amenities: B-
Food: B   Value: A
www.laquintalakeside.com

This Mediterranean-style hotel features 651 rooms scattered throughout 24 tropically landscaped acres, with over half the rooms featuring either pool, lake, or garden views. All rooms feature refrigerator, coffeemaker, and Playstation. The hotel features three pools, four on-site tennis courts, miniature golf, a fitness center, complimentary paddleboats, and four restaurants including a deli and Pizza Hut Express. The Keenta Kids' Club offers supervised activities for kids, allowing parents some much-needed time alone. Pets are welcome. Discounts: AAA.

RADISSON RESORT PARKWAY
$89-109
2900 Parkway Blvd., Kissimmee, 407/396-7000 or 800/634-4774
Room Quality: B   Amenities: B
Food: B-   Value: A
www.radissonparkway.com

With nicely landscaped grounds and spread-out rooms that were remodeled in 2001, this has more of a resort atmosphere than many of the Kissimmee motels, and yet is only 1.5 miles from Disney. The hotel's amenities include a giant free-form pool with a waterslide, two whirlpools, two tennis courts, volleyball courts, jogging and fitness facilities, and two full-service restaurants plus a 50's themed diner offering Pizza Hut, Krispy Kreme, Edy's, and Starbucks.

HOMEWOOD SUITES BY HILTON
$71-199
3100 Parkway Blvd., Kissimmee, 407/396-2229 or 800/CALL-HOME
Room Quality: B+   Amenities: C+

Food: B-   Value: A-
homewoodsuites.hilton.com

Spacious suite accommodations and a much-coveted location just east of I-4 off 192, the Homewood Suites offers fully equipped kitchens with fridge, stove, microwave, and coffeemaker, along with two televisions and video games. There's also a pool and a complimentary continental breakfast each morning, a manager's reception in the afternoons, and complimentary transportation to Disney. Discounts: AAA, AARP, Government, military.

Top Ten International Drive Hotels

RENAISSANCE ORLANDO RESORT AT SEA WORLD
$149-317
6677 Sea Harbor Drive, 407/351-5555 or 800/327-6677
Room Quality: B+   Amenities: B
Food: A-   Value: C+
www.renaissancehotels.com

This AAA Four Diamond award winning resort offers luxurious, plush rooms that measure 500 square feet and overlook Sea World or of the hotel's gorgeous atrium, which includes koi ponds and an aviary. Rooms offer high-speed Internet access, balconies, Playstation, minibar, and Bed Bath & Body Works amenities. As the Official Hotel of Sea World, the Renaissance offers exclusive length of stay admissions and ride-again passes that allow repeat rides on Sea World's marquee rides.

The hotel's facilities include a full-service spa, fitness center, a recreation area with a recently-renovated pool, kiddie pool, whirlpool, sauna, tennis courts, basketball, game room, volleyball, and an impressive all-sand playground with tire swings, slides, swinging rings, and a jungle gym. Children are greeted with a plush dolphin on check-in as well. Guests have tee time privileges at three area golf courses.

The impressive restaurants under the direction of award-winning executive chef and ice sculptor Hiroshi Noguchi include the signature **Atlantis**, AAA Four Diamond winner and home of a fantastic Sunday champang brunch and nightly harp music; **Tradewinds**, a moderately priced American bistro, a deli, and poolside bar and grill. Discounts: AAA, Government, military, seniors (62+). Best rate guarantee on www.marriott.com.

PEABODY ORLANDO

$150-440
9801 International Drive, 407/352-4000 or 800/732-2639
Room Quality: B+   Amenities: B-
Food: A+   Value: C-
www.peabodyorlando.com

The impressive Peabody, winner of both the AAA Four Diamond and Mobil Four Star awards, offers luxurious accommodations that feature the Peabody Dream Bed by Simmons Beautyrest, wireless high-speed Internet access, sitting areas, and marble bathrooms equipped with television and bathrobes. The hotel is aimed primarily at conventioneers on expense accounts,

Hotel amenities include a health club, spa, lap pool, salon, several shops, and four tennis courts, as well as a wealth of dining options such as the 24-hour **B-Line Diner**, featured on the Food Network and home of the best omelet I have eaten in my life, the spiffy **Capriccio Grill** for prime steaks and chops from Ruprecht's of Chicago, and **Dux**, the only Mobil Four Star restaurant in town, serving American haute cuisine with global accents. The latter two restaurants access a Wine Spectator Award of Excellence-winning cellar featuring over 12,000 vintages and premium cigars.

Be sure to check out the **Royal Duck March**, during which a butler leads the Peabody's duck mascots off a private elevator, down a red carpet, and into a fountain in the lobby. The ducks make their entrance at 11am daily and their departure at 5pm. Discounts: AAA.

DOUBLETREE CASTLE HOTEL

$99-170
8629 International Drive, 407/345-1511 or 800/95-CASTLE
Room Quality: B   Amenities: C+
Food: C+   Value: B-
www.doubletreecastle.com

Definitely one of the best family options for lodging in the area, the Doubletree is an eye-catcher, that's for sure. Designed to resemble a medieval summer palace (sort of), the hotel carries out the theme with European artwork and authentic Renaissance era music inside. As for the rooms, each has two queen-size beds with pillow-top mattresses, a six channel stereo system, 25" television with a Sony Playstation, high-speed Internet access, and a refrigerator and coffeemaker. While the Doubletree's onsite restaurant offerings are limited to one café, there are two excellent restaurants next door (Vito's Chop House and Café Tu Tu Tango). The hotel offers free transportation to Disney, Universal, and Sea World, and you've got a winner on your hands. Best rate guarantee on www.doubletreecastle.com.

ROSEN CENTRE HOTEL

$109-209
9840 International Drive, 407/996-9840 or 800/204-7234
Room Quality: B   Amenities: B+
Food: B+   Value: C
www.rosencentre.com

This 24-story behemoth towers over International Drive across from the Convention Center. Primarily geared to that audience, this hotel features plush accommodations with Floridian décor, coffeemaker, and high-speed Internet access, along with prime steaks and fresh seafood at the **Everglades Restaurant**, as well as a buffet restaurant and a 24-hour deli. The hotel includes the full-service Body & Sol spa, a swimming grotto, and tennis courts. Guests here have teetime privileges at Shingle Creek Golf Club. Discounts: AAA, Florida residents.

EXTENDED STAY DELUXE ORLANDO – CONVENTION CENTER/ POINTE*ORLANDO

$74-170
8750 Universal Blvd., 407/903-1500 or 800/830-4964
Room Quality: A-   Amenities: C+
Food: C   Value: A-
www.extendedstaydeluxe.com

Nestled beside I-Drive's premier shopping destination, Extended Stay (formerly Sierra Suites) is a smaller, attractive choice that opened in summer 1999, featuring full kitchens, two phone lines in each suite, high-speed Internet access, free local calls, VCRs, and even a bean bag chair. Guests here enjoy a complimentary breakfast, and facilities include an exercise room, swimming pool, and gourmet coffee bar. This hotel is pet-friendly. Best rate guarantee at www.extendedstaydeluxe.com.

SHERATON WORLD RESORT

$89-279
10100 International Drive, 407/382-1100 or 800/327-0363
Room Quality: B   Amenities: B+
Food: B   Value: B
www.sheratonworld.com

Renovated in 1998, this peaceful 28-acre complex, just three blocks from the Convention Center, has long been one of my favorites. The 1,102 rooms here have been decorated in a Mediterranean motif, and come equipped with a Sealy Posturepedic pillowtop mattress, hypoallergenic feather and down pillows, in-room movies, Nintendo games, refrigerators, ergonomic chairs, boards. The grounds include three pools (including a lagoon pool with waterfall), three tennis courts, a full-service salon and spa, health club, and a miniature golf course, along with four bars and restaurants, including Pizza Hut Express and deli items. The Sheraton offers a "Love That Dog" pet policy, with custom designed food and water bowls, beds, and accessories. Discounts: AAA, AARP, Government. Best rate guarantee at www.sheratonworld.com.

WYNDHAM ORLANDO
$116-156
8001 International Drive, 407/351-2420 or 800/421-8001
Room Quality: B   Amenities: B
Food: B+   Value: B-
www.wyndhamorlando.com

This hotel consists of 16 buildings across lagoon-dotted 48 acres at the corner of International Drive and Sand Lake Road, one block from I-4. Although that is one of the busiest intersections in the area, the Wyndham has a surprisingly away-from-it-all feel. Rooms include pillow-top mattresses, Playstation, and Herman Miller Aeron work chairs. Some suites have bunk beds perfect for kids. The hotel includes five bars and restaurants, an exercise room, jogging trails, three pools, volleyball, and a full health club with sauna and massage. Discounts: AAA, AARP, Government, military. Best rate guarantee on www.wyndham.com.

ENCLAVE SUITES
$89-219
6165 Carrier Drive, 407/351-1155 or 800/457-0077
Room Quality: A   Amenities: B
Food: B-   Value: A
www.enclavesuites.com

Located on a quieter side street near Wet 'N' Wild and Sand Lake Drive, the Enclave offers perfect location and spacious accommodations at a great price. Choose from deluxe studio suites, 2-bedroom, 2-bath suites sleeping six, or KidQuarter suites with bunk beds and themed murals. The Enclave includes a food court, a breakfast buffet, two pools, a playground, tennis court, exercise room, and more.

DOUBLETREE HOTEL UNIVERSAL ORLANDO
$98-163
5780 Major Blvd., 407/351-1000 or 800/843-8693
Room Quality: B-   Amenities: B-
Food: B   Value: C+
www.doubletreeorlando.com

Formerly the Radisson, this landmark hotel opposite the entrance to Universal has 760 rooms, each with high-speed Internet access, coffeemaker, and spacious work area, many with great Universal views, a junior Olympic sized pool, sauna, steam room, Jacuzzi, two restaurants, and a food court with TCBY, Pizza Hut, and Java Boost counters. Complimentary transportation to Universal, Sea World, and Wet'N'Wild is available. Discounts: AAA, AARP, Government, military. Best rate guarantee at www.doubletreeorlando.com.

LA QUINTA INN & SUITES
$65-125
8504 Universal Blvd., 407/345-1365 or 800/221-4731
Room Quality: B+   Amenities: B-
Food: C+   Value: B
www.orlandolaquinta.com

This brand-new hotel is located just off International Drive, by Mercado, Ripley's, Pirate's Cove, and a ton of other fun restaurants, shops, and activities, all within easy walking distance. La Quinta offers complimentary continental breakfast and spacious two-room suites and king rooms, each with microwave, fridge, coffeemaker, and recliner. Amenities include a pool, spa, and fitness center.

Off the Beaten Path

In recent years, Orlando has tried to revitalize and gentrify its tourism trade, adding premium malls, gourmet restaurants, and as listed here, a selection of unique hotel and resort properties that offer mind-boggling amenities, plush luxury, and impressive décor.

WESTIN GRAND BOHEMIAN
$209-818
325 S. Orange Ave., 407/313-9000 or 866/663-0024
Room Quality: A   Amenities: B+

Food: A-   Value: C+
www.grandbohemianhotel.com

So hip it almost hurts, the Grand Bohemian is an eye-popping luxury hotel in downtown Orlando, named to AAA's roster of Four Diamond Award winner and both Conde Nast Traveler's Gold List and Travel &

Another Option – Vacation Homes

Story time. When I was thirteen, my parents, my two brothers took a vacation to a four-season resort in the Poconos. It rained the first day. And the second. Kinda the third too. We spent three days cooped up in a hotel room, sniping at one another until tensions built to the point where we abandoned the whole vacation and checked out of the hotel four days early. What doomed this trip wasn't bad weather – it was cramped quarters. Never underestimate the value of peace, quiet, and solitude to take the edge off an overdose of family togetherness.

Vacation homes solve this problem by providing condominiums or spacious single-family homes, for about what you'd pay for an average decent hotel room. Enter **All Star Vacation Homes** (www.allstarvacationhomes.com, 888/249-1779), who offer 100 two- and three-bedroom condos and private pool homes with up to seven bedrooms. Prices range from $109 to $449, and the homes, which range from 1,400 to 3,450 square feet, can accommodate anywhere from 8 to 16 people.

All Star's homes offer fully-equipped kitchens, washers and dryers, private pools and spas, and multiple master bedrooms, as well as themed bedrooms, tasteful, attractive décor, and even home theater systems. Some homeowners even stock their home theaters from their personal DVD collection. Concierge service is provided by friendly and helpful staff who will ensure that you never miss traditional hotels. As for location, each of the 100 homes is located within 4 miles from Disney, and less than 2 miles from the All Star Welcome Center at 7822 W. Irlo Bronson Highway in Kissimmee, which also offers convenient access to supermarkets, drugstores, and restaurants.

Other companies offering AAA-rated vacation homes are the **Florida Store** (www.floridastorevacationrentals.com, 407/846-1722), **Absolute Premiere** (www.premierrentalhomes.com, 407/396-2401), **Alexander Holiday Homes** (www.floridasunshine.com, 407/932-3683), and **Loyalty Homes** (www.loyaltyusa.com, 407/397-7475).

Leisure's T&L 500 lists of the top hotels in the world. The hotel's aesthetic amenities include over 100 rare works of classic and contemporary art and Italian mosaic tiles, while rooms provide impeccable style, with Java wood, silver, and velvet furnishings. Rooms offer sumptuous luxury and, including Westin's exclusive Heavenly Bed, high-speed Internet access, the super posh Heavenly Bathroom (with dual showerheads, curved shower rods, and swanky bath amenities), AM/FM/CD clock radio, complimentary in-room Starbucks, and an interactive television system that includes digital music and Web TV.

The Westin is also home to the **Grand Bohemian Gallery** (see chapter 20), the AAA Four Diamond award winning **Boheme Restaurant**, serving stellar new American and continental cuisine, as well as a weekly jazz brunch. Last, but certainly not least, the Westin's bar, the **Bosendorfer Lounge**, was voted the Best Place to Sip Martinis by the Orlando Business Journal. Best rate guarantee on www.grandbohemianhotel.com.

JW MARRIOTT & RITZ-CARLTON ORLANDO GRANDE LAKES

Marriott:
$189-369
4040 Central Florida Parkway, 407/206-2300 or 800/576-5750.
Room Quality: B+   Amenities: A
Food: B+   Value: C

Ritz-Carlton:
$229-399
4012 Central Florida Parkway, 407/206-2400
Room Quality: B+   Amenities: A
Food: A-   Value: C

www.grandelakes.com

These two ultraluxe hotels, located on opposite ends of 500 lush acres at the headwaters of the Florida Everglades, combines exhilirating recreational options with European-style luxury that JW Marriott and the Ritz-Carlton names are known for worldwide. Both are attractive options for conventioneers and vacationers alike, with a relatively secluded location just east of the action on International Drive. The two resorts share the **Ritz-Carlton Golf Club**, 18 holes of Greg Norman golf specially designed to preserve the area's wetland ecosystem, integrating it into the course. The course was named one of 2005's Top 10 New Courses by Golf Magazine. Guests here can also take advantage of the 40,000 square foot **Ritz-Carlton Spa**, which includes the Parisian export, full-service Carita Salon, an exclusive 4,000 square foot lap pool and healing waters, 40 treatment rooms, and a 6,000 square foot Wellness Center. Spa Finder named this one of North America's ten most luxurious in 2004.

The **Ritz-Carlton** has racked up an impressive array of raves including the AAA Four Diamond, the Mobil Four Star, and Zagat's #1 Florida Hotel and #1 New Hotel awards. Its 584 rooms are 480 or 490 square feet, featuring hand-painted Italian furniture, marble bathrooms with separate shower and bathtub and dual sinks, plush terry robes and slippers, CD players, flat-screen television, and private balconies. Service amenities include twice-daily housekeeping and nightly turndown. Six dining options include **Norman's**, the AAA Four Diamond winning eponymous New World cuisine gem of Norman Van Aken, and the **Vineyard Grill**, offering organic steaks and Atlantic seafood and a phenomenal champagne brunch on Sundays.

The 26-story, 1000-room **JW Marriott**, another AAA Four Diamond winner, features Spanish architecture and many of the same amenities as the Ritz-Carlton, including flat-panel televisions, CD players, balconies, marble bathrooms, video games, high-speed Internet access, and two-line speaker-phones with voicemail. Restaurants here include Marisa Kelly's **Primo**, emphasizing contemporary Italian cuisine made from local ingredients, and **Citron**, an brasserie featuring innovative signature dishes that twist on American classics. Discounts: AAA, Government, military, seniors (62+). Best rate guarantee on www.marriott.com.

CHALET SUZANNE
$169-229
3800 Chalet Suzanne Dr., Lake Wales, 800/433-6011
Room Quality: B+   Amenities: B-
Food: A   Value: B+
www.chaletsuzanne.com

This award-winning bed-and-breakfast, named one of Uncle Ben's top ten country inns, features a 75-year tradition of peace, quiet, romance, and hospitality. And soup. Oh, the soup. The restaurant here serves twelve varieties of legendary soups so coveted that they were included on the Apollo moon flight. Like Seinfeld's Soup Nazi, you can order the Chalet's soup on the Internet. Unlike Seinfeld, you won't get banned for hesitating. Activities at Chalet Suzanne include volleyball, horseshoes, bird watching, swimming, and fishing. Each of the 30 rooms is decorated uniquely, and several special rooms feature things like king size beds, whirlpool tubs, and striking lake views Discounts: AAA.

REUNION RESORT & CLUB
$205-835
1000 Reunion Way, Reunion, 407/662-1100 or 888/418-9611
Room Quality: A+   Amenities: A
Food: C+   Value: B-
www.reunionresortandclub.com

A sparkling and striking new mixed-use community only 5 miles south of Disney via I-4, Reunion combines gorgeous villa and vacation home accommodations with 54 holes of golf designed by Tom Watson, Arnold Palmer, and Jack Nicklaus. Accommodations feature DVD player, full-sized kitchen (with dishwasher, stove, blender, corian or granite countertops, and more), oversized bathtub, and more.

Resort amenities include in-room Swedish, deep tissue, or golfer's massage, fitness center, walking and biking trails, pro shop, a tennis complex, and multiple swimming pools and Jacuzzis, including a multi-level swimming pavilion. There's also the Kids' Crew program, featuring fun, family-friendly events to make Dad feel less guilty about that mulligan.

SUMMER BAY RESORT
$149-239
25 Town Center Blvd., Clermont, 352/242-1100 or 888/742-1100
Room Quality: A+   Amenities: B+
Food: C   Value: B+
www.summerbayresort.com

Those willing to tolerate a six-mile drive to Disney can enjoy spacious lakefront accommodations at reasonable prices at this brand-new resort complex west of Disney, at the intersection of US 192 and US 27 in Clermont. Accommodations include huge 1- and 2-bedroom condominiums, equipped with full kitchen, stereo, whirlpool bath, washer and dryer, as well as 2-bedroom villas and vacation homes. Amenities include four pools with hot tubs, a fitness center, and watersports including jetskiing, canoeing, and pontoon boating on 68-acre Crooked Lake.

OMNI ORLANDO RESORT AT CHAMPIONSGATE
$161-289
1500 Masters Blvd., Championsgate, 407/390-6664 or 800/THE-OMNI.
Room Quality: B+   Amenities: A
Food: B+   Value: B
www.omniorlandoresort.com

Five miles from Disney World is Championsgate, a master-planned community built around 36 holes of Greg Norman-designed golf, named one of America's 10 Most Distinctive Places to Play by Golf Magazine. Towering over the links, and surrounded by natural wetlands, the Omni features tastefully appointed rooms with DirecTV, video games, complimentary high-speed Internet access, oversized lounge chairs, coffeemaker, balcony, bathrobes, and luxurious beds.

Amenities at the Omni include a European spa, full-service health club, a formal pool and a family pool with slides, an 850-foot lazy river, volleyball, tennis, basketball, jogging, hiking, and biking trails, and the headquarters of the David Ledbetter Golf Academy. The resort features several restaurants, including the pan-Asian **Zen**, the Mediterranean **Trevi's**, featuring a working herb garden, a sports bar, deli, and several bars. Discounts: AAA, AARP.

Chain Hotels

It goes without saying that out of the 200+ hotels in Orlando, the majority of them are local iterations of national chains. If you've been to one, you pretty much have an idea of the level of service you can expect from all of them. Of course there is variation within the establishments (some chains showing more consistency than others), but if you're familiar with the offerings of a particular company, you have a general idea what to expect. Each chain is listed with the number of locations in each location: Walt Disney World, Lake Buena Vista, Kissimmee, or International Drive (including Universal area) and the chain's website. Chains are listed in order of preference in each price category, from most to least strongly recommended.

Budget chains

Expect basic accommodations, cable TV, swimming pool, bare-bones amenities, sometimes a continental breakfast.

1. **Hilton Garden Inn:** 2 INT – www.hiltongardeninn.com
2. **Fairfield Inn:** 1 LBV, 2 INT – www.fairfieldinn.com
3. **Hampton Inn:** 1 LBV, 2 KIS, 4 INT – www.hamptoninn.com
4. **Red Roof Inn:** 1 KIS, 1 INT– www.redroof.com
5. **Comfort Inn:** 1 LBV, 1 KIS, 2 INT – www.comfortinn.com
6. **Country Inn:** 1 LBV, 1 KIS, 1 INT – www.countryinns.com
7. **Ramada:** 4 KIS, 1 INT – www.ramada.com
8. **EconoLodge:** 3 KIS, 1 INT – www.econolodge.com
9. **Rodeway Inn:** 2 KIS, 2 INT– www.rodewayinn.com
10. **Sleep Inn:** 1 KIS, 2 INT– www.sleepinn.com

11. **Best Western:** 1 WDW, 2 KIS, 3 INT – www.bestwestern.com
12. **Travelodge:** 5 KIS, 2 INT– www.travelodge.com
13. **Days Inn:** 1 LBV, 6 KIS, 3 INT – www.daysinn.com
14. **Howard Johnson:** 6 KIS, 4 INT – www.hojo.com

Moderate chains

Expect comfortable accommodations, quieter facilities, some amenities, sometimes a full-service restaurant.

1. **Doubletree:** 1 WDW, 1 LBV, 1 KIS, 2 INT – www.doubletree.com
2. **Courtyard by Marriott:** 2 LBV, 1 INT – www.marriott.com
3. **Holiday Inn:** 1 WDW, 2 LBV, 3 KIS, 3 INT – www.holiday-inn.com
4. **La Quinta:** 1 KIS, 3 INT – www.laquinta.com
5. **Radisson:** 1 LBV, 1 KIS, 2 INT – www.radisson.com
6. **Clarion:** 1 KIS, 1 INT– www.clarioninn.com
7. **Quality Inn:** 5 KIS, 4 INT – www.qualityinn.com

Upscale/luxury chains

Expect posh furnishings and décor, expanded amenities and services, and multiple restaurants.

1. **Loews:** 3 INT – www.loewshotels.com
2. **Renaissance:** 1 INT – www.renaissancehotels.com
3. **Hyatt:** 1 LBV – www.hyatt.com
4. **Marriott:** 1 LBV, 1 INT – www.marriott.com
5. **Westin:** 1 WDW – www.westin.com
6. **Hilton:** 1 WDW – www.hilton.com
7. **Wyndham:** 1 WDW, 1 KIS, 1 INT – www.wyndham.com
8. **Sheraton:** 1 WDW, 2 LBV, 3 INT – www.sheraton.com
9. **Crowne Plaza:** 2 INT – www.crowneplaza.com

All suite/extended stay chains

Expect complimentary American breakfast buffets and 1- or 2-bedroom suites with kitchens or at least microwave and refrigerator, along with a swimming pool, sometimes a fitness room.

1. **Embassy Suites:** 1 LBV, 2 INT – www.embassysuites.com
2. **Homewood Suites:** 1 LBV, 1 KIS, 2 INT – www.homewoodsuites.com
3. **Amerisuites:** 1 LBV, 2 INT – www.amerisuites.com
4. **Residence Inn:** 1 LBV, 3 INT – www.residenceinn.com
5. **Hawthorn Suites:** 1 LBV, 1 INT – www.hawthorn.com
6. **Spring Hill Suites:** 1 LBV, 1 INT – www.springhillsuites.com
7. **Extended Stay Deluxe:** 1 LBV, 1 INT – www.extendedstaydeluxe.com
8. **Comfort Suites:** 2 KIS, 2 INT – www.comfortsuites.com

Chapter 12

WHERE TO EAT

There are more than 3,800 restaurants in and around Orlando, and after sampling them all, I am now too morbidly obese to ever fit on a theme park ride again. Oh well. At least I can share the fruits of my research with you, provided I can extricate my keyboard from within these new folds of fat.

In all seriousness, gourmet opportunities abound. There's a few restaurants with celebrity chefs, others still with less-known but equally-renowned culinary maestros. Cuisines from all over the world can be sampled and enjoyed, and there's a particularly strong emphasis here on steak and seafood, thanks to Orlando's easy access to fresh Atlantic and Gulf catches, and central Florida's cattleman's history.

Best of Theme Park Eats

See the individual chapters on the Magic Kingdom, Epcot, Disney-MGM, Universal, Islands of Adventure, and Sea World for detailed information about the dining options there. Here are my "best of" lists:

Magic Kingdom
  Best sit-down meal: Tony's Town Square
  Best counter-service meal: Columbia Harbour House
  Best snack: Aloha Isle

Epcot
  Best sit-down meal: San Angel Inn

Best counter-service meal: Sunshine Seasons

Best snack: Boulangerie Patisserie

Disney-MGM
Best sit-down meal: Hollywood Brown Derby
Best counter-service meal: ABC Commissary
Best snack: Min & Bill's Dockside Diner

Restaurant Price Key

$ = Under $10
$$ = $10-20
$$$ = $20-30
$$$$ = $30 and up

Animal Kingdom
Best sit-down meal: Rainforest Café (by default)
Best counter-service meal: Flame Tree Barbecue
Best snack: Tamu Tamu Refreshments

Universal Studios
Best sit-down meal: Finnegan's Bar & Grill
Best counter-service meal: Café La Bamba
Best snack: San Francisco Pastry Co.

Islands of Adventure
Best sit-down meal: Confisco Grille
Best counter-service meal: Blondie's
Best snack: Frozen Desert

Sea World
Best sit-down meal: Sharks Underwater Grill
Best counter-service meal: Spices
Best snack: Sand Bar

Disney Character Dining

One of the highlights of many a Disney trip is the chance to meet-and-greet favorite characters. Combining a delicious buffet meal with character interaction can be a very wise investment of time and money. There are lots of different offerings. Choose your character experience based on meal, location, or by character, if there's someone specific your kids want to see. See the theme park chapters for specifics on character dining experiences.

Reservations for all character meals can be made 90 days in advance by calling 407/WDW-DINE.

•Magic Kingdom: Crystal Palace (B,L,D): Pooh, Tigger, Eeyore, Piglet

- Magic Kingdom: Cinderella's Royal Table (B): Cinderella, Fairy Godmother, Disney princesses
- Magic Kingdom: Liberty Tree (D): Mickey, Minnie, Pluto, Meeko, Chip & Dale
- Epcot: Garden Grill (L,D): Mickey, Chip, Dale
- Epcot: Akershus (B): Disney princesses
- Animal Kingdom: Restaurantosaurus (B): Mickey, Donald, Goofy, Pluto
- Beach Club: Cape May Café (B): Goofy, Pluto, Chip & Dale
- Contemporary Resort: Chef Mickey's (B,D): Mickey, Goofy, Chip & Dale
- Dolphin: Coral Café (B, Sunday only): Goofy, Pluto, Chip & Dale
- Grand Floridian: 1900 Park Fare (B): Mary Poppins, Alice, Mad Hatter, Pooh, Eeyore
- Grand Floridian: 1900 Park Fare (D): Cinderella, Prince Charming, Fairy Godmother
- Polynesian: 'Ohana (B): Mickey, Chip, Dale
- Swan: Garden Grove Café (B, Saturday only): Goofy, Pluto
- Swan: Gulliver's (D): Rafiki, Timon, Goofy, Pluto

Disney Resort Dining

Disney's Deluxe resorts each contain at least one great restaurant, sometimes more than that. These are definitely places worth checking out, even though they tend to be pricier than similar restaurants elsewhere. The sit-down restaurants in Disney's Moderate resorts, however are nothing particularly special worth seeking out if you're not staying there. For priority seating at any WDW restaurant, call 407/WDW-DINE.

Animal Kingdom Lodge

Two of the most daring restaurants in Disney World are found here. The AAA Four Diamond Award-winning **Jiko** ($$-$$$) offers flavorful fare from across the African continent à la carte, specializing in grilled meats, while the bountiful **Boma** ($$) buffet provides guests a chance to broaden their palates in dozens of different ways.

Boardwalk

Disney's waterfront entertainment, shopping, dining, and hotel complex contains four tempting restaurants: **Spoodles** ($$-$$$), a Mediterranean restaurant featuring tapas items, pasta dishes, seafood, and oak-fired flatbread pizzas; **Big River Grille** ($-$$), a brewpub featuring classic bar fare, sandwiches, salads, and grilled meats presented with a gourmet twist; and the

ESPN Club ($), serving up ballpark fare and family-friendly American cuisine with a tongue-in-cheek flair straight out of SportsCenter. The menu includes a little bit of everything but the best bets are the Bloody Mary chili, "Overtime" fries (prepared like nachos), half-pound burgers, and delicious BBQ pork sandwiches. The ESPN Club are features interactive games and a gift shop. Last, the **Flying Fish Café** ($$) specializes in creatively prepared seafood dishes.

Contemporary

Perched on the 15th floor of the hotel, the **California Grill's** ($$-$$$) spectacular views of the Magic Kingdom play backdrop to a California/Asian menu of sushi and sashimi, spit fired chicken, salmon, tuna, grouper, pork, and beef entrees. The **Concourse Steakhouse** ($$-$$$) features chipotle glazed ribeye, St. Louis spare ribs, seared yellowfin tuna, and prime rib.

Dolphin

New in 2004, **Todd English's bluezoo** ($$$-$$$$) combines fresh seafood with coastal cuisines from around the world – like Cantonese lobster, miso glazed Chilean sea bass, tuna-wrapped sashimi-grade tuna steak, and other daring dishes. **Shula's Steakhouse** ($$$$) offers a proper atmosphere for consumption of such eye-popping red meat indulgences as a 12 oz. filet mignon, 22 oz. cowboy steak, a 32 oz. prime rib, and a 48 oz. porterhouse. The menu also includes lamb loin, chicken, salmon, and yes – you guessed it – Dolphin. Anyone else mildly disturbed by this?

Grand Floridian

Victoria & Albert's ($$$$) is the only AAA Five Diamond Award winning restaurant in the entire metropolitan area, offering a prix-fixe seven-course dinner. The menu changes daily but always impresses, as do the service and settings: maid and butler at each table, Schlott-Zweisel crystal, Royal Doulton chinaware, Sambonet silver, and hand-printed souvenir menus presented with long-stemmed roses and Godiva chocolates to round out the evening. Expect to pay $90 or more per person, $30-45 more to add wine pairings. There is also a chef's table seating for the epi-curious. **Citrico's** ($$$) and **Narcoossee's** ($$-$$$) are other good options here, the former for French- and Italian-influenced fare, and the latter for fresh seafood creations.

Polynesian

At **'Ohana** ($$) guests laugh, smile, and feast family-style on hot and cold appetizers and 3-foot skewers of shrimp, sirloin, mesquite turkey, and pork loin. The **Kona Café** ($) here is renowned for its banana-stuffed Tonga Toast.

Swan

Palio ($$-$$$) is a fine Italian bistro clad in bright, vivid banners representing the Italian counties that competed in the races for which the café is named. Strolling mandolin players regale guests who dine on specialties including brick oven pizza, fettuccine Alfredo, linguini topped with shrimp and scallops, and an awesome stuffed veal chop.

Wilderness Lodge

Artist's Point ($$$) presents a breathtaking array of new American cuisine served up in an inspiring setting with Northwestern flavor. Cedar planked salmon is the house specialty here, along with grilled buffalo sirloin, free-range chicken, pan-seared scallops, and more. The **Whispering Canyon Café** ($$)offers delectable family-style skillets and à la carte offerings at all three meals.

Yacht & Beach Club

The **Cape May Café** ($$) features a festive nightly all-you-can-eat clambake with farm-raised clams in garlic butter, Prince Edward Island Sound mussels, peel and eat shrimp, and landlubber entrees. The pricey but top-notch **Yachtman's Steakhouse** ($$$) offers delectable cuts of beef including filets, strip steaks, T-bones, and tenderloins.

Downtown Disney Dining

The Downtown Disney area offers a good selection of exciting restaurants offering delectable options for every taste bud. In addition to the restaurants listed here, counter-service eateries from Bongo's, Wolfgang Puck, and Ghirardelli make quick bites just as rewarding as sit-down meals.

Downtown Disney Marketplace

On board the Empress Lilly riverboat, permanently moored at the edge of Village Lake, is **Fulton's Crab House** ($$$), specializing in unusual varieties of crab and lobster, prepared in simple ways to bring out their natural flavor. The Dungeness crab cakes, seafood boil (a lobster bake in a pot), and flown-in-daily twin Maine lobsters are highlights of the menu. The **Rainforest Café** ($$) offers family-friendly American fare in a wild setting (see Chapter 10 for full description of the Animal Kingdom location). **Cap'n Jacks** ($$) offers raw bar specialties and a small menu of seafood. **Earl of Sandwich** ($) offers signature hot and cold sandwiches on hearth baked bread.

Downtown Disney Pleasure Island

The **Portobello Yacht Club** ($$-$$$) offers regional Italian cuisine and an award-winning wine list. Start with any of a half dozen delectable antipasti dishes, and special entrees created every week by the restaurant's chefs. House specialties include spaghettini alla Portobello - tossed with scallops, shrimp, clams, and Alaskan king crab, char-grilled center cut filet with white truffle butter, and a dynamite white chocolate crème brulée variation. PI admission is not required to eat here. For a theme restaurant, **Planet Hollywood** ($$) offers surprisingly good burgers, pasta, and grilled specialties.

Downtown Disney West Side

The **Wolfgang Puck** ($-$$$$) restaurant here has four sections: an Express counter-service annex at the Marketplace, a sushi bar, casual dining at the Café, and upscale food at the upstairs Dining Room. The Café offers sandwiches, pizza, and pasta dishes, while the Dining Room offers such Puck signatures as rare tuna Nicoise, tandoori-spiced lamb chops, pumpkin risotto, and more. For reservations at the Dining Room call 407/938-9653. The **House of Blues** ($$) offers an appealing blend of Cajun, Creole, and American cuisine in a dark, appealing, well – bluesy – atmosphere. The Sunday Gospel Brunch is particularly rousing. **Bongo's Cuban Café** ($$), owned by Emilio and Gloria Estefan, serves classically prepared beef, pork, chicken, and seafood dishes in an environment that recalls both Havana and Miami Beach.

Universal Orlando Dining

Several good theme restaurants and a few great gourmet options can be found in the Universal Orlando resort, between the Citywalk complex and the three luxury hotels on the property. For reservations at any Citywalk restaurant, call 407/224-FOOD or visit the Citywalk dinner reservation cart. See Chapters 10 and 11 for discussion of USF and IOA restaurants.

Tops here is **Emeril's Orlando** ($$$-$$$$), kicking your dinner up a notch with imaginative and sophisticated cuisine, building off Creole and Old World influences as chefs bustle around an open show kitchen. Even better than Lagasse's namesake restaurant is **Tchoup Chop** ($$-$$$, 407/503-CHOP), another Emeril eatery, this one located in the Royal Pacific Resort. Asian and Polynesian fusion dishes are treated to the bold flavors of his inimitable style. Favorites here include the Kiawe smoked pork ribs, Kobe beef burgers, Kalua braised pork, and seared yellowfin tuna. The wonton skins and peanut sauce served as a warmup are particularly addictive. This is one of my personal favorites in Orlando.

Emeril does not corner the market on fine dining at Universal, however, as the posh Portofino Bay Hotel boasts **Bice** ($$$$), the eclectic locally inspired Italian boutique restaurant. This cozy gem offers innovative and flavorful northern Italian cuisine, and outdoor seating along the shore of Portofino Bay is particularly lovely. At the Hard Rock Hotel, the **Palm Steakhouse** ($$$$) brings its 70-year New York tradition to sunny Florida along with prime cuts of beef and Nova Scotia lobsters. The Hard Rock's **Kitchen** ($$) offers Kobe beef burgers and specialties dreamed up by visiting celebrities.

Moving back to Citywalk, there are a number of more casual dining options that provide great fun. Named the Best Theme Restaurant by the Orlando Sentinel, **NBA City** ($$) contains a themed game area and a phenomenal gourmet menu, including such dishes as grilled veggie and mozz sandwiches, BLT pizzas, grilled salmon pasta, and Southwestern Cobb salad. The **NASCAR Café** ($-$$) offers race and driver memorabilia and a no-frills menu of burgers, sandwiches, BBQ chicken and ribs, and seafood. The **Motown Café** ($$) serves up soulful music and dishes like chicken and waffles, special-recipe meatloaf, pecan catfish, and more. **Jimmy Buffett's Margaritaville** restaurant features cheeseburgers in paradise – some of the area's best, conch fritters, calamari, sandwiches, and margaritas (duh!). **Latin Quarter** ($$) represents the cuisines, cultures, music, and art of all 21 Latin nations.

Bob Marley – A Tribute to Freedom ($) has got the munchies – palm heart salads, beef or vegetable patties, jerk chicken, and desserts. **Pat O'Brien's** ($) serves up po'boys, jambalaya, muffelatta, red beans and rice, and other N'awlins specialties. **Pastamoré** ($-$$) offers surprisingly good quick-service Italian specialties.

Kissimmee-Lake Buena Vista-Orlando

Gourmet Dining Experiences

In the Lake Buena Vista area, **Arthur's 27** ($$$$ - Wyndham Palace Resort, 1900 Buena Vista Dr, 407/827-3450) offers a panoramic view of Walt Disney World and cuisine that has won awards including the AAA Four Diamond, the Golden Spoon, and the Orlando Magazine Reader's Choice. The multi-tiered **Black Swan** ($$$-$$$$ – Grand Cypress Resort, 1 N. Jacaranda, 407/239-1999) is another AAA Four Diamond continental masterpiece, with delicate and bold flavors served in artistic fashion with piano accompaniment.

Near the "Restaurant Row" section of Sand Lake Road, **Chatham's Place** ($$$$, 7575 Dr. Phillips Blvd., 407/345-2992) offers continental and new American treatments of seafood, wild game, chicken, and beef. The house specialty is pecan butter crusted grouper. The Peabody Orlando's signature restaurant, **Dux** (($$$$ - 9801 International Drive, 407/345-4550), features an ever-changing selection of American regional cuisine in an elegant setting.

The Grande Lakes boasts a pair of celebrity chef restaurants. At the Ritz-Carlton, **Norman's** ($$$$, 4012 Central Florida Pkwy., 407/206-2400) is where Norman Van Aken blends Latin American, Caribbean, Asian, and continental cuisine in environs featuring local art and wood-burning ovens. Next door at the JW Marriott, the elegant, candlelit **Primo** ($$$-$$$$, 4000 Central Florida Pkwy., 407/206-2400) lets chef Melissa Kelly create dazzling Italian dishes from organic herbs and vegetables grown in the on-site garden.

The AAA Four Diamond winning **Venetian Room** room is top notch and close to WDW, Kissimmee, and International Drive ($$$-$$$$ - Caribe Royale, 8101 World Center Dr., 407/238-8060). Presentation is especially breathtaking here, and dishes offered include squab with foie gras, rack of lamb, lobster, Dover sole, and braised veal.

Venture a little further to the north and go downtown to **Le Coq Au Vin** ($$$$ - 4800 S. Orange Ave, 407/851-6980) for its stellar French dishes including a flawless execution of the eponymous dish. Diners here rave about the service as well. Also downtown is the ultraluxe **Manuels' on the 28th** ($$$$, 390 N. Orange Ave., 407/246-6580), with unreal views, especially at sunset, an unmatchably romantic setting, and contemporary world cuisine changing seasonally. Head chef Manuel Ramirez traces his family lineage back to the Executive Chef of the king of Spain. This is another AAA Four Diamond winner, as is the **Maison & Jardin** ($$$-$$$$ - 430 S. Wynmore Road, 407/862-4410) in the northern suburb of Altamonte Springs. Known locally as the Mason Jar, this restaurant serves up the dynamite new American creations of Hans Spirig, who has run this celebrated kitchen for 17 years. The new **Hue** ($-$$$ - 629 E. Central Blvd., 407/849-1800) features flavorfully prepared meats and seafood, and won a ridiculous THIRTEEN awards in Orlando Magazine's Best Of.

Finally, the **Boheme** ($-$$$ - Westin Grand Boheme, 325 S. Orange Ave., 407/313-9000) is the recipient of the Florida Trend Best New Restaurant award in addition to AAA's Four Diamonds, with outrageous and tasty menus at breakfast, lunch, and dinner. There's even a Sunday jazz brunch that's nothing short of decadent.

For true opulence, go about 20 minutes west of Disney, to historic **Chalet Suzanne** ($$$$ - 3800 Chalet Suzanne Dr., Lake Wales, 941/676-6011), a bed and breakfast serving incredible six-course dinners and four-course lunches. They sell twelve kinds of hot, delicious, and world-famous soup as well. They have won the Golden Spoon award for over 30 years running.

Surf & Turf

You can find steakhouses that range from tasteful, formal exercises in decorum, to bustling, noisy places where you throw peanut shells on the floor. At the top of the heap is **Vito's Chop House** ($$-$$$$ - 8633 International Drive, 407/354-2467), an Italian-influenced steakhouse whose steaks and chops – aged 4 to 6 weeks – are succulent, superb, and filling. Australian rock lobster tail, Tuscan T-bones and porterhouse, milk-fed veal chops, and steak Italiano are to die for, and reasonably priced for the quality.

The elegant **Atlantis** ($$$$ - Renaissance Orlando resort, 6677 Sea Harbor Dr., 407/351-5555) is a AAA Four Diamond Award eatery offering lamb and filet mignon in addition to lobster, yellowfin tuna, salmon, and more. **Morton's of Chicago** ($$$-$$$$ - 7600 Dr. Phillips Drive, 407/248-3485) has showcased great steak without the bull since 1978. The restaurant is known for its USDA prime aged beef, seafood including whole baked Maine lobster flown in fresh daily, hand picked vegetables, and elegant desserts.

The **Hawk's Landing Steakhouse** ($$$$ - Marriott Orlando World Center, 8701 World Dr., 407/238-8829) features an extensive wine list. **Hemingway's** ($$$ - Hyatt Regency Grand Cypress, 407/239-3854), overlooking a majestic pool, offers game selections in addition to steak and seafood dishes.

The **Butcher Shop** ($$$ - Mercado, 8445 International Drive, 407/363-9727) has steaks from 14-ounce filets to 28-ounce T-Bones. If you wish, you can take your raw cut of beef to the pit in the center of the restaurant and cook it to your own taste. The **Old Hickory** ($$$-$$$$ - Gaylord Palms, 6000 W. Osceola Pkwy., Kissimmee, 407/586-1600) offers Black Angus steaks served in a woodsy Everglades environment. **Timpano Italian Chophouse** ($$-$$$$ - 7488 Sand Lake Road) combines affordable cuts of beef and seafood with pasta dishes and other Old Country favorites.

Bonefish ($$-$$$ - 7830 Sand Lake Road, 407/355-7707), right down the block, offers simply prepared, lightly seasoned seafood dishes with sauces like garlic gorgonzola butter, mango salsa, or lemon basil. Not to be confused with **Moonfish** ($$-$$$ - 7525 Sand Lake Road, 407/363-7262), which has a raw bar, sashimi, and specialties cooked over an open oak-and-citrus grill. Décor here is especially notable – peep the aquarium DVDs in hi-def plasma!

The **Ocean Grill** ($$-$$$ - 6432 International Drive, 407/352-9993) offers a variety of seafood prepared in a styles ranging from Southern and Chesapeake to New England and Pacific. If you enjoy lobster, and lots of it, the restaurant offers fresh - in fact, live - Maine lobsters ranging from one to four pounds.

The **Atlantic Bay Seafood Grill** ($$ - 2901 Parkway Blvd., Kissimmee, 407/238-2323) offers live Maine lobster, seven varieties of fresh fish daily, oysters on the half shell, prime rib, steak, pasta, and poultry, plus an all-you-can-eat seafood bar and early bird specials.

The **Lighthouse Lobster Feast** ($$$ - 6400 International Drive, 407/355-3750) feeds you all the Maine lobster you can eat, plus a buffet of clam chowder, lobster bisque, peel-and-eat shrimp, oysters, mussels, and much more. The **Boston Lobster Feast** ($$$-$$$$ - 8731 International Drive, 407/248-8606; 6071 W. Irlo Bronson Mem. Hwy., 407/396-2606) has a gluttonous all-you-can-eat lobster, crab, shrimp, and raw bar buffet. **Coney Island** ($$ - 5150 W. Irlo Bronson Mem. Hwy., 407/397-7077) has a lobster and seafood feast that includes mussels, oysters, cod, and shrimp, as well as hot dogs, chicken strips, pizza, and buffalo wings. **Angel's** ($-$$$ - 7300 W. Irlo Bronson Mem. Hwy., Kissimmee, 407/397-1960) offers a more limited array of seafood dishes but makes up for it with prime rib, just outside the WDW maingate.

Vittorio's ($$ - 5159 International Drive, 407/352-1255), **Crazy Grill** ($$ - 7049 International Drive., 407/354-4404) and **Texas de Brazil** ($$$ - 5627 International Drive, 407/355-0355) offer churrascaria style dining – where servers with 3-foot long skewers carry various grilled meats around the restaurant and keep feeding you, and feeding you, and feeding you, until you say "no mas." Of these, Texas de Brazil is the best.

Unmissable from US 192 is **Magic Mining Co.** ($$ - 7763 W. Irlo Bronson Mem. Hwy., Kissimmee, 407/396-8986), a steakhouse beneath a waterfall-crossed mountain. The hearty menu includes top sirloin, prime rib, T-bone, lobster, grilled shrimp, baby back ribs, and jackleg chicken. **Key W. Kool's Open Pit Grill** ($$ - 7725 W. Irlo Bronson Mem. Hwy., Kissimmee, 407/396-1166) has an open flame for a focal point and a 32-ounce Porterhouse for a signature dish. **Darryl's** ($$ - 8282 International Drive, 407/351-1883; 5260 W. Irlo Bronson Mem. Hwy., 407/396-1901) is famous for its inventive stuffed baked potatoes. Entrees include beef, seafood, and pasta, and there's a strong kids' menu.

The best steakhouse in town as per AOL Cityguide, **Charley's Steakhouse** ($$-$$$ - 2901 Parkway Blvd., Kissimmee, 407/396-6055; 8255 International Drive, 407/363-0228) selects steaks from three-year-old grain-fed steer, aged 4-5 weeks, and broiled over a 1,100-degree wood fire. Specialties include porterhouse, T-bone, Alaskan king crab, lobster tail, and 12-ounce filet mignon. Charley's 1,000-bottle selection earned it kudos from Wine Spectator as well.

Black Angus ($-$$ - 12399 S. Apopka Vineland Rd., 407/239-4414; 7516 W. Irlo Bronson Mem. Hwy., Kissimmee, 407/390-4548, 6231 International Drive, 407/354-3333) offers the eponymous steaks, all-you-can-eat dinner specials, breakfast buffets, and salad and fruit bars. The **Cattleman's Steakhouse** ($-$$ - 2948 Vineland Rd., Kissimmee, 407/238-2333) offers a selection of mouth-watering corn-fed beef, char-broiled to your liking. **Wild Jack's** ($-$$ - 7364 International Drive, 407/352-4407) is more imaginative than most in its price range, with red chile crusted New York strip steak, adobo pork chops, New Mexico salmon, and more, along with tasty appetizers. It can have sort of a greasy-spoon, Outback-lite kind of feel to it at times though.

Well-known national steak-and-seafood chains with area locations are listed below:

Crab House ($$): Full menu of seafood dishes, plus an all-you-can-eat raw bar.
- •8496 Palm Parkway, 407/239-1888
- •8291 International Drive, 407/352-6140

Golden Corral ($): Cheap, decent food served up buffet style three times a day. An incredible array of baked goods and desserts.
- •8032 International Drive, 407/352-6606
- •8707 Vineland Ave., 407/938-9500
- •2701 W. Vine St., Kissimmee, 407/931-0776
- •7702 W. Irlo Bronson Mem. Hwy., Kissimmee, 407/390-9615

Joe's Crab Shack ($$): Dungeness, Alaskan king, Alaskan snow, and blue crabs, prepared in a variety of methods.
- •12124 S. Apopka Vineland Road, 407/465-1895
- •10 Blake Blvd., Celebration, 321/939-6880

Landry's Seafood ($$): An abundant menu of shrimp, crab, and fish dishes, plus a lot more.
- •8800 Vineland Ave., 407/827-6466

Lone Star Steakhouse ($): Inexpensive steaks and grilled items.
- •8850 Vineland Ave., 407/827-8225

Longhorn Steakhouse ($): Basic steaks, ribs, and grills.
- •5351 W. Irlo Bronson Mem. Hwy., 407/396-9556

Outback ($-$$): Serviceable, basic steaks, but oh my, that bloomin' onion.
- •7804 W. Irlo Bronson Mem. Hwy., Kissimmee, 407/396-0017
- •4845 S. Kirkman Rd., 407/292-5111
- •8195 Vineland Ave., 407/477-0098

Ponderosa ($): Steaks, seafood, ribs, chicken, and the All-You-Can-Eat Grand Buffet.
- •4024 W. Irlo Bronson Mem Hwy., Kissimmee, 407/846-3339

•7598 W. Irlo Bronson Mem. Hwy., Kissimmee, 407/396-7721
•5771 W. Irlo Bronson Mem. Hwy., Kissimmee, 407/397-2477
•6362 International Drive, 407/352-9343
•8510 International Drive, 407/354-1477
•8200 World Center Drive, 407/238-2526

Red Lobster ($$): This popular national chain offers a wide variety of seafood classics.
•12557 SR 535, Lake Buena Vista, 407/827-1045
•5690 W. Irlo Bronson Mem. Hwy., Kissimmee, 407/396-6997
•5936 International Drive, 407/351-9313
•9892 International Drive, 407/345-0018
•4010 W. Vine St., Kissimmee, 407/846-3513
•7780 W. Irlo Bronson Mem. Hwy., Kissimmee, 321/677-0191

Sizzler ($): Sizzler offers steaks, salads, chicken, fish, and the famed Buffet Court, which is especially tempting at breakfast.
•12195 S. Apopka Vineland Rd., LBV, 407/238-1551
•7602 W. Irlo Bronson Mem. Hwy., Kissimmee, 407/397-0997
•9142 International Drive, 407/351-5369
•6308 International Drive, 407/248-9711
•4006 W. Vine St., Kissimmee, 407/846-2900

Steak and Ale ($-$$): This understated and thankfully theme-less steakhouse offers excellent steaks, most notably the nine-pepper filet and Bourbon Street steak.
•6115 Westwood Blvd., 407/352-0526

Teppanyaki

Teppan table cooking, the trick-laden and ancient Japanese art of chopping and cooking steak, shrimp, chicken, lobster, and veggies over a metal grill, is practiced in many locations in and around Disney World. Watching the chefs work their magic can make children and adults go positively slackjawed.

Ran-Getsu ($$-$$$$ - 8400 International Drive, 407/345-0444) is a particularly good option, offering live entertainment on the weekends and a lovely garden atmosphere as a backdrop for teppanyaki plus sushi, sashimi, shabu-shabu, and sukiyaki. Zagat named it the 4th best Japanese restaurant in the US thanks to its neat Japanese presentation of Florida ingredients.

Benihana ($$-$$$ - WDW Hilton, 1751 Hotel Plaza Blvd., 407/827-4865) is the O.G. of teppanyaki, and **Mikado** ($$$ - Marriott Orlando World Center, 8701 World Dr., 407/238-8829) is impressive as well.

Better value and quicker seating can be had at **Kobe Steakhouse** ($$-$$$ - 8460 Palm Parkway, LBV, 407/239-1119; 8350 International Drive, 407/352-1811; 2901 Parkway Blvd., Kissimmee, 407/396-8088, 5605 S. Kirkman Road, 407/895-6868), **Shogun** ($$-$$$ - 6327 International Drive, 407/352-1607) which is at the Rodeway Inn, but better than that would suggest, or **Yoji** ($$-$$$ - 4592 W. Irlo Bronson Mem. Hwy., Kissimmee, 407/396-6858), which has great sushi.

Asian Flavors

The aesthetically obsessive-compulsive **Ming Court** ($$-$$$ - 9188 International Drive, 407/351-9988) emphasizes grilled Florida seafood and steak interspersed with regional Chinese cuisine, some of which is blended with contemporary Italian, French, south Pacific, and Latin American flavors to create innovative taste sensations. Presentation is mind-blowing, as is the restaurant's architecture and decor. There's a huge dim sum menu and live Chinese music nightly. Near Universal, **Taste of Hong Kong** ($ - 6540 Carrier Dr., 407/248-2863) specializes in dim sum.

Thai is the new Chinese, and the phenomenal **Thai Thani** ($-$$ - 11025 S. International Dr., 407/239-9733), located near Sea World, features intensely flavorful cuisine like panang curry, chili jam stir fry, duck noodle soup, and three taste fish – I like this place even better than the venerable **Siam Orchid** ($$ - 7575 Universal Blvd, 407/351-0821), with its comfortable, intimate setting in which diners feast on delectable dishes like Siam wings, curry puffs, basil seafood, and orchid roast duck.

On Restaurant Row, **Amura** ($$-$$$$ - 7786 Sand Lake Rd., 407/370-0007) offers post-modern décor and daring, innovative sushi – AOL Cityguide named it the city's best. **Hanamizuki** ($-$$ - 8255 International Drive, 407/363-7200) offers sushi and lesser-known Japanese cuisine. **Také** ($-$$ - 7818 W. Irlo Bronson Mem. Hwy., Kissimmee, 407/390-0333) offers a sushi bar, an udon bar, and a tempura bar. **Sushiology** ($-$$$ - 6400 International Dr., 407/345-0245) offers big combos at small prices.

For good, neighborhood-style Schezuan and Hunan specialties, visit **Fortune Court** ($ - 8607 Palm Parkway, LBV, 407/239-2399). The enormous **Trey Yuen** ($ - 6800 Visitors Circle, 407/352-6822) features Cantonese specialties in ornate settings.

If quantity is your goal, stuff your face at **Origami** ($$ - Pointe*Orlando, 9101 International Drive, 407/352-2788) for 40 varieties of sushi plus tempura, teriyaki, and noodles, the well-liked 100-item **Bill Wong's Famous Super Buffet** ($$ - 5668 International Drive, 407/352-5373), the **New York China Buffet** ($-$$ - 12173 Apopka-Vineland Road, 407/238-9198) and its excellent seafood selection, the **Dragon Court Super Buffet** ($$ - 12384 Apopka-Vineland Road, LBV, 407/238-9996) for all-you-can-eat sushi. Mongolian barbecue, a stir-fry of thinly sliced meats, noodles, veggies, and sauces is an appealing way to eat, especially for control freaks, who get to select every ingredient that goes into their meal. Enjoy this fun meal at **China Jade** ($$ - 7308 International Drive, 407/363-9797).

Orlando has a few quality Indian restaurants. Best of all is **Passage to India** ($-$$ - 5532 International Drive, 407/351-3456), an Orlando Sentinel Reader's Choice award winner offering a lunch buffet and authentic cuisine cooked to order, mild or spicy. **Aashirwad** ($-$$ - 5748 International Dr., 407/370-9830) specializes in Northern indian and Mughlai cuisine.

Other good bets are **Akbar Palace** ($ - 4985 W. Irlo Bronson Mem. Hwy., Kissimmee, 407/396-4836), **New Punjab** ($ - 7451 International Drive, 407/352-7887 and 3404 Vine St., Kissimmee, 407/931-2449), **Shamiana** ($-$$ - 7040 International Drive, 407/354-1160) for Bombay style cooking, and **India Palace** ($ - 8530 Palm Parkway, LBV, 407/238-2322).

Innovative, International, & Islander

One of my personal favorites is **Café Tu Tu Tango** ($$ - 8625 International Drive, 407/248-2222), an art gallery, studio, and tapas bar offering appetizer-sized dishes designed for mixing and matching, sampling and sharing. The menu includes wide varieties of dips, soups, and finger foods ranging from standbys like artichoke and crab dip and black bean soup to things like the duck salad and sesame seared tuna sashimi, along with pot stickers, spring rolls, kim chee glazed ribs, barbacoa quesadillas, delicious alligator bites, and pizzas, all with a playful twist from the norm. The carefree, festive, and noisy **Bahama Breeze** ($$ - 8849 International Drive, 407/248-2499; 8375 Vineland Ave., 407/938-9010) has free-flowing bars and island cuisine, with coconut-breaded onion rings, habanero or jerk chicken wings, conch chowder, tiger prawn and spring green salad, and ambitious pan-seared salmon pasta in passion fruit, thyme, and crean sauce. Bahama Breeze is often mobbed long into the night, and is an equal winner both as a dinner choice and an evening out.

On Restaurant Row, the **Samba Room** ($$ - 7468 Sand Lake Road, 407/226-0550) is a white-linen café accentuated by palm trees and a festive Latin menu whose specialties are paella, grilled mussels, the Cuban sandwich, sea bass, crab cakes, and other flavorful treats. The Samba Room includes a cigar bar and two outdoor patios.

Regional American and international restaurants abound in this vacationers' melting pot. The **Everglades** ($$-$$$ - Omni Rosen Hotel, 9840 International Drive, 407/354-9840) offers surprising gourmet Floridian fare such as tenderloin of buffalo, filet Key Largo topped with crabmeat, pinot noir demi-glace, and Bernaise sauce. **Roy's Restaurant** ($$-$$$ - 7760 Sand Lake Road, 407/352-4844) offers Roy Yamaguchi's signature Hawaiian fusion cuisine, like macadamia crusted mahi, hibachi salmon, and blackened ahi. Rich sauces complement the freshest seafood.

Winner of a whopping seven awards in Orlando Magazine's 2005 Dining Awards, Restaurant Row's **Seasons 52** ($-$$ - 7700 W. Sand Lake Rd., 407/354-5212) is a trendy, fun wine bar with a different seasonally inspired menu from Clifford Pleau every week of the year – each with the entire selection of entrees under 475 calories, and there's no butter anywhere to be seen – certainly a rarity with food this good, usually those with food allergies have to suffer to dine this well. Feeling decadent? Desserts clock in at 250 or less. The **Melting Pot** ($$-$$$$ - 7549 Sand Lake Road, 407/903-1100) offers cheese, main course, and dessert fondues. At **Sweet Tomatoes** ($ - 6877 S. Kirkman Rd., 407/363-1616), guests can eat unlimited soups, salads, pastas, muffins, and desserts for one low price.

Think "Rainforest Café Light" when you think **Jungle Jim's** ($ - 12501 Apopka-Vineland Road, LBV, 407/827-1258) although you'll get stiffer tropical drinks and a smaller menu of entrees alongside panini sandwiches and half-pound Angus steakburgers, grilled chicken, or Gardenburgers prepared nearly two dozen different ways. Right next door, multiple award winner **Pebbles** ($$ - 12551 SR 535, LBV, 407/827-1111) offers casual hamburgers and gourmet delicacies like strawberry glazed duck and herb crusted chicken and other California-inspired dishes.

The airy, open, and popular **Cedar's Restaurant** ($$ - 7732 Sand Lake Road, 407/351-6000) offers authentic Middle Eastern and Mediterranean dishes including a decadent kibbeh nayeh (like steak tartare with cracked wheat) and signature salmon or snapper dishes, topped with tomatoes, red peppers, onions, cilantro, garlic, and tahini. **Coconut Willy's** ($ - 4944 W. Irlo Bronson Mem. Hwy., 407/397-1455) is a British pub with a Key West flavor, offering cheap eats plus line dancing, soccer, karaoke, billiards, outdoor dining, free limo pickup, and a daily happy hour. The **Orlando George & Dragon Pub** ($ - 6314 International Dr., 407/351-3578) features a beer garden, soccer and other sports on giant screen TV, NTN games, nightly entertainment, and outdoor deck seating.

East of the main tourist drags **Jockamo's** ($ - 3042 Sand Lake Rd., 407/226-2848) features New Orleans style po'boys stuffed with roast beef, ham, chicken, sausage, shrimp, oysters, catfish, crawfish, grouper, and gator.

Would you believe that even **McDonald's** ($ - 6875 Sand Lake Road, 407/351-2185) are magical here? The World's Largest McDonald's offers the usual Mickey D's menu plus burritos, panini sandwiches, hand-dipped Breyer's ice cream, and freshly baked pizza that shockingly isn't half bad.

Italian

Italian fare is always a crowd-pleaser, and Orlando has a number of solid choices of both the independent and chain varieties. The classy

Bergamo's ($$-$$$ - The Mercado, 8445 International Drive, 407/352-3805) has won awards from Florida Trend, Wine Spectator, and Southern Living magazines. It features singing waiters and a menu of daring dishes like duck ravioli in marsala cream, roasted sea bass with truffle broth, and filet mignon with pancetta and basil with porcini sauce.

For a more over the top experience, visit the AAA Four Diamond, Wine Spectator, and Ivy Award-winning **Christini's** ($$$$ - 7600 Dr. Phillips Blvd., 407/345-8770), which is romantic and flavorful, and albeit pricey, delivers an Italian dining experience with few peers. The **Capriccio Grill** ($$$ - 9801 International Drive, 407/345-4450) is one of three stellar restaurants at the Peabody Orlando, offering steaks and chops flown in from Ruprecht's of Chicago, as well as lobster, fresh seafood, and traditional Italian favorites like osso bucco and chicken parm.

The recipient of the Orlando Magazine Readers' Choice award for Best Italian restaurant is **Enzo's on the Lake** ($$$ - 1130 South US 17-92, Longwood, 407/834-9872), situated atop a gorgeous lake. Favorite menu items here include the bucatini alla Enzo, pasta tubes in a black pepper parmesan sauce with peas, prosciutto, bacon, and mushrooms and the 15-ounce filetta di Texana, the French, Italian, and California wine selections earn acclaim as well.

Villa de Flora ($$-$$$ - Gaylord Palms, 6000 W. Osceola Pkwy., 407/586-1114) offers bountiful and delicious buffets in this festive open-air piazza at all three meals. Mondays and Fridays feature Italian fare like pesto crusted salmon, swordfish parmesan, osso bucco, and pork marsala. Wednesdays and Sundays feature French – coq au vin, pork loin au poivre, beef daube, and bistro chicken. Tuesdays and Saturdays are Spain's turn – with ropa vieja, grouper Costa del Sol, pollo con chorizo, banana leaf salmon, and Andalusian vegetables. Greece gets Thursdays with spit roasted chicken, artichoke moussaka, souvlaki, and chicken oreganato. AOL Cityguide named this the best brunch in town.

Cariera's Cucina Italiana ($$ - 7600 Dr. Phillips Blvd., 407/351-1187), named top ten for atmosphere by AOL Cityguide, offers contemporary Italian selections like seafood ravioli, Sorrento chicken, and lobster and shrimp tortellacci. **Italianni's** ($-$$ - 8148 International Drive, 407/345-8884) serves traditional dishes like spaghetti bolognese as well as more exotic choices like toasted ravioli with pomodoro and basil pesto, and chicken Milanese with gorgonzola creamed spinach and tomato caper relish.

In the town of Celebration, **Café D'Antonio** ($$ - 691 Front St., 407/566-CAFÉ) offers classics with a few interesting choices, like the parpardelle tossed with salmon, peas, brandy, and marscapone.

Pacino's ($$ - 5794 W. Irlo Bronson Mem. Hwy., Kissimmee, 407/396-8022) menu includes well-done standard family-friendly Italian fare, along with great cuts of steak like 32 oz. porterhouse, 18 oz. T-bone, NY strip, or ribeye, or a 13 oz. filet grilled on an open copper Sicilian grill. Italian specialties include shrimp and scallops in vodka sauce, frutti di mare, lasagna, shrimp scampi, wild mushroom alvino, and canneloni alla Fiorentino, filled with veal, ham, spinach, mozzerella, and Romano cheese.

Ciao Italia ($-$$ - 6149 Westwood Blvd., 407/354-0770) offers a great selection of antipasti and traditional favorites with some updates: spaghetti with fresh tomato, buffalo mozzarella, and basil, linguine with mussels or clams, a filet in a green peppercorn mustard sauce, veal scallopine, and a chicken breast stuffed with prosciutto, asparagus, mushrooms, and cheese.

Also, count on these national standbys:

The Olive Garden ($): Homestyle and safe Italian fare served up in big portions with bottomless soup, salad, and breadsticks.
- •8964 International Dr., 407/264-0420
- •1555 Sand Lake Rd. 407/851-0344
- •5021 W. Irlo Bronson Mem. Hwy., Kissimmee, 407/396-1680
- •12361 Apopka-Vineland Road, LBV, 407/239-6708

Romano's Macaroni Grill ($-$$): Stellar pasta dishes and other classical Italian entrees made in an open-view kitchen. Try not to fill up on the delicious peasant bread.
- •12148 Apopka-Vineland Road, LBV, 407/239-6676
- •5320 W. Irlo Bronson Mem. Hwy., 407/396-6155

Southwestern Styles

The flavors of Tex-Mex and the American southwest are well represented in Orlando. Adobe Gila's ($ - Pointe*Orlando, 9101 International Drive, 407/903-1477) is a lively hole-in-the-wall-looking bar and restaurant with nightly music and tons of frozen drinks, 75 different varieties of tequila, and a dirt cheap menu consisting of tacos, quesadillas, tostadas, and Gila wraps. Mercado's Guadalajara Cantina ($-$$ - 8445 International Dr., 407/352-3657) features traditional Mexican entrees plus "guadalajaritas."

Chevy's Fresh Mex ($-$$): The best chain Mexican food out there, featuring total freshness and huge portions.
- •12547 Apopka-Vineland Road, LBV, 407/827-1052
- •2809 W. Vine St., Kissimmee, 407/847-2244

Chili's ($): The baby back ribs, mushroom jack fajitas, and tostada nachos are particularly good.
- •12172 S. Apopka Vineland Road, LBV, 407/239-6688
- •5340 W. Irlo Bronson Mem. Hwy., Kissimmee, 407/396-4333
- •7021 International Drive, 407/352-7618

Don Pablo's Mexican Grill ($): Large portions of affordable Mexican classics like tacos, burritos, taquitos, enchiladas, and combination dinners cooked in an open kitchen.

●8717 International Drive. Phone: 407/345-1345

Good Sports

The best sports bar in town, **Orlando Ale House** ($-$$ - 5573 S. Kirkman Rd., 248-0000, 12371 Winter Garden Rd., 407/239-1800) features 30 TVs plus winning comfort food like a dozen burgers, boneless or traditional wings with eight sauces, and Italian and American entrees like osso bucco, cajun mahi, ribs, shrimp, and even dolphin. **Houlihan's** ($-$$ - 9150 International Dr., 407/363-0043) offers fettucine Alfredo with provolone, fontina, and parmesan, stuffed chicken breast, Cajun pork medallions, coriander salmon, and margarita shrimp.

Plenty of Orlando restaurants cater to sports fans, either by way of theming or by throwing every television show known to man on the television. The **Official All-Star Café** ($-$$ - Disney's Wide World of Sports, 407/827-8376) is the theme restaurant partially owned by Joe Montana, Tiger Woods, Ken Griffey Jr., Shaquille O'Neal, and Wayne Gretzky. Classic and current sporting events are shown, and diners enjoy salads, burgers, sandwiches, and pasta. **Dan Marino's Town Tavern** ($$-$$$ - Pointe Orlando, 9101 International Drive., 407/363-1013) serves lobster ravioli, Chicago flatiron, bacon-wrapped meatloaf, and and six fresh fish selections cooked any of five ways in a friendly, upscale atmosphere. Unlike Shula's, no dolphins on the menu here.

Al Bundy would have a stroke seeing how many **Hooters** ($ - 8510 Palm Parkway, 407/239-0900, Pointe*Orlando, 9101 International Dr., 407/355-7711, 5300 Kirkman Road, 407/354-5350, 2201 W. Vine St., Kissimmee, 407/932-2702) restaurants populate Orlando. Home of "almost famous" and overpriced wings, that aren't nearly as hot as the flirtatious waitresses in orange hotpants and push-up bras.

Rated the best sports bar in town by the Orlando Sentinel, **JB's** ($ - 4880 South Kirkman Road, 407/293-8881) boasts 11 satellite dishes and screens as large as 18 feet, with up to 30 games at one time, plus great drink specials Tuesdays, Wednesdays, and Thursdays. **TGI Friday's Front Row Sports Grill** ($ - 8126 International Drive, 407/363-1414) has the full Friday's menu plus 100 brands of domestic and imported beer, 80 TVs, two basketball hoops, pool tables, video games, shuffle boards, darts, and memorabilia.

Other sports bars in the area include **Damon's** ($-$$,at Old Town, 5770 W. Irlo Bronson Mem. Hwy., Kissimmee, 407/397-9444) offers rich, flavorful bar food including legendary ribs, melt-in-your-mouth potato skins and the world-famous Onion Loaf.

Smoke 'Em If You Got 'Em

This ain't North Cackalacky, but it is the south, and that means BBQ. Far west of WDW, **JT's Prime Time Restaurant** ($$ - 16299 W. Irlo Bronson Mem. Hwy., Kissimmee, 407/239-6555) serves downright inhalable smoked meats (the turkey is particularly good!) along with steaks and chicken. **Sonny's Real Pit BBQ** ($ - 4200 Vine St., Kissimmee, 407/847-8888) offers all-you-can-eat specials on BBQ chicken, beef, pork, and ribs Sunday through Wednesday of every week and cheap lunch specials – piping hot sandwiches served on toasted garlic bread. **Smokey Bones** ($-$$, 2911 Vineland Road., Kissimme, 407/397-7102) offers teeming combinations – the ribs and pork are particularly good, the chicken not so much – and irresistable homemade donuts.

Also, don't forget:

Tony Roma's – The Place for Ribs ($$): Valhalla for rib lovers - baby backs smothered in Carolina honey, Blue Ridge smoke, and Tony Roma's Red Hot sauces.

•12167 Apopka-Vineland Road, LBV, 407/239-8040
•Osceola Mall, 3415 W. Vine St., Kissimmee, 407/870-9299
•8560 International Drive, 407/248-0094

Casual Flavors & Comfort Foods

Combine gourmet fare like oak-fired steaks and ambitious seafood dishes with simulators, attractions, video games, a rooftop dance terrace, live DJs, and bars aplenty and you get **Pac-Man Café at XS Orlando** ($$-$$$ - Pointe*Orlando, 9101 International Drive, 407/226-8922), a bacchanalian paradise reminiscent of a grown-up Chuck E. Cheese or Dave & Buster's, with a particular accent on 80s nostalgia. The menu includes Pac-Man shaped pizzas (naturally),

Le Peep ($, 4666 S. Kirkman Rd., 407/291-4580) offers the best breakfast in town, with a ton of signatures like the breakfast banana split, omelets with names like Spinnaker, White Lightning, and Green Fields Forever, and potato skillet dishes, and panini, burgers, and crepes at lunch.

Visit the **B-Line Diner** (Peabody Orlando, 9801 International Drive, 407/345-4460) 24 hours a day for the best omelets in town and extraordinary desserts in a 1958 atmosphere. **Buffalo Wild Wings** ($ - 7004 International Dr., 407/351-6200) features 12 flavors of sauce. **Johnny Rocket's** ($ - Pointe Orlando, 9101 International Drive, 407/903-0763) is a 50's style burger joint.

Murray Bros. Caddyshack ($-$$, 5250 International Drive., 407/351-3848) is not quite a theme restaurant – not of the beat-you-over-the-head variety at least. They do feature Golden Tee and lots of sports on television, plus a super friendly waitstaff and unpretentious but well-executed family-friendly fare like burgers, ribs, seafood, and the likes. **Race**

Rock Orlando ($-$$, 8986 International Drive, 407/249-9876) is a redneck magnet in a palatial round building (that used to house an upscale Italian restaurant) – a theme restaurant owned by Kyle and Richard Petty, Jeff Gordon, Rusty Wallace, and Michael Andretti. Race Rock offers a huge collection of racing memorabilia and vehicles, but the food quality has dipped considerably in recent years. Avoid this lackluster place..

Like a low-budget Waffle House – ok, a LOWER budget Waffle House, the **Omelet House** ($ - 7618 W. Irlo Bronson Mem, Hwy, Kissimmee, 407/396-6957) serves up about a dozen omelets plus waffles and pancakes.

Sometimes it's familiarity you crave. Most of America's most popular chains operate Orlando locations:

Bennigan's ($): Irish pub-inspired restaurant with extensive, cheap menu.
- •13502 South Apopka Vineland Rd., 407/938-9090
- •5877 W. Irlo Bronson Mem. Hwy., 407/390-0687
- •6324 International Drive, 407/351-4435
- •6109 Westwood Blvd., 407/352-5657

Bob Evans ($): Homestyle favorites and big breakfasts at reasonable prices.
- •4967 W. Irlo Bronson Mem. Hwy, 407/396-7377
- •7411 W. Irlo Bronson Mem. Hwy, 407/396-8599
- •6014 Canadian Court, 407/352-2161

Denny's ($): Breakfast served all day along with burgers, sandwiches, and more at budget prices. Some locations are open 24 hours.
- •12375 SR 535, LBV, 407/239-7900
- •5855 W. Irlo Bronson Mem. Hwy., Kissimmee, 407/396-0757
- •7631 W. Irlo Bronson Mem. Hwy., Kissimmee, 407/396-0757
- •5825 International Drive, 407/351-1581
- •7660 International Drive, 407/351-1420
- •9880 International Drive, 407/351-5127
- •5827 Caravan Ct., 407/352-4527

Friendly's ($): Sandwiches, soups, and salads, but it's all about the ice cream.
- •3915 W. Vine Street, Kissimmee, 407/846-4432
- •8718 International Drive, 407/345-1655

International House of Pancakes ($): Pancakes served all day, sandwiches, burgers, and more.
- 12400 S. Apopka Vineland Road, LBV, 407/239-0909
- 6065 W. Irlo Bronson Mem. Hwy., Kissimmee, 407/396-0406
- 5184 W. Irlo Bronson Mem. Hwy., Kissimmee, 407/396-1500
- 9990 International Drive, 407/352-9447
- 6005 International Drive, 407/351-0031
- 7661 International Drive, 407/351-4090
- 5203 Kirkman Road, 407/370-0597

Perkins Family Restaurant ($): Open 24 hours, well-known for their pancakes, eggs Benedict, steak, burgers, and sandwiches.
- 5170 W. Irlo Bronson Mem. Hwy., Kissimmee, 407/396-8960
- 7451 W. Irlo Bronson Mem. Hwy., Kissimmee, 407/896-3725
- 12559 Apopka-Vineland Road, LBV, 407/827-1060
- 6813 Sand Lake Road, 407/351-0373

Shoney's ($): Offering a breakfast buffet plus burgers, sandwiches, steaks, and pasta at low prices.
- 6075 W. Irlo Bronson Mem. Hwy., Kissimmee, 407/396-4849
- 7640 W. Irlo Bronson Mem. Hwy., Kissimmee, 407/397-2779
- 12204 S. Apopka Vineland Rd., Lake Buena Vista, 407/239-5416

T.G.I. Friday's ($): Sandwiches, steaks, burgers, and over 400 different drinks. Their appetizers, especially fried cheese and potato skins, are stellar.
- 12543 Apopka-Vineland Road, LBV, 407/827-1020
- 5034 W. Irlo Bronson Mem. Hwy., Kissimmee, 407/397-2200
- 7798 W. Irlo Bronson Mem. Hwy., Kissimmee, 407/397-4300
- 8955 International Drive, 407/903-9556
- 8126 International Drive (Front Row Sports Grill), 407/363-1414
- 6424 Carrier Drive, 407/345-8822

Pizza

Pizza is like a child-sized Xanax. There are places all over Orlando where you can make everything better with a slice of pepperoni. **Fama's** ($ - 5474 Central Florida Parkway, 407/239-1500) is a spirited, family-run joint just east of International Drive. Cheap, filling lunch specials make this a good option for a midday Sea World break. **Giordano's** ($- 12151 Apopka-Vineland Road, LBV, 407/239-8900; 7866 W. Irlo Bronson Mem. Hwy., Kissimmee, 407/397-0044) makes stuffed pizzas in a dish so deep, you could lose a fork. The Central Florida locations are the only ones outside the Chicago area. **Bella Roma** ($ - 6423 International Drive, 407/352-9603) offers unpretentious Italian favorites and hand-tossed pizza.

Flipper's Pizza ($ - 7480 Universal Blvd., 407/351-5643; 4774 Kirkman Road, 407/521-0607; 6125 Westwood Blvd., 407/345-0113, 2934 Vineland Rd., 407/396-1202, 5770 W. Irlo Bronson Mem. Hwy., 407/397-9509) offers New York, Chicago, and California style pies, subs, pastas, calzones, and more, all delivered. **Hometown Pizza** ($ - 4147 W. Vine St., Kissimmee, 407/932-4411) delivers all over the Kissimmee tourist corridor.

Domino's Pizza ($): Pizza, breadsticks, and wings delivered to your hotel room. Because sometimes you just can't move another inch.
- Orlando: 407/896-3030
- 8542 Palm Parkway, Lake Buena Vista, 407/239-1221
- 8687 W. Irlo Bronson Mem. Hwy., Kissimmee, 407/238-2266
- 5461 W. Irlo Bronson Mem. Hwy., Kissimmee, 407/396-0550
- 5320 S. Kirkman Rd., 407/248-8434

Pizza Hut ($): Tasty if not overly authentic. Pizza Hut Express locations can now be found at many area hotels.
- 8699 Palm Parkway, LBV, 407/239-0950
- 5740 W. Irlo Bronson Mem. Hwy., Kissimmee, 407/396-2207
- 9100 International Drive, 407/345-8833
- 8255 International Drive, 407/354-1582
- 7060 International Drive, 407/351-0005
- 2426 S. Kirkman Rd., 407/445-4299

Pizzeria Uno ($-$$): Chicago-style deep dish pizzas, burgers, and pastas are offered here.
- 12553 Apopka-Vineland Road, LBV, 407/827-1212
- 8250 International Drive, 407/351-8667
- 5350 W. Irlo Bronson Mem. Hwy., Kissimmee, 407/396-2755

Sbarro ($): Thin, overpriced mall pies.
- 8540 International Dr., 407/363-9030

Chapter 13

NIGHTLIFE

Just because Disney World is a family destination doesn't mean that it has an early bedtime. There's a huge selection of dinner shows and fun activities suitable for the whole family, as well as nightclubs and bars for a more adult release. Note that dinner shows listed do not include tax and gratuity unless otherwise noted.

Dinner Shows

Arabian Nights
  6225 W. Irlo Bronson Mem. Hwy., Kissimmee, 800/553-6116 or 407/239-9223
  Call for showtimes.
  www.arabian-nights.com
  $47 adult, $29 kids 3-11.
  AE, DI, MC, VI
  Discounts: online booking ($10 or free upgrade), magazines ($5), AAA discount, Magicard ($10), orlandoinfo.com ($11-14).

  Arabian Nights tells the story of a princess and prince set to marry under the protection of the magical Black Stallion. Over 60 spectacular horses (eight different breeds) and performers dazzle audiences in 20 acts. The three-course meal consists of your choice of prime rib, grilled chicken breast, Black Angus chopped steak, or vegetable lasagna as well as garden salad, fresh vegetables, dinner rolls, garlic mashed potatoes, and unlimited beer, wine, and soft drinks. Dessert is wedding cake. Face-smooshing at your own peril. Arabian Nights was voted the best theme restaurant in Orlando in 2004 and 2005 by AOL Cityguide and has won similar awards from Florida Living magazine, the Orlando Sentinel reader's poll, and Orlando magazine. Previous Best of Citysearch awards include best dinner show, best B-list attraction, best family outing, and best romantic restaurant.

Capone's Dinner and Show
4770 W. Irlo Bronson Mem. Hwy., Kissimmee, 800/220-8428 or 407/397-2378
Call for showtimes.
www.alcapones.com
$43.99 adults/$29.99 kids 3-12.
AE, DI, MC, VI
Discount: Website: (50% off), AAA discount, Magicard.

Capone's Dinner and Show, a 1992 addition to the U.S. 192 landscape, features a 15-item unlimited Italian buffet including sausage and peppers, baked chicken, honey roasted ham, baked ziti, deep dish lasagna, a "brownie surprise" dessert, unlimited Budweiser, Bud Lite, sangria, soda, or "Al's Rum Runners" to the accompaniment of a show taking place in 1931 Chicago's gangland that resembles a Guys and Dolls set, as rival gangsters and G-men square off.

Chamber of Magic (at Skull Kingdom)
5933 American Way, 407/354-1564
Showtimes are 6pm and 8pm.
www.skullkingdom.com
$19.75 adults, $15.97 kids and seniors.
AE, DI, MC, VI
Discount: Website ($2), magazines ($2).

Chamber of Magic, located at Skull Kingdom just off International Dr., features illusionists performing in a state-of-the-art, intricately decorated theater with primo sound and laser lighting systems. Dinner includes unlimited pepperoni and cheese pizza and wine, beer, and soda. Combination tickets with Skull Kingdom are available.

Dolly Parton's Dixie Stampede Dinner and Show
8251 Vineland Avenue, 407/238-2777
Showtimes: 6:30pm, 7pm, or 8:30pm, depending on season.
www.dixiestampede.com

Parental Parole

It's okay to need time away from your kids. It doesn't make you a bad person. It's YOUR vacation too. But unless you've got Grandma stashed in your checked luggage (and the TSA will love you for that), you gotta scramble to get some grownup time.

If you're staying at a Disney resort, you can take advantage of the numerous children's activity centers throughout the property. The supervised programs at the Animal Kingdom Lodge, Boardwalk, Contemporary, Grand Floridian, Polynesian, Wilderness Lodge, Yacht and Beach Club, Swan, and Dolphin include dinner and activities like video games, arts and crafts, movies, puzzles, and games. At Universal Orlando, the Portofino Bay Hotel, Hard Rock Hotel, and Royal Pacific Resort offer the same service.

Elsewhere in Orlando, babysitting services are available. Contact your hotel's guest services desk or contact one of the establishments listed:

If you prefer private supervision, look into **KinderCare**. They have been the Disney-authorized, in-room babysitting service for the past 20 years. Rates are $12 and up per hour, and there is a four hour minimum. You can also utilize their services if you're staying off-site. Call 407/827-5444 or visit kindercare.com.

Kids Nite Out, at 8324 International Drive, offers a drop-off point for when the 'rents feel like cruising I-Drive after dark. Their program includes dinner in a supervised entertainment and activity center. Call 888/400-KIDS or 407/354-4664 for details, or visit kidsniteout.com. **All About Kids** also provides professional childcare services. Contact them at 407/812-9300, 800/728-5606, or all-about-kids.com.

$46.99 adults/$19.99 kids 4-11.
AE, DI, MC, VI
Discount: Website ($15 upgrade), magazines ($5), Magicard ($4), AAA.

This massive 35,000 square foot arena is the newest dinner show in Orlando, featuring country and western music, 32 horses, trick riding, comedy, and specialty acts as teams of riders and performers represent the North and South during stunt shows and competitions that stir up ersatz patriotism, while tiptoeing very carefully around explicitly refighting the Civil War. They keep saying the South's gonna do it again. I ask, do what? Lose? I have to admit that I felt kind of out of place here, but dyed-in-the-wool red-staters will find plenty to get excited about. Included in the show is a 50-minute pre-show featuring varied entertainment options, and access to the open-air stables where the show's featured performers live.

The deeply subpar (even for the dinner shows' assembly line kitchens) four-course meal includes rotisserie chicken and roast pork loin, veggie soup, biscuits, corn on the cob, herb potato, dessert, and unlimited soft drinks. This show gets revamped every November through Christmas, pitting North Pole and South Pole elves against one another. Biggie-Tupac it certainly ain't. Dixie Stampede is visible from I-4, accessible from the SR 535 exit. Vineland Road intersects with SR 535 where traffic from eastbound I-4 hits the road.

Fiascos
7430 Universal Blvd., 866/GO-FIASCO or 407/226-7220
Showtimes: 6:30pm
www.fiascos.us
$45 adults/$25 kids 3-9.
MC, VI
Discounts: Magazines ($5).

This new International Drive area dinner comedy show epitomizes Murphy's law throughout – don't worry, they don't suck, it's just the theme of the place. Jokes are corny and awful – like Jungle Cruise bad – but the menu is broad, featuring Indian, Chinese, Mexican, English, and vegetarian choices plus unlimited beer and soda.

Hoop-Dee-Doo Revue
Fort Wilderness Resort, Walt Disney World, 407/WDW-DINE
Showtimes: 5pm, 7:15pm, 9:30pm
www.disneyworld.com
$50.22 adults/$25.43 kids 3-11.
AE, MC, VI
Discount: 20% for Amex holders (late show only).

The Hoop-Dee-Doo Revue is Disney's longest-running dinner show and has quite a few devotees, although reviews in recent years have been more and more mixed. At Pioneer Hall three times a night, the immensely popular show is full of song, dance, and slapstick comedy from a six-person cast. The food is served by the pile, with all-you-can-eat fried chicken, barbecued ribs, corn-onion-pepper medley, and strawberry shortcake with unlimited beer, wine, and soda. Kids can nibble on pizza, hot dogs, and mac & cheese. Reservations are required and can be made up to two years in advance.

Magic & Mischief Theater
8815 International Dr., 407/352-3711
Showtimes: Wed-Sun 6:30pm, 8:30pm
www.magicandmischieftheater.com
$21.95 adults/$16.95 kids 3-9.
MC, VI
Discounts: magazine ($5)

This magic show features illusion and hypnosis acts from Fred Becker, Puck, and Alexander similar to offerings in Vegas, Hollywood, and cruise lines. They also have a magic shop that opens at 11am daily.

Makahiki Luau
Sea World, 7007 Sea Harbor Dr., 800/327-2424 or 407/351-3600
Showtimes: 6:30pm, 8:45pm during peak seasons
www.seaworld.com
$42.95 adults/$27.95 kids 3-9.
AE, MC, VI
Discounts: Magicard ($5).

An authentic four-course Polynesian meal is served alongside Polynesian and Hawaiian entertainment along the side of Sea World's big lagoon. Dinner includes mahi mahi in pina colada sauce, sweet and sour chicken, smoked pork loin, sides, dessert, coffee, and tea. There's also a cash bar all night long. Park admission is not required.

Medieval Times Dinner & Tournament
4510 W. Irlo Bronson Mem. Hwy., Kissimmee, 888/WE-JOUST or 407/396-2900
Showtimes: 6:15pm, 7pm, 7:30pm, 8:30pm, depending on season.
www.medievaltimes.com
$48.95 adults/$32.95 kids 3-12.
AE, DI, MC, VI
Discounts: Orlandoinfo.com ($6), magazines ($2-4), Magicard (10%), AAA

You've heard of Medieval Times before, maybe even seen it featured in *The Cable Guy*. But what's the hype all about?. Just the single most exciting dinner show in the state, that's all. The year is 1093 AD, the place is the court of His Grace, Count Don Raimundo II. Six brave knights compete in swordplay, falconry, sorcery, romance, and even a real joust. Which of the six knights do you root for? Well, your seat bears the same emblem on the shield of one of the knights. Find that one and keep an eye on him, because he's yours. The menu includes appetizers, vegetable soup, whole roast chicken, spare ribs, herb-basted potato, pastries, coffee, beer, wine cocktail, and soft drinks, all served without utensils, so roll up those sleeves, bucko. Allow extra time to get here, as the stretch of US 192 near the showplace is under construction and often bumper-to-bumper.

Murderwatch

    Grosvenor Resort, Walt Disney World, 407/827-6534
    Showtimes: 6pm and 9pm, Saturdays only.
    www.murderwatch.com
    $39.95 adults/$10.95 kids 3-9.
    MC, VI
    Discounts: Website.

Sherlock Holmes attempts to unravel a mystery, with the help of participating audience members every Saturday night alongside a bountiful dinner buffet.

Outta Control Magic Show

    Wonderworks, 9067 International Drive, 407/351-8800
    Showtimes: 6pm, 8pm
    www.wonderworksonline.com
    $21.95 adults/$14.95 children and seniors.
    AE, DI, MC, VI
    Discounts: Website ($1.50), magazines ($1.50).

Held twice each night, the dinner show at WonderWorks includes a 90-minute magic show full of audience participation and laughter, and a meal of unlimited hand tossed pizza, beer, wine, and soda. Orlando Weekly called this the best dinner show in Orlando. Combination tickets to Night of Wonder and WonderWorks and/or its laser tag game are available as well.

Pirates Dinner Adventure

    6400 Carrier Drive, 800/866-2469 or 407/248-0590
    Showtimes: 7:30pm, 8pm, depending on season.
    www.piratesdinneradventure.com
    $49.95 adults/$29.95 kids 3-11.
    AE, DI, MC, VI
    Discounts: Website ($4), Orlandoinfo.com ($7-13), magazines ($4).

I'll say it: this dinner show does not have the right to be this good. But somehow it is. In fact, it's my pick for the best dinner show in Orlando. This swashbuckling good time in the northern International Drive area features a pre-show buffet of salads, snacks, and hors d'oeuvres, followed by a shockingly tasty meal of lemon pepper chicken, beef, yellow rice, vegetables, and apple cobbler à la mode, accompanied by unlimited beer, wine, or soft drinks.

The show takes place on an elaborate set constructed to resemble a pirate galleon floating in a huge indoor lagoon. The show combines audience participation, music, staged combat, a surprisingly believable romance, and genuinely laugh-out-loud comedy through a winning storyline about nobility and honor among thieves. The family-friendly show is thoroughly entertaining and never redundant. After the performance, the Buccaneer Bash is a dance party emceed by cast members, where various desserts and coffees are served as well. Truly a sumptuous feast, and the most entertaining dinner show in Orlando by a long run.

Sleuths Mystery Dinner Show

7508 Universal Blvd., 800/393-1985 or 407-363-1985

Showtimes: 6pm, 7:30pm, 9pm, depending on day of week and season.

www.sleuths.com

$46.95 adult/$23.95 child 3-11.

AE, DI, MC, VI

Discounts: website ($2.50-5), Orlandoinfo.com ($3-7), magazines ($4), AAA

Be forewarned. Every night at Sleuths, somebody dies. But don't worry, because this is International Drive's only murder mystery dinner theater. Shows alternate but all feature audience participation, and it's up to you to solve the crime. The successful sleuth who cracks the case receives a prize. The dinner includes hors d'oeuvres, salad, crackers and cheese, rolls, honey glazed Cornish game hen, prime rib, lasagna, vegetable medley, mashed potatoes and gravy, herb stuffing, fruit garnish, "mystery" dessert, and unlimited beer, wine, and soft drinks. The *Merry Mystery* show presents a more family-friendly menu and mystery, with storylines designed especially for kids ($28 adult, $16 child).

Spirit of Aloha Luau

Polynesian Resort, Walt Disney World, 407/WDW-DINE

Showtimes: 5:15pm, 8pm Tues-Sat.

www.disneyworld.com

$50.22 adult/$25.43 kids 3-11.
AE, MC, VI

This new iteration of the classic Polynesian Luau, held twice each evening in Luau Cove, features authentic Polynesian dancing, music from Lilo and Stitch, and specialty acts, many of which are performed by artists who have studied at the Polynesian Cultural Center in Honolulu. The new show is much more kid-friendly than the previous version. The meal includes salad, sliced pineapple, coconut bread, Lanai roasted chicken, pork ribs, South Seas vegetables, Polynesian rice, and "volcano" dessert – chocolate mousse with raspberry sauce. Also included are unlimited soft drinks, beer and wine. For kids, there's PB&J, mac & cheese, chicken nuggets, or hot dogs. Like the Hoop-Dee-Doo Revue, this show requires reservations and accepts them up to 2 years.

Nighttime Attractions/Entertainment Complexes

Disney's Boardwalk
Walt Disney World, Epcot resort area, 407/939-5100.
www.disneyworld.com
Opens 9am, closing times vary by establishment.
Free admission – some clubs charge a cover.

Sprawled along the shores of Crescent Lake in between Epcot and the Disney-MGM Studios, the Boardwalk complex combines luxury accommodations, nightclubs, fine dining, midway games, and shopping in an atmosphere that recalls the 1940's. Totally coherent with the themes of the nearby Yacht and Beach Club resorts, the Boardwalk includes classic swing at the Atlantic Dance Club 35,000 square feet of sports at the ESPN Club, dueling pianos at Jellyrolls (cover varies), and plenty of fun in between, like street performers. Small boats can be rented here,

Cirque du Soleil: La Nouba
See this entry under Chapter 20.

Citywalk
Universal Orlando, 407/363-8200
Open 11am-2am.
www.citywalkorlando.com
$8.95 party pass (all club access)/$12 party pass with movie.
AE, DI, MC, VI

Universal's answer to Pleasure Island, located in between its two theme parks, this bustling entertainment complex is certainly impressive. It draws a much more local crowd than Pleasure Island does, attempting to cater to the same young, affluent demographic they're trying to reach with their theme park programming. The **Universal Cineplex** is a movie lover's dream, featuring steep stadium seating with rocking chairs, 20 wall-to-wall screens with state of the art projection and digital sound. What's more, dinner and movie deals ($19.95) make this a great bargain. For Florida residents, paid parking earns an $8 concession rebate.

Nightclubs here include **Hard Rock Live** (see below); **the groove** ($7), a spiffy but not particularly compelling dance club that doesn't draw the same breed of partier seen downtown; **CityJazz**, offering funk, blues, R&B, and jazz during the week. CityJazz becomes the Bonkerz Comedy Club stand-up comedy club on weekends; and **Bob Marley: A Tribute to Freedom**, a replica of his Kingstown home offering live reggae music and authentic Jamaican food.

Bars and restaurants here include **Jimmy Buffett's Margaritaville**, an island-themed restaurant and margarita maker for Parrotheads everywhere; **Pat O'Brien's**, known for dueling pianos and tasty but lethal Hurricanes; **NBA City**, featuring fine dining and basketball memorabilia and interactive games, **Latin Quarter**, offering tango, salsa, and samba lessons along with live entertainment and great pan-Latin food. **Emeril's Orlando** is the celebrity chef's signature restaurant, his **Tchoup Chop** is nearby. CityWalk also has a dozen shops. See Chapter 21 for details. Parking is free here after 6pm.

Pleasure Island

Downtown Disney, 407/WDW-2NITE
Open 11am-2am. Cover and age restrictions at some clubs after 7pm.
www.downtowndisney.com
$20.95 adult for all-club access, $9.95 for one club.
AE, MC, VI
Discounts: military (15%), Disney Dining Experience.

Disney's grown-up playground, celebrating its 15th anniversary in 2004, offers guests a chance to kick back, cut loose, enjoy a few drinks and a few tunes after dark. Although it was originally built to compete with the now-defunct Church Street Station, it bears much more resemblance to the newer Citywalk. This portion of the Downtown Disney area, located in between the Marketplace and West Side, features New Year's style celebration every night, along with eight nightclubs, food, and retail. There is only one full-service eatery here, the Portobello Yacht Club, but about a dozen other options and additional fun activities at the West Side and Marketplace.

All told – Citywalk and Pleasure Island are mostly comparable, but the presence of the additional sections of the Downtown Disney complex give that destination the edge.

The nightclubs on Pleasure island include **Motion**, which brings a mix of alternative and Top 40 dance music. The **Rock & Roll Beach Club** has a beach party atmosphere and live rock music, along with pool tables and a couple of lounges and snack bars. The **Mannequins Dance Palace** is a discotheque that takes its name from the dummies who stand watch across the dance floor, which is a rotating turntable. **8 Trax** features classic pop, dance, and rock from the 1970's – on Thursdays it becomes 80s Trax - score. Highlight of the evening: 12:30am, YMCA, every night. Consider yourself warned. The **BET Soundstage Club** offers urban contemporary entertainment, including R&B and hip-hop acts as well as live DJs. There's also a martini bar and a decent menu of Southern, Cajun, and Caribbean food. An Irish pub is scheduled to open here in summer 2005.

Two clubs here specialize in comedy including the quirky **Adventurers' Club**, where eccentric "explorers" recall tales of their mishaps and accomplishments. Shows here start every 30-45 minutes. The **Comedy Warehouse** stars a troupe of five decidedly off-center improvisational comedians and a musician who, five times nightly, perform skits based on audience suggestions, including riotous "how can they get away with this?" spoofs on Walt Disney World. Guests sit on stools packed like sardines in a tiered arena, so everyone has a good view. Each show is different and equally entertaining, making this one of the most popular clubs on the Island.

Another highlight of a Pleasure Island visit is the nightly New Year's Eve celebration. Dancers and live bands perform on the West End Stage, and at 11:45, guests count down from 10 and shout "HAPPY NEW YEAR!" and then PI explodes into a festive street party of fireworks, spotlights, confetti, and more. You must be 18 to enter most Pleasure Island clubs unless accompanied by a parent, and you must be 21 to enter BET Soundstage and Mannequins. Pleasure Island has a designated driver program.

SAK Comedy Lab
> 45 E. Church St., 407/648-0001
> www.sak.com
> Admission varies.
> MC, VI

Improvisational comedy is performed at this theater Tuesdays through Saturdays. Shows are at 9pm Tues-Wed, with performances at 8pm and 10pm Thu-Sat. Florida residents receive discounted admission.

Nightclubs & Bars

Orlando has had a vibrant nightlife scene for years, since the early '90s, when Sasha and John Digweed would perform in front of rabid crowds at downtown clubs, long before anyone else in America had ever heard of them. Like many cities, Orlando has experienced a nightlife crackdown by law enforcement in recent years, so it's not quite as wild a town as it was a few years ago, but there are still plenty of places to get into mischief after dark. Most of the cool places are in downtown, so be prepared to leave the tourist havens.

In Disney World
Atlantic Dance
Disney's Boardwalk, 407/939-7600
www.disneyworld.com

This club at the Boardwalk features DJs and dance parties every Tuesday through Saturday, with playing '80s, '90s, Top 40, and high-energy dance. Atlantic offers 25 signature martinis plus hand rolled cigars. Free admission.

House of Blues
Downtown Disney West Side, 407/934-2583
www.hob.com

One of Central Florida's top music venues, the House of Blues club offers top-name national entertainment across the spectrum of rock, blues, country, house, and more, several nights a week. Note that there is no cover to eat at the House of Blues. Cover varies, and advance tickets are recommended.

Jellyrolls
Disney's Boardwalk, 407/939-7600
www.disneyworld.com

Dueling pianos and singalongs make this Boardwalk club a favorite. Cover is $8.

Laughing Kookaburra Goodtime Bar
Wyndham Palace, 1900 Buena Vista Dr., 407/939-7600
www.wyndhampalace.com

"The Kook" features a wide variety of domestic and imported beers plus live entertainment and dancing at this popular Hotel Plaza establishment.

Top of the Palace Lounge
Wyndham Palace Resort, Downtown Disney, 407/872-3722
www.wyndhampalace.com

With spectacular 27th floor views, a nightly sunset party, the Wyndham Palace's festive bar is a perfect spot for a nightcap, or a Downtown Disney pregame, 27 stories above the ground.

In Kissimmee, Lake Buena Vista, & the International Drive area
Adobe Gila's
Pointe*Orlando, 9101 International Drive, 407/903-1477
www.adobegilas.com

Fishbowls, live music, and dirt-cheap Mexican food are offered up at this festive, raucous open-air bar and restaurant on the second floor of the Pointe*Orlando complex.

Backstage
Rosen Plaza Hotel, 9700 International Drive, 407/996-9700
www.rosenplaza.com

The Backstage is a popular bar with DJs spinning 80's, 90's, and Top 40 music, plus occasional live bands. There is no cover. Wednesday and Thursday are ladies' nights.

Blue Martini
Mall of Millennia, 4200 Conroy Road, 407/447-2583
www.bluemartinilounge.com

Hip and stylish, this bar boasts a martini menu with nearly thirty variations on the classic adult beverage. We like the Dirty Blonde and Caramel martinis. We also like throwing back a few of these and then wandering around the gallery at the mall.

The Cricketer's Arms
The Mercado, 8445 International Drive, 407/354-0686
www.cricketersarmspub.com

The Cricketers Arms, calling itself "the oldest and newest English pub," offers hand-drawn ales plus 15 imported British stouts, lagers, and bitters served in 20 oz. mugs,. Live entertainment is featured and a satellite dish shows football and other sports on a big screen television, often live at ridiculous hours of the day.

Glo Lounge
8967 International Drive, 407/351-0361

With an attractive Convention Center area location, the Glo Lounge offers billiards and beverages along with DJs and a popular nightly happy hour in a beachfront art deco motif.

Hard Rock Live
CityWalk, 6050 Universal Blvd., 407/351-7625
www.hardrocklive.com

Adjacent to the Hard Rock Café restaurant at Universal's Citywalk complex is this 3,000-capacity concert venue, showcasing a variety of local, national, and international comedy and music talent as diverse as the Korn, Moody Blues, Marilyn Manson, the Blue Man Group, Good Charlotte, and George Clinton. Cover varies, purchase tickets in advance.

Lucky Leprechaun Irish Pub
7032 International Drive, 407/352-7031
www.luckyleprechaunirishpub.com

This pub, located on the north side of International Drive, carries a wide selection of ciders and well over a dozen beers on tap. There's Irish music and karaoke nightly, and Celtic football.

Matrix & Metropolis
Pointe*Orlando, 9101 International Drive, 407/370-3700
www.metropolismatrix.com

Nightclub & Bar named this stylish I-Drive duo to its Top 100 of 2005 list. The industrial and contemporary **Matrix** offers 15,000 square feet of state-of-the-art light and sound while clubgoers shake their groove thangs to trance, breaks, and Top 40 dance. The club boasts one of the city's largest dance floors, plus video walls and unique art deco furniture. The sister property of the Matrix nightclub, Metropolis offers upscale billiards and music from the 80s, 90s, and today, with décor inspired by the Moulin

Rouge. Stylish attire is required, and 18+ are welcome. Men must be 21 to enter on Saturday and Sunday nights.

O'Shucks Pub & Billiards
7467 International Drive, 407/352-7892
www.oshuckspub.com

Another I-Drive Irish pub, with a full array of games like Hold 'em Poker, foosball, Golden Tee golf, billiards, darts, and football. Pizza and wings are served.

Downtown
Antigua
33 Church Street, 407/649-4270

Named Orlando's best dance club for 2005 by AOL Cityguide, Antigua features popular Friday night happy hours with hip-hop accompaniment, while Saturdays bring house music. It draws a very young, sometimes rough crowd.

The Blue Room
17 West Pine Street, 407/423-2588
www.blueroomorlando.com

The Blue Room is a newly-renovated VIP nightclub in a 100-year old building, featuring national and regional DJs playing progressive, breaks, trance, '70s, '80s, and more.

Cairo
50 E. Central Blvd., 407/422-3595

This downtown favorite provides high-energy dance music including hip-hop, house, and disco, to a young, hip, good-looking crowd. Reggae and 80s music can be found on the rooftop lounge. AOL Cityguide named Cairo to its 2005 Best Nightclubs list.

The Club at Firestone
578 N. Orange Ave., 407/872-0066

The legendary and seminal Firestone is back, 22,500 watts strong — with college nights Thursdays, Latin music on Fridays, hip-hop and eclectic dance music at Saturday's gay Free4All nights, and ladies' night on Sundays.

Club Paris
122 W. Church St., 407/832-7409
www.clubparis.net

Now you don't have to be a C-list celebrity with a video camera to spend a night in Paris – or at least in her disturbingly pink namesake nightclub. Hip-hop and Top 40 dance are played to a sexy young crowd – which on any given night seems to include at least one Paris Hilton doppelganger. The former Rosie O'Grady's space has been given a fresh coat of paint and a pile of hype, and as a result is one of Orlando's most popular nightclubs.

Eli's Cribb
114 N. Orange Ave., 407/841-2008

The newest club from Thee Grotto maestro Eli Tobias, the Cribb features house, techno, and breakbeats from an impressive regional lineup of residents, and bright green and purple décor.

ICON
20 East Central Blvd., 407/649-6496
www.icon-nightclub.com

This techno club gone mainstream features local, national, and international DJs playing progressive house and more, including marquee names like Paul Oakenfold. There is a no jeans, no sneakers policy for men.

Knock Knock Martini Lounge
Central Ave. at Magnolia, 407/999-7739
www.knockknockbar.com

One of the hippest places in town, this lounge presents an eclectic assortment of DJ's specializing in chill-out, downtempo, and house music. Legendary producer Q-Burn plays here regularly.

Mulvaney's Irish Pub
27 W. Church Street, 407/872-3296

Mulvaney's features live entertainment, traditional Irish fare (including breakfast, served all day), and six imported beers on tap.

Roxy Orlando
740 Bennett Road, 407/898-4004
www.roxyorlando.com

The Roxy is three clubs in one – a two-level main dance room playing high energy and chart dance with video projection and an in-house dance team; the multi-level Cream VIP bar with plush couches and beds; and the Suede ultralounge.

Screamers
360 State Lane, 407/244-0299
www.screamersorlando.com

Located downtown just off exit 83A of I-4, Screamers is a gritty, no-nonsense music venue for punk, emo, ska, hardcore, and other alternative acts.

Tabu
46 N. Orange Ave., 407/648-8363
www.tabunightclub.com

Tabu is a raucous nightclub located in the newly-renovated, historic Beacham Theater. One of the premier upscale clubs in the city, Tabu features state-of-the-art sound and lighting systems, with DJs spinning a wide variety of dance and party music Tuesdays through Saturdays.

Thee Grotto
110 N. Orange Ave., 407/841-2008
www.theegrotto.com

Billed by jaded purists as "downtown's last great club," Thee Grotto is the place for sweet, soulful house music every night of the week. Every Tuesday night is an open-deck competition.

Chapter 14

SHOPPING

There is tremendous variety in shopping in Orlando and its surroundings. From one of a kind boutiques to bargain basement factory outlets, you'll find it all here.

Shopping & Entertainment Complexes

Citywalk
> Universal Orlando, 407/363-8200
> Open 11am-2am.
> www.citywalkorlando.com

Universal's CityWalk complex offers specialty shopping and gourmet dining in addition to the nightclubs discussed in Chapter 13. A dozen or so shops include Cigarz for a full bar and accessories, Dapy for lava lamps and novelties, Cartooniversal for character merch; Fresh Produce for apparel in vibrant colors, the Endangered Species Store for nature-themed gifts, Fossil for watches and sunglasses, Glow for all things blacklit; Quiet Flight for surfwear, Silver for jewelry and accessories, and the Universal Studios Store for theme park souvenirs.

Restaurants here include Emeril's, the Motown Café, Latin Quarter, Jimmy Buffett's Margaritaville, Pastamoré, NBA City, the Hard Rock Cafe, NASCAR Café, and more.

Downtown Disney Marketplace
   Buena Vista Drive at Hotel Plaza Blvd., 407/824-4321
   Open 10:30am-11pm
   www.downtowndisney.com

   The original destination of the current Downtown Disney complex, the Marketplace features unique boutiques and excellent gourmet dining, plus a marina where boats can be rented. Fifteen shops include World of Disney, the largest character store in the planet, and probably your single best destination for WDW souvenirs and goodies; the LEGO Imagination Center, with every kind imaginable and some you haven't even contemplated; Team Mickey's Athletic Club, selling golf, NASCAR, ESPN, and other sports-themed stuff; Pooh Corner, for all things Hundred Acre; Once Upon a Toy for playtime goodies; Disney's Pin Traders, for the World's biggest selection of collectible pins. Everything at Mickey's Mart is under $10.
   Restaurants here include Fulton's Crab House on the Empress Lilly riverboat, Wolfgang Puck Express, Earl of Sandwich, the Rainforest Café, Cap'n Jack's Restaurant, Ghirardelli Soda Fountain, and McDonald's.

Downtown Disney West Side
   Buena Vista Drive, 407/824-4321
   Open 11am-midnight
   www.downtowndisney.com

   The West Side of the Downtown Disney complex is an entertainment juggernaut, between the unforgettable Cirque du Soleil: La Nouba, the AMC Pleasure Island 24 multiplex, the House of Blues nightclub, and DisneyQuest interactive theme park. But there's also great shopping here, at the Virgin Megastore, selling any music, movies, and multimedia you could possibly want; the Guitar Gallery for axes, Magic Masters for tricks and novelties; Sosa Family Cigars for premium smoke; Hoypoloi for contemporary art and housewares; Celebrity Eyewear for designer eyeglasses; Disney's Candy Cauldron for sweets, Magnetron for fridge décor; and Mickey's Groove for Disney merchandise.
   Restaurants here include the bayouriffic House of Blues, the four-part Wolfgang Puck restaurant; Bongo's Cuban Café, and an installment of the famous Planet Hollywood.

Festival Bay
   5250 International Drive, 407/481-1944
   Open 10am-10pm Mon-Sat, 10am-7pm Sun.
   www.belz.com

Right across from Universal Orlando, this 1.1 million square foot entertainment and shopping complex is still not yet complete, but many of the shops and attractions here have already opened. The far-from-traditional anchors include a 20-screen Cinemark movie theater, a Vans Skatepark, Ron Jon Surf Shop, Steve & Barry's University Sportswear, Shepler's Western Wear, and Bass Pro Shops Outdoor World.

Restaurants here include Murray Bros. Caddyshack, Villa Pizza, A&W Root Beer, Long John Silver's, Mrs. Fields, Auntie Anne's, and more.

Market Street at Celebration

610 Sycamore Street, 407/566-4020
Open Mon-Sat 10am-9pm, Sun noon-6pm.
www.celebrationfl.com

Celebration's main retail drag combines pleasant neighborhood architecture with top notch stores like Gooding's, Barnie's Coffee, the Market Street Gallery, a jewelry store, a collectible doll and bear shop, and lots more eclectic and cute.

The Mercado

8445 International Drive, 407/345-9337
Open 10am-11pm daily.
www.themercado.com

This is an International Drive landmark, a recreated Spanish mission with red-filed roofs on stucco towers that reach far into the sky. Inside you'll find a blend of unique shops and decent restaurants, although in recent years it's practically become a ghost mall. At the time of writing Mercado had been placed on auction, so it may be closed by the time this goes to press.

Restaurants and bars include Bergamo's, La China, the Cricketer's Arms, the Butcher Shop, Mahi Mahi Bistro, Guadalajara Grill, and a half-empty food court. The twenty-some shops offer crafts, apparel, and specialty merchandise, the likes of which you're not likely to find in your local mall.

Old Town

5770 W. Irlo Bronson Mem. Hwy., Kissimmee, 407/396-4888
Open 10am-11pm daily.
www.old-town.com

If you don't mind a little seediness, the festive and bustling Old Town complex offers intriguing retail opportunities and fun rides and games. The complex includes 18 rides ($2-25 each), a haunted house, laser tag, 75 specialty shops, and restaurants including Damon's, Flipper's Pizza, A&W,

Chinese food, and more. There's also two bars here, the Blue Max and Sun on the Beach. Old Town also hosts classic car shows with live music on Friday and Saturday nights – Fridays focus on cars from 1973-1987, while Saturdays bring out an average of 325 classic cars, antiques, and hot rods. Thursdays are motorcycle nights.

Pointe*Orlando
> 9101 International Drive, 407/248-2838
> Open 10am-11pm daily.
> www.pointeorlandofl.com

The upscale Pointe*Orlando complex, located near the Convention Center, offers wild entertainment, impeccable shopping, and fine dining in a pleasant open-air atmosphere. Entertainment options include the Muvico Pointe 21 theatres, the Wonderworks attraction, two nightclubs, Matrix and Metropolis, and a restaurant/grownup arcade called Pac-Man Café, with over 100 interactive video games and booze.

Shops include a somewhat typical array of mall options like Armani Exchange, Foot Locker, Victoria's Secret, and more unusual apparel choices, as well as specialty stores like Bath and Body Works, Dapy, Yankee Candle, Sunglass Hut, and Watch Station. Popular bars here include Hooters, Adobe Gila's, and Lulu's Bait Shack. Other restaurants include Johnny Rockets, Dan Marino's Town Tavern, and Wise Guys. With its pleasant outdoor setting and stacked dining and diversion lineup, it's a befuddling shame that Pointe*Orlando is having such occupancy issues.

Inexpensive Gift Ideas

Souvenirs can add up really quickly and turn into a huge vacation expense if you go overboard, which isn't hard to do, considering the dozens and dozens of retail temptations at the theme park. One way to bring home plenty of keepsakes at a low cost is to select a low-cost item and collect as many of them as you can. Pressed pennies and trading pins are excellent bets, as are postcards, especially if you are into scrapbooking.

Disney pin trading is an activity that is often addictive to those who get into it, hunting down rare pins like retired Beanie Babies. You'll see all kinds of Pin Trading stations all over WDW, but you may want to familiarize yourself with the whole concept beforehand, as there's a lot more to it than just shiny pieces of metal. Check out www.officialdisneypintrading.com for details.

Malls, Marketplaces & Outlet Centers

Belz Designer Outlet Center

5211 International Drive, 407/352-9611
Open 10am-9pm Mon-Sat, 10am-6pm Sun.
www.belz.com

Down the block from the bigger Factory Outlet Mall, this annex offers 45 mid- to upscale shops featuring discounts up to 75%. Highlights include Kenneth Cole, Bose, DKNY, Ralph Lauren, Ann Taylor, Waterford Crystal, Fossil, Movado, Calvin Klein, Perry Ellis, and Geoffrey Beene.

Belz Factory Outlet Mall

5401 W. Oakridge Road, 407/352-9611
Open 10am-9pm Mon-Sat, 10am-6pm Sun.
www.belz.com

You won't find much atmosphere at this mall, one of the older and more run-down ones in the area. What you will find are great bargains at 170 outlet shops from the likes of Sunglass Hut, Samsonite, Bass, Vitamin World, Mikasa, Royal Doulton, Nautica, Gap, Van Heusen, Adidas, Birkenstock, Pacific Sunwear, Guess Jeans, Nike, Timberland, and London Fog.

Crossroads of Lake Buena Vista

12545-12551 SR 535, Lake Buena Vista, 407/827-7300
Open 10am-10pm.

Located at the end of Hotel Plaza Blvd., this strip mall offers the closest grocery store to Walt Disney World, a well-equipped 24-hour Gooding's. There's also 36 holes of Pirate's Cove Adventure Golf, a bunch of restaurants including Taco Bell, McDonald's, Perkins, TGI Friday's, Jungle Jim's, and Red Lobster.

Flea World

Hwy 17-92, Sanford, 407/330-1792
Open 9am-6pm Fri-Sun.
www.fleaworld.com

Billing itself as the "World's Largest Flea Market," the air-conditioned, indoor/outdoor Flea World contains 1,700 shopping booths offer-

Flea Markets

You don't have to drive all the way out to Sanford for flea market shopping – this bargain-hunting expedition can be done much closer to the main tourist drag. In fact, a few bustling markets operate along US 192 in Kissimmee.

• **192 Flea Market:** 400 booths. Open daily. 4301 W. Irlo Bronson Mem. Hwy, 407/396-4555.
• **Maingate Flea Market:** 400 booths. Open daily. 5407 W. Irlo Bronson Mem. Hwy., 407/390-1015.
• **Osceola Flea & Farmer's Market:** 900 booths. Open Fri-Sun only. 2801 US Hwy 192, 407/846-2411.

ing a wide variety of new and used merchandise to 50,000 shoppers each weekend. There's also the Kids World area featuring 8 rides aimed at kids under 6, and the Funworld amusement area, with 15 carnival type rides, go-karts, 250 video games, and miniature golf. To get here, take I-4 to Exit 98 and take Lake Mary Blvd. east to US 17-92 south.

Florida Mall

8001 S. Orange Blossom Trail, 407/851-7234
Open 10am-9:30pm Mon-Sat, 11am-7pm Sun.
www.simon.com

This mall has long been considered among the tops in Orlando. It was renovated from top to bottom in 1999, and growth since then has added anchor stores Nordstrom and Lord & Taylor to the existing lineup of Burdine's, Dillard's, JC Penney, Saks Fifth Avenue, Sears, and more than 250 specialty stores, 25 of which made their Orlando area debuts as part of the recent expansion. The roster includes Claire's, Swatch, Abercrombie, Teavana, Aveda, MAC, Sephora, Bombay, Brookstone, Pottery Barn, Williams-Sonoma, Bailey Banks & Biddle, Banana Republic, Brooks Brothers, and Hollister.

The Florida Mall also has about two dozen restaurants and eateries, including Buca di Beppo, California Pizza Kitchen, and Ruby Tuesday. The Mall is located at the corner of Sand Lake Road and the SOBT.

Kissimmee Manufacturers' Outlet Mall

4673 W. Irlo Bronson Mem. Hwy., Kissimmee, 407/396-8900
Open 10am-9pm Mon-Sat, 11am-5pm Sun.

Located one mile east of the junction of US-192 and SR-535, this 25-shop strip mall offers deep discounts on goods from Nike, Totes, Bon Worth, Dress Barn, and more.

Lake Buena Vista Factory Stores
15591 SR 535, 407/238-9301
Open 10am-9pm Mon-Sat, 10am-6pm Sun.
www.lbvfs.com

This new development features factory-direct prices with discounts up to 75% on over 300 brands. Stores include Borders, Claire's, Easy Spirit, Eddie Bauer, Fossil, Gap, Liz Claiborne, Nike, Nine West, Old Navy, Sony, Sunglass Hut, Vitamin World, and Wilson's Leather.

The Mall at Millenia
4200 Conroy Road, 407/363-3555
Open 10am-9:30pm Mon-Sat, 11am-7pm Sun.
www.mallatmillenia.com

This brand-new, visually gorgeous mall features central Florida's only Nieman-Marcus, along with Macy's, Bloomingdale's, and over 150 high-end stores like Apple, BCBG Max Azaria, bebe, Dior, Burberry, Gucci, Louis Vuitton, Crabtree & Evelyn, Cartier, Jimmy Choo, Swarovski, Crate & Barrel, Bang & Olufsen, and the Sharper Image. Great restaurants here include McCormick and Schmick's, the Cheesecake Facory, and PF Chang's. The Mall hosts a concert series the first Friday of every month.

Orlando Fashion Square Mall
3201 E. Colonial Drive, 407/896-1131
Open 10am-9pm Mon-Sat, 11am-6pm Sun.
www.orlandofashionsquare.com

Expanded by 500,000 square feet in 2000, Fashion Square Mall features over 160 specialty shops, plus a 24-screen movie theatre, along with anchors Sears, Macy's, Dillard's, and JC Penney.

Orlando Premium Outlets Mall
8200 Vineland Ave., 407/352-9611
Open 10am-10pm Mon-Sat, 10am-7pm Sun.
www.premiumoutlets.com

Home ot the best upscale outlet shopping in Orlando, the Premium Outlets Mall is an outdoor Mediterranean-themed mall featuring 110 stores offering discounts up to 65% from top-notch manufacturers like Burberry, Skechers, Banana Republic. DKNY, Giorgio Armani, French Connection, Versace, Mikasa, Movado, Ecco, Skechers, Coach, Oilily, Bose, and Kenneth Cole.

Last-Chance Souvenirs

Orlando International Airport can be a godsend for when you realize at the last minute that you've forgotten to pick up something for someone, with stores selling official merchandise from Walt Disney World, Universal Studios, and Sea World.

Chapter 15

FUN IN & ON THE WATER

Just because Walt Disney World is in a landlocked part of Florida doesn't mean that you have to stay high and dry on your vacation. There are plenty of ways to have a wet good time in and around Orlando. If you find yourself irresistibly drawn to the sea, Daytona Beach is less than an hour away via I-4.

Water Parks

Orlando and its environs are home to several excellent water parks, each of which offers something slightly different to the mix. Depending on what your agenda is – scenery, slides, waves, whatever – you can be sure to find one that's perfect for you. Personally, my favorites are Typhoon Lagoon (great scenery, great rides, less crowded than Blizzard Beach) and Wet 'N' Wild (huge number of awesome slides). Note that most water parks close for annual "rehab" and repairs for some period during the winter months. If you are traveling between October and April, call the water parks to see whether they will be open during your visit.

Another very important tip: refrain from wearing bathing suits with rivets, buckles, or exposed metal, you won't be allowed on slides.

Adventure Island
10001 McKinley Drive, Tampa, 813/987-5660
Open 10am-5pm with extended hours in the summer and holidays.
www.adventureisland.com

$32.95 adult/$30.95 kids 3-9. Two-day two-park passes with Busch Gardens cost $70.95 adult/$60.95 kids 3-9. For a third day, add $15. Parking: $5.

AM, DI, MC, VI

If Busch Gardens is on your agenda, you can relax and cool off at their next-door neighbor and sister park, also owned by Anheuser-Busch. The 30-acre park features a variety of slides and attractions of both the high-speed and chilled-out varieties.

The newest adrenaline rush is Wahoo Run, sending a 5-passenger raft down a 600 feet slide full of waterfalls and tunnels. Splash Attack is a playground with 50 interactive water elements in a massive treehouse environment, with cargo nets, bridges, and web crawl tunnels. The Gulf Scream is a 210-foot body slide where guests reach a top speed of 22mph. The Calypso Coaster is an open flume carrying inner tubes or two-man rafts. Everglides is a pair of 72-foot mega slides.for guests on toboggans.

More laid back attractions include Paradise Lagoon, a 9,000 square foot complex including a pool, cliff jumping platforms, rope walks, and waterfalls; and the gently-flowing, half-mile-long Rambling Bayou. There is also a 17,000-square foot wave pool.

Other offerings include Key West Rapids ride, sending guests down a 6-story, 700-foot plunge with twists, turns, pools, showers, gushers, and other surprises; the Aruba Tuba group raft, Fabian's Funport, a children's water play area, the three twisting tubes of the Water Moccasin, the Caribbean Corkscrew, a high-speed adventure down twin braided translucent tubes, the snaking 450-foot Calypso Coaster, the 7-story Tampa Typhoon freefall slide, the Barratuba, an inner tube slide, Runaway Rapids, a 300-foot slide down a jungle mountain.

Amenities at Adventure Island include an arcade, a gift shop, a championship white-sand volleyball complex, several stretches of beach, and three snack bars. From Orlando, take I-4 west, exit to I-75 North, take I-75 to exit 54 (Fowler Ave.), and follow signs to Busch Gardens. It's about an hour and a quarter drive.

Disney's Blizzard Beach
    Near the Animal Kingdom, 407/824-4321
    Open 10am-5pm with extended hours during the summer.
    www.disneyworld.com
    $34 adults/$28 kids 3-9.
    AM, MC, VI
    Discounts: AAA.

The newest crown jewel in Disney's water park crown, 66-acre

Blizzard Beach, opened in 1995 and combines the chills of a Northern ski resort with the thrills of a high-tech water park near the Animal Kingdom. The Imagineers behind the park put quite a bit of off-center humor into the park, which was pretty much a given, what with the theme of an Alpine ski lodge surrounded by friggin' palm trees. As the legend goes, a freak snowstorm gave some genius the idea of creating a ski lodge. Of course the snow melted as soon as the lodge was built, but the runoff from the melting snow on the former toboggan, bobsled, and slalom trails created – what else? Black diamond water slides. There's even a chair lift to take you to the top of Mt. Gushmore, or stairs, if you so prefer.

Summit Plummet is a ski jump that sends you screaming 120 feet straight down the side of Mt. Gushmore at heart-stopping speeds up to 60 miles an hour. Slush Gusher is a 90-foot high double-humped slide on which women sometimes start in two-piece bikinis and end in one. Fun for riders and spectators! Teamboat Springs offers families a chance to navigate six-passenger whitewater rafts down a twisting 1,200-foot slide with series of waterfalls. The eight-lane Toboggan Racer sends guests racing over "moguls" as they zoom down the "slopes" on a water-slick mat. The three Snow Stormer flumes wind down the mountain, following a switchback course through slalom gates. There's also a pair of open Runoff Rapids slides plus a third enclosed, "black hole" style.

Kids can enjoy miniature versions of Blizzard Beach's most popular attractions at Tike's Peak. Preteens can enjoy special attractions at Ski Patrol Training Camp. Melt-Away Bay is a one-acre wave pool at the base of Mt. Gushmore, constantly fed by "melting snow" waterfalls. The Cross Country Creek offers a lazy ride around the park, through caves and grottoes. The Beach Haus shop offers souvenirs and sundries, while there are a few dining options as well, although you can bring your own food, and many prefer to do just that. To get here, take I-4 exit 64B (US 192 West), take the Magic Kingdom exit, and follow signs.

Disney's River Country

After 25 years, Disney's "Ol' Swimmin' Hole" water park went on a hiatus in 2002 and will remain closed indefinitely.

Disney's Typhoon Lagoon

Near Downtown Disney, 407/824-4321
Open 10am-5pm with extended hours during the summer.
www.disneyworld.com
$34 adults/$28 kids 3-9.
AM, MC, VI
Discounts: AAA.

The second eye-popping Disney water park, the 56-acre Typhoon Lagoon's theme is what you might expect from the name: The wrath of God hits an unfortunate seaside town, in the form of a typhoon and subsequent earthquake and volcanic eruption (What, did they elect Schwarzenegger mayor?). When the dust settled, once-impenetrable rock had been carved into chutes down the side of 85-foot high Mount Mayday, upon which is the incredible sight of the Miss Tilly, a shrimp boat out of Safen Sound, Florida, impaled on the rocks. Every few minutes the craft attempts to free itself by sending a 50-foot stream of water into the air.

New in 2005 is the Crush'n'Gusher, sends one- or two-person tubes down three sets of flumes and spillways which take divergent paths through an abandoned fruit packing house. The three slides range from 410 to 420 feet in length.

The featured attraction here is the eponymous Typhoon Lagoon. At 2.75 million gallons and 2 acres, it's America's largest wave pool. Released every ninety seconds, waves are either gentle bobbing waves or the kind of waves adored by surfers and dreaded by landlubbers, alternating every hour. During the bobbing periods, tubing is allowed on the 2- to 3-foot waves. However, when the waves switch, ditch your tube and bear down for a 4-to 6-foot wave.

Something you won't find anywhere else is Shark Reef, offering a taste of snorkeling. For no extra fee, guests are equipped with fins, mask, snorkel, and wetsuit, then given instruction and plunged into the 72-degree salt-water pool, chock full of some 4,000 creatures, including nurse and bonnethead sharks, rays, and others, all clustered around the coral reef and the sunken tanker in the center of the pool. Visit Shark Reef first thing in the morning, as crowds build quickly. Plus, sometimes the morning dives are allowed to linger more than in the more crowded hours.

Slides abound at this park, including Humunga Kowabunga, a 30-mile-an-hour free-fall, dropping you 51 feet down the 214-foot slide; three Storm Slides that put guests in a 20 mph downhill corkscrew through about 300 feet of waterfalls, forests, caves, and rocky crags. Three inner-tube flumes offer the chance to board inner tubes for a journey down the mountain. Keelhaul Falls takes the 400-foot slide at a tame pace. Gangplank Falls sends six-foot-wide, four-passenger tubes for a trip down a 300-foot slide. Mayday Falls is the most exciting of the three, with a quick beginning, a catch pool, and steady acceleration for the rest of the 460-foot voyage. If the excitement of the scuba, surf, and slides has left you sapped, you will adore the 2,100-foot circuit tour of Castaway Creek. A round trip takes 30 minutes and soothes the soul. The young'uns can enjoy Ketchakiddie Creek, with watered-down versions of slides (pun intended), boats, fountains, waterfalls, a rapids ride, raft rides, bubbling jets, and assorted floating toys.

The park also includes a scenic overlook, a few small shops, and a pair of snack bars. Picnicking is allowed here and is a preferable option to the mediocre and overpriced snack food here. Note that the park is considerably less crowded on weekdays, especially closer to the beginning of the week than the end. Take Exit 67 and follow Downtown Disney signs.

Splash Island

Scheduled to open at Cypress Gardens in summer 2005. this $10 million, Polynesian-themed water park will include slides, a wave pool, lazy river, and kids' play area. Visit cypressgardens.com for updates.

Water Mania

6073 W. Irlo Bronson Mem Hwy, Kissimmee, 800/527-3092 or 407/396-2626

Open 10am-5pm daily.

www.watermania-florida.com

$32.05 adults/$28.84 kids 3-9. Parking: $6.

MC, VI

Discounts: Website ($3-4), magazines ($3-4), AAA.

The lightweight among water parks currently operating in the Orlando area, the 36-acre Water Mania just celebrated its 20th birthday, and still offers a good variety of straightforward slides at a very good price with special convenience for guests staying in Kissimmee. However, be aware that there's no theming here, just lots of concrete and plastic, and the quality of the rides is a notch below the technologically advanced Wet'n'Wild.

Thrill rides here include the Wipe Out, letting guests bodyboard against a continuous, perfect wave; the Double Berzerker speed slides, the 72-foot freefall Screamer, the Twin Tornadoes twist and wind a pair of 320-foot flumes. Also, visit the Abyss, a 380-foot dark slide, the Anaconda, a 400-foot family slide with a 50-foot drop, and the Banana Peel tandem slide.

More relaxing wetness can be found in the 850-foot Cruisin' Creek circuit and the 720,000-gallon Whitecaps Wave Pool, while children get two dedicated interactive play areas, the Rain Forest, featuring a pirate ship; and the new Rain Train, with fun interactive play elements, slides, and more.

Water Mania's dry-land amenities include miniature golf, volleyball nets, a beach, an arcade, basketball courts, a playground, and a wooded picnic area. Snack bars and a gift shop are also available. Season passes are available for $53.45 per person, $74.85 per person for a pass that includes parking. To get here, take I-4 Exit 64A (US 192 East/Kissimmee), it comes up pretty quickly on the left.

Wet 'N' Wild
> 6200 International Drive, 800/992-WILD or 407/351-WILD
> Opens between 9 and 10am, closes between 5pm and 9pm. Summer closing on Friday and Saturday nights is 11pm.
> www.wetnwild.com
> $33.95 adults/$27.95 kids 3-9/$16.98 seniors 55+. Parking: $6.
> AE, DI, MC, VI
> Discounts: Orlandoinfo.com ($3-5), Florida resident ($5), AAA.

This 25-acre park, recently purchased and assimilated in Borg-like fashion by Universal, has the best assortment of water rides in the area. It lacks the elaborate landscaping, natural beauty and aesthetic theming of the Disney water parks, but if you "don't need that Pirates of the Caribbean bull****," you can kick it old-school here, at the best-attended water park in America.

The newest attraction here is Disco H2O, where raft riders spin around a circle in an enclosed aqua nightclub surrounded by music, lights, and disco balls. Also new is the Blast, a two-person tube ride with colorful scenery, pipe bursts, water spouts, and sound effects leading up to a final waterfall plunge. Thrill rides include the intertwining 300-foot chutes of the 6-story Blue Niagara, the Bomb Bay, which drops you like a human cannonball, 30 miles an hour at a near-vertical pitch; Der Stuka, the park's original signature thrill ride, a six-story speed slide; the half-mile long Knee Ski kneeboarding course; the Mach 5's three quarter-mile flumes; the Roaring Rapids white water rafting ridel the Hydra Fighter water swing, and the Storm, a swirling body coaster. For an additional fee the Wild One lets guests ride inner tubes behind a waverunner in the park's lake. Other rides include the two-man rafts of the Black Hole, a 500-foot journey through the darkness; the Bubba Tub, a six-story triple dip; the 450-foot Flyer water toboggan ride; and the Lazy River and Wave Pool. Bubble Up and the newly-renovated 3,200 square foot Kids Park offer junior sized versions of the park's most popular rides. Snack bars and a gift shop are located on the premises.

If you're planning on visiting Universal and Wet 'N' Wild, consider the Orlando FlexTicket, which combines fourteen days worth of admission to Sea World, Universal Studios Florida, Islands of Escape, Wet 'N' Wild, and (optionally) Busch Gardens; see Chapter 2 for details. Annual passes are available, for weekdays only ($45) or all week long ($89.95). To get to Wet'n Wild, take exit 75A (Kirkman Road south) to International Drive and turn right. The park is located at the corner of I-Drive and Universal Blvd.

Wild Waters

5656 E. Silver Springs Blvd., Silver Springs, 352/236-2121
Open 10am-5pm, extended til 6pm during summer.
www.wildwaterspark.com
$23.99 adults/$20.99 kids under 48".
MC, VI
Discounts: $7 off with a Coke can.

Adjacent to Silver Springs (about 90 miles from Orlando), this laid-back park recently added three new flumes: the 6-story Twin Twister and the 3-story dark and enclosed Tornado and Thunderbolt, in addition to a 450,000-gallon wave pool, the Hurricane whitewater flume, and the Silver Bullet 220-foot racing flume. Family activities include the Mini Monster, Bunyan's Bend, and Osceola's Revenge slides, the themed Tad-Pool freeform wading pool and the nautical-themed Cool Kids Cove, a 1-acre play area. To get here, take I-4 East to Florida's Turnpike north. Take the Turnpike north to I-75 north. I-75 north to exit 69, U.S. 40 east. Discounted combination tickets to Wild Waters and Silver Springs are available, as are annual passes ($39.99).

Orlando's Best Pools

Orlando hotels offer all kinds of whimsy, just like the theme parks do – some of them have particularly impressive swimming pools, and given that many kids remember the hotel swimming pool more than the amusement parks, picking a hotel with a great pool can be an easy way to create cherished experiences for your whole family. The best of the best:
• Holiday Inn Family Suites
• Disney's Yacht & Beach Club Resorts
• Hyatt Regency Grand Cypress
• Disney's Polynesian Resort
• Disney's Port Orleans – French Quarter
• Caribe Royale Suites

See Chapter 11 for full details on these hotels and many more.

Rent a Boat

Pretty much every waterfront Disney resort has a marina with a variety of watercraft available for rent. All craft are not available at all locations. Call 407/828-2204 for specific availability. Boats are available at Downtown

Disney Marketplace, Boardwalk, Contemporary, Polynesian, Grand Floridian, Yacht Club, Wilderness Lodge, Fort Wilderness, Port Orleans, Caribbean Beach, Coronado Springs, Old Key West, and Dolphin.

Typical prices are:
- Sea Raycer (holds 2): $22.53/half hour, $28.16/45 minutes. $30.98/hour
- 21' Suntracker pontoon boat (holds 10): $34.74/half hour
- 12' or 14' sailboat: $18.77/ hour – 12', $23.47/hour – 14'
- Canopy boat: $24.88/half hour
- Pedal boat: $6/half hour
- Specialty cruises (holds up to 12): $117 and up

Water Sports

At Disney's Contemporary Resort, the **Sammy Duvall Water Sports Centre** offers water-skiing and parasailing opportunities. Parasailing options include regular flights, lasting 8-10 minutes at a top height of 450 feet ($90 solo/$140 tandem); or premium flights, getting you an extra two minutes and 150 feet ($112.50 solo/$162.50 tandem). Water-skiing and wakeboarding are also available. Prices per boat (for up to 5 guests) are $80 for a half hour, $140 an hour. Personal watercraft are also available. Guided tours for up to three guests are $100, as are hour-long free rides. Half hour tours are $65. Note that half-hours can not be reserved in advance. Sammy Duvall is open from 8am to 5:30pm seven days a week. Hours may be extended during the summer. Call 407/939-0754 or visit www.sammyduvall.com for reservations and information.

Outside Disney, **Buena Vista Water Sports** (13245 Lake Bryan Drive, Kissimmee, 407/239-6939, www.bvwatersports.com) offers wakeboard and waterski ($45-80) rentals, lessons, charters ($70-120), and equipment on the shores of Lake Bryan, five minutes from Disney on SR 535, between I-4 and US 192.

Ski World downtown (1413 N. Orange Ave., 407/447-7547) offers wakeboard instructions, ski school, and equipment, as does the **Orlando Watersports Complex** (8615 Florida Rock Rd., 407/251-3100, www.orlandowatersports.com).

Go Fish

Fishing excursions are available from many of the Disney resorts. For reservations call 407/WDW-PLAY. Here's a rundown of what's available where:

•**Beach Club, Boardwalk, and Yacht Club:** 2-hour excursion on Crescent Lake, $195-210. Includes guide, equipment, boat, and refreshments.

•**Contemporary, Fort Wilderness, Grand Floridian, Polynesian, Wilderness Lodge:** 2-hour trip on Bay Lake, $180-210. Includes rod, reel, artificial bait, 1 dozen live bait of shiners, and a beverage.

•**Downtown Disney, Old Key West, Port Orleans, Saratoga Springs:** 2-hour excursion on Village Lake, $180-210. Includes reel, rod, artificial bait, and beverages.

•**Kids' Fishing Around the World** program sends boats of five 6 to 12 year olds on a one-hour trip, $28.16. Pickup is available at the Contemporary, Polynesian, Wilderness Lodge, and Ft. Wilderness (Saturdays and Sundays only), and the Yacht and Beach Club, and the Boardwalk resorts (Monday through Friday).

Outside Disney World, bass fishing is king. Guides and fish camps are plentiful here:

Guides

•A#1 Bass, 800/707-5463, a1bassguideservices.com, Indian Lake Estates

•Bass Anglers, 407/656-1052, Windermere

•Capt. Travis Tanner, 407/468-0701, indianriverredfish.com, Christmas

•First Strike, 321-624-2398, firststrikebass.com, Kissimmee

•Fish With Robbie, 407/847-9157, fishwithrobby.com, Kissimmee

•Fly Envy Fishing Charters, 386/479-3429, mosquitolagoonflyfishing.com, Deltona

•Jay's Bass Bustin Guide, 407/892-5962, St. Cloud

•Lake Toho Tackle, 407/928-2529, laketohoetackle.com, Kissimmee

Deep Sea Excursions

•Incentive Fishing, 321/676-1948, www.incentivecharters.com, Melbourne

•Sea Spirit Deep Sea Fishing, 386/763-4388, www.seaspiritfishing.com, Ponce Inlet

•Sea Venture, 800/455-0333 or 407/453-6764, www.seaventurecharters.com, Merritt Island

Camps

•Big Toho Marina, 407/846-2124. 101 Lakeshore Blvd., Kiss.

•East Lake Fish Camp, 407/348-2040. 3705 Big Bass Rd., Kiss.

•Richardson's Fish Camp, 407/846-6540. 1550 Scotty's Rd., Kiss.

•St. Cloud Fishing Pier, 407/957-7243. 1104 Lakeshore Blvd., St. Cloud

Take a Cruise

If you're skittish about actually driving an airboat, there are plenty of firms in Kissimmee who will be more than happy to give you the tour, pointing out gators, birds, turtles, and other wildlife. Among those companies are **Boggy Creek Airboat Rides** offers shared ($18.95 adult/$14.95 child 3-12), and 45-minute private tours ($45) in 18-passenger boats from two locations (3702 Big Bass Road, 407/344-9550 and 2001 E. Southport Road, 407/933-4337 – www.bcairboats.com). Night tours are available from March to October and require a 3-day advance reservation. Cost is $29.95 adult/$24.95 kids. $2 off coupons can be found at their website.

Glades Adventures ($29.95 adult/$19.95 child for 1 hour), has a super-friendly staff, an interactive alligator nursery display in their office, and knowledgeable guides on smaller, quieter, six-passenger boats that give an air of intimacy and friendliness while providing the agility and precision to attempt hard-to reach areas along the water, delivering great views of egrets, herons, bald eagles, snail kites, wild boars, Osceola turkeys, and more (4715 Kissimmee Park Rd., St. Cloud, 407/891-2222 – www.gladesadventures.com). They offer a $2.50 discount on their website and via magazine coupons.

TJ Airboats offers 40 minute tours ($21.40 adult/$17.12 child under 12) of huge Lake Tohopekaliga (1550 Scotty's Rd., Kissimmee, 407/846-6540). **Big Toho** offers 45 minute tours ($27/day, $40/night) and nighttime alligator hunts ($1200) (1800 Queens Court, Kissimmee, 321/624-2398 – www.firststrikebass.com).

Further out, just east of Titusville, **A-Awesome Airboat Rides** (PO Box 333, Christmas, 407/568-7601 - www.airboatride.com) explores the St. John's River in six-passenger boats. **Old Fashion Airboat Rides** also traverses these same areas ($37 adult, $20 child).

The artsy suburb of Winter Park also offers a **Scenic Boat Tour** (407/644-4065 – www.scenicboattours.com). This narrated pontoon boat cruise spends an hour winding through historic canals and leaves every hour on the hour from 10am to 4pm daily. Cost is $8 adult, $4 kids 2-11. Boats depart from the dock at the east end of Morse Blvd. in Winter Park, 5 minutes from Park Avenue.

If you prefer your boats big and majestic, take a ride on the **Rivership Romance** (433 N. Palmetto Ave., Sanford, 407/321-5091 or 800/423-7401 – www.rivershipromance.com), which is celebrating its 20th birthday. The Rivership offers trips down the St. John's River during 3-hour lunch cruises,

4-hour dinner cruises, or Moonlight Magic dinner dance cruises on weekends. Prices start at $36.75 for 3-hour lunch cruises, $47.25 for 4-hour lunch cruises, $45 for special event shows, and $52.50 for the Saturday moonlight dining & dancing cruise.

Just because you came here instead of Vegas doesn't mean you can't send a shout out to your inner degenerate. The **Sterling Casino Lines** (180 Jetty Dr., Cape Canaveral, 800/765-5711 or 321/783-2212, www.sterlingcasinolines.com) offers free bus transportation from International Drive to Cape Canaveral, where you'll sail for free aboard a casino ship with complimentary deli buffet, drinks, and entertainment, and gambling at 1000 slot machines and table games like baccarat, roulette, craps, and blackjack. **SunCruz** (610 Glen Cheek Dr., Cape Canaveral, 321/799-3511 or 800/474-DICE – www.suncruzcasino.com) offers free cruises with comped entertainment and snacks, or a buffet ($7-10). They do not offer shuttle service from the tourist corridor, but make it up with a private poker room.

Scuba, Snorkel & Dive

Manatee tours, scuba diving, snorkeling, and dive tours can be arranged through various Orlando-area providers, inclduing:

•**Fun 2 Dive**, www.fun2dive.com, 407/322-9696 or 888/588-DIVE, providing scuba and snorkel tours on both Florida's coasts. Intimate full-day manatee tours limited to six people are available ($85). Also available are 4-day deep-sea diving charters as far away as the Keys. Scuba training is also offered.

•**Orlando Dive & Snorkel Tours**, www.diveorlando.com, 407/466-1668 or 877/GO-DIVIN, offering a variety of spring and river diving tours plus scuba instruction and Crystal River manatee tours ($74) or snorkel adventures ($40).

Chapter 16

GREAT GOLF & MORE!

Hundreds of holes of golf dot the landscape of Central Florida. Inside Disney World itself are 99 holes of golf, and many, many more are scattered throughout the rest of the area.

Inside Disney World

With the 1992 addition of the **Bonnet Creek Golf Club**, there are now 99 holes of golf inside the Walt Disney World complex. There are 45 holes at Shades of Green, 18 at Saratoga Springs, and 36 at Bonnet Creek. The golf here is so spectacular that it is an annual stop on the PGA Tour, and was named to Golf Magazine's 2002 Gold Medal list, one of only 22 resorts worldwide to earn this distinction. For information on Disney golf, visit golf.disneyworld.com.

Shades of Green

This hamlet just west of the Grand Floridian Resort houses the original WDW links. The Magnolia offers 18 holes at distances ranging from 5,232 to 7,190 yards and the *Palm*, rated one of the nation's top 100 courses by Golf Digest Magazine, has 18 holes measuring 5,311 to 6,957 yards. Both par-72 layouts were designed by Joe Lee. The Palm differs from the Magnolia in that the fairways at the former are shorter, narrower, and wooded, and the Palm has nine water hazards. There are driving ranges at both courses. Also located here is Oak Trail, a nine-hole, 45-acre course designed specifically for the beginner. There are water hazards and bunkers on the par-36, 2,913-

yard course, and the cost for 18 holes here is substantially lower than at the other courses. This is a walking course only.

Downtown Disney

Tucked away between the quiet villa retreat and the shores of Buena Vista Lagoon is the 18-hole *Lake Buena Vista* course. Also designed by Joe Lee, the par-72 links range in distance from 5,194 to 6,819 yards. This is a particularly pretty course as it winds through the Saratoga Springs and Old Key West resorts, and scrubby forests and streams.

Eagle Pines & Osprey Ridge

In January 1992, this pair of courses, located next to Fort Wilderness at the northeast corner of the World, opened with great fanfare. *Osprey Ridge*, designed by Tom Fazio, is rather unusual. Start with the natural terrain that surrounds the links. "Some of the factors that have us excited about the project are the vegetation, the water areas, and the wetlands which will become part of the background and framing for the holes," Fazio said. The par-72 Osprey Ridge ranges from 5,402 yards to 7,101. Environmentally conscious duffers will be glad to know that the circulating 18-hole design of the course uses the existing land patterns to their fullest while preserving all of the adjacent wetlands and other natural areas. Other things that make the Ridge unique are its paths, winding through remote areas and the use of high ridges and mounding, with some tees, greens, and viewing areas 20 to 25 feet above grade. The ridge that gives the course its name has quite a bearing on play.

Eagle Pines, designed by Pete Dye, is another 18-hole, par-72 affair. But this one differs quite a bit from Osprey Ridge. First of all, the course is laid out with a low profile, to be at the same level as or lower than the surrounding land. Second, the yardage is substantially shorter: 4,838 to 6,772 yards. Also, in an interesting touch, the areas outside the fairways are not rough, but pine straw. The low, dished fairways are surrounded with tall, spindly pines, giving it a secluded feel. Note that this is a traditional course in the sense that golfers can return to the clubhouse after the out nine.

Half-hour lessons with PGA professionals are available by appointment at the rate of $50 per half hour for adults and $30 per junior (17 and under). Tee times can be reserved up to 90 days in advance by calling 407/WDW-GOLF.

Walt Disney World Golf Rates

Disney World offers discounts on golf for resort guests. Also, twilight specials apply after 3 or 5pm. All greens fees except Oak Trail include electric cart rental. Oak Trail is a walking trail only. Same-day replay rates are discounted 50%, are subject to availability, and can not be reserved in advance. Specially booked Price Slice teetimes (after 10am) are eligible for a 50% discount. Visit www.disneygolf.com for details.

	Osprey Ridge	Eagle Pines	Magnolia	Palm	Lake Buena Vista
Resort guests (Mon-Thu)	$99	$89	$79	$74	$69
Resort guests (Fri-Sun)	$109	$99	$89	$84	$79
Day Guest (Mon-Thu)	$109	$99	$89	$84	$79
Day Guest (Fri-Sun)	$119	$109	$99	$94	$89
3 PM Special	$35	$30	$30	$30	$25
5 PM Special	$30	$25	$25	$25	$25

Oak Trail is open to resort guests only. Prices are $38 adult/$20 for juniors under 17. After 10am rates drop to $20/$15. At 3pm, $15/10. After 5pm, you can play for $10/$5. Replay rates are $19/$10.

Outside Disney World

Listed below is a sampling of clubs open to the public. The best resource on the Web for Orlando golf opportunities is www.orlandogolfer.com. There's a golf reservation service you can use called Tee Times USA, 888/GOLF-FLO or www.teetimesusa.com.

Celebration Golf Course
701 Golf Park Dr., Celebration, 407/566-4653
www.celebrationgolf.com
Length: 4,933 to 6,792 yards, Par: 72
Fees: $75, $65 after noon, and a $40 twilight rate.

This Golf Digest four-star course and two-time , designed by Robert Trent Jones/RTJ Jr. course and built in 1996, features both open and narrow fairways with Bermuda grass just 5 minutes from Disney World in Celebration. Florida residents receive $20 off tee times, $10 off twilight rates. Greens fees include half cart rental and range balls. Amenities include a practice putting green, aqua driving range, practice chipping hole, and a 3-hole juniors' course. Juniors camps and a golf academy are also available with classes geared towards golfes of every skill level ($269-299) and private lessons ($80-100/hr) and playing lessons ($200-375).

Championsgate

1400 Masters Blvd., Championsgate, 888/558-9301 or 407/787-GOLF
www.championsgate.com
Length: 5,937 to 7,363 yards, Par: 72
Fees: $85-140 weekdays before 1pm, $65-110 after; $90-155 weekends before 1pm, $70-110 after.

The brand-new 36-hole Championsgate complex, 10 minutes south of Disney and Orlando, features Greg Norman design on the links-style International course and the US-style National. The International includes very few trees, while the National blends with Florida's natural terrain with woodland and wetland holes. Amenities include ProLink GPS, putting green, short game practice area, driving range, and pro shop. The International was named to Golf Magazine's Top 10 New Upscale Courses list in 2001.

Eagle Creek

10350 Emerson Lake Blvd., 407/273-4653 or 866/324-5342
www.eaglecreekgolf.info
Length: 5,324 to 7,198 yards, Par: 73
Fees: $65-110, $28-50 twilight rates.

Travel & Leisure Golf was named one of the best Florida courses of the 21st century following its March 2004 opening. The course boasts Mini Verde greens, auld-style bulkheads, five par-fives, and over 90 bunkers. Amenities include Parview GPS, Precedent golf carts, a two-sided driving range, and the Graves Golf Academy. Eagle Creek is located just off the Central Florida Greeneway.

Falcon's Fire

3200 Seralago Dr., Kissimmee, 407/239-5445
www.falconsfire.com
Length: 5,417 to 6,901 yards, Par: 72
Fees: $70 before noon, $50 after, $40 twilight rates.

Strategic bunkering and an abundance of water hazards enhance the challenge of this course, convenient for and popular with both residents and tourists. The course is suitable for players of all skill levels. Amenities include Shortgrass Technologies GPS, Practice Caddie system, driving range, and complimentary valet parking. Falcon's Fire hosts the Back to Basics Golf Academy, with 1/2 to 2-day programs ($250-695) plus half- and full-hour private lessons ($45-85) and playing lessons by appointment ($150-295).

Golf Gear

Bass Pro Shops Outdoor World (at Festival Bay, 5156 International Drive, 407/563-5200) offers a huge selection of gear, an indoor driving cage, and a putting range. Edwin Watts Golf Shops (8330 International Drive, 407/351-1444) features all the top brands. Discounts can be found at the Greg Norman Outlet, with two locations (Belz Factory Outlet World, 4976 International Drive, 407/351-9335 and Orlando Premium Outlets, 8200 Vineland Dr, 407/239-2515).

Hawk's Landing

8701 World Center Dr., LBV, 407/238-8660
www.golfhawkslanding.com
Length: 4,890 to 6,810 yards, Par: 72
Fees: $95-155 before 2pm, $88-109 after 2pm, $45-55 twilight rates.

Robert E. Cupp redesigned the original Joe Lee layout at this course surrounding the Marriott Orlando World Center in 2002, adding landscape enhancements and new challenges to the course. Fifteen holes include water play, and the course is sure to challenge golfers of every skill level. Golf carts include the ProLink electronic caddy system, which tracks yardage, pin placement, and hazards. Guests here and at other area Marriotts receive discounts of 20-25%. Bill Madonna, a Golf Magazine Top 100 Teacher, holds court at the golf academy here. Offerings include golf clinics ($25), short game workshops ($90-100), private and playing lessons ($90-100/hr).

Kissimmee Bay Country Club

2801 Kissimmee Bay Road, Kissimmee, 407/348-4653
www.kissimmeebaycc.com
Length: 5,171 to 6,846 yards, Par: 71
Fees: $55-80

Golf Digest nominated this course as one of America's best new courses and it was twice ranked among the top fifty in the state by Golfweek. The fast greens are double-cut daily.

Kissimmee Golf Club

3103 Florida Coach Dr., Kissimmee, 407/847-2816
www.kissgolfclub.com
Length: 5,083 to 6,537 yards, Par: 72
Fees: $34-54, with $20-35 twilight rates.

Adjacent to the Kissimmee Municipal Airport, this course has long been a favorite for locals and visitors alike. Facilities include a lounge, pro shop, and the county's largest driving range. Lessons are available for $35/half hour and $60/full hour.

Marriott's Grande Pines Golf Club

6351 International Golf Club Rd., 407/239-6909
www.grandepinesgolfclub.com
Length: 5,418 to 7,012 yards, Par: 72
Fees: $62-130

Renovated completely in 2003 from the former International Golf Club, this Nick Faldo/Steve Smyers-designed course is located conveniently off the southern end of International Drive and gives conservative and daring players options for challenging each hole, while the course features such player-friendly and -frustrating features as contoured fairways, bunkered approach shots, and multi-tiered greens. Each cart comes equipped with ProLink. Web special rates are periodically sent to their mailing list. The Grande Pines also hosts the Orlando outpost of the Faldo Golf Institute.

Metrowest Country Club

2100 S. Hiawasee Rd., 407/299-1099
www.metrowestgolf.com
Length: 5,325 to 7,051 yards, Par: 72
Fees: $74-79, twilight rates of $49.

Designed by Robert Trent Jones Sr. and operated by Arnold Palmer's company, Metrowest features 100-foot elevations that roll around water hazards and expansive bunkers. Amenities include complimentary valet parking, Parview GPS and Practice Caddie, premium rental clubs, automobile detailing service, and an expansive practice facility featuring a 20-station all-grass putting area, 12 target greens, and a chipping green. Discounts are available to Orlando area residents.

Mystic Dunes Golf Club

7850 Shadow Tree Ln., Celebration, 407/787-5678 or 866/311-1234
www.mysticdunesgolf.com
Length: 5,893 to 7,012 yards, Par: 72
Fees: $65-115, depending on time of day.

Just two miles south of WDW, this Gary Koch-designed club includes a "low country" style front nine reminiscent of Carolina courses, and a back nine that recall the links of the British Isles. Golf and Leisure Magazine called holes #15-18 "four of the best finishing holes you'll find anywhere." GolfDigest named it one of 2004's Best New Courses and awarded it four stars. Florida Golf Guide named it Orlando's #2 course.

Orange County National Golf Center

16301 Phil Ritson Way, Winter Garden, 407/656-2626
www.orangecountynationalgolf.com
Length: 5,094 to 7,295 yards, Par: 72
Fees: $60-75 for Crooked Cat, $70-85 for Panther Lake, $15-25 for Tooth with a junior playing free with each adult.

The 45 holes at Crooked Cat and Panther Lake courses were both awarded 4 1/2 stars by Golf Digest. Additionally, OC National has been named to the prestigious "Top Ten You Can Play" list in Golf magazine, as well as a two-time winner of the Best Public Course award from Citysearch. Add to that the Golf Digest 50 Best Conditioned Courses and you've got yourself guaranteed great golf. Great play not guaranteed. The Tooth 9-hole course is a par-3, 1,563 yard affair.

Orange Lake Country Club

8505 W. Irlo Bronson, Kissimmee, 407/239-1050
www.orangelake.com
Length: 5,525 to 7,072 yards, Par: 72
Fees: $77-87, juniors $25. Twilight rates of $37. Crane's Bend is $30-32 with replay rates of $12. Legends Walk is $20/$8 for juniors.

The Resort course was completely redesigned in 2005, just prior to press time. Golf Week Magazine named this one of Florida's Top 50 courses. The Arnold Palmer-designed Legends course, which opened in late 1998, features nine holes of Scotland-style play and nine inspired by the pine and oak woodlands of North Carolina, with multi-tiered greens and spacious fairways. The courses are lit for nighttime play. Orange Lake also features Crane's Bend, 1,901 yards of par-3 golf sculpted out of pristine landscaping alongside the resort's eponymous lake. Legend's Walk is a 9-hole executive walking course, measuring 1,581 yards with so much water, woods, and sand that you'd think you were in Phuket. Multiple-round and unlimited play passes are available to guests at the resort.

Ridgewood Lakes

200 Eagle Ridge Dr., Davenport, 863/424-8688
www.ridgewoodlakesgolf.com
Length: 5,217-7,016 yards, Par: 72
Fees: $50-100

Golf Digest named these Ted McAnlis designed links the best new course when it opened in 1994, and since then it has earned accolades like a five-star rating and a Top 30 Florida Courses designation. It's about 20 minutes southwest of Disney.

Shingle Creek

9939 Universal Blvd., 407/996-9933 or 866/996-9933
www.shinglecreekgolf.com
Length: 5,081 to 7,228 yards, Par: 72
Fees: $69-119, $39-65 twilight rates.

Only 1/2 mile east of the Convention Center, David Harman's pristine new Shingle Creek features interconnecting waterways and undulating fairways along the headwaters of the Everglades. Shingle Creek features the Uplink GPS system.

Saving Money on Golf

There are ways to enjoy the Sport of Kings for less than a prince's ransom. Whether you want to play onsite at Disney or at one of the many top-notch clubs in and around the Orlando area, there are ways to minimize your expenses.

•Almost all Orlando golf courses (including Disney courses) offer twilight rates for late-afternoon play. Some charge a premium for early-morning tee times, so later starts can save $10-20 or more.

•Florida residents are often offered discount rates as well.

•Disney is currently offering "Price Slice" tee times after 10am daily, offering 50% discounts off the sticker price. These are subject to change and may not be available during peak seasons.

•Visit eGreensFees.com to bid on golf course gift certificates via eBay. If you've ever used restaurant.com, you'll know what to expect here. You can snag 18 holes on a local course for as little as $9.99.

•Some golf-centric resorts offer unlimited play packages that offer a golfer the run of the links for the duration of a guest's stay.

Spectator Sports

Maybe golf's not your thing, but basketball? Baseball? Football? Ice hockey? All that and more can be found within an hour or 90 minutes' drive.

Baseball

During the regular season, the nearest MLB hardball action can be found at Tropicana Field in St. Petersburg, where the **Tampa Devil Rays** play. Tickets can be ordered by calling 813/282-7297 or by visiting www.devilrays.com.

While minor league baseball no longer makes a home anywhere in central Florida, several big-league teams have their spring training facilities in the area, playing and practicing during the month of March:

•**Atlanta Braves:** Cracker Jack Stadium, Disney's Wide World of Sports, Kissimmee, 407/939-2200

•**Cleveland Indians:** Chain of Lakes Park, Winter Haven, 863/293-3900

•**Houston Astros:** Osceola County Stadium, Kissimmee, 321/697-3200

Basketball

The **Orlando Magic** play NBA games at the TD Waterhouse Centre, located in the Centroplex downtown, at 600 West Amelia Ave. Tickets can be ordered by calling 407/89-MAGIC or 800/4-NBA-TIX. Check out www.orlandomagic.com for more information.

Football

There's an arena football team here, the **Orlando Predators**. They also play at the TD Waterhouse Centre. For tickets consult www.orlandopredators.com or call 407/44-PREDS. NFL action can be found an hour west of Orlando, where the **Tampa Bay Buccaneers** play. Check out buccaneers.com or call 800/795-2827 for tickets, schedules, and info. Although good luck getting any (except via brokers) if you're not in for the whole season.

College football bowl games are a big deal here. The **Capital One Bowl** pits Big Ten and SEC squads against one another on New Year's Day, while the **Mazda Tangerine Bowl** features teams from the ACC and Big Twelve in late December. Tickets go on sale September 1. For more information, visit www.fcsbowls.com or call 407/423-2476.

Golf

Orlando hosts several major PGA tournaments. They are the **Bay Hill Invitational**, presented by Office Depot, held at Arnold Palmer's Bay Hill Country Club less than a mile from the junction of Sand Lake Road and International Drive. The tournament, which takes place every March, solicits some of the top names in the sport. Daily and tourney-long tickets are available, call 866/764-4843 or visit www.bayhill.com.

The **Walt Disney World Classic**, sponsored by Funai, is played in late October every year and involves the big names of the PGA, including former winners Tiger Woods, Ryan Palmer, and Vijay Singh. The tournament is played on three of Disney World's courses, the Magnolia, Palm, and Lake

Buena Vista. For ticket information, visit www.disneygolf.com or call 407/ 835-2525.

Hockey

If the NHL ever resumes play, the **Tampa Bay Lightning** will finally get the opportunity to defend their 2004 Stanley Cup at the St. Pete Times Forum. Call 813/287-8844 or check out www.tampabaylightning.com for info.

Chapter 17

AMUSEMENTS & DIVERSIONS

Look deeper than the major theme parks that dominate the vacation landscape here, and you will see a thriving second tier of fun things to do, some for an hour, some for an afternoon. The Orlando Convention & Visitors' Bureau estimates that it would take no less than 62 days to see and do everything in and around Orlando. If you've got the inclination to explore beyond the obvious, these places may be worth a peek.

Busch Gardens Tampa

3605 Bougainvillea Avenue, Tampa, 800/423-8368 or 813/987-5082
Open 10am to 6pm, extended during peak seasons.
www.buschgardens.com
$55.95 adult/$45.95 child 3-9. Multi-day, multi-park passes available, see Chapter 2.
Parking: $7.
DI, MC, VI
Discounts: Orlandoinfo.com ($2-3) AAA, AARP, Florida residents, 7-day advance eTicket purchase (10% off), twilight bonus (dinner included).

This attraction has always been one of Florida's most popular, with good reason. Busch Gardens is one part African safari-themed park, one part accredited zoo. With the introduction of the Animal Kingdom and the explosion of new theme park development in Orlando itself, Busch Gardens has kind of dropped off the radar for many Orlando guests. Those who make the 75-minute drive are rewarded with things that you won't find anywhere else –making Busch Gardens one of the most popular theme parks in the state for its residents – who admittedly have a lot to choose from.

New in 2005 is SheiKra, the first dive coaster in North America, a three-minute, half-mile ride that takes you 200 feet up and then 90 degrees straight down at 70mph, with ride elements including an Immelmann loop (loop and roll) and a second 90 degree drop into an underground tunnel. Another new addition is R.L. Stine's Haunted Lighthouse 4-D, a family-friendly movie combining 3D effects and theater surprises.

Busch Gardens is divided into nine themed sections, the Bird Gardens, Crown Colony, Morocco, Nairobi, Serengeti Plain, Stanleyville, The Congo, Timbuktu, and Egypt. Marquee attractions here are the Congo River Rapids, in which 12 riders in a gigantic inner tube set off on a wild journey punctuated by geysers; leaky caves, white water, drops, rapids, and other wet wonders; the Gwazi, a huge double wooden roller coaster, each 7,000 foot track with its own distinct flavor; the Kumba, the largest and fastest roller coaster in the Southeast, including three first-of-a-kind elements, a diving loop, a camelback loop, and a vertical loop; the Rhino Rally, an unforgettable Land Rover adventure through the area's wide-open, 80-acre tract of land, home to 800 African animals; the Montu, an inverted roller coaster that sends riders through four first-of-a-kind elements including a 60-foot vertical loop at a top speed of 60 mph and up to 3.85 G's; the Python, a 1,200-foot roller coaster with a 360-degree double spiral that cars travel at speeds up to 50 miles an hour; the Scorpion, with a 60 foot drop and 360 degree loop; the Stanley Falls log flume; and the even wetter Tanganyika Tidal Wave.

As a zoo, Busch has received many awards including certificates for the first North American captive breeding of at least 13 species of animal, plus thirteen Gold Propagator certificates for breeding 50 of a species, both awarded by the American Association of Zoological Parks & Aquariums. Zoological habitats are found in all areas of the park, but are concentrated in several sections: Myombe Reserve: The Great Ape Domain, the Bird Gardens, Nairobi, the Serengeti Plain, the Koala Habitat, the Clydesdale Hamlet, and the Elephant Habitat. All told, the collection houses over 2,700 animals.

It's about 75 minutes to Busch Gardens from Orlando and Disney: take I-4 west to I-75 north. Take I-75 to exit 54, Fowler Avenue. Bear left on the exit ramp and take Fowler Ave. west to McKinley Avenue. Turn left on McKinley and follow it to the parking lot and main entrance to the park. Another option is to take the Busch Shuttle Express, which offers round-trip transportation from Sea World for only $10 per person round trip, free with the purchase of an Orlando FlexTicket. Allow a full day for Busch Gardens, and throw in a trip next door to Adventure Island if you need to cool off.

Daytona USA

1801 W. International Speedway Blvd., Daytona Beach, 386/947-6800
Open 9am to 7pm, extended during peak seasons.
www.daytonausa.com
$21.50 adult/$15.50 child 6-12/$18.50 senior 60+
MC, VI
Discounts: Magazines ($2)

Adjacent to the Daytona Speedway, the "Ultimate Motorsports Attraction" features 60,000 square feet of simulators, hands-on activities, and exhibits. The Toyota Tundra Thunder Road (with a 360 degree flip!) and Daytona Dream Laps simulators are the cream of the crop. Films shown here include *Daytona 500: The Movie* and *NASCAR 3D: The IMAX Experience*. At *You Call the Race*, which gives guests the opportunity to play sportscaster and call the finish of a major race; the Pit Stop Challenge, where 16 seconds tick down quickly; Time Trials, an interactive activity where guests design and virtually race their own stock cars; Technology of Speed, which goes under the hood to reveal the inner workings of NASCAR vehicles; and more, and the art of Sam Bass. In a NASCAR tradition, the winner of each year's Daytona 500 is displayed at the museum for the following year. Acceleration Alley offers super-realistic head-to-head racing at speeds of over 200mph for an additional fee.

There is also a location of Richard Petty Driving Experience (see below) here. Take I-4 east about an hour to exit 129, or I-4 to exit 261-A. Allow about two to three hours to see everything.

Disney Quest

Downtown Disney West Side, 407/WDW-PLAY
Open 11:30am-11pm Sun-Thurs, 11:30am-midnight Fri-Sat
www.disneyquest.com
$34.08 adults/$27.69 children 3-9.
AM, DI, MC, VI
Discounts: Annual Passholder, Disney Vacation Club

This huge blue building on the edge of the West Side houses five stories of interactive entertainment, a "virtual" theme park loaded with techno-heavy adventures. Which is all very nice PR to say that this is like a big fat injection of video game smack. In addition to current arcade favorites and classics from the 80s and 90s, Disney Quest hosts all kinds of virtual reality games and activities.

Some of the must-see rides here include Pirates of the Caribbean: Battle for Buccaneer Gold, a 3D surround sound collaborative battle against pirates, living and dead; the Virtual Jungle Cruise, which involves significantly more paddling than the real one; CyberSpace Mountain, where guests can design and ride their own roller coasters; Aladdin's Magic Carpet Ride, where you soar over the streets of Agrabah looking for Genie's lamp; a life-sized Mighty Ducks Pinball Slam game; and Ride the Comix, where you don a VR helmet and battle supervillains with a laser sword; and a game based on the now-defunct ExtraTERRORestrial Alien Encounter. There are also creative stations where you can design your own toy à la Toy Story's Sid; record a karaoke song; or create your own artistic masterpiece on a Living Easel. Of course, you can purchase the fruits of your creative labors and take them home with you. A gift shop and two restaurants round this out – Cheesecake Factory desserts are available.

To avoid crowds here, go early in the day. Disney Quest is most crowded from 9pm until closing, when all the theme park guests find their way here. This is, however, a perfect rainy day activity.

Haunted Grimm House of Old Town

At Old Town, 5770 W. Irlo Bronson Mem Hwy, 407/847-7552
Open 10am-midnight.
$7 adult/$5 child 3-10, seniors.

Located in the ghetto-but-fun Old Town shopping complex, the 4,000-square foot Haunted Grimm House features over 20 rooms featuring live actors, creepy sets, and special effects. Definitely a step below Skull Kingdom.

Richard Petty Driving Experience

At WDW Speedway, 800/BE-PETTY
Open 8am-1pm, closed Tues, Thurs.
www.1800bepetty.com
Prices vary by program, see below.

AM, DI, MC, VI
Discounts: AAA.

This attraction, located at Walt Disney World Speedway at the parking lot of the Magic Kingdom, offers NASCAR fans the chance of a lifetime to ride in or even drive a stock car around the 1-mile track at blistering speeds. The Ride-Along ($99) seats you shotgun in a Winston Cup style qualifying run. The three-hour Rookie Experience ($379) puts you in the driver's seat for 8 laps. The five-hour King's Experience ($749) gives you 18 thrilling laps on the track. The Experience of a Lifetime ($1249) is 30 laps of pure adrenaline.

Seminole Hard Rock Casino

5223 Orient Road, Tampa
Open 24 hours.
www.seminolehardrockcasinotampa.com
Free.

Ahhh, Indian gambling. What better way to turn colonialist guilt into addictive behavior? The Hard Rock is a luxurious property that includes a hotel and a 90,000 square foot casino, featuring 1,850 slot machines and 50 poker tables. The Hard Rock also includes a full-service spa, a fitness center, live entertainment, and fine dining and is located just off I-4 at North Orient Rd. on the Seminole reservation in Tampa.

Skull Kingdom

5933 American Way, 407/354-1564
Open 10am-5pm and 6pm-midnight.
www.skullkingdom.com
$8.99 day show/$14.04 night show
AM, DI, MC, VI
Discounts: Website ($2), magazines (50% off second admission), AAA discount.

This elaborate spookhouse, located at the corner of Universal Blvd., and International Drive, is well-done and surprisingly frightening even for the most jaded and toughened. Dark rooms, well-placed special effects, live actors, and a macabre sense of humor make this 20-minute elaborate haunted house exhibit a fun way to give yourself insomnia. Skull Kingdom recently added a family-friendly show during the daytime, where children are led through the castle under the enchanted protection of a giant as they tour the chambers of the haunted castle. The **Chamber of Magic** dinner show is performed here nightly, see Chapter 20 for details.

Vans Skate Park

5220 International Drive, 407/351-3881
Open 24 hours.
www.vans.com
Admission varies.

A fully equipped indoor-outdoor skate park for public consumption! You'll feel like Tony Hawk's Underground has come to life at this skatepark featuring innovative and unique features. The **Doe Boy** is an aboveground bowl inspired by the old school pools. The skate park also includes 31,000 square foot indoor wood street course with many street features and small bowls, 40-foot vert ramp, and an 11,000 square foot outdoor concrete street course. Located at Festival Bay on International Drive.

Miniature Golf

Other than bowling, there is probably no activity on earth that levels the playing field between boys and girls, young and old, the athletic and the uncoordinated, more than miniature golf. If your vacation needs a little healthy competition, this is one of the best ways in town to while away a few hours while enjoying family togetherness, cool scenery, and a fun game – so long as you remember to breathe when you flub a six-inch putt. Just keep telling yourself "it's a bright orange ball and Astroturf, this shouldn't bother me."

Disney recently added 72 holes of miniature golf to its array of recreational activities, with two 18-hole courses at both **Fantasia Gardens** and **Winter Summerland**. Fantasia Gardens, which opened in 1996. draws its inspiration, of course, from the surreal, classic Disney musical *Fantasia*. The Gardens course is more geared towards beginners, and recreates five of the musical sequences from the film. The more challenging Fairways course includes exaggerated contours, water hazards, and holes up to 75 feet long. The Fantasia Gardens courses are located near the Dolphin hotel in the Epcot resort area.

Like the similarly-confused Blizzard Beach water park next door, Winter Summerland combines snowy elements and warm weather, as the story goes, this is a vacation spot for Santa's off-duty elves. Therefore, it's kinda Christmas the whole year round here, at least on the Sand/Summer course, where oversized ornaments hang from palm trees. The Snow/Winter course adds incongruous snowcaps to the Florida landscape. Winter Summerland, which opened in 2001, is located next to the Boardwalk complex, in the Epcot resort area. Both are open from 10am-11pm daily ($10.65 for day guests/$8.52 kids 3-9). Same-day second rounds are half-price. WDW annual passholders receive 50% discounts.

New is **Putting Edge**, an indoor glow-in-the-dark 18-hole course with music piped in and psychedelic black light artwork. It's like cosmic bowling, with smaller balls. Putting Edge is located at Festival Bay, a new mega-mall entertainment complex at 5250 International Drive ($8.50 adult/$7.50 youth 7-12, $6 child 5-6 or senior). Also new is **Tiki Island Adventure Golf** (7460 International Drive, 407/248-8180), with a four-story volcano that erupts regularly surrounded by bubbling pools and a river that runs across this 36-hole layout strewn with fake animals and rushing waterfalls ($9 adult, $8 kid, $13/12 for 36 holes, half off *Entertainment* coupon).

With 2004-new locations in Lake Buena Vista (13529 S. Apopka Vineland Rd., 407/239-8300) and near the Convention Center (8969 International Drive, 407/351-7733), **Hawaiian Rumble** features impressive musical fountains, a 100-foot volcano with waterfall, mist-shrouded lakes and streams, and lush tiki theming that makes this a new favorite ($9.95 adult, $7.95 kids 4-10, 50% off second 18 holes, 50% off second admission coupon on hawaiianrumbleorlando.com and in magazines). Add a Ben & Jerry's Scoop Shop and an internet café and this becomes destination putt-putt.

My favorite for a long time was **Pirate's Cove Adventure Golf**. *Orlando* magazine named the Orlando location the Best Miniature Golf in Florida. At each of three locations (8601 International Drive, 407/352-737; Crossroads of LBV, 407/827-1242; 2845 Florida Plaza Blvd., Kissimmee (off US 192), 407/396-7484), challenging and fun courses wind up, down, around, and through mountains, waterfalls, underwater pirate dungeons, streams, lakes, and more. No windmills here, just lush tropical landscaping, shimmering water, and Burma-Shave type signs telling the stories of Captain Kidd and Blackbeard, for whom the courses are named ($8.95 adult/$7.95 child 4-12, $1 cheaper at the Kissimmee course, *Entertainment* discounts). Second rounds are $5. The International Drive location could use a bit of sprucing up at this point, but the location overlooking I-4 in Lake Buena Vista is particularly fun these days. Note that most of the coupons floating around for Pirate's Cove are only good at I-Drive and LBV locations.

Other notable miniature golf courses include:

1. **Pirate's Island** (4330 W. Irlo Bronson Mem Hwy, 407/396-7484) is like Pirate's Cove, only less so, with mysteriously blue 2000 Flushes water

($8.49 adult/$7.49 child 4-12, $9.95 for all day play), and farther out to the east of the first hotel clusters.

2. River Adventure (4535 W. Irlo Bronson Mem Hwy, 407/396-4666) is a very-well liked, well-maintained, and out-of-the-way course recalling a pleasant, low-key, tasteful Southern riverfront featuring 18 challenging holes ($6.42 adult/$5.35 child 3-9).

3. Congo River Golf (4777 W. Irlo Bronson Mem Hwy, 407/396-6900 & 6312 International Drive, 407/352-0042) looks like a more barren Pirate's Cove but is still fun. The 18-hole course at their Universal location (5901 International Dr., 407/248-9181) is brand-new and offers a unique gator feeding experience. Be sure to count your fingers as you depart ($7.95 adults, $11.50 for two games).

4. Bonanza Golf (7761 W. Irlo Bronson Mem Hwy, 407/396-7536), with two 18-hole courses of little originality or dificulty in a kitschy red rock Wild West mining setting atop a steakhouse, backed by a 20,000 gallon per minute waterfall ($7 adult/$6 child 3-9, 50% discount on second 18 holes). Maintenance at Bonanza has suffered in recent years, but it's a cheap and sometimes underpopulated option.

Movies

High-end theaters dot the tourist areas. Here's some of the best bets:

•**Universal Loews Cineplex:** At Citywalk, this 20-screen multiplex offers all stadium seating, state of the art surround sound, and beer and wine at the concession stand, as well as free parking after 6pm. Citywalk restaurants often offer good dinner-and-movie specials (at Citywalk, 407/354-5998).

•**Muvico Pointe 21:** Wall-to-wall curved screens, amphitheater seating, digital sound, and one large-format screen (10x the size of a normal 35mm frame) with a giant 5.1 surround system (9101 International Drive, 407/92-MOVIE).

•**Enzian Theater:** (1300 S. Orlando Ave., Maitland, 407/629-1088) the metropolitan area's home for independent and alternative films. Seating is in swivel chairs around small tables, and waiter service is available. The Enzian is the home of the Orlando Film Festival

•**Cinemark at Festival Bay:** Stadium seating in all 20 theaters in this brand-new facility (5150 International Drive, 407/351-3117).

•**AMC Pleasure Island 24:** Stadium seating is available at 18 of 24 theaters here, adjacent to Pleasure Island and Downtown Disney West Side (1500 Buena Vista Drive, 407/298-4488).

Midways, Carnivals, Go-Karts, & Stuff

There's plenty of no-frills fun in Orlando as well – if noisy go-karts and carnival rides are your thing, there's no shortage of that here. Here's some of the best options.

•**Magical Midway:** Down the block from Wet 'N' Wild, this features I-Drive's only elevated go-kart tracks, classic midway rides, thrill rides like the Space Blast, giving you a 3G liftoff to a height of 180 feet, laser tag, and more (www.magicalmidway.com, 7001 International Drive, 407/370-5353). A la carte rides cost $3-6. Armbands range from $14.95-$24.95.

•**Fun Spot Action Park:** Located right off the north side of International Drive, this park offers four multi-level go-kart tracks, 7 thrill and family rides, 6 kids rides, and a huge arcade (www.fun-spot.com, 5551 Del Verde Way, 407/363-3867). Armbands are $4/95-$29.95. ($2.50 off armband coupon on website.)

•**Happy Days:** At the front of the Old Town complex, this attraction includes a 365-foot slingshot vertical accelerator ride, laser tag, go-karts, bumper cars, and over 100 video and redemption games (www.old-town.com, 5770 W. Irlo Bronson Mem Hwy, 407/397-1980).

Chapter 18

BACK TO NATURE

It can be hard sometimes to realize that all of Central Florida isn't made of Audio-Animatronic robots. But indeed, there are some breathtakingly beautiful places in the area. Here are some places that you can immerse yourself in nature during your vacation from the real.

Bok Sanctuary

1151 Tower Blvd., Lake Wales 863/676-1408
Open 8am to 6pm.
www.boksanctuary.org
$8 adult, $3 child 5-12
AM, DI, MC, VI

This National Historical Landmark combines 200 acres of gardens and grounds with the 205-foot marble and coquina tower, complete with a 60-bell carillon on peninsular Florida's highest point. Recitals are heard daily at 3pm with clock music on the half hour starting at 10am. The Pine Ridge Preserve offers a mile-long trail where guests can enjoy the flora and fauna of the region. Special events include live musical performances from bluegrass, jazz, and folk artists throughout the year, plus the Orlando Philharmonic and various carillon artists. Check the website for details. It's about 55 miles from Orlando – to get here, take I-4 west to Exit 55, then go south on US 27 for 23 miles. Turn left on Mountain Lake Cutoff Road and follow signs.

Central Florida Zoo

3755 NW US 17-92, Sanford, 407/323-4450
Open 9am-5pm daily.
www.centralfloridazoo.org
$8.95 adult, $6.95 seniors over 60, $4.95 child 5-12
MC, VI
Discount: AAA.

First established in 1923 as the Sanford Zoo, and celebrating its 30th anniversary in its current location 45 minutes north of Orlando, this zoo now hosts over 400 animals. Rare, threatened, and endangered species include cheetahs, clouded leopards, Asian elephants, brown and red ruffled lemurs, cotton-top tamarins, American crocodiles, eastern indigo snakes, Grand Cayman rock iguanas, and wreathed hornbills. Weekends are particularly good times to visit the zoo, as feeding programs, demonstrations, and shows are held throughout the day. To get here, take I-4 east to exit 104 (Orange Ave.). Exit right, turn left at Lake Monroe Rd. (CR 15). Turn right on US 17-92 and proceed about 1/8 mile.

Cypress Gardens

6000 Cypress Gardens Blvd., Winter Haven, 863/324-2111
Open 10am-6pm, with extended hours on weekends and during peak seasons.
www.cypressgardens.com
$38.95 adult/$31.95 child 3-9 or senior 55+.
AM, DI, MC, VI
Discounts: Twilight rates after 5pm, AAA, military, second day free.

It was a sad day when Cypress Gardens closed its doors in the post-911 tourism slump. As Florida's first theme park, it had a special historical significance. It reopened under new ownership in December 2004, and they are trying to revitalize this one-time must-see attraction with 39 new rides and a water park currently under construction.

Newly renovated is the **Nature's Way** wildlife area, home to over 150 animals, including a 75-year old alligator named Tarzan. The Cypress Cove Ferry Line docks here as well for scenic water views. Also new this year is the **Treasure of Cypress Cove** three-man pirate show. The park's signature wooden coaster is the classic-style **Triple Hurricane.** In 2006, the historic **Starliner** roller coaster will be carefully transferred to Cypress Gardens, imported from Panama City Beach, where it has sent guests screaming since 1963. Classic ice skating and water ski shows are presented, along with a wild west gunfight, a farm-themed magic and illusion show, and of course, the park's traditional Southern belles.

The park also features four restaurants and 19 shops. It's about an hour from Orlando – take I-4 west to exit 55 (US 27 south), turn right on SR 540 (Cypress Gardens Blvd.), the park is four miles ahead on the left.

Discovery Cove

6000 Discovery Cove Way, 877/434-7268 or 407/370-1280
Open from 9am to 5:30pm. Reservations are required.
www.discoverycove.com
Prices vary, see below.
AM, DI, MC, VI

In 2000, Sea World opened Discovery Cove, an theme park unlike anything there has ever been before. Intimate, exciting animal encounters are offered, highlighted by the once-in-a-lifetime opportunity for guests to swim with bottlenose dolphins! The experience begins with an orientation during which guests learn about the lives of dolphins and the ways that trainers communicate with them. After wading into shallow water to meet the mammals, guests are encouraged to swim and play with them. Twenty-six dolphins in all call Discovery Cove home. Other animal encounters include a coral reef fully stocked with tropical fish. There's even a shipwreck and hidden grottoes. A tropical river where you can hand-feed exotic birds, a sunny beach, and pool round out the attractions on this gorgeous property.

Attendance is limited to 1,000 per day, so Discovery Cove is intimate like no other. Upon entry guests get their pictures taken for souvenir photo ID, are greeted by a guide and personally escorted around the park for an orientation tour. The park promises a high level of personal service, and the soothing island music and secluded walkway to the entrance hint to you just how unique this experience will be. Admission is all-inclusive here, including a buffet lunch at Laguna Grille. Unlike most theme park buffets, this one is seriously gourmet – you can get everything from salads and burgers to smoked salmon to freshly made desserts here, and it's included. You can even stop in here early in the day for continental breakfast and coffee. The package also includes seven days' unlimited admission to either Busch Gardens or Sea World. For $30 extra you can have two weeks' unlimited access to both.

There are several admission options here. The all-inclusive package costs $229-259, depending on season. Without the dolphin swim component, the price drops to $129-159. There is also a Trainer for a Day program similar to the one offered in Sea World ($399-459). The Twilight Discovery program is different than just a late-day discount – it includes hand-feeding birds in the aviary, welcome reception with hors d'oeuvres and cocktails, dinner with Caribbean music and tropical drinks, beachfront desserts and an optional shallow-water dolphin interaction ($259 with, $159 without). At least one dolphin swim is required with each reservation. Saturday night sleepover packages are $389 per person.

Note that kids must be six years old to participate in the dolphin swim, though all ages are welcome at the park. Reservations are required, and can be made online or via phone.

Dinosaur World

5145 Harvey Tew Road, Plant City, 813/717-9865
Open 9am to 5pm daily.
www.dinoworld.net
$9.75 adult/$7.75 child/$8.95 senior 60+
AM, DI, MC, VI

An hour-plus west, towards Tampa, this may be worth a stop if your kids ooh and ah over the dinosaur rides in Disney and Universal and need another fix. Dinosaur World features 100 life-sized and scientifically accurate models representing over 60 species, as well as foliage designed to mimic what was found on earth during the reign of the thunder lizards, although don't expect the elaborate animatronic movements seen in the big-ticket attractions. Take I-4 west to Exit 17, turn right onto Branch Forbes Road, and immediately turn left onto Harvey Tew. Allow one to two hours to see this if you do stop by.

Gatorland

14501 S. Orange Blossom Trail, 800-393-JAWS or 407/855-5496
Open 9am to 6pm daily.
www.gatorland.com
$19.95 adult/$9.95 kids 3-9
AM, DI, MC, VI
Discounts: Florida ($5), pre-purchase ($2-3), Orlandoinfo.com ($2-6), magazines ($2.50), AAA discount, Magicard (20%).

This 110-acre theme park and wildlife preserve, named the best non-major attraction in the state by Florida magazine in 2003, stars the famed

Florida carnivores. Alligators, crocodiles, and snakes are everywhere in this zoo – guests even walk through a grotesquely large pair of gator jaws to enter the park. When inside, reptiles sunbathe in swamps on either side of the pleasant boardwalks.

There are four headlining shows here: the oldest being the famed Gator Jumparoo, in which reptiles leap out of the water for slabs of meat being dangled over the water. You can almost picture Steve-O getting his skivvies eaten by the beasts. Upclose Animal Encounters puts guests up close and personal with snakes, reptiles, and other creatures. Gator wranglers square off in the "Florida cracker" style against a 6- to 8-foot gator in the Alligator Wrestlin' show. The Jungle Crocs show lets the ferocious predators show their stuff. Beyond the shows, there's a petting zoo, a mini water park, the self-guided Swamp Walk tour, an alligator breeding marsh, and a train ride. Gatorland has a Trainer for a Day program available for $100.

Pearl's Smokehouse sells gator ribs and gator nuggets, and several snack bars offer more traditional theme park fare. Also, for souvenirs, visit the gift shop at the main entrance. For those of you who aren't revolted by the thought of Gatorland Zoo selling alligator leather, there's a boutique for that sort of thing as well. To get to Gatorland from Walt Disney World or Kissimmee, take U.S. 192 east until you reach the South Orange Blossom Trail. Turn left, the zoo will be on your right.

Green Meadows Petting Farm

1368 S. Poinciana Blvd., Kissimmee, 407/846-0770
Open 9:30am to 5:30pm daily.
www.greenmeadowsfarm.com
$19 per person
DI, MC, VI
Discounts: Magazines ($2)

The Green Meadows Children's Farm in rural Kissimmee offers a two-hour hands-on tour of the 50-acre farm, with more than 300 pigs, cows, chickens, turkeys, ducks, geese, donkeys, and other animals. Everyone gets to milk the farm's cow, and the kids get pony rides. From I-4, take Exit 64A (US 192 east). Take it three miles and turn right on Poinciana Blvd. Take Poinciana 5 miles, on your right. Realize that the tour group is in transported in a tractor-drawn hay wagon. If you are allergic, you might want to reconsider this one.

Harry P. Leu Gardens

1920 N. Forest Ave., 407/246-2620
Open 9am to 5pm daily.
www.leugardens.org
$5 adults, $1 for kids.
AM, MC, VI
Discounts: AAA, free Mon before noon.

The 50-acre Leu Botanical Gardens include miles of scenic walkways taking visitors through tableaus that include America's largest Camellia collection outside California (best seen Nov-Mar), palm and bamboo gardens, the new Tropical Stream and Kitchen Herb gardens, and an 1880s-era Leu House museum, listed on the National Register of Historic Places. The rose garden peaks in Dec/Jan, Apr/May, and Oct/Nov. There's a holiday display from Dec to mid-Jan. Guided tours are available ($7) and must be scheduled at least 21 days in advance. Take I-4 east to exit 85 (Princeton St.), turn right on Mills (US 17-92), left at the second light (Virginia Drive)., the gardens are approximately 1 mile ahead on the left.

Horse World Riding Stables

3705 S. Poinciana Blvd., Kissimmee, 407/847-4343
Open 9am-5pm daily.
www.horseworldstables.com
Prices vary, see below.
AM, MC, VI
Discount: Website ($3), magazines ($3).

This facility, located 12 miles south of US 192, features 750 acres of wooded trails. The **Nature Trail** ($39 for adults & kids 6 and up, $16.95 for kids 5 and under) lets kids as young as 6 ride their own horse on a 45-50 minute tour. The hour-long **Intermediate Trail Ride** ($47) includes walking and trotting. The 75-90 minute **Advanced Trail Ride** ($69) is by reservation only, and is customized to a rider's skill level. Pony rides and hayrides are also available.

Ivey Groves Fresh Citrus

2220 Boggy Creek Road, Kissimmee, 407/348-4757

Call for reservations.
$3.32 adults/$2.41 kids 3-12, seniors 55+

Why not check out a working citrus grove while in the Sunshine State? Ivey Groves offers an educational and scenic tram tour of their grove. The tour includes free juice and citrus samples, and you can ship the delicious fresh oranges home.

Nature Conservancy's Disney Wilderness Preserve

2700 Scrub Jay Trail, Kissimmee, 407/935-0002
Open 9am to 5pm daily, weekdays only from June through September.
www.nature.org
$3 adult/$2 child 6-17.

Set aside in 1992 as a partnership between Disney, the Nature Conservancy, and the Greater Orlando Aviation Authority, this 12,000 acre preserve at the top of the Everglades ecosystem offers over seven miles of hiking trails through pine flatwoods and wetland habitats plus off-road buggy tours ($10 adult/$5 child). To get here, take I-4 exit 68, go south on SR 535. Turn right on Poinciana Blvd. and 15 miles later, turn right on Pleasant Hill Road, left onto Old Pleasant Hill Road, and left on Scrub Jay Trail.

Reptile World Serpentarium

5705 E. Irlo Bronson Mem. Hwy., St. Cloud, 407/892-6905
Open 9am-5:30pm Tues-Sun.
$5.50 adult/$4.50 student 6-17/$3.50 child 3-5.

Snakes! Why do there have to be snakes? To the east is this quirky little zoo, featuring over 50 snakes from around the globe, ranging from harmless to lethal. There's also a working venom farm, and snakes are milked throughout the day. Fascinating stuff if you're into these creepy crawlies.

Silver Springs

5856 E. Silver Springs Blvd., Silver Springs, 800/234-7458 or 904/236-2121
Open 10am to 5pm daily.

www.silversprings.com
$32.99 adult/$23.99 child 3-9/$29.99 seniors 55+. Parking is $6.
Discounts: Orlandoinfo.com ($5-10), magazines ($10), promotional discounts (i.e., Coke cans).
AM, DI, MC, VI

Recently observing its 125th birthday, Silver Spring claims to have drawn visitors for 10,000 years for the waters' rejuvenating powers. I don't know anything about a fountain of youth, but Silver Springs is a blessedly calm attraction that can serve to repair and recover nerves frayed by a typical WDW vacation.

New here are the Fort King River Cruise, which covers 10,000 years of natural history with interactive displays of a Seminole Indian village, 1830's Fort King Army stockade, and a Florida Cracker homestead; the Lighthouse Ride, with gondolas rising to an 80-foot vantage point over the headwaters of the Silver River' and the Fantastic Fountains Water Show, with 1,000 water nozzles pumping 1,000 gallons per minute, the fountains' movement synchronized with music and lighting effects.

Major attractions here include the Jungle Cruise. Unlike the Jungle Cruise at the Magic Kingdom, all the animals you will encounter on this boat jaunt are real. Six continents are represented by the animal population of this placid river voyage. The Glass Bottom Boats take you through waters of the largest artesian spring in the world, actually 14 springs so clear that sunlight can penetrate to depths of 83 feet. And now for something completely different, the Jeep Safari puts you in a convertible, tiger-striped Jeep Wrangler for an exciting venture through the jungles where the original Tarzan movies were filmed. On your safari, you may see deer, zebras, monkeys, macaws, and deer, with absolutely nothing coming between you and the animals, not even a cage, not even a pane of glass. The botanical gardens here are also a highlight.

The Lost River Voyage takes you back thousands of years into a pristine Florida ecosystem, home to wild boar, deer, gators, osprey, wild turkeys, hawks, eagles, and 29 varieties of waterbirds. Doolittle's Petting Zoo would make its namesake proud. Younger kids also seem to enjoy this section of Silver Springs. Several different animal shows are performed daily as well. Silver Springs is 72 miles north of Orlando. Take Florida's Turnpike north to I-75 north. From I-75, take exit 69, SR 40 east.

Wekiwa Springs State Park

1800 Wekiwa Circle, Apopka, 407/884-2008
Open 8am til sundown.

www.floridastateparks.org
$5 per vehicle. $3 for single occupant vehicles.

This 7,800 acre state park about 35 minutes north of International Drive offers a bucolic setting at the headwaters of the Wekiwa River, providing a glimpse of how the area looked under the stewardship of the Timacuan Indians. Activities include biking, camping, canoeing, kayaking, fishing, hiking, a 1/8 mile boardwalk nature trail, snorkeling, and swimming in the crystal-clear 72-degree springs. Take I-4 east to exit 79 (SR 423), turn left on the John Young Parkway, left on the Orange Blossom Trail, right on Piedmont Wekiwa Road, and left on Wekiwa Circle.

A World of Orchids

250 Old Lake Wilson Road, Kissimmee, 407/396-1881
Open 9:30am to 4:30pm. Closed Mondays.
www.aworldoforchids.com
Free.

People who love orchids, LOVE orchids. If you are one of the many who is entranced by the exotic beauty of this delicate flower, put this stop on your agenda. Thousands of orchids are displayed in the lushly landscaped acre conservatory and 22,500 square foot greenhouse, and there's plenty available for purchase.

Chapter 19

AIRBORNE ADVENTURES

Perhaps no fantasy of man's has been such an obsession as that of flight (except maybe for Britney Spears in that schoolgirl outfit, but whatever).

Air Attractions

Fantasy of Flight
1400 Broadway Blvd. SE, Polk City, 863/984-3500
Open 10am to 5pm daily.
www.fantasyofflight.com
$24.95 adult/$13.95 child/$22.95 senior 60+
AM, MC, VI
Discounts: $3 coupon on website, military rates.

This interactive art-deco museum attraction takes guests back to the dawn of flight, World War I, World War II, and beyond with a fantastic collection of dozens of fully restored planes all the way up to the 1950s. Activities include a backlot tour, the Aircraft of the Day presentation, and the Restoration Shop Tour. In Fightertown simulators, guests can participate in a full-motion dogfight over the South Pacific. Biplane ($57.95-189.95) and hot air balloon rides ($160) are available. Fantasy of Flight about a half hour west of Disney. Take I-4 west to exit 44 (SR 559 North/Polk City/Fantasy of Flight).

Flying Tigers Warbird Restoration Museum
231 N. Hoagland Blvd., Kissimmee, 407/933-1942
Open 9am to 5pm daily.
www.warbirdmuseum.com
$9 adult/$8 child 8-12 and seniors
DI, MC, VI
Discount: AAA.

This museum's collection consists of over a dozen flyable aircraft, eight restoration projects, and about a dozen displays. Eras represented range from World War I to 1960. The facility also includes a museum containing airplane memorabilia and a gift shop. Special events and programs are held here throughout the year. Take I-4 to exit 64A (US 192 East), go 8 miles and turn right on Hoagland. The museum is less than 1 mile ahead on the left.

Skycoaster
2850 Florida Plaza Blvd., Kissimmee, 407/397-2509
Open noon-midnight, 2pm-midnight during off-peak seasons.
www.skycoaster.cc
$40 single/$70 double/$90 triple, $65 for two flights.
MC, VI
Discounts: Website ($3-5), magazines ($5).

Three hundred feet in the air you'll pull a rip cord and free fall to earth, swinging high above the ground before eventually returning to earth. There's a top speed of 85 mph, a 120-foot freefall, and an incredible view from the top. Skycoaster Park also features the G-Force ride, a competitive drag racing attraction where guests zoom from 0 to 110 mph in less than 2 seconds, with 4.5 G's created by 3,000 hp of air thrust power ($30 driver, $10 passenger).

Skyventure
6805 Visitors Circle, 800/SKY-FUN-1 or 407/903-1150
Open 2pm-midnight weekdays, noon-midnight weekends.
www.skyventureorlando.com
$38.50 adult/$33.50 child 4-12
AM, DI, MC, VI
Discounts: Website ($5), magazines ($5), Magicard ($5).

Experience the simulated sensation of skydiving in this vertical wind tunnel, located just off International Drive near Wet 'N' Wild. The experience is so authentic that teams of professional and amateur skydivers can often be found using Skyventure as a practice facility. First, you'll learn the basics of skydiving, including proper body positioning, and hand signals from Skyventure's professional instructors. Then you'll put on gear provided by the attraction and step into a 120 mph column of air. The whole program takes about an hour and includes two simulated dives.

Hot Air Balloons

One of the most breathtaking ways to survey the landscape is in a hot air balloon. These graceful craft float almost silently over farms, theme parks, hotels, swamps, marshes, and whatever else the winds of fortune decide to show you. These establishments all offer champagne balloon flights that depart at dawn. One of the most romantic things you can do in Orlando, it's also completely suitable for families – although it does get expensive. Call for reservations, you may be able to get them even the day before your desired sunrise flight..

•**Blue Water:** Tel. 800/586-1884 – www.bluewaterballoons.com – $175-200. AAA, Internet, military, and gift certificate discounts. Offers a refreshing champagne picnic following landing. Flights rise as high as several thousand feet.

•**Bob's Balloons:** Tel. 877/824-4606 – www.bobsballoons.com - $165/adult, $75/child. Internet and gift certificate discounts. Champagne toast and all-you-can-eat breakfast buffet follows a ride on these more intimate four- or six-person balloons, which rise to approximately 1,000 feet. Afternoon flights are offered seasonally.

•**Orange Blossom:** Tel. 407/239-7677 – www.orangeblossomballoons.com - $175/adult, $95 kids 10-17, kids under 9 free. Upon landing, guests enjoy a champagne toast and then a breakfast buffet at the Best Western Lakeside, their base of operations.

•**Skyscapes:** Tel. 407/856-4606 – www.skyscapesballoontours.com - $165/adult, $95/kids 6-12. Landing is followed by a champagne toast and continental breakfast. Mmm, mimosas.

Helicopter & Airplane Rides

Warbird Adventures, next to the Flying Tigers museum, offers guests the chance to actually fly in a WWII-era North American T-6/SNJ Texan/ Harvard plane. Guests take the controls in the front seat of the plane for an unforgettable flight Reservations are highly recommended, especially for summer weekends (www.warbirdadventures.com – 233 N. Hoagland Blvd. – 800/386-1593 or 407/870-7366). Prices are $170 for 15 minutes/$280 for 30 minutes/$510 for 60 minutes. **Fantasy of Flight** offers biplane rides (see above) as well.

Firms offering helicopter rides are plentiful in and around Orlando. Thanks to post-911 security regulations, the choppers can no longer fly over the Disney theme parks. However, they still are a fascinating and fun way to see the lay of the land. If you'd just like to experience the thrill of riding in a helicopter, many of the companies offer brief, 3-minute rides at a reasonable price. You won't see much on these teaser flights but you'll get a taste. More extensive tours are available as well, and can be quite fun – like seeing the world's most elaborate model train set. Check out these helicopter tour providers:

•**Air Florida:** 9 tours, $20-325. 8990 International Drive, 407/354-1400 – www.airfloridahelicopters.com

•**Orlando Helitours:** 4 tours, $15-125 adult, $15-75 child. 5519 W. Irlo Bronson Mem. Hwy., 407/397-0226 – www.orlandohelitours.com

•**Magic Air Adventure:** 5 tours, $20-130. 5069 W. Irlo Bronson Mem. Hwy., 407/390-7502.

Hang Gliding

You don't expect that you'd be able to do hang gliding on such a flat piece of real estate as central Florida, but sure enough, you can do just that at the laid-back **Wallaby Ranch Flight Park** ranch, located about a half hour from Disney World. Guests fly as high as 2,000 feet for 15 minutes in specially designed ultralights thanks to the latest aerotowing techniques. No experience is necessary. The best times to fly, weather-wise are early morning and late afternoon. Cost is $95 for a tandem flight with instruction. Multi-lesson packages are also available.

Wallaby Ranch offers a friendly atmosphere and tons of amenities including camping, swimming, golf instruction, massage therapy, ATV's and minibikes, mountain bike trails, a climbing wall, volleyball, horseshoes, RC instruction, and a lot more. To get to Wallaby Ranch, take I-4 west to Exit 55, turn North on US 27. Turn left on Dean Still Road and go 1.7 miles. Turn left at the mailbox labeled 1805. Visit www.wallaby.com or call 800/WALLABY or 863/424-0070.

Chapter 20

MUSIC, ART & CULTURE

There's a town here beyond the mouse, you know. And Orlando's a pretty vibrant little town, thank you very much – several good live music venues drawing national touring acts, a surprising array of art galleries, and attractions celebrating heritage and culture abound. This chapter will show you how to enrich your mind with unexpected and unusual sights, sounds, and experiences in a town not known for this sort of thing.

Cultural Attractions

Cirque du Soleil: La Nouba
> Downtown Disney – West Side, 407/939-7600
> Showtimes: 6pm, 9pm, Tues-Sat
> www.cirquedusoleil.com
> $59-87 adults, $44-65 kids 3-9
> AE, MC, VI
> Discounts: orlandoinfo.com ($7-10).

Whether you've seen one of their incomparable touring shows, seen *O* or *Mystère* in Vegas, witnessed their spectacle on the Bravo network, or if you've not experienced their wonder, Cirque du Soleil offers something to make every heart soar and put a smile on every face. This spellbinding show, featuring 60 performers, artists, and dancers, is performed twice a day in the huge white theater at the edge of Lake Buena Vista, looking from the distance like a linen tent built onto a UFO. The show is the single most breathtaking thing I've ever experienced in Disney World, and even though ticket prices are steep, I believe it to be worth **every penny**. If you've seen any of Cirque's other offerings and are worried about whether the show is appropriate for children, no worries. This is Disney World. The sensuality and sexuality of the show, while still present, are much less intense than Cirque shows elsewhere. But the show is still absolutely gorgeous, evocative, moving, and totally stunning. Try to arrive at the theater 30 minutes prior to showtime.

Enzian Theater

1300 S. Orlando Ave., Maitland, 407/629-0054
Call for showtimes.
www.enzian.org
Ticket prices vary. Regular admission is $8.
MC, VI

The non-profit Enzian has been Orlando's premier showplace for independent and alternative cinema for the past 18 years, and is the home base of the Florida Film Festival each spring (see Part 2, pages 325 and 332 for details) as well as several other annual events. The Enzian has a full-service kitchen including pizza, pasta, burgers, sandwiches, salads, and beer and wine. Take I-4 east to exit 88 (Lee Road) and go east. Turn left on US 17-92 and right at the second light, Magnolia St.

Holy Land Experience

4655 Vineland Road, 866/872-4659 or 407/367-2065
Opens 10am Mon-Fri, 12pm Sat, 9am Sun. Closing hours vary from 5-9pm.
www.theholylandexperience.com
$29.99 adults, $19.99 kids 6-12
AE, DI, MC, VI
Discounts: Magazines ($2).

This controversial 15-acre, $16 million theme park is a living biblical museum that lets guests experience exhibits like A Day in the Life of a Monk and the world's largest scale model of the walled city of Jerusalem, plus replicas of such biblical icons as the Garden Tomb and the Qumran Dead Sea Caves. Actors perform throughout the park in passion plays and musical revues like Praise Through the Ages. The Scriptorium Center for Biblical Antiquities, a 18,000 square foot museum in the Byzantine style, houses rare cuneiform, manuscripts, scrolls, and Bibles presented up close. To get here, take I-4 east to Exit 78. Turn left on Conroy. Turn right on Vineland. The park's entrance is on the right. In case of the rapture, remember where you parked.

Lakeridge Winery and Vineyards
    19239 US 27 North, Clermont, 800/768-WINE or 352/394-8627
    Open 10am-5pm Mon-Sat, 11am-5pm Sun.
    www.lakeridgewinery.com
    Free.

I am NOT drinking any Merlot! Florida isn't generally known for its wines, but that doesn't mean that they don't have some worthwhile offerings off the vine. At this 127-acre winery, the state's largest, you can participate in a tour of the 22,000 square foot facility and take part in a tasting that involves five or six of the winery's award winning vintages. The vineyard's Lakeridge and Lakeridge Reserve brands have won over 300 awards for winemaking excellence. The tours start every 15 to 20 minutes and last 45 minutes to an hour.

Medieval Times Living Museum
    4510 W. Irlo Bronson Mem. Hwy, 407/396-1518
    Open 4pm-8pm nightly.
    www.medievaltimes.com
    $8 adults, $6 kids 3-9. Included in Medieval Times dinner admission.
    AE, DI, MC, VI

Described as a "step back in time," this is the only permanent medieval village in the United States. It's easy to spend an hour or two wandering the cobblestone streets of Raymondsburg and observing the artisans, potters, blacksmiths, millers, carpenters, and glassblowers working their trade with

Orlando International Fringe Festival

Voted the "Best Outdoor Event" and "Best Cultural Festival" by the readers of Orlando Weekly, this ten-day May festival has been held every year since 1992. Performing artists from all over the world descend upon Orlando for this non-juried, first-come first-served festival, with over 70 groups performing at nine venues, 40 bands and musicians, and multiple dining and drinking options. All nine venues are located within a mile of "Fringe Central," at Heritage Square, downtown at the corner of Magnolia Ave. & Central Blvd. A $6 Fringe button is necessary to check out any of the indoor shows, although individual tickets are usually required as well. Visit their website – orlandofringe.org – to reserve tickets or view show schedules. You can also call them at 407/648-0077.

the materials and techniques of their ancestors. The craftsmen explain the nuances of their craft in fascinating detail, and falconry demonstrations are particularly intriguing. Truthfully though there's not much to this ... get to the dinner show early and check this out, for sure – but is it worth doing on its own? Probably not.

Pinocchio's Marionette Theater
525 S. SR 436, Winter Park, 407/788-8468
Performances Thu-Sun. Call for showtimes.
www.pinocchios.net
$9 adult, $8 for children under 12 and seniors.
AE, DI, MC, VI

Classic children's stories and fairy tales are performed with puppets at this unique professional repertory marionette company in Winter Park. Take I-4 east to exit 83B (Amelia St.). Bear right onto W. Colonial Dr. and take that four miles to Semoran Blvd. Turn left. It's about a half hour from International Drive.

Titanic: Ship of Dreams
8445 International Drive, 407/248-1166
Open 10am-8pm
www.titanicshipofdreams.com
$17.95 adult, $12.95 kids 6-12
AE, MC, VI
Discounts: Orlandoinfo.com ($3), magazines ($2), Magicard (10%).

You'll feel like the king of the world when you visit its first permanent Titanic attraction. Located at the Mercado shopping center, this museum features the only full-scale re-creations of the Titanic's staterooms and facilities, including her world-famous Grand Staircase. You'll also find over 200 priceless artifacts, Leonardo DiCaprio's costume from the film Titanic, and live interactive interpretations by storytellers in period costume. For those of you who paid for James Cameron's kids' platinum-and-diamond-encrusted orthodontics from repeated viewings of the schmaltzy movie, it's a must see. If your t-shirt says "THE BOAT SANK, GET OVER IT," you may want to skip this one.

Wordspring Discovery Center
11221 John Wycliffe Blvd., 407/852-3626
Open 9am to 4pm weekdays and 10am to 4pm every other Saturday.
www.wycliffe.org
Free.

This attraction presents the past, present, and future of the Bible with multimedia exhibits, interactive computer games and simulations, audio dramas, and hands-on activities. There is a café serving lunch and a gift shop. To get here, take the Central Florida Greeneway (SR 417, toll road) to Exit 22 (Narcoosee Road). Turn left on Narcoosee, right on Moss Park Road, and the center is 2 1/2 miles ahead on your left.

Art Galleries & Museums

Albin Polasek Museum & Scultpure Gardens
633 Osceola Ave., Winter Park, 407/852-3626
Open 10am-4pm Tues-Sat, 1pm-4pm Sun.
www.polasek.org
$5 adults, $4 seniors, $3 students. Kids under 12 free.

Slightly north of Orlando, Winter Park is host to the sculpture of Czech artist Albin Polasek, best known for "Man Carving His Own Destiny." The museum is listed on the National Register of Historic Places and contains 200 of his works scattered across three acres of gardens plus four galleries, all on the shores of beautiful Lake Osceola. A nice change of pace if your kids can stand a little culture, and you can't beat the price. Take I-4 east to Exit 86, Par Ave. Turn right on Par, left on Clay, right on Berkshire, left on Orange, and right on Fairbanks.

Charles Hosmer Morse Museum of American Art
445 Park Ave. North, Winter Park, 407/645-5311
Open 9:30am-1pm Tue-Sat, 1pm-4pm Sundays,
extended Friday hours in the summer.
www.morsemuseum.org
$3 adults, $1 students, free kids under 12.

The Morse Museum hosts the world's most comprehensive collection of the works of Lewis Comfort Tiffany, he of Tiffany glass and jewelry, pottery, paintings, etc. There is also a major exhibition of arts and crafts and American paintings from the past 200 years. Take I-4 east to Exit 86, Par Ave. Turn right on Par, left on Clay, right on Berkshire, left on Orange, right on Fairbanks, and left on S. Park.

Gallery at Avalon Island
37 & 39 S. Magnolia Ave., 407/992-1200
Open 8am-12am Tues-Fri, 12pm-12am Sat.

www.avalonisland.cc
Free.

Affiliated with the Orlando Modern Art Collection, the Gallery at Avalon Island includes striking modern pieces and rotating exhibitions as well as a coffee house with live entertainment. The gallery is located downtown at the corner of Pine St. & Magnolia Ave., in the historic Rogers Building, which dates back to 1886. Take I-4 east to Exit 82C (Anderson St.). Turn right on Anderson and left on Magnolia.

Grand Bohemian Gallery

325 S. Orange Ave., 407/581-4801
Open 9:30am-5:30pm Mon, 9:30am-10pm Tue -Sat, 10am-3pm Sun.
www.grandbohemiangallery.com
Free.

Orlando's most eclectic fine art gallery can be found downtown in the Westin Grand Bohemian Hotel. The museum features paintings, art glass, jewelry, and sculpture from the late 19th and early 20th centuries. To get here, take I-4 east to Exit 82C (Anderson St.). 2 blocks to Magnolia, turn left. 2 blocks to Jackson, turn left. The Westin is at the end of the block, on the left.

Menello Museum of American Folk Art

900 East Princeton Street, 407/246-4278
Open 10:30am-4:30pm Tues-Sat, 12pm-4:30pm Sun
www.mennellomuseum.com
$4 adults, $3 seniors, $1 students. Parking: $3.50.
AE, MC, VI
Discounts: AAA.

This small museum, located on the grounds of Lake Eola Park downtown, features exhibits from the permanent collection of paintings by Earl Cunningham as well as other traditional and contemporary folk artists. Traveling exhibitions are also featured. Take Exit 85 from I-4 East and turn right on Princeton St.

Millenia Gallery

4190 Millenia Blvd., 407/226-8701
Open 10am-6pm Tue-Thu, 10am-7pm Fri-Sat, noon-5pm Sun.
www.milleniagallery.com

New in 2004, this 10,000 square foot gallery is located by the Mall at

Millenia near Universal. will display contemporary sculpture and the work of modern masters, including Warhol, Chihuly, Libensky, and Statom. Monthlong exhibitions keep things interesting here. Take Exit 78 (Conroy Rd.) from I-4, turn right on Conroy and left on Millenia.

Museum of Fine Arts of St. Petersburg
    255 Beach Drive NE, St. Petersburg, 727/896-2667
    Open Tue-Sat 10am-5pm, Sun 1pm-5pm.
    $8 adults, $7 seniors, $4 college students and youth 7-18.
    www.fine-arts.org

This comprehensive art collection, celebrating its 40th anniversary in 2005, includes European and American art as well as photography, Greek and Roman antiquities, and pre-Columbian and Asian art. Featured artists include Monet, Cézanne, Renoir, Rodin, and Gauguin. The museum is located about two hours southwest of Orlando. Take I-4 to I-275 south, get off at exit 23A. Follow signs for the Pier, the Museum is one block north.

Orlando Museum of Art
    2416 N. Mills Ave., 407/896-4234
    Open 10am-4pm Tues-Fri, 12pm-4pm Sat-Sun.
    www.omart.org
    $8 adults, $7 seniors/students. $5 kids 6-18. Parking: $3.50.
    Discount: $1 coupon on website.

This museum in downtown Orlando features rotating exhibits from three collections: the American Art collection, including paintings, drawings, prints, photos, and sculptures from the last 300 years; the Art of the Ancient Americas collection, with 30 different cultural groups represented, from 2000 B.C. all the way up to 1521 A.D.; and the African Art collection, containing ceremonial and utilitarian artifacts and beads, tapestries, masks, carvings, and more. And who says you can't take it with you? The Museum Shop contains gifts, books, and artwork to brighten your home. To get here, take I-4 east to Exit 83A (Robinson St.). Turn right onto Robinson and drive approximately 1 mile.

The First Thursdays program brings an eclectic mix of locals to explore areaaartists' work, listen to live music, sip on beer and wine, and sample cuisine from various area restaurants. It happens the first Thursday of every month from 6 to 9pm.

Polk Museum of Art
    800 E. Palmetto St., Lakeland, 863/688-7743
    Open Tue-Sat 10am-5pm, Sun 1pm-5pm.

$5 adults, $4 seniors, students free.
Free admission Sat before noon.
www.polkmuseumofart.org

Two galleries and several annexes worth of historic and contemporary artwork are featured at this museum, and includes traveling and artist spotlight exhibits. The Sculpture Garden is well worth a look. The permanent collections include modern and cotemporary art, Asian art, European and American decorative arts, and pre-Columbian art. Take I-4 west to Exit 33 (SR 33). Turn left onto SR 33. Take the road to its end, at Lake Morton. Turn left there and again on East Palmetto.

Salvador Dali Museum
1000 Third St. S, St. Petersburg, 800/442-3254 or 727/823-3767
Open 9:30am-5:30pm Mon-Sat, open til 8pm Thu (and summer Fridays). Open Sun noon-5:30pm.
$14 adults, $12 seniors, $9 students, $3.50 for kids 5-9.
$5 admission after 5pm Thu. $2 coupon on website.
www.salvadordalimuseum.org
Discounts: Magazines ($1).

Over 200 of the incomparable Salvador Dali's oil paintings, watercolors, and drawings are on permanent display at this rehabilitated marine warehouse in the downtown area. An additional 1,300 objects include graphics, photographs, and sculptures, as well as archival footage. The collection is rotated occasionally, so the museum reains novelty on repeat visits. Six public tours are scheduled daily, and a 50 minute audio tour is available as well.

Timothy's Gallery
236 Park Ave N., Winter Park Tel. 407/629-0707
Open 10am-5:30pm Mon-Sat (open til 9pm Thu), 1pm-5pm Sun.
www.timothysgallery.com

Located in the eclectic suburb of Winter Park, Timothy's was voted to the Top 100 Galleries of American Craft list every year since 1997, and includes over 300 artists' work, ranging from jewelry and blown glass to wood and ceramics. Take I-4 east to Exit 45 (Fairbanks Ave.), two miles up turn left onto Park Ave.

Live Music Venues

For up to date concert listings anytime, I recommend **Pollstar.com**. It provides venue, date, and artist information through an easy search interface. You can run a search of all performances in an entire metropolitan area for a specified date range – thus granting you a bird's eye view of all the music coming to O-town during your visit. Some of the liveliest venues for touring acts are listed below.

•**Back Booth**, backbooth.com, 407/999-2570, 37 W. Pine St., Downtown

•**Hard Rock Live**, hardrocklive.com, 407/351-5483, Universal Orlando Citywalk

•**House of Blues**, hob.com, 407/934-2583, Downtown Disney West Side

•**Improv** (comedy club), www.orlandoimprov.com, 321/281-8000, 129 W. Church St., Downtown

•**Social**, thesocial.org, 407/246-1419, 54 N. Orange Ave., Downtown

•**Tanqueray's**, 407/649-8540, 100 S. Orange Ave., Downtown

•**TD Waterhouse Centre**, www.orlandocentroplex.com, 407/849-2001, 600 West Amelia St., Downtown

Performing & Fine Arts

Orlando has the kind of rich and diverse arts scene that you would expect from a metropolis of 1.6 million. Local groups, both professional and amateur, put on music, dance, performances throughout the year. Check their websites or call to find out what they'll be performing during your visit. Also, be sure to check out the list of annual festivals, concert events, and traditions in Part 2, pages 324-333. For a complete listing of performing and fine arts in Orlando, visit orlandoinfo.com or call 407/363-5872 and request the *Unexpected Orlando* guide.

Dance
Central Florida Ballet, www.centralfloridaballet.com, 407/849-9948
Orlando Ballet, www.orlandoballet.org, 407/426-1733

Music
Festival of Orchestras, www.festivaloforchestras.com, 407/896-2451
FL Symphony Youth Orchestra, www.fsyo.org, 407/999-7800
Orlando Chorale, www.theorlandochorale.org, 407/896-8624

Orlando Opera, www.orlandoopera.org, 407/426-1700
Orlando Philharmonic, www.orlandophil.org, 407/896-6700

Theater

Mad Cow Theater, www.madcowtheatre.com, 407/297-8788
Orlando Black Essentials Theatre, 407/491-9762
Orlando Repertory Theatre, www.orlandorep.com, 407/823-1500
People's Theater, www.peoplestheatre.org, 407/426-0545
Suntrust Broadway in Orlando, www.broadwayacrossamerica.com, 407/841-4675
Theatre Downtown, www.theatredowntown.net, 407/841-0083
UCF Civic Theater, www.ucfcivictheatre.org, 407/896-7365
Winter Park Playhouse, winterparkplayhouse.org, 407/645-0145

Chapter 21

SCIENCE, DISCOVERY & LEARNING

If the adventures at Epcot have given your kids (or you) the learning bug, there's plenty of places in Orlando where you can broaden your mind.

Holocaust Memorial Resource & Education Center

851 N. Maitland Ave., Maitland, 407/628-0555
Open Mon-Thu 9am-4pm, Fri 9am-1pm, and Sun 1pm-5pm.
www.holocaustedu.org
Free.

This sobering museum includes displays consisting of photos, text, artifacts, art, and short film presentations across twelve exhibits that each shed light on a different theme of the Holocaust. The museum is located north of Orlando – take I-4 east to exit 90A, bear right at W. Maitland Blvd., and right onto N. Maitland Ave.

Kennedy Space Center

NASA Parkway, Cape Canaveral, 321/449-4444

Open 9am-7pm daily.

www.kennedyspacecenter.com

$30 adult, $20 kids 3-11 for stamdard admission. $7 more includes the Astronaut Hall of Fame and interactive space flight simulators.

AE, DI, MC, VI

Discounts: Orlandoinfo.com ($3-5).

The Kennedy Space Center's popular visitor center features a variety of exhibits, films, and tours.

The Astronaut Encounter gives you a chance to get up close and personal with a real astronaut, every day of the year. The program includes mission briefings, space artifacts, personal anecdotes, and a Q&A session. The Astronaut Memorial space mirror is a high-tech tribute to fallen heroes. The Astronaut Hall of Fame (included in maximum access admission) includes interactive exhibits that bring to life the stories of America's space pioneers as well as simulators that let guests experience G-force training, moonwalks, and Mars rover rides. The Mad Mission to Mars is a live-action show that features 3-D CGI animation and theatrical effects in this comedic tale of a 2025 expedition to the Red Planet.

KSC also hosts the world's only back-to-back IMAX theatres, featuring two films presented on 5-story tall screens. *Space Station 3-D* is a breathtaking film about the construction of the International Space Station, narrated by the man who puts the science into Scientology, Tom Cruise. *The Dream Is Alive* offers an insider's view of the space shuttle program, with 37 minutes of footage from 3 separate missions, narrated by Walter Cronkite.

Three tours are available – the Kennedy Space Center tour is included in admission and includes the LC-39 Observation Gantry and Apollo/ Saturn V Complex. The NASA Up Close and Cape Canaveral: Then and Now tours are available for an extra fee – the former includes unparalleled access to the inner workings of the Kennedy Space Center, plus a full-scale mockup of the International Space Station's Habitation Module while the latter includes the launch sites for the Mercury, Gemini, and Apollo programs.

For a true hands-on visit, enroll in the Astronaut Training Experience (ATX) program ($225). This full-day program includes training and simulation activities including a multi-axis trainer and the 1/6 gravity chair, as well as an exclusive tour of NASA facilities. Participants must be 14 years of age or older, those under 18 must be accompanied by an adult. Advance reservations are required, call 321/449-4400.

To get to Kennedy Space Center, take SR 528 (Beeline Expressway) east to SR 407 north, turning right on SR 405, following signs nine miles to KSC.

Orange County Regional History Center

65 East Central Blvd., 407/836-8500
Open 10am-5pm Mon-Sat, noon-5pm Sun.
www.thehistorycenter.org
$7 adult, $3.50 kids 3-12, $6.50 seniors 60+ and students.
MC, VI
Discounts: Website (buy 1 get 1), magazines (buy 1 get 1), AAA.

The History Center takes a look at 12,000 years of history in Central
Florida, with fascinating permanent and traveling exhibits on such topics as
citrus farming, cattle ranching, the Seminole Indians, African-American
contributions, Orlando Air Base's WWII significance, WDW's construction, and many more. The History Center is located downtown, off Exit 82C
(Anderson Street). Turn left on Magnolia and right on Central.

Orlando Science Center

777 East Princeton Street, 888/OSC-4-FUN or 407/896-4234
Open 9am-5pm Mon-Thu, 9am-9pm Fri-Sat, noon-5pm Sun.
www.osc.org
$14.95 adults, $9.95 youth 3-11, $13.95 senior 55+ or student.
Parking: $3.50.
MC, VI
Discounts: Orlandoinfo.com ($1-2.50), magazines (free kids' admis-
sion), AAA, Friday and Saturday nights after 4pm ($5).

This 207,000 square foot hands-on learning center features a constantly evolving series of interactive exhibits including the BodyZone area,
which includes a 3D movie and exhibits about the functioning of the human
body; Dr. Dare's Laboratory, where computers and instructors guide parents
and children through hands-on experiments; Touch the Sky, a Lockheed-
Martin sponsored exhibit uncovering the math and science behind flight;
ShowBiz Science, covering topics like CGI and make-up effects; Science
City, with themed areas about math, physics, electricity, and magnetism,
DinoDigs, featuring eight full dinosaur skeletons donated from the Animal
Kingdom; and the Inventors' Workshop, using three 15-minute experi-
ments to reveal scientific method.

Three films are shown daily at the Dr. Phillips Cinedome and DigiStar
II planetarium, which features 28,000 watts of digital sound. *Mystery of the
Nile, WSKY Radio Station,* and *ESPN Ultimate X* were the current offerings

at press time. The Crosby Observatory offers public access to night sky viewing through this powerful telescope on Friday and Saturday nights. This is a great rainy day option in downtown Orlando. Take I-4 east to exit 85 (Princeton St.,), turn right.

Ripley's Believe It ... Or Not!

8210 International Drive, 407/363-4418
Open 9am-1am.
www.ripleysorlando.com
$16.95 adults, $11.95 kids 4-12.
AE, MC, VI
Discount: Orlandoinfo.com ($2), magazines ($1-1.50), Magicard ($1-2)

Robert Ripley is famous for the cartoons, books, television specials, and museums that bear his name. The intrepid Ripley spent his whole life crisscrossing the globe searching for oddities to satisfy his never-ending appetite for the unusual. The fruits of his labors are on display here at this satisfying and fascinating landmark museum on International Drive, just north of Mercado Mediterranean Village.

Items on display include a replica of Leonardo Da Vinci's Mona Lisa constructed of inch-square pieces of toast; a two-thirds scale model of a 1907 Rolls Royce made of over a million matchsticks; a Van Gogh self-portrait made of postcards; shrunken heads; clothing made of human hair; masks representing cultures from all over the globe, a dinosaur exhibit; a 10-foot square portion of the Berlin Wall; a vast miniatures collection including a grain of rice with a tropical sunset painted on it; an Egyptian mummy; and many more. It takes approximately an hour and a half to tour the museum at your own pace.

The building that houses the eclectic 8,900-square foot museum is as off-center as the exhibits — literally. Constructed on a slant, it appears as if it is descending into one of Florida's infamous sinkholes.

Trainland Train & Trolley Museum

8990 International Drive, 407/363-9002
Open 10am-6:30pm Mon-Thu, 10am-7pm Fri-Sat.
$6 adult/$5 kids under 12 and seniors.
AE, DI, MC, VI

Near the convention center, this museum is a hobbyist's dream, with 14 continuously operating model trains transversing 3,000 feet of track across 4,800 square feet of exhibit space. The detail is immaculate and often incredible, sometimes with a touch of humor, always with a smile. There's a scavenger hunt game that challenges you to search the scale model layout for specific items, where guests compete for prizes.

Winter Park Historical Museum

200 W. New England Ave., Winter Park, 407/647-8180
Open Thu-Fri 11am-3pm, Sat 9am-1pm, and Sun 1pm-4pm.
www.winterparkhistorical.com
Free

This muesum details the history of Orlando's eclectic, artistic, and historic urban village with photos, collectibles, and memorabilia. Take I-4 east to exit 87 (Fairbanks Ave.), turn right, then turn left on S. New York Ave. and take that to New England.

Wonderworks

9067 International Drive, 407/351-8800
Open 9am-midnight.
www.wonderworksonline.com
$18.95 adults, $12.95 children 4-12 & seniors.
AE, DI, MC, VI
Discount: Website ($1.50), magazines ($1.50).

WonderWorks is the single most unbelievable architectural achievement I have ever seen. At the north end of the Pointe*Orlando complex is this interactive, hands-on entertainment center, which is in an UPSIDE DOWN building. For maximum shock value effect, drive south from Sand Lake Road onto International Drive, watch your kids' jaws go halfway to the floor upon seeing the Ripley's museum, and then seal the deal by continuing south past this classically designed building, which according to storyline, was a research facility in the Bermuda Triangle until swept up by a tornado and dropped on top of a warehouse in its present location in Orlando.

Once you get over the shock of the building's appearance, buy a ticket and head inside. There you'll find three levels containing over 85 different hands-on experiences and activities. At the WonderCoaster, you can design your own roller coaster and then ride it. Experience a simulated 5.3

earthquake or hurricane force winds, virtual combat in the Global VR exhibit, the Bridge of Fire, which sends 250,000 watts of electricity through your body, a bed of 3500 nails, and a virtual hoops game played via the magic of the blue screen (really a hoot!). In addition to these exhibits, there's also a 10,000 square foot laser tag arena with arcade on the top-floor "basement," available for an additional fee of $4.95 per person. Combinations with Wonderworks admission, and/or with the Outta Control dinner show (pizza and magicians) are available.

Part 2

PLANNING YOUR TRIP

When to Visit

Once you've decided to make like a Super Bowl MVP and declare yourself destined for Disney World, this is the first question you need to answer. What time of year are you going to plan your visit?

Don't take this decision lightly. It can mean the difference between stress-free touring and a trip from which you'll need a vacation to recover. Most people gauge the quality of their Disney vacation by how much stuff they do. If you pick a less crowded time of year, you spend less time in lines and more time on rides – practically guaranteeing you enjoy your vacation more. Sounds like common sense, I know. But a lot of parents have the knee-jerk reaction to schedule their trip for summer vacation or over the holidays, even though these are the most infuriatingly crowded times of year.

The first time my parents took my brothers and me to Disney World, we visited in the month of August. By visiting right in the middle of the summer, we dealt with torrential thunderstorms, oppressively hot temperatures, and huge lines.

When we returned two years later, my parents did just about the coolest thing in the world for us. They pulled us out of school for a week in November for the trip. Nicer weather plus fewer crowds equals better vacation. It's as simple as that.

You may be hesitant to pull the kids out of school, but the alternative is spending half the day in line. You don't want that. They don't want that. Really, how many cherished stories do you have of waiting in lines?

Attendance

Scheduling your trip to minimize the crowds you have to deal with is the single biggest favor you can do for yourself when it comes to hitting Disney. The biggest crowds of the year, by far, are found during the last week in December. Over 75,000 people can enter the park on these days. The summer months are nearly as busy. The weeks of Easter and Thanksgiving round out the most crowded times of the year at Disney World. President's Week draws enough crowds to be avoided as well.

Better touring times include March through mid-May (except for Easter week) and September through November (except for Thanksgiving week).

The best time of year to tour Disney World with the minimum crowds is in December and January (except for Christmas week, of course). Another benefit of visiting during off-peak periods is that hotel rooms are often cheaper. Disney's resorts are priced the lowest during the months of January, September, November, and parts of February and December.

It used to be that Disney parks did not run their nighttime events during off-peak seasons. This is no longer the case, as the Magic Kingdom, Epcot, and Disney-MGM Studios end each day with their respective nighttime spectaculars year-round. With this final factor falling into place, it's nearly impossible to recommend peak-season touring unless your family has no other workable choices.

Weather

Another reason to avoid summertime touring is that it can get insanely hot, and it rains almost every afternoon. Dry, temperate months are best

Orlando Weather Chart

	Low	High	Rain	Humidity
Jan	48.6	70.8	2.30	56%
Feb	49.7	72.7	3.02	52%
Mar	55.2	78.0	3.21	50%
Apr	59.4	83.0	1.80	49%
May	65.9	87.8	3.55	49%
Jun	71.8	90.5	7.32	57%
Jul	73.1	91.5	7.25	58%
Aug	73.4	91.5	6.78	60%
Sep	72.4	89.7	6.01	60%
Oct	65.8	84.6	2.42	56%
Nov	57.5	78.5	2.30	56%
Dec	51.3	72.9	2.15	57%

suited to theme park touring. The chart on the previous page shows the average daily highs and lows, as well as the average monthly rainfall and 1pm humidity. While Orlando is landlocked, it is not immune from tropical storms, as the brutal 2004 hurricane season proved three times in a month. Hurricane season generally runs from June 1 through November 30, and while it's impossible to anticipate if and when they will hit central Florida when planning your trip, it's always a good idea to keep the possibility in mind.

What to Do If It Rains

Q. It's raining! &^%#(*! Help!

A. You can purchase rain ponchos at most sundry-selling stores in each of the theme parks for about $7. Or you can get 'em beforehand at 7-Eleven for $2.

Q. How necessary is a poncho?

A. You can live without it, unless you're visiting during the rainy summer months. If you suffer from a cat-like hydrophobia and still want to experience rides like Splash Mountain and the Kali River Rapids, bring one regardless of weather.

Q. I'm at the park, and the clouds look threatening. Should I call it a day?

A. Not in most cases. Especially in the summer, Orlando is subject to afternoon thunderstorms that blow across the sky, black and ominous, only to fade into the horizon just as quickly. Everything picks back up at that point, and the crowds are usually thinner and the temperature a little cooler. It's a win-win situation.

Q. They're predicting rain for tomorrow but I still want to go out. Which theme park is least affected by rainy weather?

A. The overwhelming majority of Epcot's attractions are indoors, so rain doesn't take many options off the docket. Universal Studios is also a mostly indoor park.

Q. They're predicting rain for tomorrow. Find me something cool to do!

A. The best rainy-day options are covered in Part IV. Here's a list of my favorites.

Wait out short rains at Ripley's Museum or get off your feet for a couple of hours and catch a movie at the multiplexes at Pleasure Island, Citywalk, Pointe*Orlando, or Festival Bay. If you're looking at a longer rain delay, consider Wonderworks, Disney Quest, or Museum Row downtown – the Orlando Art Museum, Orange County Historical Museum, and Orlando Science Center.

Special Events

Orlando and Disney World are fun places at any time of the year, but there are a handful of annual events worth arranging your trip around, if properly inclined.

Epcot's Annual Festivals

Annual events at Epcot transform this enlightening attraction into an extra-special place with dozens of new reasons to smile. The **Epcot International Food & Wine Festival** (Oct 1 through mid-Nov), now in its eighth year, is a must for epicureans, and my personal favorite annual Disney World event. World Showcase's already impressive dining options are supplemented by more than 20 international food and wine stands all around the lagoon that enable you to snack your way around the world, one appetizer-sized, budget-priced portion at a time. For the armchair somelliers, 45-minute wine tastings and seminars are available, with over 70 wineries participating over the course. The festival also includes a specialty beer garden and the Eat to the Beat Concert Series.

For the serious gourmet, there's a bunch of other ticketed events that may tempt your palate. Education programs, celebrity chef demonstrations, food and wine tastings, themed evening prix fixe dinners, reserve dinners, and food/wine pairings at Epcot's restaurants are all available. Note that Epcot admission is required for all ticketed events.

Also popular is the **Epcot Flower & Garden Festival** (mid-Apr through mid-June), now in its 12th year. The festival spotlightselaborate display fields, including exotic internationals around World Showcase. Seminars, Q&A sessions, and demonstrations help develop green thumbs, and the Flower Power Concert Series at the America Gardens Theater features folk, pop, and rock acts from the 60s and 70s. There's also special activities suitable for the whole family.

Artistic, Musical, Cultural, & Ethnic Events

Downtown Disney plays host to the **Festival of the Masters** (mid-Nov), a juried art competition that celebrates its 30th anniversary in 2005. Over 150 artists representing media like jewelry, painting, sculpture, photography, clay, and glass participate in this eclectic, open-air festival that includes folk art, sidewalk chalkings, performance art, and children's activities. Admission is free. Annual art events include the trendy and eclectic **Winter Park Sidewalk Art Festival** (Mar); the **Winter Park Autumn Art Festival** (Oct), a juried, community-oriented art show; the free **Osceola Art**

Festival in downtown Kissimmee (Nov); and the **Mount Dora Arts Festival** (Feb), a quirky, juried event less than an hour's drive from Disney.

A few of the more interesting Hollywood-themed special events of the year are held at the Disney-MGM Studios. The popular **Star Wars Weekends** (weekends in May-Jun) allows guests to mingle with 40 characters from the Holy Trilogy (and its bastard children, Episodes I-III) in themed Rebellion and Empire zones, along with a special Star Wars edition of the *Who Wants to Be a Millionaire: Play It!* Attraction, meet-and-greets, and other fun events.

In the fall, the **ABC Super Soap Weekend** provides guests with an opportunity to meet the stars of ABC daytime dramas, purchase one-of-a-kind memorabilia, a "casting call" experience, and experience other assorted elbow-rubbing. 98 Degrees and the Backstreet Boys notwithstanding, Orlando is a decent town for live music. This is never more true than during some of the year's excellent annual events. The **Bach Festival** (Feb) has been held at Rollins College since 1935 and features over 100 singers and musicians. Citywalk's **Bob Marley Reggae Fest** (Feb) features performances from the likes of Sean Paul and Rita Marley along with Caribbean food and specialty shopping. Admission is $22 for one day or $30 for two.

If you're craving more of an American original sound, head to Kissimmee Lakefront Park for **Jazzfest Kissimmee** (Apr) or the **Kissimmee Bluegrass Festival** (Mar). The **Festival of Rhythm and Blues** (Feb) features R&B, gospel, jazz, Caribbean, and African music as part of Black History Month. The **WLOQ Jazz Jams Summer Concert Series** brings monthly performances to Central Park in Winter Park.

If music gets you closer to God, consider a September visit. **Night of Joy** and **Rock the Universe** are two extremely popular celebrations of contemporary Christian music held on the weekend after Labor Day at the Magic Kingdom and Universal Studios, respectively. These usually sell out in advance and require a separate admission, as they are held after the parks close to the general public. However, both events' admission will get you into the respective parks after 4pm. Night of Joy showcases artists like Nicole C. Mullen, Mercy Me, and Audio Adrenaline, and costs $37.95 for one night or $61.95 for two. Rock the Universe features a harder edge, focusing more on Christian rock (2005 headliners: Michael W. Smith, David Crowder, Third Day, Reliant K). Tickets run $35.95 for one night or $58.95 for two.

Other noteworthy cultural events include the award-winning **Fringe Festival** (May), which features hundreds of shows from over 50 groups across ten days, along with visual art exhibits. **Gasparilla Pirate Festival** (Jan), where re-enactors have staged pirate invasions of Tampa for the past 100 years; the **Scottish Highland Games** (Jan), celebrating the area's rich Scottish heritage with authentic activities, food, music, and games; the **Florida Film Festival** (Apr), featuring over 100 films along with seminars, tributes, and a gala; and Orlando's annual **Gay Days** festivities; which include plenty of music at over 40 activities citywide during the first week of June.

Car aficionado? Over 150 rare and exotic cars are on display at the annual **Concours d'Elegance** (Oct) in Winter Park. If motorcycles are more your thing, **Biketoberfest** brings 12,000 Harley-Davidson enthusiasts to Daytona Beach.(Oct). There's also **Daytona Bike Week** (Mar), a 64-year tradition.

Local Fairs and Festivals

Face it, Floridians love a good party. And they'll use any excuse to throw a festival. The **Grant Seafood Festival** (Feb), **Zellwood Sweet Corn Festival** (May), and **Florida Strawberry Festival** (Mar) celebrate some of the area's favorite native foods, served with side dishes of music, shopping, and rides. Winter Haven's **Florida Citrus Festival** (Jan) features the Miss Florida Citrus pageant and entertainment. But best of all is the **Orlando Beer Festival** (Nov) at Citywalk, drawing 10,000 bacchanalians for live festival performances, awards, sample-size snackery from Citywalk restaurants, and oh yeah, over 150 specialty and handcrafted brews. Tickets are $25 for Saturday and $20 for Sunday, an extra $5 at the gate. The Gaylord Palms hosts the **Best of Summer Florida Fest** (July-Aug) on weekends over the summer, featuring stunt shows, laser spectaculars, live entertainment, kids' activities, and street entertainers inside the resort's massive atrium.

Sporting Events

ESPN: The Weekend is a chance for sports fans to mingle with personalities from the seminal sports network, witness live on-site telecasts, and interactive sports exhibits across the Disney-MGM Studios (late Feb), including a sports edition of the *Who Wants to Be a Millionaire?* attraction.

Central Florida hosts several major sporting events every year. Biggest of all is NASCAR's highest-profile race, the **Daytona 500** (Mar), held 45 minutes east of Orlando as the culmination of a week-long Speed Week celebration. If you prefer your racing done without cars, the **Walt Disney World Marathon** is open to the public in January of each year.

The **Capital One Bowl** pits Big Ten and SEC squads against one another on New Year's Day, while the **Champs Sports Bowl** features teams from the ACC and Big Twelve in late December. Ticket information and prices are announced around October 1.

Another high-profile championship event is the annual **Walt Disney World Golf Classic** (Oct), this year under new sponsorship from Funai. It lures top name PGA talent – including past winners like Vijay Singh and Tiger Woods – with $4 million in prize money. *Note that if you're planning on hitting the Disney World links yourself, you ain't getting a tee time over Tiger,* *so plan accordingly.* Also, the **Bay Hill Invitational** (Mar) has drawn top PGA golfers for 25 years – including four-time champion, Tiger something-or-other.

Before it was the gateway to the World, Kissimmee was something of a cow-town. Relive those days with the **Silver Spurs Rodeo** (Feb, Oct), a tournament that draws cowboys from all across the country to compete for $100,000 in a brand-new arena at Osceola Heritage Park on US 192.

Disney's Wide World of Sports complex plays preseason host to the NFL's **Tampa Bay Buccaneers** (Jul-Aug) as well as the **Atlanta Braves** (Mar) spring training. The **Houston Astros** (Mar) also hold their spring training locally, at Osceola County Stadium in Kissimmee.

Christmas in Disney & Orlando

White Christmas is overrated. There, I said it. Orlando and Disney World prove that you don't need cold, wet, heavy, road-slicking white chaos to enjoy the holiday season. Christmas week is so crowded that stress-free touring is about as realistic as a flying reindeer, but there's a ton of extra-curriculars that make this one of the most special times of year to visit, if you can overlook the hour-long lines and claustrophobic crowds. Fortunately, most of the special events run for most of the month of December, so you can witness the holiday cheer minus the maddening crowds.

MAGIC KINGDOM: On selected evenings throughout December, **Mickey's Very Merry Christmas Party** takes place. After the park closes to the general public, popular attractions throughout the park remain open, guests thrill to a nightly snowfall on Main Street USA, and entertainment in the form of stage shows, carolers, fireworks, and the Very Merry Christmas Parade. Santa Goofy greets kids on Main Street, the smell of cocoa and cookies permeates the air, and families receive a souvenir photo and button. The party runs from 7 pm to 1 am, and tickets are $46.81 for adults, $37.23 for kids 3-9, plus tax. Advance tickets for Sundays through Thursdays are about five bucks cheaper, and Annual Passholders get discounts of about $10 on selected nights. Note that only 20,000 tickets are available for each night, so the park is considerably less crowded than during regular hours. Also, this means that many nights sell out in advance.

Holiday fun in the Magic Kingdom isn't limited to the after-hours party. There's a nightly tree lighting ceremony on Main Street, as well as special holiday editions of the Country Bear Jamboree and Diamond Horseshoe Revue shows. Other festive entertainment includes the daily **Mickey's Very Merry Christmas Parade**, Mickey's Night Before Christmas (in Tomorrowland), and the Celebrate the Season musical revue.

EPCOT: Epcot's **Holidays Around the World** is a multiculti celebration of the customs, stories, songs, and traditions of the world's various peoples. The walkway linking Future World and World Showcase displays "Lights of Winter," an animated display of illumination synchronized with classic Christmas songs, and each World Showcase pavilion hosts storytellers. *Storyteller performances are generally scheduled to enable you to see them all in succession as you proceed around the lagoon, if you'd like.*

The other jewel in the Epcot holiday crown is the **Candlelight Processional.** Now in its 35th year, this is a reading of the Christmas story performed by celebrity narrators along with the Voices of Liberty choir and a 50-piece orchestra. Past emcees have included Jim Caviezel, Joe Mantegna, Gary Sinise, Edward James Olmos, Brian Dennehy, and many more Hollywood B-listers. Performed three times a night at the America Gardens Theater, the Processional is included in regular park admission, and we recommend showing up at least 15 minutes in advance to ensure seating. However, priority seating is available as part of a dinner package at one of many top Epcot restaurants ($28.99-$44.99 adults, $10.99 kids 3-9).

DISNEY-MGM STUDIOS: After being declared a public nuisance in 1994 by the Arkansas Supreme Court, Jennings Osborne's five-million light Christmas display has been transplanted here from Little Rock. The park is decked out with over 5 million lights, in the shape of everything carousels, flying angels, reindeer, and glittering Mickey Mouse figures. The **Hollywood Hollyday Parade** decks out the daily parade in a festive Noel veneer. Even the Disney villains look like they're angling for mistletoe kisses. Santa arrives in a pimped out 1929 Cadillac. What did you expect, an Escalade?

ANIMAL KINGDOM: Camp Minnie-Mickey is the holiday HQ here, with Disney characters decked out for the occasion, plus hands-on fun like making cookies and Christmas ornaments. The daily **Jingle Jungle Expeditions** parade is a safari-style celebration. Since the Animal Kingdom isn't open after dark, there's nothing to light. Park's closed, folks. Mouse out front should've told you.

UNIVERSAL ORLANDO: Universal Studios runs a parade featuring balloons and floats from **Macy's Holiday Parade.** Dr. Seuss's favorite creations come to life in this Whoville style celebration, **Grinchmas,** at Islands of Adventure.

ELSEWHERE AROUND TOWN: The theme parks do not have a monopoly on Christmas, of course. There's plenty of other worthwhile stuff to check out. The **International Drive Fantasy of Lights** features dazzling displays, decorations, and seasonal activities – most of which are free. The **Pinewood Estate** at Historic Bok Sanctuary southwest of Orlando in Lake Wales, lavishly decorates a 20-room, 12,000-sq. foot Mediterranean Revival mansion in holiday attire ($13 adults, $8 kids 5-12). Bok Sanctuary also features special Xmas Eve and Day performances from the 60-bell carillon along with seasonal readings, luminaries, and more. The spectacular new **Gaylord Palms** resort features the spectacular ICE! attraction, with 2 million pounds of ice carved into whimsical holiday sculptures and intereactive displays throughout eight themed exhibits. Silver Springs hosts its annual **Festival of Lights** (included in park admission), making Florida's "natural attraction" glimmer with festive cheer.

Traditional holiday performances downtown include the Orlando Philharmonic's holiday concert, and the Orlando Ballet's **Nutcracker**. A less traditional offering is the First Baptist Church's **Singing Christmas Trees** combines 45-foot trees with a full orchestra, choir, and a 118-rank Schantz pipe organ. The FBC also hosts the **Walk Through Bethlehem** narrated tour depicting the life of Jesus, with a costumed cast of 250 and live animals.

A favorite among locals is the **Kissimmee Holiday Extravaganza** at Kissimmee Lakefront Park, featuring a nighttime street parade, arts and crafts, a food festival, fireworks, and 20 tons of snow.

New Year's in Disney, Universal, & Orlando

There's no lack of family-friendly ways to ring in the New Year in and around Disney World. Three of the four Disney parks are open until 1am, with complimentary hats and horns offered to guests. At the **Magic Kingdom**, there's extra performances of SpectroMagic and the Wishes fireworks display along with dance parties for the kids throughout the park. **Epcot** features multiple areas of music – techno, rock, big band, swing, euro, and more. At **Disney-MGM Studios** Fantasmic! is performed three times and the Sorcery in the Sky fireworks cap the night off – all these festivities are included in normal admission.

If you're looking for something a little more intoxicating, **Pleasure Island** is worth consideration. Their 2004 blast featured Tone Loc, Cheap Trick, and Kurtis Blow. Parties are also held at Bongo's Cuban Café, the California Grill (at the Contemporary), and Narcoosee's at the Grand Floridian. **Universal Orlando** also hosts a New Year's party geared more towards adults.

One of the hottest tickets in town is the Gaylord Palms' **Grande Masque** ($275). It's a black-tie masked ball produced jointly by the Orlando Ballet, Orlando Opera, and the Orlando Philharmonic Orchestra, featuring open bar, a five course dinner, live and silent auction, and a champagne toast at midnight.

Halloween in Disney, Universal, & Orlando

Mickey's Not-So-Scary Halloween Party is a tame but fun celebration at the Magic Kingdom. It's a separate ticketed event ($42.55 adult, $35.10 kids 3-9), and the party includes five hours of after-house access to rides and attractions plus special Halloween fireworks, a twice-nightly parade of costumed Disney characters, and trick-or-treating across the park. Add spooky stories, live music, and lots of special touches, and you've got the makings for a fun night for the whole family. But be sure to get your tickets in advance, as this sells out. Sunday night editions of the Halloween Party seem to be the least crowded. Friday nights seem to be particularly mobbed, as do the last few nights in October, especially Halloween proper. Purchase your tickets in advance and save approximately $5 per person. Annual Passholders receive a $10 discount for the party on specified nights.

Downtown Disney also hosts free celebrations on the weekend around Halloween proper. Pleasure Island's **Dance the Fright Away** event adds "goodie tosses," magicians, witches, ghosts, and stiltwalkers to the complex's formidable entertainment lineup. As always, there is no charge for admission to Pleasure Island itself, only the nightclubs on it. Kids can also trick-or-treat at various locations in Downtown Disney, and thrill to magicians, jugglers, and balloon artists.

"THIS EVENT IS NOT INTENDED FOR YOUNG CHILDREN." So screams the caveat on the web page of Universal's **Halloween Horror Nights**, now in its 13th year. If the promise of "gut-wrenching scares and blood-curdling frights" raises your eyebrows in addition to your heart rate, check out this after-hours party at Islands of Adventure. Creep through themed haunted houses and scare zones, including the Field of Screams, the Hellgate Prison, Castle Vampyr, and more. There's also a new live show for 2003 – Bill and Ted's Excellent Halloween Adventure.

Halloween Horror Nights

Q. How much does Halloween Horror Nights cost?

A. Admission in 2003 cost $54.95, $10 less for Florida residents.

Q. Can I bring my kids?

A. Can you afford psychotherapy? Parental discretion is strongly suggested. It's not intended for children, which is why there's no child ticket price.

Q. Can I order in advance?

A. You absolutely should! Many of the weekend nights and some of the weeknights sell out in advance. Purchase your ticket on the website, www.halloweenhorrornights.com.

Q. When does Halloween Horror Nights run?

A. It runs on selected nights during the month of October – all weekends, plus many weeknights, running more frequently closer to the end of the month. It starts at 7pm, after the park closes to the general public. From Sunday through Thursday, it runs til midnight. On Fridays and Saturdays it runs til 2am.

Q. Is it included in regular Universal admission?

A. No, but if you're in a Universal park during the day, you can get a "Stay and Scream" pass allowing day/night admission for $37.95 on Friday and Saturday or $21.95 on weeknights nights, in addition to your daytime admission.

Q. Are there any discounts?

A. Decisions on discount availabilities were not available at press time, but in the past Floridians could get $20 weeknight/$15 weekend discounts from coupons on Coke cans or at area Burger Kings. Check the website for the most up-to-date coupon locations. Universal's annual passholders also get a discount.

Q. Is there any kind of season pass?

A. Frequent Fear passes allowing unlimited admission Sundays through Thursdays have been available in years past.

Q. Can I wear a costume?

A. Nope. They'll turn you away at the gate.

Sea World hosts the **Spooktacular Family Sleepover**, designed for families with kids from kindergarten through the fifth grade. It includes trick-or-treating, family-friendly activities, a sleepover at an animal habitat, a pizza snack, and a continental breakfast. It costs $107 per person including next-day admission to the theme park, $75 for just the sleepover.

Mardi Gras in Orlando

Fat Tuesday celebrations abound in Orlando. In addition to rowdy parties all across the downtown nightclub district, there's also **Pleasure Island**, with stilt-walkers, beads, jugglers, live bands, and Cajun cuisine – included in regular admission. Named the #6 Mardi Gras celebration in the country by AOL Cityguide, **Universal Studios**' month-long event features a 10-block long parade, street performers, beads, and lots and lots of alcohol on Friday and Saturday nights. There's also musical performances from big names (2005 included the Go-Gos, Jason Mraz, O.A.R,). Very popular with locals. The Mardi Gras celebration is included in Universal admission, alternately guests can purchase a special "Mardi Gras After Five" ticket, offering late-day admission for the discounted rate of $39.95 ($10 less for FL and GA residents).

Website/Phone Information – Special Events

Epcot Food & Wine Festival - www.disneyworld.com/foodandwine – 407/824-4321

Bach Festival – www.bachfestivalflorida.org – 407/646-2182

Jazzfest Kissimmee – www.kissimmeeparksandrec.com – 407/933-8368

Night of Joy – www.nightofjoy.com – 407/939-7639

Rock the Universe – www.rocktheuniverse.com – 866/788-4836

Gasparilla Pirate Festival – www.gasparillapiratefest.com – 813/353-8108

Scottish Highland Games – www.flascot.com – 407/426-7268

Winter Park Sidewalk Art Festival – www.wpsaf.org – 407/672-6390

Osceola Art Festival - www.ocfta.com

Mount Dora Art Festival - www.mountdoracenterforthearts.org – 352/383-0880

Florida Film Festival - www.floridafilmfestival.com – 407/629-1088

Gay Days – www.gaydays.com – 407/896-8431

Cours d'Elegance - www.tscevents.com – 352/383-1181

Biketoberfest - www.biketoberfest.com – 386/271-3120

Bike Week – www.daytona.bikeweek.com

Grant Seafood Festival - www.grantseafoodfestival.com – 407/723-8687

Zellwood Sweet Corn Festival – www.zellwoodsweetcornfest.org

Florida Strawberry Festival – www.flstrawberryfestival.com – 813/752-9194

Florida Citrus Festival – www.citrusfestival.com

Orlando Beer Festival – www.orlandobeerfestival.com – 407/224-2690

Daytona 500 – www.daytona500.com – 904/254-2700

Capital One Bowl/Champs Sports Bowl – fcsbowls.com – 407/423-2476

Funai Classic – www.disneyworldsports.com –407/835-2525

Bay Hill Invitational – www.bayhillinvitational.com – 407/876-7774

Silver Spurs Rodeo – www.silverspursrodeo.com – 407/67-RODEO

Buccaneers Preseason – www.disneyworldsports.com – 407/939-7810

Braves Spring Training – www.disneyworldsports.com – 407/939-4263

Astros Spring Training – www.astros.com – 407/839-3900

I-Drive Fantasy of Lights – www.internationaldriveorlando.com – 407/248-9590

Christmas at Pinewood – www.boksanctuary.org – 863/676-1408

Gaylord Palms ICE! – www.gaylordpalms.com – 407/586-0000

Silver Spring Festival of Lights – www.silverspring.com – 352/236-2121

First Baptist Church – www.fbcorlando.org – 407/849-6269

Orlando Ballet (Nutcracker) – www.orlandoballet.org – 407/839-3900

Kissimmee Holiday Extravaganza – www.kissimmeeparksandrec.com – 407/933-8368

Grande Masque – www.grandemasque.org – 407/426-7360

Halloween Horror Nights – www.halloweenhorrornights.com – 888/467-7677

Sea World Spooktacular Family Sleepover – www.seaworld.com – 866/4SW-CAMP

Preparation

The key to a successful vacation anywhere is preparation. Perhaps nowhere is this more the case than at Orlando and Disney World, where the unparalleled multitude of attractions, restaurants, and hotels include a lot of good choices, and a few that you may want to skip. Orlando is the kind of destination where a little bit of knowledge can pay serious dividends, so if you get there knowing what you want to do, when you want to do it, and how to do it plus cheap, minus crowded, you start off ahead of the game.

Thanks to the Internet, it's much easier to gather information on your destination before you arrive. Not only will educating yourself make for a better-planned, better-executed trip, but it'll get the excitement about the trip building. Now's the time to get excited – whether it's your first trip to Orlando or simply your first time since childhood. So consider your research here the most thrilling and rewarding homework assignment you'll ever have.

Disney vs. Universal

Universal's programming is geared much more towards locals, and more specifically, young adult locals – not families. Not to say that Universal isn't family-friendly, but grown-ups are made to feel like this is THEIR park, THEIR vacation, much more so than at Disney, which spins itself much more as the FAMILY destination, grownups and kids together, which in reality all too often means "mom and dad sacrifice their own happiness to amuse the spawn."

Universal's hotels are a small step above Disney's Deluxe Resorts in terms of quality – Loews knows how to run a hot hotel. Much more refined and luxurious, with every bit as much pervasive theming, and great restaurants at each. Universal also offers better perks to its guests – namely, Universal Express access parkwide all day long.

If I had to choose one – either a Disney vacation or a Universal vacation, I would choose Universal. In recent years, Disney seems to have slipped badly in terms of development and programming that enhances a guest's experience – seems like they're all simply designed to part guests from their a larger chunk of their money. Of course, only the most naïve would even suggest that the best new buzz-generating attraction isn't designed to do the same thing, but the choice of emphasis that Disney has applied to their recent development efforts is telling.

And Disney has definitely fallen behind in the innovation department, with Universal boasting attractions like Spiderman, the Hulk, and Revenge of the Mummy, although Mission: SPACE makes things interesting again, Eisner and co. have certainly been playing catchup.

Visitor Info & Discount Resources

Extensive information about the entire **Walt Disney World** resort can be found on its website, from which you can order a vacation planning kit, that includes a video plus information on WDW lodging and packages. **Universal Orlando** also provides extensive information about its hotel, theme park, and vacation offerings on their website.

Official tourism boards are excellent sources of both information and savings, as their member businesses often make available deep discounts. **OrlandoInfo.com** is the Internet face of the Orlando/Orange County Convention and Visitors' Bureau. While you're here, be sure to order an Official Visitors' Guide and download or order an **Orlando Magicard**, which entitles you to savings of up to $500 at over 100 area attractions, hotels, restaurants, and shops. When in town, visit the Official Visitor Center at 8723 International Drive for hotel and restaurant information, discount attraction tickets, or make last-minute reservations.

Take advantage of your **AAA** membership if you have one. Order a Florida Tourbook, which contains detailed, objective listings of hundreds of area hotels and restaurants with ratings for each. AAA members can also get discounts on car rental, hotels, and attractions.

The **Kissimmee Convention & Visitors' Bureau** offers a free vacation planning kit, although the information it contains is more bare-bones than the Orlando guide, but Kissimmee contains a lot of inexpensive options for lodging and dining and is particularly convenient to the Magic Kingdom and the rest of Disney World, so if you're trying to conserve cash on the trip, this is a more essential bit of information.

Not to be outdone, the bustling **International Drive Resort Area** has its own tourism office, publishing a must-have guidebook that's loaded with coupons for hotspots up and down this brightly lit tourist mecca.

Your Planning Timeline

6 months to 1 year in advance (peak seasons), or 90 days in advance (off-peak seasons)
- Select a hotel and make reservations.

60 days in advance
- Make Advance Dining Reservations at Disney restaurants.

30 days in advance
- If you have not already made flight reservations, do so now to take advantage of 21-day advance fares.
- Order tickets for Disney World and other area attractions.

7 days in advance
- Plan out your week – decide which parks you'll visit on each day.
- Shop for sundries you'll need (see packing checklist in this chapter.)
- Use Web to confirm park hours for the dates you'll be visiting.

2 days in advance
- Pack everything you'll need, except for toiletries, medications, eyeglasses, or other stuff you'll need up til the last minute.

1 day in advance
- Be sure all your confirmations, vouchers, tickets, and other important documents are accounted for. Sleep easy knowing you're ready to go.

The Orlando Sentinel's visitor info site, **Go2Orlando.com**, provides tools like budget planners and reservation search engines, in addition to discounts and deals and editorial content from Sentinel writers.

If you'd like to include more than just the Central Florida vicinity in your trip, check out the **Visit Florida** website, where the state maintains a portal to information about destinations across the state.

Some of the best information, though, comes from unofficial sources. **AllEarsNet** is one of my personal favorites, as Deb Wills and her army of correspondents keep their finger on the pulse of all things WDW. It's a particularly good resource for trip reports from the different hotels, as well as full menu listings from most, if not all, of the park and hotel restaurants. **MouseSavers.com** is a great site for the budget-conscious, as it exhaustively details the different ways you can cut costs at WDW.

But if you prefer a more interactive forum in which to conduct your research, I highly recommend the **DIS Boards**. This bulletin board community contains enthusiastic, opinionated, and helpful folks whose immense expertise about Walt Disney World blows MY mind. And I wrote a book on the subject! Anyway, this is the place to take questions and dilemmas, and to get personalized suggestions and advice.

Another good resource that includes more local-oriented options as well as tourist classics is **AOL Cityguide**, which lists current entertainment options, best-ofs in every category imaginable,

Available through local charities as fundraisers or online pretty much year-round, **Entertainment** books ($10-25) offer half-price meals at dozens of restaurants and deep discounts at various hotels nationwide.

Just about every business in Orlando and Kissimmee, it seems, has a rack of cheesy tourist magazines out front. Don't dismiss these – the magazines contain plenty of ideas for meals, activities, and retail therapy – along with lots of coupons. Grab as many as you like – many of them feature different advertisers, and thus reveal to you more choices on how to spend your vacation dollar. Some of the magazines even put their advertiser offers online. Others will mail you their magazines for a couple of bucks, but that really isn't necessary. A lot of these magazines come and go, but some of the more dependable mags are **See Orlando** and **Best Read Guide**. For hotel discounts, the best resource is the **Roomsaver** guide, featuring hundreds of printable coupons for discounts up to 50% off rooms up and down the main

Web & Phone Visitor Info & Discount Resources

Walt Disney World – www.disneyworld.com – 407/824-4321
Universal Orlando – www.universalorlando.com – 407/363-8000
Orlando/Orange CVB – www.orlandoinfo.com – 407/363-5872
American Automobile Association (AAA) – www.aaa.com
Kissimmee/St. Cloud CVB – www.floridakiss.com – 888/333-KISS
I-Drive: www.internationaldriveorlando.com – 407/248-9590
Go2Orlando – www.go2orlando.com
Visit Florida – www.flausa.com – 941/922-3575
AllEarsNet – www.allearsnet.com
Mouse Savers – www.mousesavers.com
DIS Boards – www.disboards.com
AOL Cityguide – www.digitalcity.com/orlando
Entertainment – www.entertainment.com
See Orlando – www.see-orlandoflorida.com
Best Read Guide – www.bestreadguides.com
Roomsaver – www.roomsaver.com
Inside Central Florida – www.icflorida.com
Orlando Citysearch – orlando.citysearch.com
Orlando Sentinel – www.orlandosentinel.com

highway corridors of Florida and the rest of the country. The print editions are also a great resource if you're driving to Orlando, as you can find lodging discounts right off just about any highway you'll take to get there.

Several other worthwhile websites include **Inside Central Florida**, an exhaustive, Yahoo-style portal for information from a variety of Orlando media outlets; **Orlando Citysearch**, Ticketmaster's site network including info on arts, attractions, bars, hotels, concert and movie listings, shopping, sports, restaurants, and more; and the **Orlando Sentinel**, the area's leading daily newspaper, with up-to-the-minute event information, traffic, and weather.

Online Ticketing

Many area attractions make their admission media available online, either on their own sites or through a reseller. Often the tickets are sold at a discount, adding value to the convenience and peace of mind provided by actually having your tickets beforehand, and not having to wait in line to purchase them during precious moments that could be spent on rides.

Disney World's website walks you through the process of customizing and purchasing the parks' new "Magic Your Way" tickets. There is no discount for purchasing the tickets online, but you can save substantial time by not having to purchase tickets at the gate.. **Universal Orlando** offers an exclusive Bonus Pass that offers five consecutive days' admission for $99.95, less than the cost of two single-day admissions. **Sea World** offers a print-at-home e-ticket that's discounted 10% with a seven-day advance purchase.

Other tickets can be bought cheaply through the Orlando CVB at **OrlandoTicketSales.com** site (or call 877/460-OTIX). They range from discounts of $10 on multi-day Disney passes to deep discounts for dinner shows and the quieter attractions. Also recommended is the Orlando Sentinel's ticketing portal, **OfficialTicketCenter.com**.

There are plenty of other sites out there offering various discounts on lodging and accommodations. Some of these companies may be more reputable than others, so when venturing off on your own, look for companies that are listed with the Better Business Bureau or Dun & Bradstreet.

Thumbs up for **UndercoverTourist.com**, **FloridaOrlandoTickets.net**, **MapleLeafTickets.com**, and **KnowBeforeUGo.com**.

We do not recommend buying tickets at the booths you find scattered across souvenir shop parking lots. Most "too-good-to-be-true" ticket deals are usually either come-ons for timeshare visits, or are resold or used admission media that may or may not work. With the addition of biometric verification at the gates, used admission media can no longer be resold – not that it was legal in the first place. Disney tickets are a big enough ticket item that you don't want to get burned on it. Caveat emptor.

With that chilling warning, there are a few places where you can get discount or advance tickets once in Orlando? They include:

- Your hotel's Guest Services desk.
- Official Visitor Center, 8723 International Drive.
- Florida Vacation Center, 8445 International Drive (Mercado).
- Know Before You Go, 4720 US Hwy 192, 8000 International Drive, and 8957 International Drive.
- Maple Leaf Tickets, 4647 US Hwy 192.

Walt Disney World Ticketing

Disney made everything a lot more complicated in early 2005 where they introduced a new system of admissions. The new **Magic Your Way** program allows guests to customize their tickets, which sounds great on paper until you realize that what it boils down to is Disney charging extra for things that used to be included in the tickets themselves. It's only at the level of week-long or longer tickets that the new system adds value for the consumer compared to the old tickets.

Admission starts with the "base ticket," which allows for admission to one theme park per day, with no "hopping" between parks. The base tickets are good for 14 days from the date of first use. Guests can then add on the Park Hopper option for a flat fee of $35 per person per pass, allowing them to visit multiple parks in the same day; or the No Expiration option, which lifts the 14-day restriction; or Magic Plus Options, which allow anywhere from 2 to 5 additional admissions to water parks, Pleasure Island, Disney Quest, or Wide World of Sports. The number of actual visits allotted depends on the original number of days on the pass, and do not have to be used on the same day as admission to the four major theme parks. Add-ons are priced based on how many days are originally on the pass. Guests can upgrade all three options at any point during the life of the ticket, but do not pay a pro rated price based on how many days remain.

Buying a six-to-ten-day pass with the No Expiration option lets you get two vacations' worth of admission for one price, which takes some of the sting out of such a big-ticket purchase. We recommend adding the Park Hopper option, as the flexibility in touring that it enables is worth paying for. Breakdown of prices are given in the table on the next page:

Days	Base Ticket (Adult/Child 3-9)	Park Hopper	Magic Plus	No Expiration
1	$63.33/$51.12	$35	$45 (2 visits)	N/A
2	$126.74/$102.24	$35	$45 (2 visits)	$10
3	$182.12/$145.91	$35	$45 (2 visits)	$10
4	$197.03/$157.62	$35	$45 (3 visits)	$15
5	$205.55/$165.08	$35	$45 (3 visits)	$35
6	$208.74/$167.21	$35	$45 (4 visits)	$45
7	$211.94/$170.40	$35	$45 (5 visits)	$55
8	$215.13/$172.53	$35	$45 (5 visits)	$100
9	$218.33/$174.66	$35	$45 (5 visits)	$100
10	$222.59/$177.86	$35	$45 (5 visits)	$100

As you can see from the tables on the next two pages, the longer-term tickets provide a better value in the long run. Here's how the individual tickets are priced with option add-ons, and cost per-day breakdowns follow for each set of options. Five-day or longer passes are discounted from $7-11 for adults, $6-9 for kids if purchased in advance of arrival.

Florida residents can purchase Magic Your Way tickets with a choice of perks – either a 10% discount off a one-day ticket, free park hopper option on a one-day ticket, or three days for the price fo two.

Annual passes are also available. Prior to the introduction of the Magic Your Way passes, these were the cheapest way to pull off the two-vacations-for-one thing, but the caveat with that method was that you had to take the second vacation within 365 days of the first. With these passes you can return at your leisure.

Disney gives annual passholders benefits like complimentary parking discounts to hard-ticketed events, minor attractions, park tours, selected restaurants, and Downtown Disney shops, reduced rates at Disney resorts, and Alamo Rent-a-Car. Rates are $420.68 for adults, $357.84 for kids 3-9 (renewals are $378.08 and $321.63 respectively.)

Also offered are premium annual passes, which also include a year's admission to Typhoon Lagoon, Blizzard Beach, Disney Quest, Pleasure Island, and Wide World of Sports. Cost is $548.49 for adults and $466.49 for kids 3-9 (renewals are $495.25 and $420.69 respectively). Disney Vacation Club members save up to $125 off annual passes when purchased online at the DVC Member website.

Florida residents receive discounts on passes, paying $315 and $415 for regular and premium annual passes, $268 and $353 for children. Floridians can also purchase a Seasonal Pass, which is valid year-round except for peak-season blackout dates; i.e., spring break/Easter, summer, and Christmas/New Year's. Prices are $209 for adults, $178 for kids.

Universal Orlando/Sea World Ticketing

Like Disney, Universal offers advance ticketing on its website, saving you time and money. A one day admission is $59.75 per adult, $48 for kids 3-9, The 2-Day, 2-Park Bonus Pass offers five consecutive days' admission for $99.95 per person. Save shipping fees and time at the gate by choosing the Print @Home Ticket option. Otherwise, an electronic will call retrieves your reservation and spits out the tickets at the gate.

If Sea World and Wet 'N' Wild are on your agenda, consider the 4-Park Flex Ticket, offering 14 days' consecutive admission to those parks plus the two Universal theme parks ($184.95 adults/$150.95 kids). Add Busch Gardens for a 5-Park Flex Ticket ($224.95/$189.95).

Days	Base Ticket	+PH	+ PH, MP	+ PH, NE	+ PH, MP, NE
1 (adult)	$63.33	$98.63	$143.63	N/A	N/A
1 (child)	$51.12	$86.12	$131.12	N/A	N/A
2 (adult)	$126.74	$161.74	$206.74	$171.74	$216.74
per day	$63.37	$80.87	$103.37	$85.87	$108.37
2 (child)	$102.24	$137.24	$182.24	$147.24	$192.24
per day	$51.12	$68.62	$91.12	$73.62	$96.12
3 (adult)	$182.12	$217.12	$262.12	$227.12	$272.12
per day	$60.71	$72.37	$87.37	$75.71	$90.71
3 (child)	$145.91	$180.91	$225.91	$190.91	$235.91
per day	$48.64	$60.30	$95.40	$63.64	$78.64
4 (adult)	$197.03	$232.03	$277.03	$247.03	$292.03
per day	$49.25	$58.01	$69.26	$61.76	$73.01
4 (child)	$157.62	$192.62	$237.62	$207.62	$252.62
per day	$39.41	$48.16	$59.41	$51.91	$63.16
5 (adult)	$205.55	$240.55	$285.55	$275.55	$320.55
per day	$41.11	$48.11	$57.11	$55.11	$64.11
5 (child)	$165.08	$200.08	$245.08	$235.08	$280.08
per day	$33.02	$40.02	$49.02	$47.02	$56.02
6 (adult)	$208.74	$243.74	$288.74	$288.74	$333.74
per day	$34.79	$40.62	$48.12	$48.12	$55.62
6 (child)	$167.21	$202.21	$247.21	$247.21	$292.21
per day	$27.87	$33.70	$41.20	$41.20	$48.70

Days	Base Ticket	+PH	+ PH, MP	+ PH, NE	+ PH, MP, NE
7 (adult)	$211.94	$246.94	$291.94	$300.94	$346.94
per day	$30.28	$35.28	$41.71	$42.99	$49.57
7 (child)	$170.40	$205.40	$250.40	$260.40	$305.40
per day	$24.34	$29.34	$35.77	$37.20	$43.63
8 (adult)	$215.13	$250.13	$295.13	$350.13	$395.13
per day	$26.89	$31.27	$36.89	$43.77	$49.39
8 (child)	$172.53	$207.53	$252.53	$307.53	$352.53
per day	$21.57	$25.94	$31.57	$38.44	$44.07
9 (adult)	$218.33	$253.33	$298.33	$353.33	$398.33
per day	$24.26	$28.15	$33.14	$39.26	$44.26
9 (child)	$174.66	$209.66	$254.66	$309.66	$354.66
per day	$19.41	$23.30	$28.30	$34.41	$39.41
10 (adult)	$222.59	$257.59	$302.59	$357.59	$402.59
per day	$22.26	$25.76	$30.26	$35.76	$40.26
10 (child)	$177.86	$212.86	$257.86	$312.86	$357.86
per day	$17.79	$21.29	$25.79	$31.29	$35.79

Universal also offers annual passes: a **2-Park Annual Power Pass** is $119.95 and includes admission to Universal Studios and Islands of Adventure for a year, with blackout dates around Easter/spring break, summer, and Christmas/New Year's. A **2-Park Preferred Annual Pass** ($179.95) has no blackout dates and offers perks like free self-parking and discounts on everything from 10-15% reductions in merchandise and restaurant prices to 30% discounts on Universal resorts. Universal gives guests the Flex Pay option, allowing them to buy a preferred annual pass with monthly payments of $15.97 instead of one lump sum.

Discounts on Universal Admission

A few easy ways to score a few bucks off Universal admission:

•AAA members can visit www.aaa.com/universal to purchase special Third Day Free of 2-Day, 2-Park passes for $93.45 adult, $83.17 for kids 3-9.

•Buy your passes in advance on www.orlandoinfo.com and save about $2 on a 1-Day, 1-Park ticket, $8 on a 2-Day, 2-Park pass, or $10 on a 3-Day, 2-Park pass. FlexTickets are discounted about $15-20. Once you get into town, you can visit the Official Visitor Center and purchase them for the same price. Multi-day passes come with value-added special offers.

•Discounts are often available for Florida residents on the back of Coca-Cola cans, in fast food restaurants, or elsewhere. Such promotions are often advertised on the radio, so keep 'em peeled.

•Universal periodically runs special deals that they advertise on their website, tickets.universalstudios.com.

To purchase Sea World tickets alone, visit www.seaworld.com. Admission options include single day tickets with second day free ($59.75 adult, $48 child 3-9), which can be purchased online as an e-ticket with a 7 day advance for a 10% discount. 2-day, 2-park tickets in conjunction with Busch Gardens are available for $94.95 adult, $84.95 child. The Fun Card offers unlimited admission for the calendar year ($64.95 adults, $54.95 kids). Add Busch Gardens for $50 per person, add Adventure Island for $10 more.

Passports convey perks in addition to just the park access offered via Fun Card. Silver and gold passports offer one year of park admission, complimentary general parking, 50% off preferred parking, $8 off single-day guest tickets, 10% off food and merchandise, discounts on strollers, wheelchairs, and select Adventurecamp amd Animal Interaction program.

Discounts on Sea World Admission

A few easy ways to score a few bucks off Sea World admission.

•Specially marked Pepsi cans offer all-in-one admission that includes lunch and a couple of Pepsi products.

•Wendy's offers coupon codes that permit discounts to be made on www.seaworld.com ticket purchases.

•Buy the One Day eTicket online at a 10% discount.

•Orlandoinfo.com offers $2-3 discounts on one-day tickets.

•AARP members can get up to $10 off tickets.

Package Deals

Package deals offer convenient one-stop shopping for your hotel, park admissions, and sometimes other features as well. However, they don't offer as much of a financial incentive as they used to.

Visit www.disneyworld.com for full details, up-to-date prices, and availability of vacation packages. Along with the introduction of the Magic Your Way tickets, Disney has replaced theirprevious array of packages with a more simplified, à la carte system.. Guests choose the length of stay, the hotel, and the ticketing options. Note that most packages are designed less as a vehicle for savings and more as a convenient one-stop shopping opportunity. If your bottom line is the bottom line, consider booking the elements of your trip separately.

The basic **Magic Your Way** plan includes accommodations at a Disney resort and the Magic Your Way base ticket (with your choice of options). Prices for a 7-day, 6-night vacation start at $474 for adults, $213 for juniors (10-17), and $170 per child. The **Magic Your Way with Dining** upgrade adds meals and snacks from over 100 participating eateries. Each day your party gets one table-service meal (including appetizer, entrée, dessert, and a non-alcoholic beverage, with tax and tip included; one counter-service meal (including entrée or combo meal, drink, and dessert), and one snack, like popcorn or ice cream. Guests can exchange two table-service meal credits for one signature dining experience (A-list restaurants, some character breakfasts, and dinner shows). 7-day, 6-night prices start at $684 per adult, $423 per junior, and $230 per child.. The posh **Magic Your Way Premium** plan provides breakfast, lunch, and dinner every day, unlimited use of recreational facilities including golf, tennis, fishing, and water sports; admission to Cirque du Soleil: La Nouba, use of children's activity centers, and theme park tours. Prices for 7 days and 6 nights of the royal treatment start at $1,382 per adult, $1,121 per junior, and $811 per child. AAA members can book flights and rental cars together with the Magic Your Way package.

Through the end of the Happiest Celebration on Earth 50th anniversary festivities, all Disney resort packages and accommodations include the **Magical Express** feature, which offers complimentary motorcoach transfer and (with participating airlines) baggage claim bypass, enabling you to check your bags with a special tag at the departure airport, and have the bags delivered directly to your room. Allow an hour's travel time to get to Disney World from the airport, and allow one to two hours after check-in for your bags to be delivered. When you're ready to head home, you can check in your luggage and receive your boarding pass before leaving the hotel. Motorcoaches depart about 2:30 to 3:00 before your scheduled flight. Allow a half hour to check in for your flight before you leave the hotel. Current participating airlines include American, Continental, Delta, Song, United, and Ted. Although be aware, taking advantage of this program strands you on Disney property with no car – which makes it very difficult to get to off-site shops, restaurants, and attractions – which is kind of Disney's whole idea, after all, there's no customer like a captive.

Disney also offers the **Great Golf Escape**, which includes three or more nights' accommodations, one round of golf per night's stay (including greens fees, cart rental, club cleaning and storage, and a bucket of range balls), and one of the following per person per night: DisneyQuest or Pleasure Island admission, water park admission, or choice of breakfast or lunch at selected restaurants. Prices start at $469 per adult for three nights.

As a full-service resort destination, **Universal Orlando** offers some compelling package deals of its own, and knowing that they're the underdog, their packages often wind up being better discounts than their Disney counterparts. Note that Universal packages do **not** include Disney admission. Note that staying at a Universal hotel gets you Universal Express ride access to pretty much everything at both theme parks – a very significant perk.

Universal vacations can be booked buffet style, where you select your hotel, the number of days, and then add on transportation (airfare, car rentals, and transfers are available) and options like including five-day passes (for the price of two), VIP tours, 4- or 5-park Orlando Flex Tickets, gourmet, theme restaurant, and character dining experiences, and one-day admission to most of the major central Florida parks (besides Disney). Floridians can sign up on the Universal website to receive an email newsletter with resident-only special offers, including surprisingly low rates on hotels. AAA members who book hotel-and-tickets Universal vacations receive special discounts and freebies at restaurants and shops around Universal.

If you're thinking about more of a long weekend than a lengthier getaway, check out **Site59.com**, which offers deep discounts on last-minute weekend travel packages, including hotel and optional air and car. The Convention and Visitors Bureau offers several varieties of vacation package on **OrlandoInfo.com**. This is highly recommended because in addition to the hotel and adimssions included in the selected package, the CVB offers discounted tickets to many area attractions, and can all be purchased at once.

Other good, trusted sites for package deal vacations are **Expedia, Travelocity, Orbitz**, and **Hotels.com. GolfPacTravel.com** offers packages including accommodation and multiple rounds of golf at courses across the metro area.

Packing Tips

In the parks, dress comfortably. T-shirts and shorts are the norm most of the year. However, as it grows colder, clothes grow thicker and longer. Above all: wear comfortable sneakers. You are going to get your walk on. Plan accordingly. No, your sandals aren't comfortable. only a few of the most chichi restaurants in the Orlando area require anything more than resort dress.

A bathing suit is a necessity, regardless of the timing of your visit. On winter nights, temperatures can dip into the 40s or lower (my last visit found morning temperatures in the mid-30s in February), so bring a lightweight sweater or jacket. Such an item isn't a bad idea in the dog days of summer because most Florida hotels have arctic air conditioning.

Other items that you may want to bring: cameras or camcorders, batteries and film or extra digital media, sporting equipment, a laptop or PDA. Two-ways, walkie-talkies, and cell phones can enable families to stay connected. Remember, toiletries and other sundries are always more expensive closer to the theme parks. Stick to supermarkets and drugstores for anything you've forgotten.

Getting to Orlando

Whoever said that getting there was half the fun never spent 19 hours in a minivan with three obnoxious children – like my parents did when I was 12. The journey should be about building anticipation and excitement for your family's arrival, but it can be quite draining both to your wallet and sanity. Whether you're driving to Orlando or flying into town, a little foresight and planning can go a long way in easing both burdens.

Flying into Orlando

Orlando International Airport (MCO – orlandoairports.net, 407/ 825-2001) is America's fourth busiest and one of its "best liked," according to Conde Nast Traveler magazine, with over 31 million people flying in and out every year on 53 airlines. The main terminal has three floors, below seven levels of parking, a heliport and a Hyatt. Here's what you'll find on each:

Level 1: Ground transportation – rental car pickup and delivery, courtesy phones, tour operators, shuttles, limousines, taxis, Lynx buses.

Level 2: Baggage claim, curbside pickup, tour operators, and courtesy phones.

Level 3: Ticketing and all gates - food court, shops, curbside drop-off., shuttles to airside terminals. Restaurants include: Macaroni Grill, Chili's,, Nathan's, Sbarro, Miami Subs, Villa Pizza, McDonald's, Burger King, Fresh Attractions, Freshens, Carvel, TCBY, Cinnabon, Pepito's, Seattle's Best, and Starbucks. There are also over 30 shops and kiosks selling theme park merchandise, news and sundries, or gifts and specialty goods.

Airfare Discounts

Okay, it may not be half the fun, but in many cases, getting there can be half the cost of the whole trip. There are only so many ways that you can minimize this necessary and large expense, but they are out there for savvy travelers.

•Do your research on flight times on a site like Orbitz, Travelocity, or Expedia – but book your flight through your selected airline's website. Often this way you can save the $5 or more booking fee that the online services add to the ticket prices. Plus, some airlines give bonus frequent flyer miles for online bookings. Sometimes airlines offer web-exclusive rates you can't find elsewhere.

•If you've got a little flexibility about departure times, consider purchasing tickets on Priceline or Hotwire. Priceline allows travelers to name their own price and bid on airline tickets for a trip between two points on a certain day, but don't get to specify an airline or departure time, and also offers an option for those who need a little more control over the booking process. Hotwire works a little differently – you put in your search parameters and then they quote you a price that you can accept or reject. After your purchase you're notified all the relevant details of the flight.

•Consider a discount airline if they offer service from your city. Airlines like Independence (offering connecting flights from dozens of cities through Dulles) Southwest (offering nonstop service from 25 cities) Song (offering service from Washington, New York, Hartford, Boston, Las Vegas, and Los Angeles), and JetBlue (serving JFK and Boston nonstop), in addition to offering great rates, also are renowned for their efficiency and customer satisfaction.

•If you have multiple airports in your area, consider leaving from a less popular alternate – the price difference, for example, between a BWI and

Reagan National departure, can be fifty dollars or more. Consider off-peak travel as well. Saturday and Sunday flights are often the most expensive.

•Consider www.cheaptickets.com or another consolidator – they often run ads in newspaper travel sections. Note that these tickets often come with stricter rules and less perks (i.e., miles). Some of them even sell their wares on eBay. If you do purchase tickets from eBay, be sure to know what the tickets are worth to avoid overpaying, check the seller's feedback and use a credit card or Paypal to avoid getting stiffed.

•Earn frequent flyer miles with linked credit cards or special airline promotions to earn free travel or bonuses, even if you don't fly enough to earn them that way.

Renting a Car

Renting a car is not necessary for a Disney World vacation, regardless of whether you're staying on WDW property or off it. Granted – it's a pain in the butt to get around without a car (especially for guests at offsite hotels – although the flip side of that is that WDW guests without cars are pretty much at the mouse's mercy for the duration), but with a little planning and a little patience you can get yourself where you need to be. It'll still cost ya though. Unless you stay at a hotel that offers complimentary transportation to the theme parks. While this is a substantial perk that can save you a bunch of money over the course of a trip, it's not always convenient, as you sacrifice flexibility in terms of your arrival and departure times. Guests in many of the hotels in the Kissimmee, Lake Buena Vista, and International Drive areas all can take advantage of multiple dining options within walking distance.

If you do rent a car, consider these avenues for discounted rides:

•Generally speaking, the companies located at the airport charge more than offsite firms.

•Collision damage waivers are often redundant – check your credit card and auto insurance policies, as you may already be covered for rental car incidents.

•*Entertainment* books offer coupons for many of the major companies, offering discounts, upgrades, or extra days.

•Various discounts are available to members of AAA, AARP, USAA, Costco, Sam's Club, BJ's, and many labor unions, frequent flyer programs, and credit card holders.

•Use Google, Yahoo, or another search engine to scour the Net for current discount. Promotion, and coupon codes. Try searching for "Orlando rental car codes," or if you'd prefer, add a specific company to the query.

There are six rental companies located on Level 1 of the airport. Those are Alamo, Avis, Budget, Dollar, L and M, and National. The rest are located nearby, with courtesy phones on Levels 1 and 2 of the airport and frequent shuttle service to and from the rental office. Dollar and National get the best marks for service of the on-site rental agencies. **Remember to bring proof of insurance.**

You've got a couple options as you leave the airport. If you are headed to Kissimmee or Walt Disney World, take the south exit from the airport and follow the access road to the Greeneway (SR 417 south). If you're headed to International Drive, Sea World, or Universal Orlando, take the north exit and get onto the Beeline Expressway (SR 528). As you might guess from the name, the Beeline Expressway is a pretty straight shot into the heart of the tourist district. Note that there is a toll for both roads.

If you want to travel in style, or in what the kids call a "pimp ride," call **Luxury Rental Cars of Orlando** (www.luxrentals.com, 307/909-0800 or 888/641-9211). They offer luxury SUVs and sports car convertibles with perks like GPS, OnStar, Playstation 2, and E-Pass. You can rent anything from a Mini Cooper (from $119 per day, $699 per week), Plymouth Prowler (from $199/day, $995/week) or Corvette (from $269/day, $1250/week) to a Cadillac Escalade (from $189/day, $949/week) or Hummer H2 (from $269/day, $1450/week). They can arrange airport pickup, or deliver and pick up your vehicle at your local hotel. Just be sure not to say "rollin' on dubs" in front of your kids, you'll sound like an idiot.

Airport Transfers

Mears Transportation (www.mearstransportation.com) offers airport transfers via private town car or shared shuttle van service. Book a ride at the counters on the second floor of the airport. Mears' current tariff shows fares of $15 one way and $25 round trip to I-Drive ($11/$18 for kids); $17/$29 to Lake Buena Vista, WDW, or US 192 west ($13/$21 for kids); and $23/$41 to Kissimmee east of SR 535 ($19/$32 for kids). They also offer private sedan services that range from $40 to $60 for a one way transfer. Limousine, van, or town car service is also a viable option that can be surprisingly cost-effective for larger parties. Expect to pay around $110 an hour.

Several taxi providers service the airport as well. Expect to pay $60 for a trip to WDW, $43-60 to Kissimmee, $47 to Lake Buena Vista, $33-39 for a ride to I-Drive. To arrange taxi transportation, call:
- Ace Metro/Luxury Cab – 407/855-1111
- Diamond Cab – 407/523-3333
- Star Taxi – 407/857/9999
- Town & Country Transport – 407/828-3035
- Yellow/City Cab – 407/422-2222

A dirt-cheap alternative, the **Lynx** public transportation system also serves the airport every half hour from 5:30am to 11:30pm. From the A side of Level 1, take the 11, 41, 42, and 51 bus to downtown Orlando or International Drive. While the $1.25 bus fare is practically nothing, you can't say the same about the 60 minutes that it'll take to get there. I mean, really – who wants to spend an hour on a city bus after a pile of hours in a plane?

For Disney resort guests, the **Magical Express** program allows you to skip the baggage claim and board a motor coach directly from the airport to your hotel, while your specially pre-checked luggage makes its way to your hotel room automatically, usually within 1 to 2 hours of your check-in. Disney has announced that this service will be complimentary through the end of 2006.

Driving into Orlando

Orlando is less than a day's drive from most parts of this country east of the Mississippi (and a few west of it too). It can be a bit grueling to some – but it can save a ton of money, especially if you are traveling with a large party. Have three kids, but don't trust them to spend 12 hours in the backseat of your Accord without fratriciding all over the place? Consider renting a mini-van. Weekly rates are not so prohibitive (so long as you have unlimited mileage) and you save the wear and tear on your own vehicle.

In-state, the major approach routes to Orlando are I-95 to westbound I-4 from the Daytona area and the east coast., eastbound I-4 from the Gulf Coast, and I-75 to Florida's Turnpike from the panhandle and beyond.

Be sure to properly equip yourself for the trip – music for those maddening moments in between cities where all you have on the radio is static. Snacks and drinks for those never-convenient hunger pangs. Diversions like books, toys, games, cards to keep the "Are we there yet?" to a minimum. The iPod's iTrip accessory or other FM transmitters also help take the edge off a long road trip.

Getting Around Orlando

Driving

Thankfully, orientation in and around Orlando isn't difficult at all to get a hang of, especially the more tourist-oriented parts of town. Getting to the major theme parks is pretty straightforward. However, if you've got any off-the-beaten-path attractions, restaurants, or diversions on your agenda, directions are your friend. Visit Mapquest (www.mapquest.com) or Yahoo Maps (maps.yahoo.com) to get directions from any point A to point B. One caveat though: these sites don't always handle correctly driving directions to

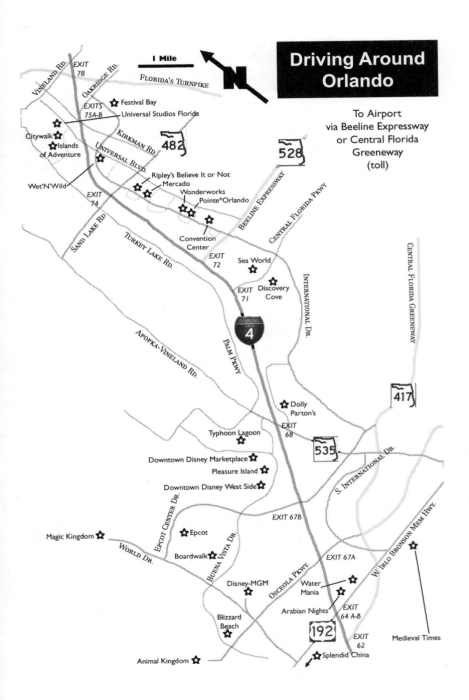

or from Disney hotels, sometimes sending you along service roads instead of main thoroughfares. Don't just rely on website directions – get yourself an up-to-date map. Here's a quick-and-dirty guide on getting around Orlando.

Driving in Disney World

Disney World is a major metropolis all on its own – 43 square miles of property, with a comprehensive series of limited-access highways and back roads that efficiently connect all the guest areas on the property. World Drive, the "maingate," is located on US 192 (just west of I-4, take exit 64B), but other entrances include SR 535 in Lake Buena Vista and the Osceola Parkway in Kissimmee.

Hess gas stations can be found at Pleasure Island, at the Disney MGM Studios and Boardwalk, and near the Magic Kingdom on World Drive. Also near the magic kingdom is the AAA Car Care Center, offering minor automotive repairs, towing, and services like fuel and flat tire assistance, battery jumps, and winch-outs.

Interstate 4

The main arterial in the city, I-4 is an east-west route that actually runs more north-south through Orlando, the midpoint on the highway between Tampa and Daytona, where it hits I-95. NOTE: The junction of I-4 and US 192 is scheduled to remain under construction through 2007, and individual ramps may be closed for lengthy periods of time, necessitating detours. To see if any detours will affect you, visit www.trans4mation.org or contact your hotel or the Kissimmee-area business you plan on visiting.

Here is a list of important local I-4 exits in each direction, and a sampling of the landmarks accessible at each. Note that this does not include all exits in the downtown area.

Exit 55: US 27, Clermont/Haines City (Cypress Gardens, Bok Tower Gardens)

Exit 58: Osceola CR 532, Kissimmee (Reunion, Championsgate)

Exit 60 (opens in 2006): SR 429 N (toll), Citrus Ridge/Winter Garden (Central Florida Expressway)

Exit 62: World Drive South, Celebration, Disney World, and from I-4 eastbound only: SR 417 N (Central Florida Greeneway) (toll), Airport, Sanford

Exit 64A: US 192 E, Kissimmee/Celebration (Old Town, Medieval Times, Arabian Nights, Water Mania)

Exit 64B: US 192 W, Magic Kingdom, Disney-MGM Studios (Kissimmee, WDW main gate, Clermont)

Exit 65: Osceola CR 522 Osceola Parkway, Animal Kingdom, Wild Word of Sports

Exit 67: SR 536 to SR 417 N (Central Florida Greeneway) (toll), Epcot, Downtown Disney, Airport (International Drive S)

Exit 68: SR 535, Lake Buena Vista (Downtown Disney, Hotel Plaza, Crossroads, Vista Centre, Dixie Stampede)

Exit 71 (eastbound only): Central Florida Parkway, Sea World (Discovery Cove, Grande Lakes)

Exit 72: SR 528 E (Bee Line Expressway) (toll), Airport, Cape Canaveral (International Drive, Convention Center, Sea World, Pointe*Orlando)

Exit 74A: SR 482 Sand Lake Road/International Drive (Official Visitor Center, Restaurant Row)

Exit 74B (westbound only): Universal

Exit 75A: SR 435 S, Kirkman Road/International Drive, Universal (Festival Bay, Belz, Wet'n'Wild).

Exit 75B: SR 435 N, Kirkman Road

Exit 77: Florida's Turnpike, Miami, Ocala (toll)

Exit 78: Conroy Road (Mall at Millennia)

Exits 80, 80A, 80B: US 17/92/441, Orange Blossom Trail

Exit 82A: SR 408, East-West Expressway, Ocoee, Titusville (toll)

Exit 82C: Anderson St. E, Church Street Station, Historic District (Downtown, Capital One Bowl, nightclubs)

Exit 83A (eastbound only) SR 526, Robinson St.

Exit 83B & 84: Ivanhoe Blvd., US 17/92/SR 50, Colonial Dr., Centroplex (Downtown, Bob Carr Auditorium, TD Waterhouse Centre)

Exit 87: SR 426, Fairbanks Ave. (Winter Park)

You may be able to get a traffic update on demand via your cell phone. Simply dial 511 from your AT&T, Cingular, Sprint, Nextel, or Voicestream mobile. There's also plenty of overhead signs providing early warning of traffic snags. In the morning, you can tune your radio to 580 AM (WBDO) for traffic reports every six minutes.

Alternate route: To circumvent the traffic on I-4 from the Universal/I-Drive and WDW areas, take Sand Lake Road about 2 miles west of I-4, turn left on Apopka-Vineland Road, and take that south to the back side of WDW, turning right onto Hotel Plaza Blvd.

US 192

Location, location, location right outside the gates of the Magic Kingdom, US 192 (aka the W. Irlo Bronson Memorial Highway, and further east, Vine Street) is home to a colossal array of inexpensive (and sometimes downright ghetto) motels, well-known national chain restaurants, enormous department stores selling souvenirs, sundries, and kitsch, and some of Orlando's best-known non-theme park attractions.

In years past, US 192 was a cluster of the highest magnitude. Congested, narrow, and ugly, this road was the scourge of Disney visitors – maddening delays in the mornings when you HAD to get to the park early, and frustrating and stressful stop-and-go traffic in the afternoons. In 2002, the $29 million "BeautiVacation Project" was complete, widening the highway and adding wide sidewalks, improved lighting, substantial landscaping, and impossible-to-miss 25-foot high milepost guide markers. Those guidemarkers serve as handy points of reference for many area businesses – it's much easier to find a place "1000 feet past Marker 12" than it is to crane your neck to look for street numbers to figure out how close you are.

US 192 crosses I-4 at milepost 64, about 1 1/2 miles west of the WDW maingate. The road continues west another seven miles, where it meets US 27. To the east, once you get past the glut of motels, restaurants, and gift shops, you reach downtown Kissimmee (around mile marker 15) and further to the east, St. Cloud.

Alternate route: the Osceola Parkway (CR 522) is a traffic-free, limited-access toll road running from Epcot Center Drive east to the edge of East Lake Tohopekaliga. You can zip along this road, bypassing all of the US 192 traffic. Access points between the two roads include South International Drive, Seralago Blvd., and Poinciana Blvd.

International Drive

Further to the north, International Drive runs from Universal Orlando and the Belz Factory Outlet Mall south, winding through countless outlet centers, hotels, attractions, and eateries to the Convention Center, Sea World, the Beeline Expressway. It runs to the east of I-4 and is accessible from pretty much any exit from mileposts 71-75.

Note that on the half of International Drive north of Sand Lake Road, traffic is a major headache at pretty much any time of day. Left turns can be difficult and dangerous. Traffic is still heavy on the southern half, but it flows much better.

Alternate route: Universal Blvd. (formerly Republic Drive) runs parallel to International Drive just to its east. Recently extended from Pointe*Orlando (where it used to merge with I-Drive) to the Beeline Expressway, this is an underdeveloped stretch of road offering an easy bypass.

S.R. 535

S.R. 535, the Apopka-Vineland Road, runs along the western side of Orlando, going south from the smalltown suburb of Winter Garden, to the west of Universal, Sand Lake Road, Lake Buena Vista, the back entrance to Downtown Disney, crossing I-4, and then intersecting with International

Drive South, the Central Florida Greeneway, Osceola Parkway, and ultimately ending at US 192 near Celebration. The area between US 192 and I-4 is the newest area, while the area north of I-4, including the Crossroads and Vista Centre complexes is more gridlocked.

Alternate route: Palm Parkway runs parallel to S.R. 535, just west of I-4, turning into Turkey Lake Drive and crossing Sand Lake Road, offering a good alternative route to Universal. For the stretch between I-4 and US 192, International Drive South is a good alternative.

Getting Around Without Your Car

You're on vacation. Who says you have to deal with the stress of driving in an unfamiliar town at all? It's not that difficult to get around Orlando without a car. It's certainly not convenient, but the option is there if you want it. If, however, you're staying onsite at Disney and are not planning to leave the premises – you don't even need to sweat it. The Mouse has your back.

Disney Transportation

Walt Disney World's 47 square miles encompass so many destinations, hotels, and activities that the place requires a mass transit system as robust as that of many major cities. Unlike the rat-infested NYC subway, however, WDW's mouse-friendly transit system is clean, safe, and reliable. Pick up a WDW property map at any park or hotel's guest services desk or at the Ticket and Transportation Center for full details on the entire system.

The best-known and best-loved of Disney's transit fleet are the sleek, quiet monorail trains that glide across elevated rails that connect the Transportation and Ticket Center with Epcot as well as the Magic Kingdom and the three hotels on the line – the Contemporary, Polynesian, and Grand Floridian. The monorails run every 15 minutes starting at 7:30am and until one hour after park closing, moving of up to 20,000 passengers every hour – that's as many as a 22-lane freeway. There are three monorail lines. One connects Epcot and the TTC. The Express line connects the TTC to the Magic Kingdom, while the Local line adds the Contemporary, Polynesian, and Grand Floridian resorts to the route. If you come up to the platform as the Express line is leaving, feel free to line up for the Local. Chances are it'll still get you there sooner than if you'd waited for the next Express.

If you want to add a little something special to the monorail ride, ask an attendant to seat you in front with the driver. The view is awesome, the narration is entertaining, and your kids will be impressed at what a baller you are. (Note to tragically unhip parents: That's a good thing)

Boats are also plentiful and efficient means of transportation. Two grand ferries get guests' pulses racing as they move across Seven Seas Lagoon between the TTC and MK in a 5-minute ride that departs every 12 minutes.

The Magic Kingdom can also be reached nautically from the monorail hotels, Fort Wilderness, and the Wilderness Lodge. Epcot and the Disney-MGM Studios are connected via FriendShip launches (the same boats that transverse World Showcase Lagoon) from the Yacht & Beach Club, Boardwalk, Swan, and Dolphin resorts.

It's impossible to go from point A to point B in WDW without passing at least one of the 280 buses that move thousands of guests across the property each and every day. All of the bus routes usually run every 20 minutes and connect virtually all guest areas that are not serviced by the flashier modes of movement. Allow 40 minutes to get from hotels to theme parks and vice versa, or an hour to get from one hotel to another via bus, as in almost all cases this will require a transfer.

I-Ride Trolley

If you're staying in the International Drive area, getting around is easy. Brightly painted trolley buses make a circuit around the entire length of the drag, moving over 1.6 million guests a year. There are 85 clearly marked stops on the route, and buses run every 15 minutes from 7am til 11:30pm. Note that a second route, the Green Line, runs up and down Universal Blvd. every 30 minutes. Single fares are 75 cents for adults, 25 cents for seniors, and free for kids under 12. Exact change is required, but $1 bills are accepted. You can also purchase a pass good for unlimited rides at over 100 locations around I-Drive, but not on the trolley itself. Prices are $3 for a single day pass, $5/three days, $7/five days, $9/seven days, or $16/two weeks. Visit www.iridetrolley.com for details, pass availability, and stop locations.

Lynx

While more suitable for commuting than tourism, LYNX, the Central Florida Regional Transportation Authority, offers inexpensive travel across the entire metropolitan area, including the tourist corridor. Single ride fares are $1.50. Daily passes are $3.50, weekly passes are $12, passes are available at Albertson's grocery stores, CCS Financial Services stores, or online at www.golynx.com. Call them at 407/841-LYNX.

Shuttles

Many hotels offer complimentary or paid shuttle transportation to the theme parks, although as mentioned above, they aren't always convenient to your schedule. Contact your hotel's guest services desk for details. Expect to pay around $12-14 per person round trip via Mears Transportation. Mears' SuperPass entitles a guest to round-trip airport transfers and unlimited transportation between International Drive and US 192 hotels and Disney World, Universal, and Sea World for three nights or more. Prices start at

$63/adult and $56/child for three nights and $107/adult, $100/child for seven.

Taxi Service

Taxis are plentiful in Orlando, though not necessarily cheap. Prices run about $2.50 for the first mile and $1.50 each additional.. To arrange a taxi, call your hotel's guest services desk or refer to the contact information listed above. Figure about $5-10 to go between destinations on US 192 or International Drive, $12-20 to get to Universal or Disney World. This can add up quickly, so don't look at this as a potential money-saving method of transportation, but certainly fine in small doses. See above for taxi contact information, or contact your hotel's guest services or front desk.

Index

AASHIRWAD, 229
A-Awesome Airboat Rides, 271
ABC Super Soap Weekend, 325
Adobe Gila's, 232, 249
Adventure Island, 262-263
Adventureland, 23-26; attractions, 23-25; dining, 46; shopping, 25-26
Affection Section, 109
Africa (park section), 108-109; attractions, 108-109; dining, 114; shopping, 109
air attractions, 301-303
airboats, 271
air travel, 346-350; discounts, 347; renting a car, 348-349; transfers, 349-350
Akbar Palace, 229
Albin Polasek Museum & Sculpture Gardens, 309
AllEarsNet, 335
All-Star Sports, Music, Movies Resorts, 186-187
Amazing Adventures of Spiderman, 136-137
American Adventure, 69-70
AmeriSuites Orlando/Lake Buena Vista South, 203
Amura, 228
Angel's, 225
Anheuser-Busch Beer School, 155-156
Animal Kingdom, 102-116; attractions and shopping, 102-111; characters, 112; Christmas, 328; dining, 112-115; entertainment, 111-112; FastPass, 116; hours, 115; location, 115; money, 115; package pickup, 115; parking, 115; security, 115; services, 116; smoking, 116; tickets/admission, 338-342
Animal Kingdom Lodge, 166-168; dining, 218
Animal Planet Live!, 126
Antigua, 251
AOL Cityguide, 336
Arabian Nights, 238-239
art galleries & museums, 309-312
Arthur's 27, 222
Asia (park section), 110-111; attractions, 110-111; dining, 114-115; shopping, 111
Asian cuisine, 228-229
Astro Orbiter, 41
Atlantic Bay Seafood Grill, 224-225
Atlantic Dance, 248
Atlantis, 224
attendance, 322

BACH FESTIVAL, 325
Backlot Tour, 92-93
Backstage, 249
Bahama Breeze, 229
barbecue, 234
Barnstormer at Goofy's Wiseacre Farm, 36
baseball, 280-281
basketball, 281
Bay Hill Invitational, 327
Beauty & the Beast – Live on Stage, 95
Beetlejuice's Graveyard Revue, 123
Beluga Interaction Program, 156
Bella Roma, 237
Belz Designer Outlet Center, 258
Belz Factory Outlet Mall, 258

Benihana, 227
Bergamo's, 230-231
Best of Summer Florida Fest, 326
Best Read Guide, 336
Best Western Lake Buena Vista Resort, 190-191
Big Thunder Mountain Railroad, 26-27
Biketoberfest, 326
Bill Wong's Famous Super Buffet, 228
Black Angus, 225
Black Swan, 222
B-Line Diner, 234
Blue Horizons, 154
Blue Martini, 249
Blue Room, 251
Blues Brothers, 121-122
boating, 268-269
Bob Marley Reggae Fest, 325
Body Wars, 62
Boggy Creek Airboat Rides, 271
Boheme, 223
Bok Sanctuary, 292
Bonanza Golf, 290
Bonefish, 224
Boneyard, 106
Boston Lobster Feast, 225
Buena Vista Suites, 198
Buffalo Wild Wings, 234
Busch Gardens Tampa, 283-285
Butcher Shop, 224
Buzz Lightyear's Space Ranger Spin, 39

CAFÉ D'ANTONIO, 231
Café Tu Tu Tango, 229
Cairo, 251
Camp Jurassic, 140-141
Camp Minnie-Mickey, 107-108; attractions, 107-108; dining, 114
Canada (pavilion), 73; dining, 81
Capone's Dinner and Show, 239
Capital One Bowl, 326
Capriccio, 231
Caribbean Beach Resort, 184-185
Caribbean Tidepool, 155
Caribe Royale Resort Suites, 197
Cariera's Cucina Italiana, 231
Caro-Seuss-El, 144
Cat in the Hat, 144

Cattleman's Steakhouse, 225
Cedar's Restaurant, 230
Celebration Golf Course, 275
Celebration Hotel, 201-202
Central Florida Zoo, 293
Chalet Suzanne, 212, 223
Chamber of Magic, 239
Championsgate, 276
Champs Sports Bowl, 326
Charley's Steakhouse, 225
Charles Hosmer Morse Museum of American Art, 309
Chatham's Place, 222
childcare and babysitting, 240
China (pavilion), 68; dining, 77
China Jade, 228-229
Christini's, 231
Christmas, 327-329
Ciao Italia, 232
Cinderellabration, 32
Cinderella Castle, 33
Cinderella's Golden Carrousel, 35
Circle of Life, 60
Cirque du Soleil: La Nouba, 303-304
Citywalk, 245-246, 254
Club at Firestone, 251
Club Hotel by Doubletree, 200
Club Paris, 252
Clyde and Seamore Take Pirate Island, 153
Clydesdale Hamlet, 154
Coconut Willy's, 230
Comfort Suites Maingate East, 203-204
Concours d'Elegance, 326
Coney Island, 225
Congo River Golf, 290
Conservation Station, 109
Coronado Springs Resort, 185-186
Contemporary Resort, 174-175; dining, 219
Country Bear Jamboree, 28
Cranium Command, 61
Crazy Grill, 225
Cricketer's Arms, 249-250
Crossroads of Lake Buena Vista, 258
Curious George Goes to Town, 126
Cypress Gardens, 293-294

DAMON'S, 233
Dan Marino's Town Tavern, 233

Day in the Park with Barney, 127
Daytona 500, 326
Daytona Bike Week, 326
Daytona USA, 285
dining, inside theme parks:
  Animal Kingdom, 112-115
  Disney-MGM Studios, 97-100
  Epcot, 75-81
  Islands of Adventure, 145-147
  Magic Kingdom, 44-49
  Sea World, 157-159
  Universal Studios Florida, 129-131
dining, outside theme parks, 216-237:
  at Disney resorts, 218-220
  at Downtown Disney, 220-221
  at Universal Orlando, 221-222
  in Kissimmee, Lake Buena Vista, and
    Orlando, 222-237
dinner shows, 238-245
Dinoland U.S.A., 105-107; attractions, 107;
  dining, 113-114; shopping, 107
Dinosaur, 105
Dinosaur World, 295
DIS Boards, 335-336
Discovery Cove. 294-295
Discovery Island, 103-104; attractions, 103-
  104; dining, 113; shopping, 104
Discovery Island Trails, 104
Disney character dining, 217-218
Disney-MGM Studios, 84-101;
  attractions and shopping, 84-96;
  characters, 96-97; Christmas, 328;
  dining, 97-100; entertainment, 96;
  FastPass, 101; hours, 100; location, 100;
  money, 100-101; package pickup, 101;
  parking, 100; security, 101; services,
  101; smoking, 101; tickets/admission,
  338-342
Disney Quest, 285-286
Disney's Blizzard Beach, 263-264
Disney's Boardwalk, 245
Disney's Boardwalk Resort & Villas, 175-
  177
    dining, 218-219
Disney's FastPass, 50
Disney's River Country, 264
Disney Stars and Motorcars Parade, 96
Disney's Typhoon Lagoon, 264-266

Disney's Wide World of Sports, 327
Disney transportation, 355
Doctor Doom's Fearfall, 137-138
Dolly Parton's Dixie Stampede, 239-241
Dolphin Nursery, 155
Donald's Boat, 37
Doubletree Castle Hotel, 206-207
Doubletree Guest Suites Resort, 190
Doubletree Hotel Universal Orlando, 209
Downtown Disney: golf, 274; hotels, 187-
  191; Marketplace, 255; dining, 220-221;
  West Side, 255
Dragon Court Super Buffet, 228
driving around Orlando, 351-355
driving into Orlando, 350
Dudley Do-Right's Ripsaw Falls, 139
Dueling Dragons, 141-142
Dumbo, the Flying Elephant, 35
Dux, 222-223

EAGLE CREEK, 276
Eagle Pines, 274
Earthquake: The Big One, 123
Echo Lake/Streets of America, 86-90;
  attractions, 86-90; dining, 97-99;
  shopping, 90
Eighth Voyage of Sindbad, 142-143
Eli's Cribb, 252
Ellen's Energy Adventure, 56-57
El Rio del Tiempo, 66-67
Embassy Suites LBV Resort, 198
Enclave Suites, 208
Entertainment books, 336
Enzian Theater, 306
Enzo's on the Lake, 231
Epcot, 52-83; attractions and shopping,
  52-73; characters, 74; Christmas, 328;
  dining, 75-81; entertainment, 73-74;
  FastPass, 82; Flower & Garden Festival,
  324; hours, 81; International Food &
  Wine Festival, 324; location, 81; money,
  82; package pickup, 82; parking, 81;
  security, 82; services, 83; smoking, 82;
  tickets/admission, 338-342
ESPN: The Weekend, 326
E.T. Adventure, 126
Everglades, 229
Expedition: Everest, 110

Extended Stay Deluxe Orlando – Convention Center/Pointe*Orlando, 207
Extreme Ghostbusters: The Great Fright Way, 122

FALCON'S FIRE, 276
Fama's, 237
Fantasia Gardens, 288
Fantasmic!, 94-95
Fantasyland, 31-36; attractions, 31-36; dining, 47-48; shopping, 36
Fantasy of Flight, 301
Fear Factor Live, 123
Festival Bay, 255-256
Festival of Rhythm and Blues, 325
Festival of the Lion King, 107
Festival of the Masters, 324
Fiasco's, 241
Fievel's Playground, 127
fishing, 269-271
Flag Retreat, 44
flea markets, 259
Flea World, 258-259
Flights of Wonder, 111
Flipper's Pizza, 237
Florida Film Festival, 325-326
Florida Mall, 259
Florida Citrus Festival, 326
Florida Strawberry Festival, 326
Flying Tigers Warbird Restoration Museum, 302
Flying Unicorn, 142
football, 281
Fortune Court, 228
Fort Wilderness Resort & Campground, 181-182
France (pavilion), 71-72; dining, 79-80
Frontierland, 26-29; attractions, 26-29; dining, 46-47; shopping, 29
Frontierland Shootin' Arcade, 28-29
Fun Spot Action Park, 291
Future World, 52-65; attractions, 52-64; dining, 75-76; shopping, 65

GALLERY AT AVALON ISLAND, 309-310
Gasparilla Pirate Festival, 325
Gatorland, 295-296

Gay Days, 326
Gaylord Palms, 200-201; Christmas, 329
Germany (pavilion), 68-69; dining, 77-78
Giordano's, 237
Glades Adventures, 271
Glo Lounge, 250
Go2Orlando.com, 335
golf, 273-280; inside Disney World, 273-275; rates, 274-275; outside Disney World, 275-280; discounts, 280; pro events, 281-282
gourmet dining, 222-223
Grand Bohemian Gallery, 310
Grand Floridian Resort & Spa, 173-174; dining, 219
Grant Seafood Festival, 326
Great Movie Ride, 85-86
Green Meadows Petting Farm, 296
Grosvenor Resort, 189
Guadalajara Cantina, 232

HALL OF PRESIDENTS, 30
Halloween, 330
Halloween Horror Nights, 330-331
Hanamizuki, 228
hang gliding, 304
Happy Days, 291
Hard Rock Hotel, 194-195
Hard Rock Live, 250
Harry P. Leu Gardens, 297
Haunted Grimm House of Old Town, 286
Haunted Mansion, 29-30
Hawaiian Rumble, 289
Hawk's Landing, 277
Hawk's Landing Steakhouse, 224
helicopter & airplane rides, 303-304
hidden Mickeys, 37
Hilton in the WDW Resort, 188
hockey, 282
Holiday Inn in the Walt Disney World Resort, 191
Holiday Inn Sunspree Resort LBV, 199
Hollywood (park area), 128-129; attractions, 128-129; dining, 131; shopping, 129
Hollywood Boulevard, 85; attractions, 85-86; dining, 97; shopping, 86

Holocaust Memorial Resource & Education Center, 315
Holy Land Experience, 306
Hometown Pizza, 237
Honey, I Shrunk the Audience, 57-58
Honey, I Shrunk the Kids Movie Set Adventure, 89
Hoop-Dee-Doo Revue, 242
Hooters, 233
Horse World Riding Stables, 297
hot air balloons, 303
Hotel Royal Plaza, 190
hotels, 161-215:
  best, 15-16
  chains, 214-215
  discounts, 163
  International Drive, 205-209
  Kissimmee, 200-205
  Lake Buena Vista, 195-200
  off the beaten path, 209-214
  Universal, 191-195
  Walt Disney World, 163-191
Houlihan's, 233
House of Blues, 248
Hyatt Regency Grand Cypress, 195-196

ICON, 252
If I Ran the Zoo, 144
Illuminations: Reflections of Earth
Imagination!, 57-58
Impressions de France, 72
Incredible Hulk Coaster, 137
Indiana Jones Epic Stunt Spectacular, 88-89
India Palace, 229
Innoventions, 63-64
International Drive, 354; Fantasy of Lights, 329; hotels, 205-210; Resort Area, 334-335
I-Ride Trolley, 356
Islands of Adventure, 134-149; attractions and shopping, 135-145; characters, 143; dining, 145-147; hours, 148; location, 148; money, 148; package pickup, 148; parking, 148; security, 148; smoking, 148-149; tickets/admission, 340, 342-343
Italian cuisine, 230-232
Italianni's, 231

Italy (pavilion), 69; dining, 78
It's a Small World, 32-34
It's Tough to Be a Bug, 104
Ivey Groves Fresh Citrus, 297-298

JAMMINATORS, 74
Japan (pavilion), 70-71; dining, 78-79
Jaws, 122-123
Jazzfest Kissimmee, 325
JB's, 233
Jellyrolls, 248
Jim Henson's Muppet*Vision 3D, 86-87
Jockamo's, 230
Johnny Rocket's, 234
Journey Into Imagination with Figment, 58
Journey to Atlantis, 151
JT's Prime Time Restaurant, 234
Jungle Cruise, 24
Jungle Jim's, 230
Jurassic Park, 139-141; attractions, 139-141; dining, 146; shopping, 141
Jurassic Park Discovery Center, 140
Jurassic Park River Adventure, 139-140
JW Marriott Grande Lakes, 211-212

KALI RIVER RAPIDS, 110-111
Kennedy Space Center, 315-316
Key West at SeaWorld, 154
Key W. Kool's Open Pit Grill, 225
Kidcot Fun Stops, 66
Kilmanjaro Safaris, 108
Kissimmee Bay Country Club, 277
Kissimmee Bluegrass Festival, 325
Kissimmee Convention & Visitors Bureau, 334
Kissimmee Manufacturer's Outlet Mall, 259-260
Kissimmee Golf Club, 277
Knock Knock Martini Lounge, 252
Kobe Steakhouse, 228
Kraken, 151-152
Kristos, 74

LAKE BUENA VISTA GOLF COURSE, 274
Lake Buena Vista Factory Stores, 260
Lakeridge Winery and Vineyards, 307
La Quinta Inn & Suites, 209

La Quinta Lakeside, 204
Land, the, 58-60
Laughing Kookaburra Goodtime Bar, 248-249
Le Coq Au Vin, 223
Le Peep, 234
Liberty Square, 29-31; attractions, 29-31; dining, 47; shopping, 31
Liberty Square Riverboat, 31
Lighthouse Lobster Feast, 225
Lights, Motors, Action! Extreme Stunt Show, 89
Living Seas, 62-63
Living with the Land, 59-60
Lost Continent, 141-143; attractions, 141-143; shopping, 143
Lucky Leperchaun Irish Pub, 250
Lucy: A Tribute, 129
Lynx, 356

MAD TEA PARTY, 35-36
Maelstrom, 67
Magical Midway, 291
Magic Carpets of Aladdin, 25
Magic Kingdom, 20-51; character greetings, 42-43; Christmas, 327-328; dining, 44-49; entertainment, 42; FastPass, 50; hours, 49; location, 49; money, 50; package pickup, 51; parking, 50; security, 51; smoking, 51; tickets/admission, 338-342
Magic Mining Co., 225
Magic of Disney Animation, 92
Magnolia (golf course), 273-274
Maharaja Jungle Trek, 110
Main Street, U.S.A., 21-23; attractions, 21-22; dining, 45-46; services, 23; shopping, 22
Main Street Vehicles, 22
Maison & Jardin, 223
Mall at Millenia, 260
Making of Me, 62
Manatee Rescue, 154
Manuel's on the 28th, 223
Many Adventures of Winnie the Pooh, 34
Mardi Gras, 331
Marine Mammal Keeper Experience, 156
Market Street at Celebration, 256

Marriott's Grande Pines Golf Club, 278
Marvel Superhero Island, 136-138; attractions, 136-137; dining, 145; shopping, 137
Matrix & Metropolis, 250-251
McDonald's, 230
Medieval Times, 242-243, 307-308
Melting Pot, 230
Menello Museum of American Folk Art, 310
Mercado, 256
Me Ship, the Olive, 139
Metrowest Country Club, 278
Mexican cuisine, 232-233
Mexico (pavilion), 66-67; dining, 76
Mickey Avenue/Animation Courtyard, 90-93; attractions, 90-93; shopping, 93
Mickey's Country House & Judge's Tent, 37
Mickey's Jammin' Jungle Parade, 111
Mickey's Not So Scary Halloween Party, 330
Mickey's Philharmagic, 31-32
Mickey's Toontown Fair, 36-38; attractions, 36-38; dining, 48; shopping, 38
Mikado, 227
Millenia Gallery, 310-311
Ming Court, 228
miniature golf, 288-290
Minnie's Country House, 37
Mission: SPACE, 53-54
Moonfish, 224
Morocco (pavilion), 71; dining, 79
Morton's of Chicago, 224
Mount Dora Arts Festival, 325
MouseSavers.com, 335
movies, 290
Mulvaney's Irish Pub, 252
Murray Bros. Caddyshack, 234-235
Museum of Fine Arts of St. Petersburg, 311
music venues, 16, 313
Mystic Dunes Golf Club, 278

NATURE CONSERVATORY'S DISNEY WILDERNESS PRESERVE, 298
New Punjab, 229
New Year's Eve, 329

New York (park area), 120-122; attractions, 121-122; dining, 129; shopping, 122
New York China Buffet, 228
Nickelodeon Family Suites by Holiday Inn, 196
nightclubs & bars, 248-253
nightlife, 238-253; best, 17
Night of Joy, 325
Norman's, 223
Norway (pavilion), 67; dining, 76-77

OAK TRAIL, 273-274
Oasis, 103; dining, 112; shopping, 103
O Canada!, 73
Ocean Grill, 224
Odyssea, 153
Official All-Star Café, 233
Old Hickory, 224
Old Key West Resort, 177-178
Old Town, 256-257
Omelet House, 235
Omni Orlando Resort at Championsgate, 213-214
One Fish Two Fish Red Fish Blue Fish, 143
Orange County National Golf Center, 279
Orange County Regional History Center, 317
Orange Lake Resort & Country Club, 202-203, 279
Origami, 228
Orisi Risi, 74
Orlando Ale House, 233
Orlando Beer Festival, 326
Orlando Fashion Square Mall, 260
Orlando George & Dragon Pub, 230
OrlandoInfo.com, 334
Orlando International Fringe Festival, 307, 325
Orlando Magicard, 334
Orlando Museum of Art, 311
Orlando Premium Outlets Mall, 260
Orlando Science Center, 317-318
Orlando World Center Marriott, 196-197
Osceola Art Festival, 324-325
O'Shucks Pub & Billiards, 251
Osprey Ridge, 274
Outta Control Magic Show, 243

PACIFIC POINT PRESERVE, 154
Pacino's, 231-232
package deals, 344-346
packing, 346
Pac-Man Café at XS Orlando, 234
Palm (golf course), 273
Pangani Forest Exploration Trail, 108-109
Passage to India, 229
Peabody Orlando, 206
Pebbles, 230
Penguin Encounter, 155
Peter Pan's Flight, 34
Pets Ahoy, 153-154
performing & fine arts, 313-314
Pinewood Estate, 329
Pinocchio's Marionette Theater, 308
Pirates Dinner Adventure, 243-244
Pirate's Cove Adventure Golf, 289
Pirate's Island, 289-290
Pirates of the Caribbean, 23-24
pizza, 237
planning timeline, 335
Playhouse Disney: Live on Stage, 91-92
Pleasure Island, 246-247; dining, 221; Halloween, 330
Pocahontas and Her Forest Friends, 107-108
Pointe*Orlando, 257
Polk Museum of Art, 311-312
Polynesian Resort, 171-173; dining, 219
Pop Century Resort, 187
Popeye and Bluto's Bilge Rat Barges, 138
Port of Entry, 135-136; dining, 145; shopping, 135-136
Portofino Bay Hotel, 192-193
Port Orleans Resort – French Quarter, 183
Port Orleans Resort – Riverside, 183-184
Poseidon's Fury: Escape from the Lost City, 142
Primeval Whirl, 106
Primo, 223
Production Central, 119-120; attractions, 119-120; dining, 131; shopping, 120
Pteranadon Flyers, 141
Putting Edge, 289

RACE ROCK ORLANDO, 235
Radisson Resort Parkway, 204-205

Ran-Getsu, 227
Reflections of China, 68
Renaissance Orlando Resort at Sea World, 205
Reptile World Serpentarium, 298
Residence Inn Orlando/Lake Buena Vista, 198-199
restaurants, best, 17
Reunion Resort & Club, 213
Revenge of the Mummy, 121
Richard Petty Driving Experience, 286-287
Ridgewood Lakes, 279
Ripley's Believe It ... Or Not!, 318
River Adventure, 290
Ritz-Carlton Grande Lakes, 211-212
Rivership Romance, 271-272
Rock 'n' Roller Coaster Starring Aerosmith, 95-96
Rock the Universe, 325
Roomsaver, 336
Rosen Centre Hotel, 207
Roxy Orlando, 252
Royal Pacific Resort, 193-194
Roy's Restaurant, 229-230

SAK COMEDY LAB, 247
Salvador Dali Museum, 312
Samba Room, 229
San Francisco/Amity (park area), 122-124; attractions, 122-123; dining, 129-130; shopping, 124
Saratoga Springs, 180-181
Scottish Highland Games, 325
Screamers, 253
scuba diving & snorkeling, 272
Seabase Alpha, 63
Seasons 52, 230
SeaWorld of Orlando, 150-160; Animal Connections Programs, 156; animals, 154-156; dining, 157-159; educational tours & programs, 156-157; hours, 160; location, 159; money, 160; package pickup, 160; parking, 160; rides, 151-152; security, 160; shows, 152-154; smoking, 160; tickets/admission, 340, 342-343

See Orlando, 336
Seminole Hard Rock Casino, 287
Seuss Landing, 143-145; attractions 143-144; dining, 147; shopping 144-145
Shades of Green, 182; golf, 273-274
Shamiana, 229
Shamu Adventure, 152
Shamu Rocks America, 153
Shamu's Happy Harbor, 155
Share a Dream Come True Parade, 43
Shark Encounter, 155
Sharks Deep Dive, 156
Sheraton Safari Hotel, 199-200
Sheraton World Resort, 207-208
Shingle Creek, 280
Shogun, 228
shopping, 254-261
Shrunken Ned's Junior Jungle Boats, 25
shuttles, 356-357
Siam Orchid, 228
Silver Springs, 298-299
Silver Spurs Rodeo, 327
Skull Kingdom, 239, 287-288
Skycoaster, 302
Skyventure, 302-303
Sleuths Mystery Dinner Show, 244
Smokey Bones, 234
Snow White's Scary Adventures, 34-35
Soarin', 59
Sonny's Real Pit BBQ, 234
Sounds Dangerous, 89
Space Mountain, 38-39
Spaceship Earth, 54-55
special events, 324-333; best, 15
spectator sports, 280-282
SpectroMagic, 43
Spirit of Aloha Luau, 244-245
Splash Island, 266
Splash Mountain, 27-28
sports bars, 233
Star Island Resort & Club, 203
Star Tours, 87-88
Star Wars Weekends, 325
steak & seafood, 224-227
Sterling Casino Lines, 272
Stitch's Great Escape, 39-40
Storm Force Accelatron, 137

Storytime with Belle, 44
Summer Bay Resort, 213-214
SunCruz, 272
Sunset Boulevard, 93-96; dining, 99-100
Sushiology, 228
Sweet Tomatoes, 230
Swiss Family Treehouse, 24
Sword in the Stone, 44

TABU, 253
Také, 228
Taste of Hong Kong, 228
Tarzan Rocks!, 106
taxi service, 357
Terminator 2: 3D Battle Across Time, 128
Test Track, 55-56
Texas de Brazil, 225
TGI Friday's Front Row Sports Grill, 233
Thee Grotto, 253
theme parks, 20-160; best, 16
teppanyaki, 227-228
Thai Thani, 228
Tiki Island Adventure Golf, 289
Timekeeper, 40
Timothy's Gallery, 312
Timpano Italian Chophouse, 224
Titanic: Shop of Dreams, 308
TJ Airboats, 271
Tomorrowland, 38-42; attractions, 38-41;
    dining, 48-49; shopping, 42
Tomorrowland Indy Speedway, 41
Tomorrowland Transit Authority, 41
Tom Sawyer Island, 28
Toon Lagoon, 138-139; attractions, 138-
    139; dining, 146; shopping, 139
Top of the Palace Lounge, 249
Trainland Train & Trolley Museum, 318-
    319
Trey Yuen, 228
Triceratops Encounter, 140
TriceraTop Spin, 106-107
Tropical Serenade, 25
Tropical Reef, 155
Turtle Point, 155
Turtle Talk with Crush, 63
Twilight Zone Tower of Terror, 93-94
Twister... Ride It Out, 121

UNITED KINGDOM (PAVILION), 72-
    73; dining, 80
Universal Express, 118
Universal Horror Makeup Show, 128-129
Universal Orlando: Christmas, 328; dining,
    221-222; hotels, 191-195; hotels,
    benefits, 191-192; tickets/admission,
    340, 342-343; VIP Tours, 118
Universal Studios Florida, 117-133;
    attractions and shopping, 119-129;
    characters, 128; dining, 129-131; hours,
    132; location, 132; money, 132; package
    pickup, 132; parking, 132; security,
    132; smoking, 132-133;
    tickets/admission, 340, 342-343
U.S.A. (pavilion), 69; dining, 78

VACATION HOMES, 210
Vans Skate Park, 288
Venetian Room, 223
Villa de Flora, 231
Visit Florida, 335
Vito's Chop House, 224
Vittorio's, 225
Voyage of the Little Mermaid, 90-91

WALLABY RANCH FLIGHT PARK, 304
Walt Disney: One Man's Dream, 91
Walt Disney's Carousel of Progress, 40
Walt Disney World:
    Dolphin, 179-180; dining, 219
    Golf Classic, 326
    Railroad, 21-22, 29, 38
    Marathon, 326
    resorts, 163-187; benefits, 163-166;
    Deluxe & Disney Vacation Club, 166-
    183; dining, 218-220; Moderate, 183-
    186; reservations, 164; Value, 186-187
    Swan, 178-179; dining, 220
Water Mania, 266
water parks, 262-268
water sports, 268
weather, 322-323
Wekiwa Springs State Park, 299-300
Westin Grand Bohemian, 209-211
Wet 'N' Wild, 267
when to visit, 321-333

Who Wants to Be a Millionaire? – Play It!, 90

Wild Arctic, 152

Wilderness Lodge & Villas, 168-170; dining, 220

Wild Jack's, 226

Wild Waters, 268

Winter Park Autumn Art Festival, 324

Winter Park Historical Museum, 319

Winter Park Scenic Boat Tour, 271

Winter Park Sidewalk Art Festival, 324

Winter Summerland, 288-289

Wishes, 44

WLOQ Jazz Jams Summer Concert Series, 325

Wonders of Life, 60-62

WonderWorks, 243, 319-320

Woody Woodpecker's Kidzone, 125-128; attractions, 125-127; dining, 131; shopping, 127-128

Woody Woodpecker's Nuthouse Coaster, 127

Wordspring Discovery Center, 308-309

World Expo, 124-125; attractions, 124-125; dining, 130; shopping, 125

World of Orchids, 300

World Showcase, 65-73; dining, 76-81

Wyndham Orlando, 208

Wyndham Palace Resort & Spa, 188-189

Wyndham Palms Resort & Country Club, 202

YACHT & BEACH CLUB RESORTS & VILLAS, 170-171; dining, 220

Yoji, 228

ZELLWOOD SWEET CORN FESTIVAL, 326